STUDENT ACTIVISM AND CIVIL RIGHTS IN MISSISSIPPI

STUDENT ACTIVISM
AND
CIVIL RIGHTS
IN
MISSISSIPPI

Protest Politics and the Struggle for Racial Justice, 1960–1965

JAMES P. MARSHALL

WITH A FOREWORD BY STAUGHTON LYND

Louisiana State University Press
Baton Rouge

Published by Louisiana State University Press
Copyright © 2013 by Louisiana State University Press
All rights reserved
Manufactured in the United States of America
First printing

DESIGNER: Michelle A. Neustrom
TYPEFACE: Chaparral Pro
PRINTER: McNaughton & Gunn, Inc.
BINDER: Dekker Bookbinding
MAPS: Mary Lee Eggert

LIBRARY OF CONGRESS CATALOGING-IN-PUBLICATION DATA

Marshall, James P., 1942–
    Student activism and civil rights in Mississippi : protest politics and the struggle for racial justice, 1960–1965 / James P. Marshall ; with a foreword by Staughton Lynd.
    p. cm.
    Includes bibliographical references and index.
    ISBN 978-0-8071-4984-3 (cloth : alk. paper) — ISBN 978-0-8071-4985-0 (pdf) — ISBN 978-0-8071-4986-7 (epub) — ISBN 978-0-8071-4987-4 (mobi) 1. Civil rights movements—Mississippi—History—20th century. 2. Student movements—Mississippi—History—20th century. 3. African Americans—Mississippi—Politics and government—20th century. 4. College students—Political activity—Mississippi—History—20th century. 5. African American college students—Political activity—Mississippi—History—20th century. 6. African Americans—Civil rights—Mississippi—History—20th century. 7. Mississippi—Politics and government—1951–58. Mississippi Freedom Democratic Party. I. Title.
    E185.93.M6M27 2013
    323.1196'0730762—dc23

                                                                    2012026512

For Rev. Herbert Lee and those martyrs
of the Mississippi movement who gave their lives
to win freedom from racist oppression

For my wife, Esther, and my children, Dan, Gad, and Yael

For my parents who raised me to fight for civil rights and
to live believing that "Justice Must Be Done"

and

For Staughton Lynd, without whom this life project
would never have come to fruition

There is a street in Itta Bena called Freedom
There is a town in Mississippi called Liberty
There is a department in Washington called Justice

(Sign posted at many civil rights offices)

CONTENTS

FOREWORD

Staughton Lynd

James Marshall undertook this study in the 1960s, when he was a Yale undergraduate and I taught American history there.

I had been a teacher at Spelman College in Atlanta from 1961 to 1964 and, no doubt because of this experience, was invited to become the coordinator of Freedom Schools in the 1964 Mississippi Summer Project.

As I have reflected on that summer's experience I have formulated certain questions that, so it appears to me, have yet to be fully answered. This process of reflection began when I was walking across the New Haven green in June 1967 and encountered Dave Dennis, who in 1964 had been the principal representative in Mississippi of the Congress of Racial Equality (CORE) and assisted Bob Moses in directing the Council of Federated Organizations (COFO). At breakfast the next morning, Dave told me that the Student Nonviolent Coordinating Committee (SNCC) and CORE staff had initially voted down the idea of inviting hundreds of white college students to Mississippi in summer 1964. The concern of those who opposed the idea was that a multitude of articulate white college students would disrupt the efforts of SNCC and CORE to nurture the self-confidence of Mississippi African Americans in beginning to play a public role as citizens.

Dave said that, after Mississippi staff of the two organizations rejected the idea, he and Bob Moses had insisted that there be another vote and that the project go forward. This was conduct completely uncharacteristic of the extremely democratic, self-effacing Bob Moses I knew. Years later, first in reading Taylor Branch's biography of Dr. King and then in consulting other sources, it became clear to me that the crucial staff meeting in Hattiesburg where these votes were taken about the Summer Project had been interrupted by a telephone call for Moses. He was informed that Louis Allen, who as an eyewitness to the murder of Herbert Lee had asked the FBI for protection and was about to leave the state, had himself been murdered. Bob left the meeting and drove to southwestern Mississippi, where he talked with Mrs. Allen. When he came back he told his colleagues that there had to be another vote. His conviction as I came to understand it was that the voter registration strategy then being pursued, besides leading to the registration of very few black voters, had brought about the deaths, not of civil rights staff workers, but of courageous black Mississippians like Lee and Allen.

I began to see the 1964 drama in which I had played a small part not as a melodrama in which Good triumphed over Evil, but as a tragedy in the classical Greek sense. Those who feared that the influx of white college students would have a chilling effect on the empowerment of blacks were right, especially when about eighty white volunteers stayed on in Mississippi after Freedom Summer ended, almost doubling the size of the Mississippi SNCC staff. But those who, like Bob Moses, were concerned that the civil rights movement could not responsibly continue a strategy that led to the deaths of the very persons the movement sought to assist, were right also. This, I now believe, was one of several existential dilemmas that the movement had confronted as best it could at the time, but which it was the business of responsible inquiry to assess in retrospect.

I

There are several questions the reader might wish to keep in mind that this book seeks to clarify.

The first is: Was the effort to seat Mississippi Freedom Democratic Party (MFDP) delegates at the Atlantic City convention of the national Democratic Party in August 1964 an organic outgrowth of the step-by-step process that had led to the Freedom Vote in November 1963? When Bob Moses first visited Mississippi at the suggestion of Ella Baker in 1960, he did not pursue a preconceived organizing strategy. Instead he talked with Amzie Moore in the Delta, E. W. Steptoe in Amite County, and other African American local leaders. They told him that they were more interested in voter registration than in equal access to public accommodations, as this was the established practice of NAACP activists in the 1950s.

Mr. Marshall describes how the first two years of organizing around voter registration (1961–63) led to stalemate, although black candidates had tested the waters by running in the 1962 Congressional primaries. Then he tells how movement organizers improvised an organic, step-by-step process that led to "freedom votes" in August and November 1963.

Frustrated in their persistent efforts to take Mississippians down to the courthouse to register, movement staff discovered an old Mississippi law that might make possible a process of parallel voting. The words of the statute indicated that a person who thought he was entitled to vote but was denied the opportunity to do so could make out an affidavit. Thousands of such affidavits, it was hoped, would demonstrate the intense desire of excluded African Americans to vote.

The first opportunity to apply the new tactic was the Democratic Party gubernatorial primary in early August. But, in contrast to organizers' hope that something like 20,000 would-be-voters would take part, only about 1,000 persons braved hostility at the local polling place to participate in this "vote-in."

A run-off primary between Democratic candidates for governor was required. Avoiding the intimidation and violence that greeted blacks at the official polling places, on August 25, 1963, more than 27,000 black Mississippians went to churches and other places where they felt less threatened and cast freedom votes between a so-called white moderate and a white racist.

The obvious drawback of this tactic was that, in choosing between two unsatisfactory white candidates, the African American freedom voter was unable to support a candidate truly of his or her choice. Again proceeding "in an experimental, step-by-step manner," the movement persuaded Aaron Henry, state president of the NAACP, to run for governor, and Reverend Ed King, white chaplain of Tougaloo College, to be a candidate for lieutenant governor, at the general election in November 1963. Their platform included the right to vote, a $1.25 per hour minimum wage, better schools, impartial enforcement of the law, and government aid to small farmers.

This time, more than 83,000 black Mississippians cast freedom votes. The figure was equal to the difference in the votes cast for the two official candidates.

A novel aspect of the campaign was that Democratic Party activist Allard Lowenstein recruited more than eighty Yale and Stanford students to help out. These volunteers carried their stories back north and garnered considerable media attention.

Not surprisingly, the Freedom Vote of November 1963 segued into plans for a Freedom Summer in 1964. Hundreds of volunteers would be recruited with two major objectives. The first would be to help with voter registration. The second would be to staff Freedom Schools. Freedom Schools, Marshall shows, had their roots in the "Nonviolent High" in McComb in the fall of 1961 after Burglund High School students refused to sign a pledge not to participate in direct-action activities in order to be accepted back in school.

In making the decision to embark on Freedom Summer, however, the organic, step-by-step process followed by the movement during the summer and fall of 1963 began to break down.

For the most understandable of reasons but nevertheless quite arbitrarily, Bob Moses and Dave Dennis insisted that SNCC and CORE staff, who had rejected the idea of a Summer Project, take a second vote and approve it. Charles Payne states flatly that most staff, "including MacArthur Cotton, Charlie Cobb, Ivanhoe Donaldson, Hollis Watkins, Willie Peacock, and Sam Block, opposed the idea," while Moses, Dennis, and two influential Mississippians, Lawrence Guyot and Mrs. Fannie Lou Hamer, supported it. The difference is ordinarily presented as a disagreement about working with whites, but I think that class, and an apprehension that fast-talking northern college students would "gravitate to leadership positions, supplanting local people," may have been more important.[1]

In any event, Payne concludes flatly: "The way in which Moses and Dennis forced the issue was a long-term source of anger within COFO precisely because it was the opposite of SNCC's usual consensual style."[2]

The difference of opinion within SNCC about inviting hundreds of white volunteers to Mississippi is a familiar topic. There was a lesser-known controversy within SNCC as to whether the Atlantic City strategy was a good idea. It demonstrates the further breakdown of an organic, consensual process of decision-making.

Going to Atlantic City was different from the Freedom Vote of November 1963. November 1963 was the creation of a symbolic political process for the marginalized and excluded parallel to the official electoral proceedings. Those who cast "freedom votes" supported candidates other than those on the ballot for the Democratic Party. The purpose was to demonstrate how many African Americans desired to vote but were not permitted to do so.

In summer 1964, by contrast, the movement sought to assist Mississippi African Americans to become part of the national Democratic Party. On the eve of the 1964 Summer Project, SNCC staff expressed deep uneasiness with the idea of seeking to be seated at Atlantic City. The following are desperately brief extracts from the minutes of a SNCC staff meeting on June 9–11, 1964.[3]

Ruby Doris Smith opened a discussion on goals with the words: "We could begin with discussion of whether we're working to make basic changes within existing political and economic structure. . . . What would the seating of the delegation mean besides having Negroes in the National Democratic Party?" Here were some of the responses:

IVANHOE DONALDSON. Disagrees with just making more Democrats and more Republicans. Perhaps the way is to create a parallel structure. . . . Our problem is that our programs don't change basic factors of exploitation. Perhaps it's better to create a third stream. . . . [W]hat is the point of working within the Democratic Party? It is not a radical tool.

CHARLIE COBB. Feels there would be negligible value in merely being part of the Democratic Party structure. . . . There is a danger of Negroes being manipulated by the national parties. . . . It is bad if you make people part of a decadent structure.

JOHN LEWIS. He is not sure that we can get what we want within "liberal politics." The basic things we want to achieve are equality for Negro and white, liberate the poor white as well as the Negro.

JIM FORMAN. We should agitate for dignity. . . . Dignity is an umbrella concept. E.g., a man without a job has no dignity.

JIM JONES. SNCC's program is limited to desegregating facilities and voter registration.

LAWRENCE GUYOT. If our goal is just voter registration then we should stop. We have to organize around something.

Only days later, we learned that James Chaney, Andrew Goodman, and Michael Schwerner were missing and had in all probability been murdered. It became much more difficult to continue the discussion begun at the SNCC staff meeting in June. On the one hand, nationwide support for actually seating MFDP delegates at the Democratic Party convention increased dramatically. On the other hand, a feeling grew within the movement that only if the delegates were seated would the sacrifice of Chaney, Goodman, and Schwerner have been worthwhile. The MFDP, in order to distinguish itself from the Mississippi regulars, felt obliged to emphasize its fidelity to President Johnson and to the program of the national, as distinct from the state, Democratic Party. Organizing materials prepared by Donna Richards, Casey Hayden, and other

SNCC staff members for MFDP precinct and county meetings accordingly called for a "loyalty pledge" to the national party.[4]

Further, in spring 1964 SNCC representatives had gone to the national convention of the United Automobile Workers (UAW) and arranged for UAW attorney Joseph Rauh to represent the MFDP at Atlantic City. It seemed a logical move at the time. Rauh was an influential Democrat. The National Lawyers Guild attorneys who were doing the day-to-day legal work in Mississippi were personae non gratae to many liberals in the national Democratic Party. No one imagined that a conflict could arise between the UAW, which had contributed heavily to the 1963 March for Jobs and Freedom, and the MFDP. As late as August 6, 1964, a summer volunteer wrote home "from the floor of the State Convention of the Mississippi Freedom Democratic Party": "Attorney Joseph Rauh . . . addressed the group. Mr. Rauh is also Walter Reuther's attorney and his appearance indicated the support of Mr. Reuther who is, of course, one of the powers of the Democratic Party."[5]

This was the latent or suspended state of dialogue within the movement when, at Atlantic City, Lyndon Johnson and Walter Reuther betrayed the hopes of the MFDP would-be delegates who had made the long bus trip from the South. Nelson Lichtenstein in his biography of Reuther, and Taylor Branch in his biography of Dr. King, tell the identical story.[6]

At Johnson's request, Reuther broke off negotiations with General Motors and flew to Atlantic City by chartered plane. Arriving at 3 a.m., Reuther went into session with Hubert Humphrey and Walter Mondale. They agreed that the MFDP would be required to accept a so-called "compromise": the Mississippi regulars would continue to be the official delegation, and the MFDP would have two "at large" delegates named by the president, who, so Humphrey made clear, would not include "that illiterate woman," Mrs. Hamer.

The next day exhausted MFDP delegates instructed their attorney, Joseph Rauh, to hold out for at least the same number of seats allotted to the regulars. However, Reuther told Rauh: "Here's the decision. I am telling you to take this deal." If Rauh did not do what he was told, Reuther added, he would terminate Rauh's employment with the UAW.

The same kind of strong-arm tactics were used with Dr. King. Reuther told him: "Your funding is on the line. The kind of money you got from us in Birmingham is there again for Mississippi, but you've got to help us and we've got to help Johnson."

The result was that no MFDP delegates were seated, causing SNCC's African American staff to give up on working within the system, working with organized labor, and working with whites.

II

From the underlying disagreements about Freedom Summer and the failure to seat MFDP delegates at the Democratic Party convention in Atlantic City, other inter-related questions follow.

Why did the Mississippi movement fail "to maintain the momentum it had created during Freedom Summer"? As Jim Marshall states, the critical time when this default occurred was during staff meetings in October and November 1964.

At the Waveland, Mississippi, SNCC conference in November 1964, Executive Secretary Jim Forman proposed a "Black Belt" voter registration effort for summer 1965 in counties across the South where African Americans were a majority. Mr. Marshall very much wishes that program had been adopted and deprecates the so-called "freedom high" participants at the gathering (who included, at least to some extent, Bob Moses and Casey Hayden). Marshall believes the Black Belt proposal was supported by SNCC staff members who came from working-class families in the South.

It is hard to be sure of a conclusion when looking back on something that did not happen. But I would add this cautionary note. Stokely Carmichael and other SNCC staff in effect carried out Forman's program in one locality. They moved into a Black Belt county in central Alabama, used black rather than white staff (as Forman had recommended), and organized the Lowndes County Freedom Organization with its Black Panther logo. In twenty months (March 1965–November 1966), Carmichael and colleagues helped local African Americans to win the right to vote in numbers that offered hope of electoral predominance in the near future. But then Carmichael and SNCC withdrew. Within a very few years African American leaders of the local movement had dropped the Black Panther logo, begun to cut deals with their white counterparts, ceased to seek authorization from their constituents, and rejoined the Democratic Party.

Hasan Jeffries describes this experience. He concludes that movement activists "believed that obtaining political power was the key to reducing racial disparities and improving local conditions," but that electing African Americans to public office "failed to create the kind of sweeping change that movement activists hoped." SNCC organizers, he adds, overestimated "the sustainability of freedom politics." In reality, "interest in freedom politics waned as soon as movement activists stopped doing political education work."[7]

Another question is: Why did SNCC fail to develop a program that, in Marshall's words, would have "tied the political elements of the movement" to the economic issues "which in turn were the outward manifestations of the Mississippi African American's lack of freedom"?

This book offers a survey of various experiments in economic development that SNCC staff and others attempted after 1964. It would not have been an easy task to put together a comprehensive, effective economic program, but local initiatives that were in fact undertaken by various Mississippi communities suggest some of the elements that could and should have been projected statewide. One component of the road not taken would have been economic boycotts by African American consumers with the goal of rounding out achievement of the vote by non-discriminatory hiring, the appointment of African Americans as police officers, assured access to public accommodations, and the use of courtesy titles.[8] A second element of a long-run program, begun with considerable success but then not continued, would have been a pre-school program for black children preparing the youngsters for the jobs of the future.[9]

Marshall stresses that, after Freedom Summer, the nation tended to forget Mississippi and the white governing class was given time to catch its breath. But I think the difficulties facing the Mississippi movement were aggravated by so many civil rights organizers leaving the state. When they left, middle-class blacks and whites with aspirations that were less radical and more self-interested tended to come to the fore.

Why was this? Why did veteran civil rights staff leave Mississippi in such large numbers after the 1964 summer project?

A crucial cause of the organizers' exodus was an organizing philosophy shared in the 1960s by the trade union movement, by the community organizing movement sponsored by Saul Alinsky, by SNCC in the South and Students for a Democratic Society (SDS) in the North. Chuck McDew, first chairperson of SNCC, explained that many SNCC staffers had always viewed the committee as a short-lived group of organizers who would eventually organize themselves out of a job: "We said that if we go more than five years or if we go without an understanding or feeling that the organization would be disbanded, we will run the risk of becoming institutionalized and spending more time trying to perpetuate the institution than having the freedom to act and do."[10]

Much the same rationale was offered by Stokely Carmichael when, after his brilliant work in Lowndes County, Alabama, he (and other SNCC staff) left the county after less than two years there: "Our way is to live in the community, find, train, or develop representative leadership within strong, accountable local organizations or coalitions that did not exist before, and that are capable of carrying on the struggle after we leave. When we succeed in this, we will work ourselves out of a job. Which is our goal."[11]

I am inclined to think that in the new movement young people are trying to create today they would do well to be guided by the philosophy of "accompaniment" articulated in Latin America by, among others, Monsignor Oscar Romero. In essence, this philosophy says that, if you want to bring about basic social change, you must develop a useful skill like medicine, teaching, or law, move to a community where poor and oppressed people need that service (which might, of course, be the community where you were born and grew up), and stay there.

III

Read *Student Activism and Civil Rights in Mississippi,* and, whether or not you were there physically, put yourself back in that context as best you can. Ask yourself what we can learn from that experience to help in creating the other world that is possible.

And finally, I want to be sure the reader understands that, to the best of my knowledge, I am no kin of Theron Lynd, voter registrar of Hattiesburg, Mississippi.

ACKNOWLEDGMENTS

My acknowledgments have grown over the years as this project moved from Yale College and Law School, to the civil rights organizations SNCC and CORE, to the American Studies and History programs at the Hebrew University in Jerusalem and Tel Aviv University, to the W. E. B. Du Bois Institute for African and African American Research and its professors, fellows and staff at Harvard University, to Elaine Hall and Cynthia Lewis at the King Center in Atlanta, and through discussions with civil rights activists and numerous individuals and scholars such as Bob Zellner, Julian Bond, Marvin Rich, Norman and Velma Hill, Sally Belfrage, Tim Jenkins, William Julius Wilson, Linda Haywood, John Thornton, Doug McAdam, Clayborne Carson, Wesley C. Hogan, Connie Curry, Bruce Payne, Steve Bingham, Susie Erenrich, and John Ameer, who encouraged me along the way. This is not to forget Howard Zinn and W. Haywood Burns, who mentored me and encouraged me in my work over the years until their passing.

Julian Bond and Jack Minnis opened up the SNCC files to me in 1965 in Atlanta, and James Farmer and Marvin Rich did the same at the National CORE office in New York before anyone was putting documents away in archives. Movement people devoted their time to recording interviews with me, particularly Tim Jenkins and Bob Moses, and many many others who spent time with me clarifying facts and events. Without them I am very sure this book would never have seen the light of day. Those people I interviewed who are still with us have gratefully provided permissions for me to publish sections of what they related to me. Without them I would not have been able to delineate the process of development of the Mississippi civil rights movement.

My initial study grew from a senior paper with interview transcriptions at Yale into a very long master's thesis at the Hebrew University with documents, statistical studies, and maps. Staughton Lynd continued to critique my work;

Howard Zinn read my thesis, gave me documents from his collection, and mentored me; and Professor Henry Louis Gates read and circulated my manuscript for me. While I was living in Israel, the following professors and scholars were very helpful in keeping me focused on pushing this project forward: Yehoshua Arieli and David Ricci at the Hebrew University, Sigmund Diamond and Stanley I. Kutler as guest lecturers, Elite Olshtain and Lloyd Gartner at Tel Aviv University, and Gideon Stachel, my teaching colleague.

In the late 1980s my manuscript landed on the desk of Louisiana State University Press for the first time, and they encouraged me to turn my thesis into a publishable book. Happily I have renewed my relationship with LSU Press. There senior editor Rand Dotson, cartographer Mary Lee Eggert, and copyeditor Stan Ivester have graciously and professionally shepherded me through the processing of the book. Today I look forward to my life project finally seeing the light of day.

CITIES AND TOWNS IN MISSISSIPPI,
BY COUNTY

+*Aberdeen, MONROE
+*Batesville, PANOLA
+*Belzoni, HUMPHREYS
+Biloxi, HARRISON
+*Brandon, RANKIN
+*Brookhaven, LINCOLN
Camden, MADISON
+*Canton, MADISON
+*Carthage, LEAKE
Centreville, AMITE, WILKINSON
+*Charleston, TALLAHATCHIE
+*Clarksdale, COAHOMA
+*Cleveland, BOLIVAR
+*Columbus, LOWNDES
Como, PANOLA
+*Corinth, ALCORN
Doddsville, SUNFLOWER
+Drew, SUNFLOWER
+Durant, HOLMES
Edwards, HINDS
*Fayette, JEFFERSON
Flora, MADISON
Gluckstadt, MADISON
Goodman, HOLMES
+*Greenville, WASHINGTON
+*Greenwood, LEFLORE
+*Grenada, GRENADA

+*Gulfport, HARRISON
Harmony, LEAKE
+*Hattiesburg, FORREST, LAMAR
+*Hazlehurst, COPIAH
+Hollandale, WASHINGTON
+*Holly Springs, MARSHALL
+*Indianola, SUNFLOWER
Itta Bena, LEFLORE
+*Jackson, HINDS
+*Laurel, JONES
+Leland, WASHINGTON
+*Lexington, HOLMES
*Liberty, AMITE
+McComb, PIKE
*Magnolia, PIKE
+*Marks, QUITMAN
*Mayersville, ISSAQUENA
+*Meridian, LAUDERDALE
Mileston, HOLMES
+Moss Point, JACKSON
Mound Bayou, BOLIVAR
+*Natchez, ADAMS
+*Oxford, LAFAYETTE
Palmers Crossing, FORREST
+*Pascagoula, JACKSON
+Pass Christian, HARRISON
+*Philadelphia, NESHOBA

+Picayune, PEARL RIVER

*Poplarville, PEARL RIVER

+*Port Gibson, CLAIBORNE

*Rolling Fork, SHARKEY

+Rosedale, BOLIVAR

Ruleville, SUNFLOWER

+*Senatobia, TATE

+Shaw, BOLIVAR, SUNFLOWER

+Shelby, BOLIVAR

+*Starkville, OKTIBBEHA

Summit, PIKE

Tchula, HOLMES

Tougaloo, HINDS

+*Tupelo, LEE

Tutwiler, TALLAHATCHIE

*Tylertown, WALTHALL

+*Vicksburg, WARREN

+*West Point, CLAY

+*Winona, MONTGOMERY

+*Yazoo City, YAZOO

+Population over 2,500 in 1970
*County seat

Counties: in capital letters
Cities and towns: in upper and lowercase

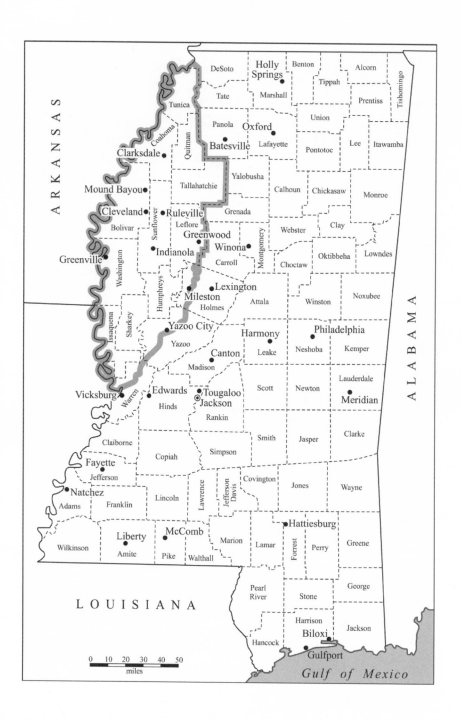

ARKANSAS

LOUISIANA

ALABAMA

Gulf of Mexico

DeSoto
Holly Springs
Benton
Alcorn
Tippah
Tishomingo
Tunica
Tate
Marshall
Prentiss
Union
Panola
Oxford
Itawamba
Batesville
Lafayette
Lee
Coahoma
Pontotoc
Clarksdale
Quitman
Yalobusha
Mound Bayou
Tallahatchie
Calhoun
Chickasaw
Monroe
Cleveland
Ruleville
Grenada
Bolivar
Sunflower
Leflore
Webster
Clay
Greenwood
Indianola
Winona
Montgomery
Oktibbeha
Lowndes
Washington
Carroll
Choctaw
Greenville
Humphreys
Lexington
Mileston
Attala
Winston
Noxubee
Issaquena
Sharkey
Holmes
Yazoo City
Harmony
Philadelphia
Yazoo
Leake
Neshoba
Kemper
Canton
Madison
Lauderdale
Vicksburg
Edwards
Tougaloo
Scott
Newton
Warren
Hinds
Jackson
Meridian
Rankin
Claiborne
Smith
Jasper
Clarke
Copiah
Simpson
Fayette
Jefferson
Covington
Jones
Wayne
Natchez
Lincoln
Lawrence
Jefferson Davis
Adams
Franklin
Hattiesburg
Liberty
McComb
Marion
Lamar
Forrest
Perry
Greene
Wilkinson
Amite
Pike
Walthall
Pearl River
Stone
George
Harrison
Jackson
Biloxi
Hancock
Gulfport

0 10 20 30 40 50
miles

ABBREVIATIONS

ACLU	American Civil Liberties Union
ADA	Americans for Democratic Action
APWR	Americans for the Preservation of the White Race
ASCS	Agricultural Stabilization and Conservation Service
CDGM	Child Development Group of Mississippi
CLAS	Lawyers Guild Committee for Legal Aid to the South
COFO	Council of Federated Organizations
CORE	Congress of Racial Equality
CORR	Commission on Religion and Race of the NCC
DM	Delta Ministry
DOC	Delta Opportunities Corporation
FBI	Federal Bureau of Investigation
FCC	Federal Communications Commission
HEW	U.S. Department of Health, Education, and Welfare
ICC	Interstate Commerce Commission
Ink Fund	NAACP Legal Defense and Educational Fund, Inc.
JD	U.S. Department of Justice
LCDC	Lawyers Constitutional Defense Committee
LSCRRC	Law Students Civil Rights Research Council
MFDP	Mississippi Freedom Democratic Party
MFLU	Mississippi Freedom Labor Union
MSU	Mississippi Student Union
NAACP	National Association for the Advancement of Colored People
NCC	National Council of Churches
NSA	U.S. National Student Association (also USNSA)
NSF	National Sharecroppers Fund
NSM	Northern Student Movement

OEO   Office of Economic Opportunity
PPC   Poor People's Corporation (also Poor People's Conference)
SCEF   Southern Conference Educational Fund
SCLC   Southern Christian Leadership Conference
SDS   Students for a Democratic Society
SNCC   Student Nonviolent Coordinating Committee
SRC   Southern Regional Council, Inc.
SSOC   Southern Student Organizing Committee
UAW   United Automobile Workers of America
VEP   Voter Education Project

STUDENT ACTIVISM AND CIVIL RIGHTS
IN MISSISSIPPI

Introduction

When you're in Mississippi, the rest of America doesn't seem real. And when you're in the rest of America, Mississippi doesn't seem real.

—ROBERT PARRIS MOSES

The closed society of Mississippi thus swears allegiance to a prevailing creed with over a hundred years of homage behind it. Based on antique assumptions no longer tenable and on a legendary past, the doctrine of white supremacy is guarded by a bureaucracy, by ceaseless, high-powered and skillful indoctrination employing both persuasion and fear, and by the elimination, without regard for law or ethics, of those who will not go along. Within its own borders the closed society of Mississippi comes as near to approximating a police state as anything we have yet seen in America.

—JAMES W. SILVER, 1964

My objective is to trace the development of student support of the civil rights movement in Mississippi from 1960 to 1965, along with the growth of protest, parallel politics, and the resultant parallel political organizations. White Mississippi resisted the movement, and to a great extent the federal government failed to meet its promises and legal commitment to protect civil rights workers and local African Americans. During the initial years of the movement, African Americans and small numbers of white workers reminded the federal government of what it could legally do to protect those who sought to exercise their inherent constitutional and statutory rights.

The movement gradually turned from freedom rides and sit-ins to voter registration as a result of prompting from local leaders such as Amzie Moore in the Delta and by promises of greater federal protection for voter registration workers. However, by the end of 1963, attempts to register African Americans in Mississippi had almost completely failed, as had the federal government's promises of protection. Mock registration of African Americans and "freedom" elections were then conducted to prove to the American public—and to African Americans themselves—that if African Americans were given the opportunity to register to vote for their own candidates in Mississippi, they would vote.

Following on the heels of the "Freedom Vote" in the fall of 1963, the movement retooled itself, decided to bring in large numbers of white volunteers, and launched the "Freedom Summer" project of 1964. During spring and summer 1964 the Mississippi Freedom Democratic Party (MFDP) was created and delegates were elected. The MFDP then challenged the right of regular Mississippi Democratic Party delegates to be seated at the Democratic National Convention in August 1964.

In addition, the MFDP questioned the right of the elected Mississippi congressmen to be seated in Congress in January 1965. Although these two challenges initially failed to accomplish their objectives, they did bring about a change in spirit on a local level and in future political developments for Mississippi African Americans with promised changes in the way future Mississippi Democratic Party delegations would be seated at Democratic National Conventions. The summer of 1964 saw the disappearance of three civil rights workers—Michael Schwerner, James Chaney, and Andrew Goodman—which put a great deal of pressure on the U.S. Congress to pass the 1964 Civil Rights Act and, after the campaign in Selma, Alabama, the Voting Rights Act of 1965.

Mississippi presented the greatest resistance to the progress of African Americans in the entire South. The Mississippi movement provides a picture of how civil rights strategy evolved organically to crack the white power structure throughout the state and to weaken its influence on the U.S. Congress.

The Mississippi movement was supported by students, and it acted on a statewide basis. Movement activists developed strategies to support local activists. These paths of action were essentially developed within the framework of the Student Nonviolent Coordinating Committee (SNCC) and the Council of Federated Organizations (COFO). Centrally decided actions were developed with local support. Movement activists, encouraged and supported by local leaders, moved into local communities and stayed to develop connections with local people and gradually create local cadres of leadership.

Although the civil rights movement caused little change in the numbers of registered African American voters before the 1965 Voting Rights Act, it did bring a change of heart for many African Americans. Local people overcame their fears and publicly expressed their desire to change the "closed society." They first used "freedom registration" in the 1963 Freedom Vote and then in the establishment of the Mississippi Freedom Democratic Party in 1964, a revolution in the minds and hearts of Mississippi African Americans and the future of local African American politics after 1965.

The movement demonstrated to local African Americans that, first, they were being denied rights that many of them never knew existed, and, second, they were capable of fighting for those rights if they were willing to risk their lives and their economic fortunes. The MFDP challenges were overt disappointments, but they were the roots of a continuing but less radical civil rights movement. After 1965 these early protest actions were directed to more conventional acts which brought about the election of more African American officials in Mississippi than anywhere else in the South.

The high numbers of African Americans who were registered to vote after 1965 were countered by gerrymandering and similar actions on the part of Mississippi authorities. Additionally, cooperative efforts and unionizing by African American farmers to relieve their economic plight were also nullified by whites who mechanized their cotton crops and threw African American farmers off the land. Many other repressive measures, on economic, physical, and legal levels, were carried out by whites in order to guarantee the continuation of the closed society. Moreover, whites who in any way tried to help civil rights workers or local African Americans were many times obliged under physical, economic, or verbal threats and actions to leave Mississippi.

Even though the student-run civil rights groups—SNCC and the Congress of Racial Equality (CORE)—left Mississippi in 1964–65 with the disintegration of COFO, local people took the movement in hand and built upon the foundations that had been expanded in 1960–65. Some of the SNCC and CORE staffers stayed on and worked with the Delta Ministry. African American Mississippians returned from the Democratic National Convention in Atlantic City and conducted a "Freedom Vote" with candidates who pledged to support the national Democratic Party and continued their economic battles for many years after 1965. Moreover, even though the congressional challenge of the seating of the regular Mississippi Democrats seemed to fail in 1965, local people continued their fight for political office as more and more registered to vote.

The Mississippi Movement

The reinvigoration of the civil rights movement in 1960–65 in Mississippi should be considered with the understanding that, whenever civil rights workers and local people were met with violence in their actions and subsequently changed their tactics to more radical ones, they did so in reaction to, or in anticipation of, and in coincidence with their frustration of not receiving federal protection for their actions to exercise basic rights of U.S. citizens. This was the state of affairs in Mississippi during the period from 1960 to 1965. This helps explain how the movement—met with such violence both officially and unofficially—reacted.

The Council of Federated Organizations,[1] the umbrella organization for the major civil rights groups in Mississippi—SNCC, the Southern Christian Leadership Conference (SCLC), NAACP, and CORE[2]—concluded its handbook for "Freedom Summer" (1964) with these words of warning to incoming volunteers: [U.S.] Justice Department litigation in Mississippi must begin in the hostile atmosphere of the Federal District Courts. The Judges who sit on the bench in the Northern and Southern Districts of Mississippi *are* Federal Judges, but they are Mississippians—and staunch white supremacists. A truly fair and objective hearing . . . is generally considered to be impossible. . . . It is the feeling of most civil rights workers that 'equal justice under law' is a farce at any level beneath the [U.S.] Fifth Circuit Court of Appeals.[3] Civil rights workers and community activists thus predicated any action on the assumption that little or no protection was available for them, except in the most extreme cases, and then only after the fact. The movement worked within this netherworld to secure those rights—guaranteed by the U.S. Constitution and federal statutes—for African Americans in Mississippi and the entire South.

The movement went from efforts to open public accommodations for African Americans with the Freedom Rides and sit-ins at local stores, to renewed efforts to register voters in order to break the white stranglehold on office holding, to symbolic voter registration in "freedom votes," when it became apparent that registering voters within the legal structure of government apparatus was not only overwhelmingly dangerous but also pointless insofar as the amount of effort expended had little bearing on the end results.

Finally, the movement established an entire network of parallel institutions—the Mississippi Freedom Democratic Party (MFDP); the Mississippi Student Union (MSU); the Mississippi Freedom Labor Union (MFLU); the *Mississippi Free Press;* the Poor People's Corporation (PPC); Freedom Schools; the Mississippi Caravan of Music; the Free Southern Theater; the Medical Committee for Human Rights (MCHR)—and other such organizations that enabled

Mississippi African Americans to join together outside of the framework of white society since they were not allowed to become part of it.

This evolution within the movement from the original efforts to win freedom of movement and commerce to work for voter registration was a slow process that involved a great deal of discussion among the movement's various individuals and groups.[4] Not all civil rights workers agreed to carrying on voter registration campaigns; some continued their direct action work.

Bob Moses in his first trip to Mississippi, in 1960, met Amzie Moore in Cleveland in the Delta; during his second trip, in 1961, he met and worked with C. C. Bryant, Webb Owens, and E. W. Steptoe in southwest Mississippi. Moses became convinced by these local NAACP veteran leaders that the best way to organize African Americans was through voter registration.

The SNCC staff decision, however, to organize African Americans through voter registration efforts was only finalized during the summer and fall of 1961 after much discussion and the arrival at a consensus decision, even though in the fall of 1960 SNCC approved Amzie Moore's and Bob Moses's plans for voter registration work. Marion Barry Jr., one of the early sit-in leaders in SNCC, and who opposed going into voter registration work in the beginning, had the following to say about how the decision was made: "The debate was between those of us who didn't want to get involved in voter registration because we thought that this was an attempt on the part of the [Kennedy] Administration to kill direct action movements, . . . and Charlie Jones, I guess, and Tim Jenkins were probably the biggest pushers on the other side, of getting involved in voter registration, . . . and so I guess what was finally decided was that the two would go on [at the same time]—direct action and voter registration."[5]

Moses, though, didn't wait and took advantage of his initial contacts to build a bridge to the local African American leaders and their communities in southwest Mississippi and the Delta. This then became the bedrock of the student-supported movement in the state which worked with the local movement's leaders. Leaders such as Moore, Bryant, Steptoe, Dr. Aaron Henry, Medgar Evers, Cleve Jordan, and Vernon Dahmer not only provided an entry into local communities but also introduced many young people into the movement who went on to become local organizers and leaders themselves. Among these young local leaders were Hollis Watkins and Curtis Hayes (Muhammad) in southwest Mississippi; Sam Block and Willie Wazir Peacock in the Delta; Anne Moody in Canton; Dorie and Joyce Ladner at Tougaloo and in Palmers Crossing;

Ida Mae "Cat" Holland, Silas and Jake McGhee and their half-brother Clarence, George and Dewey Greene and their sister Fredeye Greene, and June Johnson of Greenwood; Charles McLaurin of Jackson and Ruleville; Lawrence Guyot of Pass Christian and the Mississippi Freedom Democratic Party, and many others.

Whereas men had been the mainstay of the local NAACP leadership in the 1950s, in the 1960s women such as Mrs. Fannie Lou Hamer, Mrs. Victoria Gray, Mrs. Winson Hudson, Mrs. Hazel Palmer, Mrs. Annie Devine, Mrs. Unita Black-well, Mrs. Laura McGhee, and Mrs. Vera Pigee emerged to lead the movement locally.

By 1963, however, it had become apparent that even voter registration efforts were pointless under then-existing conditions (only the 1965 Voting Rights Act made intensive renewal of voter registration work possible in many parts of the state in spite of the continuing intimidation and violence against African Americans), and this technique of mobilizing the African American community was downgraded for a form of protest politics, the "Freedom Vote."[6]

Thus, between 1960 and 1965, a powerful grassroots movement of local Mississippi African Americans grew up and even continued to be active after the major student-supported civil rights organizations ceased their activity there in 1965–66. How this came to pass is the subject of my study.

1

The Incipient Movement

So I think that we knew that there would be violence if we tried to bring about
social change, and we certainly lived with that knowledge in our own lives.
—ALLARD K. LOWENSTEIN, 1965

The dilemma for Mississippi African Americans was whether to remain in "their place" and accept their lot or to leave that position and seek those constitutional rights denied to them by Mississippi's closed society. If they chose the latter path, it was obvious to them that a fate similar to that of Emmett Till, Mack Charles Parker, and countless other unnamed Mississippi African Americans awaited them. Nevertheless, choose they did.

Mississippi was a society with a sharp line drawn between the African American and white communities, and the student-supported civil rights movement that entered that society in 1960 crossed that line and sought to encourage African Americans to take the same bold step. The result was social upheaval. What in fact were Mississippi African Americans seeking if not those rights promised to them by the amended U.S. Constitution? Should such a search cause violent reprisals against the seekers? The rights they sought had been totally denied them since before the turn of the nineteenth century, so it is possible to understand that those demands were indeed revolutionary when seen from the point of view of White Mississippi.[1]

The movement, perhaps subconsciously, knew that it was attempting to cause a revolution to overthrow the "white power structure" in Mississippi. It knew that by stepping into the breach it would be attacking a white society that would use every conceivable power to stop that confrontation from achieving its ends. Nevertheless, the movement felt that it had justice and time on its side. John Lewis, chairman of SNCC, had wanted to ask at the March on Washington in August 1963 which side the federal government was on. To movement people and some Mississippi African Americans, it was clear that the U. S. Constitution was on the side of the African American and had been since Reconstruction.[2]

If African Americans had certain legal rights guaranteed to them by the Constitution and federal law, then why hadn't the federal government backed them in their struggle prior to 1960? In fact, the 1954 U.S. Supreme Court decision in *Brown v. the Board of Education* can be seen as a clear federal step toward equal rights for African Americans in the South. However, if the federal government were to move more quickly in enunciating a policy favorable to African Americans, then African Americans would have to show the government they were willing to fight for their constitutional rights.[3] Thus, the movement's struggle was not only against the white power structure in the South but also against the federal government, which apparently did not want to step in on the side of African Americans until there was enough public demand on a national level to justify forcing white southern society to give its African American citizens those rights that had been promised them during Reconstruction.[4]

Southern resistance to African American demands was apparent to the nation at the inception of the civil rights movement's open fight in the 1950s.[5] What was not apparent to the public was that the federal government also opposed the movement in less obvious ways. The U.S. Supreme Court had ordered school desegregation in 1954, but this and subsequent decisions required the South not to act immediately but with "all deliberate speed." A national political consensus had to be established before the federal courts would (or perhaps could) threaten the South with summary action if it did not comply with federal law without any further delay. The civil rights movement stood between southern resistance and federal inaction. Its need was to push the federal government over to the African American's side.

On March 15, 1965, it was possible for President Johnson to say to a joint session of the U. S. Congress, "We Shall Overcome" in reference to southern opposition. It was possible for an American president to openly espouse the African American's cause as the nation's cause. And it was possible because there was a national consensus for such action. In 1960 there was no such possibility. The civil rights movement, particularly in Mississippi, Alabama, and Georgia, forged that consensus by educating the American public in its forgotten promises and by reminding the nation that southern African Americans wanted to become first-class citizens without further delay.

The movement was to find its way into Mississippi in 1960 and 1961. But even before it came, White Mississippi began to organize itself for the confrontation which it instinctively knew was not far off.[6] In 1954 the first of the Citizens' Councils was founded in Indianola, Sunflower County, and in 1956 the state legislature created the Mississippi State Sovereignty Commission and provided for its funding. Professor James W. Silver calls this commission the "watchdog of segregation" and describes its functions as follows: "[It] 1) operates a public relations department to publicize the Mississippi version of the southern way of life, 2) employs trained investigators to inquire into subversive activities (conduct thought detrimental to the Mississippi image), and 3) makes periodic financial contributions to the Citizens Council."[7] Silver further states that the State Sovereignty Commission has a network of informers in black communities throughout the state; sends speakers to places throughout the United States to explain Mississippi's point of view; brings anti-Communist speakers to speak in the state; produces written and visual explications of the Mississippi way of life, such as the movie *Message from Mississippi;* and lobbies in Washington, D.C., against civil rights legislation. (In 1963 the State Sovereignty Commission contributed $120,000 toward the lobbying activities of the Coordinating Committee for Fundamental American Freedoms, which was organized to oppose the Democratic administration's civil rights bill.)[8] Governor Ross R. Barnett (1960–64) was a member of both the State Sovereignty Commission and a Citizens' Council.[9]

In addition to the Citizens' Councils and the State Sovereignty Commission, the Ku Klux Klan became active again in the state, and the grand wizard of a state Klan was known to live in Natchez, Adams County, in the southwestern part of the state, one of the most violent areas in the entire South.[10] Dr. Robert Coles, a psychiatrist close to the movement, writes of the southwestern part of Mississippi: "There were klans, councils and societies there whose daily words or deeds encouraged the burning of churches, the dynamiting of houses, the beating, ambushing and killing of men."[11] Thus, even before the movement entered Mississippi, the state and its protectors of white supremacy had readied themselves, adding new organizations as they felt necessary. (On June 25, 1963, Americans for the Preservation of the White Race was granted a state charter. It was founded in Natchez.)[12]

The movement was not as well organized as its entrenched Mississippi opposition. Ms. Ella Josephine Baker, of the Southern Christian Leadership Conference (SCLC), helped in the formation of the Temporary Student Nonviolent Coordinating Committee, which was set up at a conference at Shaw University in Raleigh, North Carolina, on Easter weekend, April 15–17, 1960. She pushed for "group-centered leadership" rather than depending on the leadership of a single individual and for independence from established civil rights organizations such as SCLC and the National Association for the Advancement of Colored People (NAACP), both of which she had worked for. An executive committee of fifteen was established, representing each of the states at the conference.[13] Many of the future leaders of SNCC, including John Lewis of rural Alabama, Julian Bond of Atlanta, Chuck McDew of Massillon, Ohio, and South Carolina State in Orangeburg, and Ivanhoe Donaldson from Michigan State University, were present, as well as observers from SCLC, the Congress of Racial Equality (CORE), the NAACP, and numerous other human relations and civil rights groups. About three hundred students from the early sit-in movement came to the conference.[14]

In May, the executive committee of SNCC met in Atlanta, with Ms. Baker, Dr. Martin Luther King Jr., and observers from the National Student Association (USNSA), the YMCA, and the American Friends Service Committee. Marion Barry Jr., of Memphis and Nashville, was elected chairman of SNCC, and an office was established in Atlanta. Jane Stembridge, a white southern graduate of the Union Theological Seminary, became the office manager of the group.[15]

In June, Robert Parris Moses, who grew up in Harlem but studied at Hamilton College for his B.A. and received his M.A. in philosophy from Harvard University in 1957, arrived at the Atlanta office, expecting to go to work for SCLC.[16] Instead, he was sent on a trip through the Black Belt counties of the South with a list of contacts supplied by Ms. Baker to find people for the October SNCC meeting in Atlanta. Ms. Baker, who advised SNCC throughout its existence, says, "I guess it was on that trip that he [Moses] got the idea he should go into Mississippi and try to start a voter registration project [there]."[17]

While Moses was in Mississippi, he met Amzie Moore, the head of the NAACP chapter in Cleveland, Bolivar County, in the Delta.[18] According to Moses, Moore convinced him of the potential effect of an all-out campaign to register African Americans in the Delta of Mississippi, which was 65 percent nonwhite and included 277,031 of the state's 920,595 nonwhites in 1960.[19] Moses invited Moore to attend the upcoming SNCC conference. With Moore's attention focused on getting SNCC to send students to do voter registration work and to involve local people as well, he attended the fall conference in Atlanta.

The need for the student-supported civil rights movement to come to rural Mississippi was imperative if African Americans were to become part of mainstream America. Tom Hayden, an early leader of Students for a Democratic

Society (SDS), writes in his pamphlet *Revolution in Mississippi*: "The adult Negro population of a remote, rural Mississippi county far removed from industrial society do not even possess means of communication among themselves, much less means of communication with the outside world. . . . But Moses and Moore saw the possibility of getting out on those dirt roads and into those old broken homes, talking the language and living the life of the oppressed people there, and persuading them to face the trials of registration. That trial passed, a Negro community with an actual voice in local, if not regional, politics, might be built, thereby acquiring the possibility for educational and social reforms."[20]

At the October meeting in Atlanta, SNCC became a permanent organization. In attendance were 235 students and young people, many from the Black Belt counties of Alabama, Georgia, and Mississippi.[21] The founding statement adopted by SNCC is an important document in the movement because it helps explain the early motivation of student civil rights workers who went to work in the rural South. Many of them were well-dressed members of the middle class who had decided to take time off from their studies to go into rural southern communities and fight the battle for all of their people. Religious inspiration was not missing from their early motivation, and it was much later, only after fighting a cruel guerrilla-type war with the white southern power structure from 1961 to 1964, that they turned to talk of Black Power and armed self-defense.

Many of these early field staff, however, supported the idea of tactical nonviolence as opposed to the nonviolent convictions expressed in SNCC's public statement below. They also accepted being guarded at night by local people who, like white Mississippians, were armed in protecting their homes and families. SNCC's original Statement of Purpose is in part: "We affirm the philosophical or religious ideal of nonviolence as the foundation of our purpose, the presupposition of our faith, and the manner of our action. Nonviolence as it grows from the Judaeo-Christian tradition seeks a social order of justice permeated by love. Integration of human endeavor represents the crucial first step towards such a society."[22]

At least publicly the early civil rights workers in the Deep South espoused the words of this statement drafted by the Reverend James Lawson of the Nashville movement and were inspired by its underlying ideals. It would be difficult indeed to understand the early student movement's actions in the sit-ins and the Freedom Rides if this were not the case because the greater part of rural southern African Americans are deeply religious.

If some of these Mississippi African Americans and civil rights workers later spoke with bitterness and hate, it was only after they had undergone the traumatic experiences of 1960–65. During this period they found ways to communicate with each other within Mississippi and with the rest of America through their demonstrations, which were viewed at times over national television networks, particularly the ones held by the Mississippi Freedom Democratic Party and its supporters in Atlantic City at the 1964 Democratic National Convention. Up to the fall of 1964, Mississippi African Americans believed that, if given the chance to present their case to a national forum, they would take their rightful place in sharing in the government of Mississippi. This was not to be the case until long after 1965.

Mississippi Law Enforcement

Law Professor Louis Lusky calls Mississippi's policy on civil rights one of obstructionism.[23] He says: "Obstructionism in the lawmaking process is sometimes hard to identify. . . . But denial of rights *after they have been established* is easy to see and understand. And being not a tactic of delay but a strategy of permanent resistance, it strikes immediately and destructively at the integrity of the whole lawmaking process."[24] Lusky indicates that the "Mississippi method" is to prosecute civil rights demonstrators on "plainly unfounded criminal charges."[25]

Jackson city officials were to use the first type of obstructionism—lawless official action—against the Freedom Riders, but they tried it out on another group first. On March 27, 1961, nine students from Tougaloo Southern Christian College, a private integrated institution of higher learning located outside of Jackson, engaged in a sit-in at the Jackson Public Library.[26] They were all arrested on charges of breach of the peace and put in jail when they refused bail. No apparent effort was made to determine whether they were engaged in constitutionally protected activities. The next day two hundred students at Jackson State College demonstrated in solidarity with the Tougaloo Nine, and when fifty of them began marching toward the jail, police broke up the march with tear gas, clubs, and dogs.[27] On March 29, the day of the trial, the police dispersed one hundred African Americans with nightsticks and dogs. The nine students were fined a hundred dollars each and given thirty-day suspended sentences.[28] In the case of the sit-in, legal obstructionism was used to protect the practice of segregation in a public place. Arresting the Jackson State demonstrators would not have served any legal purpose, but dispersing them with violence helped instill fear in the African American demonstrators.

Biloxi, in Harrison County, provides a good example of official inaction as well as lawless official action after the fact. Concerning this phenomenon, Lusky states: "For any community that contains enough willing murderers, thugs, and arsonists, lynch law provides a solution of a sort."[29] He adds that this sort of official inaction puts the federal government in a real dilemma because the government must acquiesce "in continued disregard of constitutional requirements or [impose] police state conditions."[30] In most instances of a local nature, the federal government has not taken executive or legal action, but in the case of the Ole Miss riots there really was no choice but to intervene directly, and with force, to stop the flouting of federal law.[31]

In the case of Biloxi, where the worst race riots in recent Mississippi history took place on April 24–25, 1960, the city's entire twenty-six-mile beach was closed to African Americans. A group of forty to fifty African Americans attempted to integrate the beach but were attacked by whites wielding sticks, chains, and blackjacks. Four African Americans were wounded before the crowd was dispersed by police. Later in the day two whites and eight African Americans were wounded by bullets in street clashes, and seven white Air Force personnel from Keesler Air Force Base were attacked by whites. The officials at the base then declared Biloxi off limits, except in emergency cases. On the same day police arrested four African Americans in a car for carrying a shotgun, among them Dr. Gilbert R. Mason, thirty-one, a leader of the beach demonstrators. Mason was found guilty of disturbing the peace and obstructing traffic and was fined fifty dollars. Mayor Laz Quave ordered a curfew, and police patrolled the city on April 24–25 with riot guns. Biloxi African Americans then began boycotting stores that had discriminatory policies.[32]

On April 27, the Mississippi State Legislature enacted an anti-riot law that called for prison terms up to ten years for anybody inciting a riot where there was injury or death.[33] Finally, on May 17, the U.S. Department of Justice filed suit in the Federal District Court (Southern District, Miss.) in Biloxi to compel Biloxi and Harrison County officials to open a government-reconstructed beach on the Gulf of Mexico to African Americans. In its suit the Justice Department stated that $1,133,000 of federal aid had been used to repair the beach and a seawall there.[34]

Southwest Mississippi, though, provides the most extreme examples of blatant lynch law, from arson to bombings, beatings, and murder, as well as cross burnings. The U.S. Commission on Civil Rights staff report on racial violence in Pike County in 1964 indicated forty-two such incidents that occurred between January 25 and November 1, 1964.[35] In separate incidents of a cross burning, bombing of his home, and bombing of his barber shop, Curtis C. Bryant, the head of the Pike County chapter of the NAACP, was unable to get satisfaction from the law in McComb. No arrests were made, even though all events were reported to the local police and information that might have led to an arrest was provided.[36] The Civil Rights Commission's report, *Law Enforcement*, stated: "During 1963 and 1964 substantial racial violence occurred in Adams, Madison, and Pike Counties, Mississippi. The local authorities—sheriffs and police—were ineffective in controlling this violence or apprehending the persons responsible."[37]

Not every part of Mississippi was as extreme as the southwestern section, the city of Greenville being a notable exception. The *Delta Democrat-Times*, published in Greenville by Hodding Carter III, had a great deal to do with promoting racial sanity within that city.[38] This paper and those of Hazel Brannon Smith, the *Lexington Advertiser* and the *Northside Reporter*, were among the few newspapers in the state that were not blatantly segregationist.[39]

The Freedom Rides

Before SNCC's project got underway in southwest Mississippi, the Freedom Rides, organized by CORE, but with the participation of students and individuals from throughout the movement, descended on the state.[40] It was to be only the first in a long series of confrontations between the white power structure of Mississippi and the civil rights movement. Not only did "outside agitators" take part but also local African Americans, who were no longer afraid. Mississippi prepared a characteristic welcome for the Freedom Riders.

The first Freedom Ride was precipitated by the U.S. Supreme Court's decision in *Boynton v. Commonwealth of Virginia*[41] in 1960, extending the prohibition against segregation in interstate travel to cover terminal accommodations as well as buses and trains. The riders left Washington, D.C., on May 4, 1961, in two integrated groups—seven African Americans and six whites in all— via Trailways.[42] After one of the buses was burned in Anniston, Alabama, and the other was viciously attacked in Birmingham, students from SNCC and the Nashville Student Movement decided to join the ride and carry it through to

Mississippi. On May 23, James Farmer, the National Director of CORE, returned to the South and joined with SNCC and SCLC in forming the Freedom
Ride Coordinating Committee. They decided to carry on the Freedom Ride, even
if it meant filling the jails of Montgomery, Alabama, and Jackson, Mississippi.

On May 24, Farmer and 26 other riders desegregated the white terminal restaurant at the Montgomery Trailways station and then left for Jackson in two
well-guarded buses. They were arrested for trying to use white facilities in the
Jackson bus station and were found guilty of breach of the peace; when they
refused to pay the fines, they began to serve sixty-seven-day terms in jail. By
the end of the summer, 328 Freedom Riders had been arrested in Jackson. Two-
thirds of the riders were college students, three-fourths of whom were male
and half of whom were African American, mostly from the South. On June
15, male riders were transferred to the maximum-security wing of Parchman
State Penitentiary in Sunflower County—the home county of Senator James O.
Eastland. Jail conditions both in Jackson and at Parchman were poor, but the
psychological pressures on the riders were even worse.

At this point the real battle between the Freedom Riders and the State of
Mississippi began.[43] Instead of serving their full sentences in jail, the overwhelming majority chose to be bailed out after thirty-nine days—the maximum period one could stay in jail and still appeal the conviction. CORE's bill by
the end of July reached $138,000, mainly for bail bonds and legal fees. Then, on
August 4, Mississippi officials told CORE to have the 196 riders who had been
bailed out back in Jackson for arraignment in ten days' time. Only 6 failed to
appear in court; there the Freedom Riders were informed that they were to be
tried at a rate of 2 per day. After the trials were conducted, the jail terms were
generally doubled to four months and the fines tripled to $1,500. When this
became known, Farmer tried to withdraw his appeal, but the Mississippi courts
refused this action. CORE had to raise $372,000 in cash for bail bonds.

In order to cut down on these immense costs, which would have driven
CORE into bankruptcy, the National Action Council of CORE asked the riders
to plead *nolo contendere* (no contest), resulting in a suspended sentence and a
$200 fine that CORE agreed to pay. This arrangement was accepted by 118 of
the riders and saved CORE a substantial amount of money. A few of the riders
decided to remain in jail, but the majority insisted on appealing the case up
to the U.S. Supreme Court. In November 1961, the NAACP Legal Defense and
Educational Fund agreed to pay much of the bail money and took over the trial

costs. The trials continued from August 1961 to May 1962. The appeals were not reviewed by the U.S. Supreme Court until April 1965, when the convictions were overturned in *Henry Thomas v. Mississippi*.

CORE's original strategy had been to force the federal government to act against the South,[44] and on May 29 U.S. Attorney General Robert Kennedy asked the Interstate Commerce Commission (ICC) to abolish segregation in interstate transportation. On September 22, the ICC issued its order prohibiting the use of Jim Crow facilities in interstate travel. The order became effective on November 1. Then SNCC and CORE began to test this order. On November 9, five New Orleans CORE members attempted to enter the white waiting room of the McComb, Mississippi, Greyhound bus terminal. Their way was barred. Freedom Rider George Raymond and others were kicked, and Jerome Smith, who had been in jail at Parchman for eighty days after refusing bail, was beaten with brass knuckles. While FBI agents stood by taking notes, an African American truck driver and African American cab drivers helped them get away from the mob. Baton Rouge CORE members successfully integrated the bus terminal on December 1. At the same time as the Freedom Rides were taking place, SNCC's voter registration program in southwest Mississippi had begun.

Southwest Mississippi

In August 1961, Bob Moses returned to Mississippi, but not to the Delta as he had previously arranged with Amzie Moore in the summer of 1960. (He was unable to find a church in the Delta for a voter registration school.)[45] He went instead to southwest Mississippi at the invitation of E. W. Steptoe, the founder and leader of the Amite County NAACP; Curtis C. Bryant, the head of the Pike County NAACP; and Webb Owens from McComb, who introduced him to local people and helped him raise money to finance voter registration work. These three had read about Moses's project in the November 1960 issue of *Jet* and wrote Moses suggesting that he come to southwest Mississippi instead of the Delta. Moses arrived in August. At that time only 38 of the nonwhite voting age population of 6,936 in Pike County were registered to vote, and only 1 of the nonwhite voting-age population of 3,560 in Amite County was registered. Walthall County was little better with 4 of 2,490 nonwhites registered.[46]

The voter registration drive that Moses helped start in Pike County spread quickly to Amite and Walthall counties. During the first week in August, John Hardy, of Nashville and the sit-in movement, and Reggie Robinson, of Baltimore, joined Moses in Burglundtown—the African American section of Mc-Comb—to help set up a voter registration school, which opened on August 7. Everything went well for the first few days, with a number of African Americans registering, but then on the evening of August 10 a local African American was shot at by a white after an article about the voter drive appeared in the *McComb Enterprise-Journal*. The school's attendance dropped off quickly, and the first of a series of harassments against the voter registration workers began to occur. On August 15, Moses was arrested after he had taken three African Americans down to the courthouse in Liberty, the county seat of Amite County, and was on his way back to McComb. He spent two days in jail, where he was able to protect himself by putting through a collect call to John Doar at the Department of Justice in Washington.

On the same day Gwendolyn Green of Washington, Travis Britt of New York, William Mitchell of Atlanta, Ruby Doris Smith of Atlanta, James Travis of Jackson, and Douglas MacArthur Cotton of Kosciusko and Jackson came to Pike County to work. On August 18, John Hardy set up a voter registration school in Walthall County, and thirty people attended the first day. That day Marion Barry also arrived in McComb. He formed the Pike County Non-violent Movement, and on August 26 he staged a sit-in at the local Woolworth's at which Curtis Hayes, twenty, and Hollis Watkins, twenty, both of McComb, were arrested and sentenced to thirty days in jail.

On August 29, a mass meeting of two hundred was led by Rev. James Bevel. The following day three young people were arrested while trying to sit-in at the McComb bus terminal. Three local African Americans—Brenda Travis, sixteen, Robert Talbert, nineteen, and Isaac Lewis, twenty—were convicted on charges of breach of the peace and spent thirty days in jail.

And this was only the beginning. On August 29, Moses was beaten by Billy Jack Caston, a cousin of the Amite County sheriff and the son-in-law of State Representative E. H. Hurst, while he was taking people down to the courthouse. On August 31, Caston was acquitted, but before the decision was brought in, the sheriff escorted Moses and Hardy to the county line. (The courtroom was packed with armed white farmers, and the sheriff felt he had no other way to protect Moses's and Hardy's lives.) During the day of the trial, two shots were fired outside the Liberty courthouse, where Moses and Travis Britt had taken three African Americans to register, but nothing came of the incident. On September 5, Britt was beaten when he and Moses took four African Americans down to the courthouse in Liberty.

On September 7, 1961, John Hardy accompanied some African Americans down to the courthouse in Tylertown, the county seat of Walthall County, to help them register to vote.[47] During the confrontation that took place, Hardy was pistol-whipped by the registrar, John Q. Wood. When Hardy staggered into the street, he was arrested by the sheriff and charged with disturbing the peace. Then he was transferred to the Pike County jail because it was too dangerous to keep him in Tylertown overnight. On September 21, two days before Hardy was to appear for trial in Tylertown, the Justice Department filed an appeal with the U.S. Fifth Circuit Court of Appeals in Montgomery, Alabama, for a temporary restraining order against the prosecution of John Hardy. The restraining order had been denied by Federal Judge W. Harold Cox, of Mississippi (a Kennedy appointee), the same day in Hattiesburg, Mississippi. Judges Richard T. Rives, of Alabama, and John R. Brown, of Texas, wrote the majority opinion granting the restraining order under the Civil Rights Act of 1957, which authorizes the U.S. attorney general to seek equitable relief to combat discriminatory denials of the right to vote. Judge Ben F. Cameron, of Mississippi, dissented. On the morning of September 22, Hardy and Bob Moses again escaped, this time from a Tylertown mob after they had appeared at Hardy's trial and the stay was announced. Rarely after this instance was this type of injunction sought by the Justice Department.

Southwest Mississippi was in turmoil over the Freedom Rides and the voter registration drive that Moses was conducting. Then on September 25, Herbert Lee of Amite County was shot and killed by State Representative E. H. Hurst.[48] Lee had spent the preceding week in Amite County with lawyers from the Justice Department investigating incidents and taking affidavits from people who had been down to register in Liberty, the county seat. The night prior to the murder, John Doar, of the Civil Rights Division of the Justice Department, had been informed by Moses and E. W. Steptoe that Hurst had threatened to kill Lee, Steptoe, and George Reeves, also a local African American. The coroner's jury freed Hurst after the three witnesses to the killing, fearing for their lives, had lied at the inquest. About a month later Lewis Allen, one of the witnesses, came to Moses in McComb and asked him if it were possible to get protection if he told the truth at the grand jury hearing that day. Moses related what happened in a talk given on June 20, 1963.[49] Lewis Allen was found dead in his front yard with three shotgun holes in him on January 31, 1964, the day he had been scheduled to leave Mississippi with his family.[50]

The response to the killing of Herbert Lee was strong among McComb African Americans. When Isaac Lewis and Brenda Travis, who had just spent thirty days in jail, were not readmitted to Burgland High School, 116 students, together with Bob Moses, Charles McDew from Massillon, Ohio, and John Robert Zellner, an Alabama white who joined SNCC in September 1961, marched downtown on October 4 to city hall where everyone was arrested. Bob Zellner was brutally beaten by the white mob outside the courthouse until he passed out. While he was being beaten, the McComb chief of police was holding onto him. He regained consciousness in the police station and then was taken to Magnolia, the county seat, and let out of the car.

Brenda Travis was among those arrested and consequently received a one-year sentence to the Colored Girls Industrial School, a detention home near Oakley, Mississippi.[51] The students of Burgland refused to return to school until she was readmitted. On October 12, Moses and McDew set up classes—the forerunner of future Freedom Schools in Mississippi—for the students in an African American Masonic Temple, which they attended until they were admitted to Campbell Junior College in Jackson several weeks later.[52]

In December, Moses and the rest of the SNCC staff pulled out of McComb and went up to Jackson for the winter in order to prepare for the following spring. The McComb experience was only an introduction into what both the power structure and White Mississippi would do to break the movement.

Mrs. Unita Blackwell of Mayersville, in Issaquena County in the Delta, expresses briefly and clearly what life was like not only for outside movement people but also for local people who dared to join them: "This was a time and place where terror reigned. Civil rights activists were the targets of black-hating white people in Mississippi. If there was anything worse than an outside agitator, it was a homegrown agitator. . . . Most whites in the Delta found the NAACP loathsome enough, but SNCC and COFO just unhinged them."[53]

Memories of southwest Mississippi grated on civil rights workers' consciences throughout the long period ahead in the Delta and provided the stimulus for returning to McComb in the summer of 1964. From the winter of 1961 to 1964 the African Americans of southwest Mississippi were left to fend for themselves, and they guardedly received the movement on its return. The movement, though, had learned its lesson well, and when violence mounted in other parts of the state, it brought in reinforcements instead of pulling out.

2

The Decision to Go Into Voter Registration

[T]here wasn't any basic disagreement . . . about who you were going to attack in
terms of the white power structure. The disagreement was whether we were going
to . . . use direct action . . . or whether we were going to use voter registration. . . .
And so as a result both continued during the fall of '61.

—MARION BARRY JR., 1965

The decision to go into voter registration work in Mississippi was the
result of an internal debate within the student movement. Intermittent
discussions lasted throughout the summer of 1961 and failed to convince all workers of the correct course of attack. Even though a final decision
was not made during the summer, the voter registration program in Mississippi
was begun in August in McComb under the leadership of Bob Moses. Those who
were still not sure of the efficacy of voter registration work continued the direct
action program under Marion Barry Jr. and Diane Nash.[1] And a final decision
on whether to use direct action or voter registration as a means of organizing
African Americans was put off until a later date.

These two approaches to the problem—how to confront the white power
structure in Mississippi and how to break its lock on its African American
citizens—illustrate what came to be known as participatory democracy but in
fact was the process of decision-making which functioned by consensus of all
staff involved in deciding what actions to take. In essence, the movement was
looking for a way to open up the closed society. What the civil rights workers
eventually learned was that what was necessary was a direct attack on the
power structure through any available means. Looking back on the problem
during the winter of 1965, Marion Barry said to me, "Negroes in the state don't
have any power of any kind; they're discriminated against, segregated; they're
powerless. By organizing people to register to vote, we think that we can get

some of this power."[2] Thus, it could be said that the movement was looking for a way to get at the source of power in Mississippi. The significance of lining up at the county courthouse to register to vote on a Freedom Day—a method of organizing which came into bloom in 1964—was that this was a confrontation with the white power structure at the place where its power was symbolically located. Here was the place to which the African American's fear could be traced. Here could be found the sheriff—who was also the county tax collector—along with the judge and the registrar. As the movement began to concentrate on the backwaters of rural Mississippi, it became clear that a frontal attack had to be made on these symbols of power in order to break down the Mississippi African American's fear and apathy.

Direct Action or Voter Registration?

Much of the problem in making the decision to move into voter registration came from the movement's latent fears of the liberal white establishment in Washington. People in the Kennedy administration and the liberal wing of the Democratic Party were very much in favor of a voter registration drive in the South, if only to guarantee a larger potential vote for Kennedy in 1964. It was felt by administration members that every African American who was able to register in the South was a potential Democratic voter.[3]

During the summer and fall of 1961, two separate types of meetings were held, those within the movement and those within the liberal white establishment in Washington. Tim Jenkins, the national affairs vice-president of the U.S. National Student Association (USNSA) and later a law student at Yale, stood between the two groups. He, like Bob Moses, favored voter registration work as a way of organizing. Charles Jones, of Charlotte, North Carolina, and the sit-ins, represented SNCC at conferences between the movement and the Kennedy administration.

In discussing the push from the side of the Kennedy people, August Meier and Elliott Rudwick state: "From the time the Kennedys took office, they strongly favored a massive voter registration campaign, believing that until blacks formed a major part of the constituency of Southern congressmen, no significant civil rights legislation could be passed. . . . Simultaneously, leaders of the biracial Southern Regional Council (SRC) were also urging that a voter-registration program be accorded the highest priority."[4] The administration's proposal was drawn up by Burke Marshall, the assistant attorney general for civil rights, and Harold Fleming, the former director of the Southern Regional Council and the head of the newly created Potomac Institute.

The Kennedy administration first contacted Roy Wilkins, executive director of the NAACP since 1955. On June 9, a conference was held at Capahosic, on the eastern shore of Virginia. Present were Fleming, Burke Marshall, John Doar, and St. John Barrett of the Justice Department, various foundation executives, Tim Jenkins of the National Student Association, and Charles Jones representing SNCC. Jenkins related to me in 1965 that the administration people discussed how the "enthusiasm of the movement could be led into more direct political activity. It was agreed that it was very useful to do this, and at that time the indication from the Justice Department and from the foundation representatives was made that a special program could be jointly worked out at subsequent times."[5]

A week later, on June 16, the Kennedy Administration called a meeting with representatives of SNCC, SCLC, the USNSA, CORE, and Robert Kennedy in Washington. August Meier relates that the attorney general "asserted that in his opinion voter registration projects would be a far more constructive activity than freedom rides or other demonstrations. He assured the conferees that necessary funds would be available through private foundations, and that Justice Department personnel, including FBI teams, would provide all possible aid and cooperation."[6] When James Farmer got out of Parchman State Penitentiary, he was contacted, and on July 28 a further meeting was held. Present were Farmer, of CORE, and top leaders from the Urban League, the NAACP, SCLC, and SNCC on one side, and on the other officials from the SRC and the Taconic Foundation, Burke Marshall, and Harris Wofford of the White House civil rights staff, who spoke "of the concern of the President."[7] Meier further states that "plans were unveiled to channel foundation monies for voter registration through the SRC, and the conferees were assured that the Justice Department would act to protect civil rights workers and those who attempted to register."[8]

Parallel to these meetings, SNCC held monthly conferences throughout the summer. In June, they met in Louisville; in July, in Baltimore; and in August, at the Highlander Folk School, in Monteagle, Tennessee.[9] Throughout this period Jenkins talked with both groups. Jenkins told me that, during the winter of 1960–61 and the spring of 1961, he and others had been thinking of ways to strengthen the movement.

The sit-in demonstrators and the Freedom Riders had suffered far too much at the hands of the police and local officials. Some way had to be found to get "stronger leverage within the political system."[10] Jenkins felt that way was through voter registration, which was protected by federal law. Bob Moses, having met with Amzie Moore in the Delta in 1960, had come to the same conclusion, but for other reasons. He had seen it as a way to contact rural African Americans and bring them together at registration meetings and later at the courthouse. Jenkins thought of political leverage, Moses about bringing rural African Americans into contact with their neighbors and the outside world, from which they had been largely cut off for years.

Prior to the August SNCC meeting, Jenkins related the situation:

> We had talked with the Justice Department, and they indicated that they would have much stronger affirmative powers in protecting people engaged in civil rights activity if they weren't linked, or associated, with political activity. That is, not partisan activity [but] registering people to vote and use the franchise. It was also indicated by foundation people, at a joint session, that we would have a much stronger basis for getting funds from tax-exempt sources if we engaged in something that could be called nonpartisan political activity. It was their feeling that the demonstrations at lunch counters and so forth—however vital, would not be the kind of thing that they could fund. And as a result, they would never really get their maximum push, because they couldn't get the resources—financial resources. But the voting proposition was said to have this kind of backing from the foundation world.[11]

At the meeting in August, SNCC almost split in two over the issue of voter registration. Bob Moses, Tim Jenkins, and Charles Jones pressed for a voter registration program; James Bevel, Diane Nash, John Lewis, and Bernard Lafayette—all three from the Nashville Student Movement—Charles Sherrod (of Petersburg, Virginia, who became an inspiration to the African American people of southwest Georgia), and Marion Barry (a graduate student at Fisk) were vehement in their support of direct action. Ms. Ella Baker, who had continued to be an adviser and an inspiration to SNCC since its founding in Raleigh in 1960, was finally able to reconcile the two groups. Two arms of SNCC were forged, with Diane Nash in charge of direct action and Charles Jones in charge of voter registration.[12] Bob Moses apparently left the conference early for McComb, where he began voter registration work without waiting to see what would happen at the Highlander Folk School.

Robert Parris Moses

Through the years Bob Moses gradually became a legendary figure in Mississippi and throughout the entire movement; it is possible to understand why from this characteristic action. He is a quiet person who rarely raises his voice, is of small stature, and wears glasses. Nevertheless, many of the ideas in the Mississippi movement emanated from him.[13] According to Marion Barry, many of the movement people were unsure about how things got going in Mississippi, but when speaking to me about Bob Moses, he expressed a different sentiment:

> So, I mean unknowingly to us, this was the beginning; I think it was the beginning of a sort of grass-roots movement. . . . I mean Bob Moses certainly helped to chart a lot of these courses. . . . So I think that in terms of Mississippi politics the one person who charted that course would be Bob—sometimes we all agreed with him, sometimes we didn't. But I would attribute most of them to Bob Moses in terms of ideas. . . . I mean there were others who certainly did a lot of the work. Like, I think the whole parallel structure thing [the idea of freedom registration and freedom votes, parallel to but outside of the existing structure because it was not possible to register and vote within the existing power structure]—I first heard it from him. He was the first person who talked about that. *And it was in the winter of '62.*[14]

When Moses worked as the "submerged" campaign director for Reverend Robert L. T. Smith in his primary campaign in the spring of 1962, he did so in what had already become a customary fashion for him.[15] Reverend Smith remembered in 1965 that among other things Moses had helped out with the typing in the office and that he had "a keen mind," even though Smith apparently didn't agree with all of Moses's ideas.

Furthermore, according to Smith, Moses just showed up in Jackson to help out. William L. Higgs, the only white Mississippi lawyer—he graduated from Harvard Law School—to work with the movement, was a close adviser to Smith. When I questioned him about Moses's part in the campaign, it became clear that Moses did indeed play an important role but that he didn't say much about his achievements. While Higgs was in Jackson with Reverend Smith,

Moses would go out into the rural areas of the Third Congressional District and talk to people and organize for the election primary. He also went along with Smith when he met with people in Vicksburg, Natchez, and McComb. But then this was the sort of person Moses was. He apparently didn't say much unless he felt he had something important to say. He was normally too busy doing things that had to be done.

Moses did not stay until the end of the Highlander conference but was in McComb to welcome the SNCC staff people who came in the middle of August 1961 to help with voter registration. He was the first SNCC worker to live in Amite County—at E. W. Steptoe's farm—and the first person to start a voter registration class in the county. He was also the first person to challenge the white man's right to beat up African Americans when he filed assault and battery charges against Billy Jack Caston. And after Herbert Lee's murder on September 25, he was the last SNCC worker in the county until January 1965.[16] No volunteers lived there during the summer of 1964, and the one registered African American voter in the county—nobody from the movement knew who he was—when Moses came to Amite in 1961 remained the only one until Mississippi liberalized its voting laws just before President Johnson signed the Voting Rights Act in 1965. Steptoe was still there when the movement returned in 1965. And Marshall Ganz, a rabbi's son from Bakersfield, California, moved in with Steptoe and picked up where Moses had left off.[17]

In late October, shortly after the Burgland High School students had been accepted at Campbell Junior College in Jackson, the entire SNCC staff was arrested in McComb in connection with their demonstration after Lee's murder. Unable to pay the fourteen thousand dollars necessary to stay free pending appeal, they spent two months in the Magnolia jail, located at the county seat of Pike County. Moses wrote the following letter from that jail:

> We are smuggling this note from the drunk tank of the county jail in Magnolia, Mississippi. Twelve of us are here, sprawled out along the concrete bunker; Curtis Hayes, Hollis Watkins, Ike Lewis and Robert Talbert, four veterans of the bunker, are sitting up talking—mostly about girls; Charles McDew ("Tell the story") is curled into the concrete and the wall; Harold Robinson, Stephen Ashley, James Wells, Lee Chester Vick, Leotus Eubanks, and Ivory Diggs lay cramped on the cold bunker; I'm sitting with the smuggled pen and paper, thinking a little, writing a little; Myrtis Bennett and Janie Campbell are across the way wedded to a different icy cubicle.

Later on, Hollis will lead out with a clear tenor into a freedom song, Talbert and Lewis will supply jokes, and McDew will discourse on the history of the black man and the Jew. McDew—a black by birth, a Jew by choice, and a revolutionary by necessity—has taken on the deep hates and deep loves which America and the world reserve for those who dare to stand in a strong sun and cast a sharp shadow. . . .

This is Mississippi, the middle of the iceberg. Hollis is leading off with his tenor, "Michael row the boat ashore, Alleluia; Christian brothers don't be slow, Alleluia; Mississippi's next to go, Alleluia." This is a tremor in the middle of the iceberg—from a stone that the builders rejected.[18]

This letter smuggled out the Magnolia jail expressed the stubborn optimism of the students in the civil rights movement, even though Herbert Lee had been publicly murdered and the SNCC staffers were jailed for their actions. And even though the movement did not return to southwest Mississippi until 1965, their confidence in Mississippi being the "next to go" remained as the spirit of the movement for subsequent years. Thus, when Robert Moses moved out of Mississippi in 1965, he changed his name to Parris to avoid "charisma." However, before he left a lot of things had changed in Mississippi.

The Decision Made

Direct action and voter registration worked side by side in McComb in 1961. Sometimes one group was more effective than the other; but, in the long run, it was found that the penalties were too severe and much too costly to continue direct action through sit-ins in Mississippi. Nevertheless, direct action did not disappear but was born anew in the form of Freedom Days in which tens and sometimes hundreds of African Americans lined up together at the county courthouse to try to register to vote. If a sizeable group was taken down to the courthouse, numbers might afford protection and make it harder for the white community to retaliate. In any case, fears were easier to overcome when African Americans joined together in groups.

If African Americans could get the vote, they would be able to change the laws on public accommodations. When this became apparent, the decision to devote time and resources to voter registration had been made. But this method, too, was to become too dangerous, too costly, and too slow, and it was finally subordinated to freedom registration in late summer 1963.

3

Warming Up Mississippi
The Movement Becomes a Local Thing

The only attack worth making is an attack aimed at the overthrow of the existing
political structures of the state. They must be torn down completely to make way
for new ones. The focus of such an attack must be on the vote and the Delta of
Mississippi, including Jackson and Vicksburg.

—ROBERT PARRIS MOSES, Memo to SNCC Executive Committee

I n the winter of 1961–62, Jackson, Mississippi, was a busy planning center for
the spring and summer of 1962, and the Mississippi *Free Press* began to appear there.[1] The movement saw the necessity of forming a battle plan for the
coming months. Haphazard campaigns, which had characterized 1961, were out.
A confrontation with Mississippi's white power structure had to be created. Fear
of reprisal, which had dominated the lives of local African Americans, had to be
overcome. Local people willing to join the movement had to be found, and the
movement's commitment to staying in Mississippi had to be established.

The Delta, like southwest Mississippi, had its local movement people. Amzie
Moore, of Cleveland in Bolivar County and since January 1955 head of the local
chapter of the NAACP, had started to get involved when he returned home at
the end of World War II. In 1950 a group of African Americans from the Delta
set up the Regional Council of Negro Leadership (RCNL), which helped cut
back a wave of lynchings. In 1952 a second meeting was held, featuring a speech
by Thurgood Marshall, who was to argue the plaintiffs' case for the NAACP in
Brown v. the Board of Education (1954) and later became a Johnson appointee
to U.S. Supreme Court. (Marshall was appointed to the U.S. Circuit Court of
Appeals by Kennedy and served as solicitor general under Johnson.) Also at
the meeting, Reverend George W. Lee presented a complaint that the African
Americans of Humphreys County were not being allowed by local officials to
pay the poll tax.[2]

On October 12, 1954, the first of the Citizens' Councils was created in In-
dianola, in Sunflower County, home of Sen. James O. Eastland. During this
period Reverend Lee went to the Federal District Court (Northern District,
Mississippi) to ask the court to enjoin the sheriff of Humphreys County and allow them to pay their poll tax. On May 7, 1955, Lee was murdered in Belzoni, in
Humphreys County. In August, Lamar Smith was killed in Brookhaven, Lincoln
County, and Emmett Till was lynched in Tallahatchie County in 1955. And in
November, Gus Courts, who had been warned by whites to stop his civil rights
activity and had refused, was also shot in Belzoni. After being released from
the hospital in the all–African American town of Mound Bayou, he was advised
to leave the state, which he did.

Nevertheless, Amzie Moore and others continued their efforts to organize
and educate local African Americans about their civil rights. In 1957, the Mississippi State Legislature passed a law requiring those who wanted to register
to vote to pass a test by interpreting the Mississippi Constitution to the satisfaction of the local registrar. Local civil rights work continued, and Moore took
Moses on a trip around the Delta in 1960. In 1961, a local meeting place could
not be found to house SNCC workers, so Moses went to McComb after he was
invited by C. C. Bryant. During the winter of 1961–62, plans were made to work
in the Delta.

However, before discussing what the student-supported movement and the
local Mississippi movement decided on doing in 1961, it is critical to understand
just how decisions were made about what to do and how they were to be done.

Movement Decision-Making/
Participatory Democracy

Carol Baker argues that [Ella] Baker actually introduced the concept of participatory democracy to the progressive movements of the 1960s. Others attribute it
to Tom Hayden of the Students for a Democratic Society. Whether or not Baker
technically introduced the idea, she lived and breathed and modeled it. It was
the practice of a new type of inclusive, consensus-oriented democracy, which
opened organizational doors to women, young people, and those outside of the
cadre of educated elites.

—BARBARA RANSBY, *Ella Baker and the Black Freedom Movement*

In a participatory democracy, the political life would be based in several root
principles:

that the decision-making of basic social consequence be carried on by public groupings;

that politics be seen positively, as the art of collectively creating an acceptable pattern of social relations;

that politics has the function of bringing people out of isolation and into community, thus being a necessary, though not sufficient, means of finding meaning in personal life.

— *The Port Huron Statement*, 1962

The basic concept of participatory democracy, as defined by Ms. Ella Baker[3] and the Students for a Democratic Society (SDS),[4] calls for involving people in solving their own problems. In Mississippi the basic problem for African Americans was gaining a share of the power in running their own lives. From 1961 to 1965, SNCC generally assumed that this power might be obtained through the vote. As we have seen, it took more than a year's experience of working in the state for the most of the SNCC and COFO staff to become convinced that voter registration was probably the best way to gain the power denied African Americans after Reconstruction, even though Bob Moses was already convinced of this in 1960–61 after speaking with established community leaders in the Delta and southwest Mississippi. By the summer of 1963, state repression and private violence, together with the federal government's failure to act, stimulated a search for a new strategy.

And participatory democracy, present in some degree from the start of the Mississippi movement, came to be seen as essential to voter registration work in order to overcome the fear of the isolated and economically dependent potential African American voter. Since registering to vote exposed the African American to personal dangers, they had to find out what its value was and what it could win for them. SNCC's use of decision-making by consensus naturally involved local people in the decisions that affected their lives and exposed them to the dangers brought about by trying to improve their conditions.

While Mississippi African Americans were learning to overcome these dangers, they also needed to overcome their fears. And one of the things they did to stand up to them was to sing. Mrs. Unita Blackwell explains what singing helped people to do: "Singing was the most powerful part of our mass meetings; we sang and sang and sang—freedom songs, church songs, church songs we made into freedom songs. Singing brought the people in and held us all together. . . . We'd preach freedom and then we'd sing freedom, and everybody got it."[5]

The tactical function of participatory democracy was in overcoming fear, which in Mississippi enabled a divided and isolated African American populace to unite in fighting for common goals that had proven impossible to attain when sought individually. When people did come together, it was necessary for all of the participants to feel they had taken part in making the decisions that affected their future rather than having others make decisions for them from above.

African Americans had been led for too long by whites who did not have their interest at heart. Their self-confidence had been destroyed over the years, and they had been terrorized to such a degree that they had withdrawn within themselves, becoming functionally schizophrenic. They faced the white world with an apparent apathy and led a quite different life among their own people. Dr. Robert Coles says that African American parents "must teach their child a variety of maneuvers and postures to cope with his baffling lot. By seven or eight most African American children know the score, and I have seen them draw only faintly disguised pictures of the harsh future awaiting them."[6]

It is possible that the value of participatory democracy is not to be found in its value as a system of government; instead, it had a specific role in Mississippi as well as the rest of the civil rights movement by enabling African Americans to act as a group in fighting the terror tactics of the white power structure. Self-confidence was regained, and in Mississippi the African American did stand up to the white man, putting aside his fear and apathy because he was able to act jointly with his brothers in deciding his own future.

Furthermore, the crisis atmosphere created by the movement and its enemies brought about the conditions necessary for the effective practice of participatory democracy in Mississippi. After 1965, these severe conditions began to break down and more normal forms of decision-making became the rule. Nevertheless, by that time masses of people had learned to take part in deciding their own futures.

In the May 10, 1965, edition of *The Nation,* Jack Newfield quotes Bob Parris Moses as saying, "The people on the bottom don't need leaders at all. What they need is the confidence in their own worth and identity to make decisions about their own lives."[7] This statement explains one of the most important elements in SNCC's ideology: that indigenous leadership must be found because it has been submerged over the years; African Americans' dignity and self-respect, as well as their individualism, have been lost. In order for Mississippi African Americans to rise out of apathy and fear, they had to believe in themselves and not become followers unless they made positive and conscious decisions to do so. When they could participate in deciding their own personal future, they would no longer be led astray by ambitious politicians, and the vote they possessed would become real political power.

Participatory democracy—a process involving rank-and-file African Americans —was a natural offshoot of the process that evolved in the decision to emphasize voter registration rather than direct actions such as sit-ins. This point was made by William Mahoney, an early Mississippi Freedom Rider from Howard University and a staff member of SNCC:

> I think that participatory democracy occurred at one point in SNCC because there were people in SNCC who felt that they were a community and could communicate with one another . . . and they felt that they were a community because they were oppressed and were conscious of this oppression. . . .
>
> What's happened is that as SNCC has grown larger . . . the size of the group that was making the decisions was important. . . . At all points participatory democracy has meant structure and recognition of minority rights, letting everybody speak, getting everybody's viewpoint out.[8]

The idea, then, of participatory democracy in Mississippi was to organize African Americans effectively to act together in making conscious decisions to become a part of Mississippi, not an unequal part but an equal one that afforded the opportunity to be full participants in an open and democratic society. In 1963, African Americans began to come together not just in tens or hundreds but sometimes in thousands to tell the white power structure that they would no longer be denied their part without a fight. An Eastland or a Stennis who said that they were not being denied the right to register to vote was lying to a national audience that could in no way continue to believe Mississippi's untruths about the condition of its African Americans.

If participatory democracy was no more than an illusion (and I feel that this was not the case) and was only a way of organizing people to take part in the movement, it is of little import. Indigenous leaders did surface, and local African Americans did become increasingly more involved in their own fate. Dr. Coles contends that, until 1967, "nonviolent action [which characterized the Mississippi movement] has come naturally to African Americans, because the only alternative has been to turn their suffering in upon themselves, converting it to sullen despair. The African American is not now *becoming* angry. At some level of his mind, in its corners that are out of both the white man's sight and often enough his own, the African American has always been angry."[9] By the end of the "Freedom Vote" in the fall of 1963, if not before, it was apparent that Mississippi African Americans were becoming explicit in showing their anger about having to live in a closed society. That they were willing to risk even the little that they had to obtain their freedom proved the Mississippi myth of the contented African American to be a blatant lie. During this period the movement also began to teach the American public about Mississippi and its true nature.

Early Political Action

Carrying the ideas of decision-making by consensus forward, Moses and the SNCC staff, before going into the Delta in the summer of 1962, became involved in something quite different and no less promising, something that would lead to the protest actions of 1963. Meetings were held in Jackson, where Bill Higgs, Moses, Paul Brooks and his wife Katherine, Lester McKinnie, James Bevel and his wife Diane, and Bernard Lafayette, who later worked with his wife in Selma, Alabama, were present.[10] Higgs, who had run unsuccessfully for the state legislature in 1959, the U.S. Congress in 1960, and for Jackson city commissioner in 1961, met Medgar Evers, the NAACP state field secretary, during the last campaign. Higgs mentioned to the group that it was a relatively easy matter to get on the ballot in Mississippi. The group then approached Evers with the suggestion that he run for Congress in the June Democratic Primary. Evers turned them down, but Reverend Robert L. T. Smith was persuaded to run, and after filing with the Mississippi secretary of state, the State Executive Committee of the Democratic Party gave in to the demand to list Smith on the primary ballot with John Bell Williams, who was running from the Third Congressional District.[11]

Moses became Smith's "submerged," or unofficial, campaign director because it was felt that the campaign should appear to be a local effort and not one directed by "a New York Negro." Moses worked mostly in the rural areas and was also able to establish contacts in Hinds, Adams, Jefferson, Claiborne, Copiah, and Lincoln counties. Moses's and SNCC's strategies were characterized by "a willingness to set up shop in the rural Deep South, a focus on grassroots community organizing, and a capacity to flood the zone with activists when trouble arose."[12] These principles from 1962 onward were found wherever SNCC and COFO went in Mississippi.

During the campaign Higgs took Reverend Smith to New York, Boston, and Washington, D.C., where he met with Mrs. Eleanor Roosevelt and James A. Wechsler, the columnist and editorial-page writer of the *New York Post*, and other liberals with political influence. Mrs. Roosevelt wrote President Kennedy concerning the campaign; complaints were filed with the Federal Communications Commission (FCC) about getting network time in Mississippi; and Wechsler wrote a number of editorials in the *Post*. Finally, the FCC sent a letter to Mississippi ordering that Smith be given television time on WLBT-TV in six days or appropriate action would be taken. After this, Smith was invited to one of the local television stations and subsequently appeared on the air. In addition, Smith gave a number of speeches throughout the district, and a campaign was conducted by Diane Bevel to teach young African Americans the techniques of nonviolence.[13] This then was one of the first steps in making African American candidates visible to the community, thereby giving people hope to some day get an African American elected to political office as well as giving people a reason to be interested in the political process as more than the white man's politics.

A poll-tax campaign was also organized to confront the situation that a registered voter wishing to vote in an election had to produce poll-tax receipts from the last two years. In addition, the poll-tax could only be paid from late December of the previous year to January 31 of an election year. Furthermore, the poll tax, which was later held to be unnecessary in state elections and a bar to African American political participation in *United States v. Mississippi* (Southern District, Mississippi, 1966), was generally two or three dollars, a considerable sum for a rural farm laborer or sharecropper who did not earn much more than that for a day's work.

Reverend Theodore Trammell, a Methodist minister from Clarksdale, was convinced to run against Jamie L. Whitten and Frank Smith in the Second Congressional District. During the campaign, Trammell died of a heart attack and Reverend Merrill W. Lindsey,[14] a Methodist minister from Holly Springs in Marshall County and the brother-in-law of Aaron Henry, took over the campaign. Lindsey, however, apparently did not get many votes in his district because African Americans felt it would be better to give their votes to Frank Smith, a liberal who in the end lost to Whitten.[15] It made little difference that Smith and Lindsey received only a few thousand votes on June 5, because they had both been able to go on television and campaign widely in their districts. The real significance of the 1962 primary elections was that, for the first time within memory, African Americans had run for Congress in Mississippi. African American viewpoints were presented by candidates who offered an alternative to white supremacy slogans and the segregationist candidates of the state Democratic Party. These campaigns gave African Americans a reason not only to pay the poll tax but to go register, no matter what danger was encountered or economic intimidation used. Furthermore, African Americans could hope that, since Smith and Lindsey had run for Congress, then maybe a more moderate white or even an African American could eventually be elected after enough African Americans had registered to vote. This was particularly so in the Second Congressional District as 52 percent of the voting-age population in 1960 was nonwhite.

Thus, these campaigns became not only an opportunity for African Americans to participate in the political process but also to regain self-respect and hope. For the civil rights movement, the campaigns meant that more extensive contacts were made in the Delta as well as the southwestern part of the state. The idea of running an African American for public office came to be seen as an organizing device that would spur voter registration and would be used again during the fall of 1963 and the summer of 1964. Moreover, this type of political activity led to the parallel, protest activities of the Freedom Vote in 1963 and the formation of the Mississippi Freedom Democratic Party in 1964.

The Founding of COFO

During the Freedom Rides in the summer of 1961, the Council of Federated Organizations (COFO) was set up in order to get a meeting with Governor Ross Barnett, who refused to meet with NAACP people. COFO did meet with Barnett, but he refused to do anything about the charges against the Freedom Riders, and COFO became inactive until February 1962.[16] The organization included representatives from SNCC, SCLC, the NAACP, and CORE. Its purpose when it was brought back in 1962 was to coordinate voter registration activities throughout the state in such a fashion that it would be able to receive the tax-exempt funds that had been promised the year before by private foundations. Even though there were conflicts over policy between the participating organizations, COFO became the umbrella group for civil rights voter registration and education activities in the state as Bob Moses, Dave Dennis, Medgar Evers,

TABLE 1

Voter Registration in Counties of the Delta and Other Counties Where the Civil Rights Movement Was Active

County	White Voting-Age Population (1960)	Nonwhite Voting-Age Population (1960)	Pre-Act[a] Nonwhite Registration	Post-Act[b] Nonwhite Registration	Nonwhite Population (1970)	Nonwhite Population (1960/70)
The State	748,266	422,256	28,500[6.7]	252,519[59.8]	821,991	42.3/37.1
Adams	10,888	9,340	1,050[11.2]+	4,388[47.0]	17,865	49.5/47.9
*Amite	4,449	3,560	1[0.03]+	2,285[64.2]	6,942	54.2/50.4
Bolivar***	10,031	15,939	612[3.8]+	8,160[51.2]	30,338	67.8/61.4
*Coahoma***	8,708	14,604	1,061[7.3]+	9,713[66.5]	26,013	68.3/64.3
*Forrest	22,431	7,495	236[3.1]	5,176[67.5]	14,151	28.0/24.5
Hancock	6,813	1,129	...	724[64.1]	2,467	16.1/14.2
Harrison	55,094	9,670	2,000[20.7]+	13,864[100+]	22,731	16.1/16.9
*Hinds	67,838	36,138	5,616[15.5]	24,099[66.7]	84,026	40.0/39.1
*Holmes***	4,773	8,757	20[0.2]	6,362[72.7]	15,743	72.0/68.1
*Humphreys***	3,344	5,561	0[0.0]	2,441[43.9]	9,460	69.8/64.8
*Issaquena***	640	1,081	5[0.5]	643[59.5]	1,689	67.1/61.7
Jackson	24,447	5,113	1,400[27.4]+	5,567[100+]	14,231	19.6/16.2
*Jefferson	1,666	3,540	0[0.0]+	2,061[58.2]	6,996	75.5/75.3
*Claiborne	1,668	3,969	26[0.7]	3,092[77.9]	7,522	76.0/74.6
*Jones	25,943	7,427	...	3,347[45.1]	13,810	25.9/24.5
Lamar	6,489	1,071	0[0.0]	1,216[100+]	2,013	16.3/13.2
Lauderdale	27,806	11,924	1,700[14.3]	5,667[47.5]	20,630	35.0/30.8
Leake	6,754	3,397	220[6.5]	2,161[63.6]	6,091	43.4/35.7
Lee	18,709	5,130	231[4.5]+	1,906[37.2]	9,548	25.3/20.7
*Leflore***	10,274	13,567	281[2.1]	9,792[72.2]	24,374	64.6/57.9
Lowndes	16,460	8,362	99[1.2]	2,686[32.1]	16,226	38.1/32.6
*Madison	5,622	10,366	218[2.1]	7,037[67.9]	18,548	71.8/62.4
Marshall	4,342	7,168	177[2.5]	4,603[64.2]	14,891	70.4/62.0
Monroe	13,426	5,610	9[0.2]+	4,455[79.4]	10,382	35.4/30.5
*Neshoba	9,143	2,565	...	2,245[87.5]	4,098	28.2/19.7
*Oktibbeha	8,423	4,952	128[2.6]	4,432[89.5]	10,004	43.7/34.8
Panola	7,639	7,250	878[12.1]	3,867[53.3]	13,753	56.4/51.3
Pike	12,163	6,936	207[3.0]+	5,237[75.5]	13,827	43.9/43.5
Quitman***	4,176	5,673	436[7.7]+	2,655[46.8]	9,120	63.3/57.4
*Rankin	13,246	6,944	94[1.4]+	2,444[35.2]	12,368	37.3/28.2
*Sharkey***	1.822	3,152	3[0.1]+	1,708[54.2]	5,784	69.8/64.7
Sunflower***	8,785	13,524	185[1.4]	5,548[41.0]	23,261	67.8/62.8

TABLE 1   *(continued)*

County	White Voting-Age Population (1960)	Nonwhite Voting-Age Population (1960)	Pre-Act[a] Nonwhite Registration	Post-Act[b] Nonwhite Registration	Nonwhite Population (1970)	Nonwhite Population (1960/70)
Tallahatchie***	5,099	6,483	17[0.3]	3,377[52.1]	11,632	64.4/60.2
Tunica***	2,011	5,822	38[0.7]	2,05[35.3]	8,614	79.2/72.7
*Walthall	4,536	2,490	4[0.2]	1,805[72.5]	5,088	45.1/40.7
*Warren	13,530	10,726	2,433[22.7]	6,403[59.7]	18,355	46.8/40.8
Washington***	19,837	20,619	1,762[8.5]+	8,655[41.9]	38,460	55.2/54.5
*Wilkinson	2,340	4,120	60[1.5]+	3,300[80.1]	7,499	71.2/67.6
Yazoo***	7,598	8,719	256[2.9]+	4,692[53.8]	14,579	59.4/53.4

Sources: U.S. Bureau of the Census, *County and City Data Book* (Washington, D.C., 1973); U.S. Commission on Civil Rights, *Political Participation* (Washington, D.C., 1968).
[a]Unofficial figures showing registration as of a median date, January 1, 1964.
[b]Figures as of September 30, 1965, after passage of Voting Rights Act of 1965.
*County designated by U.S. attorney general for appointment of a federal examiner and in which examiners have been appointed.
***Delta County; in cases of Quitman, Sharkey, Tunica, Issaquena, and Yazoo there were no civil rights offices located in the county; other Delta counties had civil rights offices which at times serviced adjacent counties' nonwhite population.
+ From U.S. Civil Rights Commission, *Hearings* (Washington, D.C., 1965), vol. 1: 263–64.

Amzie Moore, and Aaron Henry led their respective organizations. COFO eventually ran the Freedom Summer program in 1964, and in many cases it served as a bridge between the civil rights leaders of the 1950s, who pushed this cooperation, and the student-supported movement of the 1960s.

The first funds for SNCC and COFO that came from the foundation world were provided through the Voter Education Project (VEP), which operated under the direction of the Southern Regional Council (SRC) in Atlanta. A grant of $5,000 was made to SNCC in June for work in the Delta, and a further $14,000 to COFO for the period of August 1, 1962, to March 31, 1963. By November 1963, when VEP cut off funds to Mississippi, some $50,000 had been provided for the movement, but it was only a small part of the overall expenses of the movement in the state.[17]

Violence, threats, and intimidation struck at the movement and at Mississippi African Americans at every step in 1962.[18] On January 3, in Clarksdale, Coahoma County, Reverend Trammell; Aaron Henry; John C. Melcher, the head of the local NAACP chapter; R. L. Drew, the president of the Clarksdale Voters League; and J. W. Wright were convicted on charges of conspiracy to harm public trade by participating in a boycott against Clarksdale stores owned by whites. They were fined $500 each and sentenced to six months in jail; all were released after paying $1,000 bail bonds.

On February 6, 1962, Clarksdale police brutally beat Bessie Turner, a young African American woman.[19] In May, Mrs. Bevel, who was four months pregnant, was convicted of contributing to the delinquency of minors for teaching African American youths nonviolent techniques. After a short stay in prison she was released. At her trial Jesse Harris, of Jackson, and Luvaughn Brown, also from Mississippi, were arrested for trying to sit on the white side of the courtroom. Both received "special treatment" during their forty-day stay at the prison farm. This sort of treatment continued throughout the summer, fall, and winter of 1962.[20]

During the spring and summer of 1962, voter registration projects were set up in Hattiesburg under Curtis Hayes and Hollis Watkins, who had joined the movement in McComb the previous year; in Laurel, under Lester McKinnie; in Holly Springs, under Frank Smith, who was studying there at Rust College but was from Atlanta; and in Greenville, Vicksburg, Cleveland, and Ruleville. The most important project, though, was established in Greenwood, the county seat of Leflore County. Sam Block, of Cleveland—thirty miles from Greenwood— and Willie Wazir Peacock, of Charleston, Mississippi, moved in and began to organize a voter registration campaign around a police brutality case.

On July 28, Welton McSwine, a local African American of fourteen, had been picked up by the police, accused of peeping into a local white woman's house, and brutally beaten while in jail. When Block learned of this after the boy was released from jail, he took pictures and had McSwine fill out affidavits which Block then sent to the Justice Department and the FBI.

The Delta

The efforts of SNCC and COFO during the remainder of 1962 were located almost entirely in the Delta. What in fact is this area, and why should the movement have concentrated its efforts there? The Federal Writers' Project described the Delta in the following way:

The most clearly defined of the eight sections [of Mississippi] are the Delta and the Coast. David Cohen has said that the Delta "begins in the lobby of the Peabody Hotel at Memphis and ends on Catfish Row in Vicksburg. . . ."

For the native Mississippian . . . the word "Delta" connotes for him persons charmingly lacking in provincialism, rather than wide flat fields steaming with fertility and squat plantation towns that are all alike. Settled on land as unstable as it is productive . . . the variable factors are the high water and the price of cotton; the constant is the Negro. . . . [T]he Delta is politically conservative and economically diverse. . . . This backdrop of overt violence, political and economic oppression, and widespread deprivation affected all of those African Americans who matured in the Delta of the 1930s through the 1960s.[21]

Every one of the eleven Delta counties (Bolivar, Coahoma, Humphreys, Issaquena, Leflore, Quitman, Sharkey, Sunflower, Tallahatchie, Tunica, and Washington) was over 50 percent nonwhite in 1960 and 1970. Eight of the ten counties adjacent to the Delta (Carroll, DeSoto, Grenada, Holmes, Madison, Marshall, Panola, Tate, Yalobusha, and Yazoo) in 1960 and six of the ten in 1970 were over 50 percent nonwhite. The eleven Delta counties were 65 percent nonwhite in 1960 and 60.3 percent nonwhite in 1970; the ten adjacent counties were 61.3 percent nonwhite in 1960 and 51.4 percent nonwhite in 1970. Between 1960 and 1970, the former area experienced a loss in its nonwhite population of 20.9 percent, while the latter area registered a drop of 17.1 percent. Part of the answer to the population drop may be that, while only 14 percent of the cotton crop in the Delta was harvested by mechanical cotton-picker in 1954, 27 percent was in 1957, and 81 percent was in 1964; and by 1967 about 95 percent was harvested this way.[22] With this, chemical defoliants came into use and the major employer of hand labor in the Delta was thus eliminated. Whether no direct cause-and-effect relationship between the movement's activities in the Delta counties and the changeover to mechanized cotton production can be proven, I believe there is such a relationship.

The median family income for nonwhites in the twenty-one Delta and ad-jacent counties in 1969 ranged from $1,921 a year in Quitman County to $3,408 in Grenada County, with the lower figure nearer the general condition. The median number of school years completed for nonwhite males over twenty-five years old in 1970 ranged from 4.2 years in Tallahatchie County to 6.4 years in Madison County. The educational situation of females in the same age group was a little better, but not much.

The only cities in the Delta with a population of more than 10,000 in 1970 were Clarksdale (21,673), Cleveland (13,327), Greenville (39,648), and Green-

TABLE 2
Mississippi County Breakdown of Population and Migration by Race

County	Population[a] (1960)	Population[b] (1970)	Number[c] of Nonwhites (1960)	Number[d] of Nonwhites (1970)	Nonwhite[e] (1960/70)	Net change[f] Nonwhites (1950–60 /1960–70)
State	**2,178,14**	**2,216,912**	**920,595**	**821,991**	**42.3/37.1**	**-7.1/-10.7**
Adams*	37,730	37,293	18,695	17,865	49.5/47.9	-16.1/-4.3
Alcorn	25,282	27,179	3,333	3,171	13.2/11.7	-14.6/-4.9
Amite*	15,573	13,763	8,443	6,942	54.2/50.4	-19.1/-17.7
Attala	21,335	19,570	9,546	7,903	44.7/40.4	-17.5/-17.0
Benton	7,723	7.505	3,609	3,149	46.7/42.0	-6.3/-12.7
Bolivar***/*	54,464	49,409	36,943	30,338	67.8/61.4	-14.4/-17.3
Calhoun	15,941	14,623	4,346	3,813	27.3/26.1	1.3/-12.3
Carroll**	11,177	9,397	6,500	4,771	58.2/50.8	-26.4/-26.5
Chickasaw	16,891	16,805	6,511	5,976	38.5/35.6	-22.7/-8.0
Choctaw	8,423	8,440	2,520	2,366	29.9/28.0	24.3/-6.0
Claiborne*	10,845	10,086	8,245	7,522	76.0/74.6	-7.7/-8.7
Clarke	16,493	15,049	6,492	5,396	39.4/35.9	-17.6/-16.6
Clay	18,933	18,840	9,719	9,306	51.3/49.4	-3.7/-4.2
Coahoma***/*	46,212	40,447	31,582	26,013	68.3/64.3	-11.4/-17.3
Copiah	27,051	24,764	14,059	12,437	52.0/50.2	-13.7/-11.5
Covington	13,637	14,002	4,741	4,565	34.8/32.6	-9.1/-3.5
Desoto**	23,891	35,885	14,643	12,609	61.3/35.1	-11.4/-13.8
Forrest*	52,722	57,849	17,752	14,151	28.0/24.5	13.0/-3.9
Franklin	9,286	8,011	3,800	3,109	40.9/38.8	-11.7/-18.1
George	11,098	12,459	1,287	1,448	11.6/11.6	4.5/12.7
Greene	8,366	8,545	1,923	1,878	23.0/22.0	27.9/-2.3
Grenada**	18,409	19,854	9,057	8,690	49.2/43.8	-7.9/-4.0
Hancock*	14,039	17,387	2,255	2,467	16.1/14.2	10.6/9.8
Harrison*	119,489	134,582	19,256	22,731	16.1/16.9	43.5/19.3
Hinds*	187,045	214,973	74,840	84,026	40.0/39.1	17.1/12.4
Holmes***/*	27,096	23,120	19,501	15,743	72.0/68.1	-20.3/-19.2
Humphreys***/*	19,093	14,601	13,335	9,460	69.8/64.8	-17.2/-28.9
Issaquena***/*	3,576	2,737	2,400	1,689	67.1/61.7	-28.3/-29.2
Itawamba	15,080	16,847	874	914	5.8/5.4	-6.7/4.8
Jackson*	55,522	87,975	10,864	14,231	19.6/16.2	61.3/31.6
Jasper	16,909	15,994	8,507	7,416	50.3/46.4	-12.5/-12.1
Jefferson*	10,142	9,295	7,653	6,996	75.5/75.3	-9.1/-8.6
Jefferson Davis	13,540	12,936	7,414	6,497	54.8/50.2	-13.9/-12.3

TABLE 2 (continued)

County	Population^a (1960)	Population^b (1970)	Number^c of Nonwhites (1960)	Number^d of Nonwhites (1970)	Nonwhite^e (1960/70)	Net change^f Nonwhites (1950–60 /1960–70)
Jones*	59,542	56,357	15,447	13,810	25.9/24.5	2.9/-10.3
Kemper	12,277	10,233	7,447	5,612	60.7/54.8	-21.0/-22.2
Lafayette	21,355	24,181	7,245	6,705	33.9/27.7	-10.4/-7.0
Lamar*	13,675	15,209	2,232	2,013	16.3/13.2	6.0/-9.8
Lauderdale*	67,119	67,087	23,484	20,630	35.0/30.8	0.4/-12.1
Lawrence	10,215	11,137	3,861	3,580	37.8/32.1	-18.9/-7.3
Leake*	18,660	17,085	8,101	6,091	43.4/35.7	-11.6/-19.7
Lee*	40,589	46,148	10,289	9,548	25.3/20.7	-3.5/-7.2
Leflore***/*	47,142	42,111	30,443	24,374	64.6/57.9	-13.8/-19.6
Lincoln	26,759	26,198	8,352	8,035	31.2/30.7	-9.1/-3.7
Lowndes*	46,639	49,700	17,768	16,226	38.1/32.6	-3.5/-8.5
Madison*	32,904	29,737	23,637	18,548	71.8/62.4	-5.2/-21.5
Marion	23,293	22,871	7,885	7,102	33.9/31.1	-6.0/-9.9
Marshall*	24,503	24,027	17,239	14,891	70.4/62.0	-2.8/-13.6
Monroe*	33,953	34,043	12,021	10,382	35.4/30.5	-12.3/-13.6
Montgomery	13,320	12,918	5,971	5,787	44.8/44.8	-4.1/-3.0
Neshoba*+	20,927	20,802	5,901	4,098	28.2/19.7	-11.5/-12.5
Newton	19,517	18,983	6,567	5,187	33.6/27.3	-16.4/-16.1
Noxubee	16,826	14,288	12,102	9,397	71.9/65.8	-18.8/-22.1
Oktibbeha*	26,175	28,752	11,448	10,004	43.7/34.8	-2.6/-12.5
Panola**/*	28,791	26,829	16,226	13,753	56.4/51.3	-7.2/-15.2
Pearl River	22,411	27,802	5,190	5,129	23.2/18.4	15.5/-0.9
Perry	8,745	9,065	2,412	2,386	27.6/26.3	9.1/-1.0
Pike*	35,063	31,813	15,408	13,827	43.9/43.5	-1.9/-10.2
Pontotoc	17,232	17,363	3,286	3,097	19.1/17.8	-13.9/-5.7
Prentiss	17,949	20,133	2,186	2,305	12.2/11.4	-6.3/5.5
Quitman***	21,019	15,888	13,304	9,120	63.5/57.4	-15.3/-31.2
Rankin*	34,322	43,933	12,818	12,368	37.3/28.2	-6.2/-3.4
Scott	21,187	21,369	8,137	7,053	38.4/33.0	-13.2/-12.8
Sharkey***	10,738	8,937	7,491	5,784	69.8/64.7	-18.5/-22.6
Simpson	20,454	19,947	7,200	6,258	35.2/31.4	-1.0/-13.0
Smith	14,303	13,561	3,247	2,888	22.7/21.3	-4.2/-10.7
Stone	7,013	8,101	1,711	1,864	24.4/23.0	25.3/9.1
Sunflower***/*	45,750	37,047	31,020	23,261	67.8/62.8	-18.7/-24.6
Tallahatchie***/*	24,081	19,338	15,501	11,632	64.4/60.2	-20.1/-24.5

TABLE 2 *(continued)*

County	Population[a] (1960)	Population[b] (1970)	Number[c] of Nonwhites (1960)	Number[d] of Nonwhites (1970)	Nonwhite[e] (1960/70)	Net change[f] Nonwhites (1950–60 /1960–70)
Tate**	18,138	18,544	10,442	8,760	57.6/47.2	0.7/-16.1
Tippah	15,093	15,852	2,756	2,581	18.3/16.3	-18.8/-5.9
Tishomingo	13,889	14,940	679	669	4.9/4.5	-15.8/-1.2
Tunica***	16,826	11,854	13,321	8,614	79.2/72.7	-24.8/-35.3
Union	18,904	19,096	3,312	2,944	17.5/15.4	-8.9/-11.1
Walthall*	13,512	12,500	6,100	5,088	45.1/40.7	-14.9/-16.6
Warren**/*	42,206	44,981	19,759	18,355	46.8/40.8	-1.7/-6.6
Washington***/*	78,638	70,581	43,399	38,460	55.2/54.5	-7.8/-10.8
Wayne	16,258	16,650	5,809	5,470	35.7/32.9	-6.6/-5.7
Webster	10,580	10,047	2,642	2,253	25.0/22.4	-1.9/-14.0
Wilkinson*	13,235	11,099	9,428	7,499	71.2/67.6	-3.4/-20.5
Winston	19,246	18,406	8,393	7,198	43.6/39.1	-9.7/-13.0
Yalobusha**	12,502	11,915	5,540	4,814	44.3/40.4	-16.8/-13.1
Yazoo***	31,653	27,314	18,791	14,579	59.4/53.4	-14.9/-22.3

[a]SNCC, *The General Condition of the Mississippi Negro* (Atlanta, 1963); based on statistics from the U.S. Bureau of the Census and the Mississippi State Board of Health.

[b]U.S. Bureau of the Census, *County and City Data Book* (Washington, D.C., 1973).

[c]SNCC, *The General Condition of the Mississippi Negro*; Blacks and nonwhites are used interchangeably as there is a less than 1 percent difference.

[d]U.S. Bureau of the Census, *County and City Data Book*; here statistics on Blacks are used.

[e]For 1960, see SNCC, *The General Condition of the Mississippi Negro*; figures for 1970 were computed by the author.

[f]For 1950–60, see SNCC, *The General Condition of the Mississippi Negro*; for 1960–70, U.S. Bureau of the Census, *County and City Data Book*.

*Counties of civil rights activity

**Counties on Delta border

***Delta counties.

+This is the only county affected by nonwhites who were not Blacks.

wood (22,400). Over 57 percent of the population of the eleven Delta counties was rural, and over 73 percent of the population in the ten adjacent counties was rural.

Thus, in 1962 the movement chose to go into an area composed of African Americans who were poor, undereducated, and subject to economic intimidation by the white power structure. Furthermore, a close examination of voter

TABLE 3

Vital Statistics, Median Schooling, and Median Family Income: The Delta and Adjacent Counties, Mississippi, 1970

County	Birth Rate Per 1,000 Pop., 1968	Death Rate Per 1,000 Pop., 1969	Median Yrs. Schooling: Persons 25+ Years	Median Family Income 1969: White ($)	Median Family Income 1969: Nonwhite ($)
The State	20.7	10.8	10.7	7,577	3,200
Bolivar*	27.8	11.0	8.7	8,129	2,534
Carroll	18.1	11.4	8.9	6,260	2,771
Coahoma*	21.8	12.4	8.7	8,824	2,479
DeSoto	21.9	7.6	10.9	9,236	3,246
Grenada	22.1	11.0	10.2	8,655	3,408
Holmes*	22.6	13.3	8.6	6,429	2,144
Humphreys*	26.0	13.3	8.3	6,141	2,230
Issaquena*	22.5	8.2	8.3	8,929	2,855
Leflore*	23.6	12.1	9.6	8,844	3,037
Madison	25.5	11.6	9.5	8,319	3,329
Marshall	22.7	10.1	8.7	6,934	2,937
Panola	22.3	12.5	9.2	7,205	2,694
Quitman*	23.2	10.7	8.0	6,454	1,921
Sharkey*	24.6	11.7	8.7	8,346	2,536
Sunflower*	26.2	11.1	8.6	7,715	2,523
Tallahatchie*	22.7	12.9	8.2	6,458	2,069
Tate	20.1	10.0	9.4	7,297	2,896
Tunica*	28.3	13.5	7.1	6,670	2,093
Washington*	23.8	11.3	9.8	9,077	3,254
Yalobusha	16.8	15.0	9.3	5,635	3,000
Yazoo*	21.2	12.6	9.2	8,179	2,188

Source: U.S. Bureau of the Census, County and City Data Book (Washington, D.C., 1973).
Note: The median family income in 1970 for whites in the South was $9,240, while for nonwhites it was $5,226. The low-income level for a nonfarm family of four was $3,743 while for a farm family it was $3,182.
*Delta county.

registration statistics for 1962 in this area reveals a range from 0.0 percent for nonwhites in Humphreys County to 8.6 percent for nonwhites in Washington County. The state average was 6.7 percent prior to the Voting Rights Act of 1965, but the Delta and the adjacent counties normally had even lower voter registration percentages for nonwhites.[23]

Greenwood became a center of voter registration activity in the Delta because of the SNCC and COFO people who went there and decided to stay no matter what happened to them.[24] Sam Block's story, although extreme, is not uncharacteristic of the movement's experiences in the northwestern part of the state.

Block went to Greenwood in June with the recommendation of Amzie Moore, who helped him make his initial contacts with local people, among them Cleve Jordan of the Citizen's League, Richard West, Louie Redd, W. J. Bishop, and Charles Golden of the NAACP, who had all been active in the 1950s. Block began to canvass in the African American section, and a police car followed him constantly. People were afraid to speak with him, but the local Elks Club gave him a meeting place, and two of its members, Ed Cochrane and W. J. Bishop, were very supportive. Willie Wazir Peacock, who worked with Block from the beginning, gives an account of their time in Greenwood: "We were hungry one day and didn't have anything to eat and didn't even have a pair of shoes hardly, and we went down and started hustling and a fellow gave me a pair of shoes. . . . We just go on and raise hell all the time. We don't have to ride, we can walk, we don't care."[25]

The stubbornness of these two workers had already become a characteristic of the movement in Mississippi. After Block got involved in the investigation of Welton McSwine's beating, he himself was beaten by three white men on August 16. Earlier in the summer, Luvaughn Brown and Lawrence Guyot, of Pass Christian, Mississippi, attended a planning session and voter registration workshop in Edwards, Mississippi, between Vicksburg and Jackson. On August 16, they arrived in Greenwood to work with Block and Peacock. The three of them fled from the SNCC office on the night of the seventeenth, after whites and local police had been milling around threateningly all evening. Peacock, who had been in Cleveland with Bob Moses during the evening of the incident, returned before sunrise to Greenwood with Moses to find the office in a shambles. Block, after fleeing by way of the rooftops and sleeping with some local people, went to Hattiesburg for the day. When he returned the following day, he was informed by the owner of the office that SNCC could no longer use it. For the next two nights he slept in a wrecked car in a local junkyard. It took Block and Peacock five months to find another office, but they remained in the city to continue the fight, keeping up a steady stream of voter registration applicants from the local community. Nevertheless, only five African Americans were declared by the registrar to have passed the test during the first six months of the project.

On August 26, COFO people met in Clarksdale with Wiley A. Branton, the lawyer for the African American school children during the Little Rock Crisis and the project director of the Voter Education Project.[26] Present at the meeting were Moses; Aaron Henry; James Forman; Sam Block; Jesse Harris; Dave Dennis of Shreveport, Louisiana and CORE's field secretary in the state, along with others. At the meeting Branton insisted that Moses be chosen state field director and Henry be chosen state president of COFO. The meeting broke up after midnight, after the Clarksdale curfew for African Americans had gone into effect. Forman and Reggie Robinson were stopped on their way out of the city. Six workers in one car were stopped a few blocks from the meeting, and they were arrested on charges on "loitering" in a moving vehicle in violation of the city curfew. Some of the occupants were held overnight in the city jail, some in the county jail. Branton tried to bail them out during the night but succeeded only the next morning.

After part of the group was released from jail, they went to Indianola to pass out leaflets for a mass meeting. Charles McLaurin of Jackson, Lafayette Surney of Ruleville, Sam Block, and Moses were among those arrested for distributing literature without a permit from the city. Moses had organized this campaign in Indianola, the birthplace of the Citizens' Councils, in order to collect signatures on a petition which stated that, if African Americans had been allowed to vote in the June 5 Democratic Party Primary, they would have voted for Reverend Lindsey. He felt that, if he could get enough signatures, he could challenge the right of Jamie Whitten to be seated as the representative of the Delta in Congress. (This was in fact another step in the development of protest politics, used again in the "Freedom Vote" in November 1963 and later used for the challenge to the Mississippi congressmen in January 1965.)

This campaign was continued through September in Indianola and Ruleville, the home of Mrs. Fannie Lou Hamer—who after going to register on August 31 was thrown off the plantation where she was the timekeeper and had lived all her life. She joined the movement shortly afterwards. Economic intimidation and violence built up during this period in an effort to stall registration work in the Delta.

In October, the Leflore County Board of Supervisors stopped distributing federal surplus commodities, cutting off twenty-two thousand people—mostly African Americans—who were dependent upon them because the cotton had already been picked and it was customary for the plantation owners not to supply "furnish" (credit against the next year's crop) until March. A national food-

and-clothing drive was then begun by SNCC and COFO, which helped alleviate the situation, but it was not a comfortable winter in the Delta. As food began to come in, people responded by going down to the courthouse to register after they had picked up the food that had been sent in from the North. And this sort of action became an important organizing device for the movement as it reached out to the poverty-stricken people of the Delta and encouraged them to support the movement's programs.

The drive was surrounded by violence and intimidation, as was typical in its occurrence. Ivanhoe Donaldson and Ben Taylor, students from Michigan State University, were arrested and charged with possession of narcotics (vitamin pills and aspirin) on December 26, in Clarksdale, after driving more than a thousand miles to get there. Their truckload of food, clothing, and medicine was never recovered. Bond was set for the two at $15,000 but was later reduced to $1,500.[27]

Mississippi Violence

Violence also occurred in other parts of the state during the last months of 1962.[28] On October 3, in Biloxi, the residence of Dr. Gilbert R. Mason was damaged by a firebomb and the gas station of Emmett Clark was attacked. On October 5, in Harmony, Leake County, shotguns were fired into eight African American homes and an African American store, slightly injuring an African American child of nine. Harmony's African Americans had recently petitioned the authorities to desegregate local schools. On October 10, in Columbus, Lowndes County, a firebomb was thrown from a speeding car into the home of Dr. James L. Allen, vice-chairman of the Mississippi Advisory Committee to the U.S. Commission on Civil Rights.

OLE MISS

Parallel to the civil rights activities that went on throughout the year, pressure built up within the state over the admission of James Howard Meredith to the University of Mississippi. Studies of the events have been written by Professors Russell H. Barrett[29] and James W. Silver.[30] The importance of the confrontation between the Mississippi government and the federal government cannot be passed over, particularly concerning the atmosphere it created for disregard of federal law in the state. Other than this, however, these events are only tangential to the civil rights movement in Mississippi. Nevertheless, local law enforcement agencies' disregard for the U.S. Supreme Court and President Kennedy, Governor Barnett's defiance of federal court orders, and the riots that took place at Ole Miss on September 30 and October 1 polarized the general atmosphere in the state and probably made things more difficult and dangerous for the civil rights movement in the Delta. Furthermore, all of Mississippi's federal representatives—James Eastland and John Stennis in the Senate and Thomas G. Abernathy, Jamie Whitten, Arthur Winstead, John Bell Williams, and William M. Colmer in the House—publicly supported Barnett in his defiance of the federal government.[31]

GREENWOOD

Throughout the winter of 1962–63, the movement continued its activities in the Delta. Then on February 28, 1963, three voter registration workers were fired on while driving from Greenwood to Greenville.[32] Thirteen .45-caliber bullets from a submachine gun were fired into their car from a white Buick, which had no license plates and had been parked outside the SNCC office in Greenwood all day. James Travis, of Jackson, was driving the car and was critically injured when a bullet lodged behind his spine at the base of his skull. Also in the car were Bob Moses and Randolph Blackwell, the field director of VEP, but they were untouched by the bullets. When the FBI began its investigations, a local white man voluntarily surrendered to the sheriff, confessed, and implicated a companion. The FBI investigation disclosed that spent bullets found inside his car were fired from the same weapon that fired the bullet recovered from Travis's neck.[33] After three six-month continuances, the trial of the self-confessed criminal was permanently adjourned in November 1964. State District Attorney Everett had judged the confession inadmissible and felt that the other evidence would not support a conviction.[34]

This incident brought the Mississippi movement to Greenwood, where it was to concentrate its actions throughout the year. James Forman, of SNCC, wrote President Kennedy from Atlanta asking him to protect voter registration workers from acts of violence in Mississippi; Dave Dennis, of CORE, wired Attorney General Robert Kennedy for protective action on the part of the Justice Department and the FBI; and Aaron Henry, the state president of the NAACP and COFO, issued a statement of protest. Wiley Branton, of VEP, asked all of the voter registration workers in the state to congregate in Greenwood and show the white power structure in Leflore County and the rest of the state that the movement would not be terrorized and intimidated by violence.[35] This gathering in Greenwood became a keystone in the movement's strategic philosophy of organizing: never again submit to Mississippi's use of violence and intimidation.

Once its members had congregated in Greenwood, the Mississippi movement began to coalesce into a more ordered structure, supported in no small part by the work of Mrs. Hamer in Ruleville and Sunflower County in her position as a SNCC field secretary under the umbrella of COFO. "Some twenty odd SNCC field workers participating in the COFO project were immediately concentrated in Greenwood, [the] NAACP sent Amzie Moore and hired five special workers from the Greenwood NAACP youth chapter, CORE sent in Dave Dennis and SCLC sent in James Bevel and Annelle Ponder of Atlanta."[36] The substance of this action was that the movement had thrown down the gauntlet in refusing to be intimidated and driven out of an area no matter how rough the situation became. This fortitude was to prove essential in the period that followed as the numbers of registrants to vote rose from the tens to the hundreds.

4

Commitment Aborted

Our Committee experience convinces us that, contrary to many a political slogan,
the Federal Government is most reluctant to intervene, even where Constitutional rights are concerned.

— MISSISSIPPI ADVISORY COMMITTEE
TO THE U.S. COMMISSION ON CIVIL RIGHTS, 1963

The Mississippi movement's decision to work on voter registration
was influenced by both the federal government and the foundation
world. By early 1963 the early fears of the direct action group that the
movement was being led astray had been proven to be justified. The promise
that more protection would be given to those working in voter registration
activities, where the federal government had clear statutory power, had been
aborted. By and large, the movement was left to protect itself.[1] Also, the promise of foundation money for nonpartisan political action in the state, although
at first fulfilled in the Voter Education Project, was revoked in the fall of 1963
when it was seen that not enough African Americans were able to register to
make the expenditure worthwhile from the donors' point of view.

Additionally, the hearings on Mississippi before the United States Commission on Civil Rights—first scheduled for October 1962—did not take place
until February 1965.[2] These hearings might be termed a failure because by 1965
their purpose—exposing Mississippi's closed society to the nation—had already been accomplished.[3] The Freedom Summer of 1964 had largely obviated
the need for the hearings, although the commission's findings might have been
helpful in drawing up the Voting Rights Act of 1965. Nevertheless, it is not entirely clear if this was true. It seems to be a case of too little, too late.

The Justice Department

William L. Higgs, the white Mississippi lawyer with the movement, verifies Tim
Jenkins' description of the federal promise of protection in 1961: "The bargain

was struck that the Attorney-General's office would help with the registration *in every possible way*, and the student movement would channel its efforts from the sit-ins and public accommodations into trying to get people registered to vote."[4]

But federal presence, in a real sense, was not to come until 1964; and then, it was only after crimes had been committed against northern whites in the movement. *Law Enforcement*, a 1965 U.S. Commission on Civil Rights publication, states: "severe self-limitations have been imposed on the scope of Federal protective action. Except where court orders have been previously obtained, the Department of Justice will not directly protect persons exercising Federal rights. Nor will FBI agents or United States marshals arrest persons for offenses committed in their presence or perform patrolling or other preventive duties in communities where there has been substantial racial violence."[5]

Justice Department dependence on and bargaining with local law enforcement authorities are notable in two cases in 1963. The first was in the investigation and trial of Byron de la Beckwith, who murdered Medgar Evers in Jackson on June 12. His trial resulted in two hung juries; he was released when the state dropped its case.[6] No federal charges were proffered against him because a state indictment had been brought and failed to return a conviction. (He was finally convicted of his crime in 1994.)

The second instance took place in Greenwood. Bob Moses, Jim Forman, Willie Peacock, and seven others were arrested on March 27 for leading a march to the courthouse. The march was broken up by police using dogs. The demonstrations continued for the next few days, with comedian Dick Gregory joining. Moses and the others were sentenced to four months in prison and fined two hundred dollars each, the maximum penalty for disorderly conduct. They were then released in return for a Justice Department promise to postpone its suit enjoining the Greenwood officials against interfering with the civil rights of movement workers.[7] The difficulty arose over the making of this sort of deal without the movement's prior knowledge. Jesse Harris, of SNCC, spoke about this: "We asked the Justice Department to come in and file an injunction against the city officials for interfering with the [rights of] civil rights workers and to release us from jail and stop the officials from arresting us . . . but the Justice Department . . . made a deal with the city officials to release us from jail, and [after] ten days in jail, we got out because the Justice Department came in. But . . . some of us got arrested again. . . . So, the Justice Department simply took the position that, well, I got you out the first time, and I promised the man [the police] that you all won't demonstrate no more, that you all won't do that again."[8]

In spite of ample available powers (see appendix), President Kennedy and Attorney General Robert Kennedy made the Justice Department primarily a fact-finding organization that filed suits concerning the denial of the right to register to vote. One such suit was against Registrar Theron Lynd of Forrest County, Mississippi.[9] It was filed by John Doar in August 1960, under the Civil Rights Act of 1960. The long process of litigation took until January 1964, when the U.S. Supreme Court upheld the Fifth Circuit Court of Appeals decision of July 15, 1963, that said it would find Registrar Lynd guilty of civil contempt unless he complied with court orders not to discriminate in registering voters. The time-consuming process of the Justice Department's suits against Lynd and other registrars required that a "pattern or practice" of discrimination be proven by the plaintiff. The first African American in eight years to register in Forrest County did so on April 26, 1962; but by July 14, 1963, only 8 more had done so, making a total of 23 African Americans out of 7,495 voting-age non-whites in the county. This pattern of discrimination was the rule in Mississippi rather than the exception.

A typical reaction of the Justice Department to discrimination in the South, as well as that of the FBI, was the reaction to the beating of five people from the New Orleans CORE on November 9, 1961, in McComb, when they sought service at the lunch counter in the Greyhound bus terminal.[10] The week before, the Interstate Commerce Commission had ruled that it was illegal to segregate interstate facilities. Nevertheless, the FBI merely stood by observing the beatings and taking notes.

Sit-in leader Marion Barry commented on the lack of federal protection for civil rights workers: "They said to us, 'Well, look now. We're not trying to tell you what to do and where to go. You can go where you want to. But if you want us to protect you, we only have so many men, so many lawyers, so much time, and so much legal power to help you. And if you want us to do this, we would suggest that you work with us to make sure we've got enough people to be around and to do things.'"[11]

In ways such as this the federal government tried to put a price on the protection it offered the movement and turn those rights inherent under the Constitution into rights conditional upon gradual change with little or no direct confrontation with the white power structure. The movement refused this compromise. Jesse Harris's comments on the situation in Greenwood in 1963 further clarify the federal position: "And our position was that we wanted to get peoples registered, and . . . we wanted cooperation from the Justice Department in terms of helping us get these people registered. And so John Doar and Burke Marshall explained the Justice Department position to us, saying that they would help us in terms of filing suits, if we went out and got affidavits and complaints that the registrar actually discriminated against Negroes, if we considered taking people [down to register] who were able to read and write."[12]

SNCC, however, felt that African Americans who had been denied an equal education ought to be allowed to vote even if they were illiterate. The Justice Department dissented from this position. Bill Higgs, who was run out of Mississippi in February 1963 on a trumped-up morals charge but in reality for his civil rights involvements, told me: "They didn't come through with the promises they'd made, in terms of protection, this that, and the other. There was almost no protection, you know, in the grossest of circumstances. We were heavily involved in Mississippi; there was just nothing that could be done. They just wouldn't help at all, even though the law was very clear."[13]

Aaron Henry, who ran for governor in the Freedom Vote of November 1963, condemned the discriminatory application of federal law. He said: "Medgar Evers was killed in June 1963, and his killer walks the street, day by day, in Greenwood, Mississippi. The Federal Government has not filed any suit against anybody for violating Medgar's civil rights. And it has not done it in any case where Negroes were involved—the only cases where the Federal Government has really used this muscle is in cases in the South where a white person was killed. I am sorry to have to make this accusation, but it's obvious that the Federal Government is much more concerned with difficulty [i.e., discrimination] when the white community is involved."[14]

The Voter Education Project

The Voter Education Project (VEP) started operating on April 1, 1962, as a subordinate agency to the Southern Regional Council. Its home office was in Atlanta. The primary objectives of the project were to register new voters in the South and do research on southern opposition to voter registration. The program was set up as a nonpartisan political organization with tax-exempt status, the impetus coming from the meetings that were held in 1961.[15]

Wiley A. Branton, a civil rights lawyer from Pine Bluff, Arkansas, was appointed project director. Randolph Blackwell, a graduate of Howard University Law School, was field director. Jack Minnis, who later became head of research at SNCC, was research director of VEP and a consultant to fieldworkers. VEP employed very few fieldworkers directly involved in voter registration work, depending instead on local organizations and the major civil rights groups to organize voter registration campaigns. The staff at VEP took field trips and held investigatory meetings for purposes of gathering information and distributing funds for its work.

VEP's financial participation in the Mississippi movement was eventually withdrawn because Mr. Branton felt that significant enough numbers of African Americans had not been registered to justify the expense involved, even though the research objectives of the project in Mississippi had been accomplished. VEP's decision to leave Mississippi, except for the NAACP program in Jackson, is explained in part in the organization's Second Annual Report:

> This state presents more resistance to would-be Negro voters than any other state and offers more intimidation and violence to Negroes than all the others combined. VEP has only been able to add 3,871 voters to the rolls in Mississippi during the past two years. . . .
>
> Mississippi has a long history of intimidation and violence against Negroes who seek to register and with the rather large number of cases of injury and death to their persons and destruction of their property, it is little wonder that Negroes developed a fear of attempting to do anything which the white people of the state were opposed to.[16]

Although the Voter Education Project purported to be a nonpartisan political program to register voters in the South, this was probably not the case. Jack Minnis took extensive notes on what went on behind the scenes at VEP, and his diary reveals the partisan objectives of the organization and its backers in the foundation world, the Democratic National Committee, and the Kennedy Administration:

> May 8, 1963 . . . He [Wiley Branton] said that everybody concerned with VEP, including the donors, the Southern Regional Council, and the Kennedy Administration realized that the research angle was just a gimmick to get tax-exemption and that nobody was at all interested in such things as methods and techniques, but in getting people registered. He said that the donors had been critical of VEP because it was not operating in areas where registration was easy . . .
>
> May 9, 1963 . . . He [Branton] said that so far as he knew the only thing

that the Administration had to fear in Mississippi was Eastland's power in the Senate.[17]

What was VEP really attempting to accomplish in Mississippi? Was its aim simply to register voters who would support the National Democratic Party, or was it trying to make a breakthrough in the status of the African American? Bill Higgs states that VEP money was responsible for the reestablishment of the Council of Federated Organizations (COFO), which was to sponsor the 1964 Summer Project: "So, very early in the game, a meeting was called in Clarksdale, at which COFO was organized, and Bob Moses was elected as executive director in charge of voter registration, and Aaron Henry was the chairman, and I guess there were about 40 of us there, almost half of whom I suppose were SNCC affil-iated people. The whole thing was set up under the influence of Wiley [Branton]. . . . Wiley just simply said, 'Either you people come together or no money.' . . . And Medgar Evers was there . . . From then on, COFO began to move."[18]

Thus it can be said that COFO was renewed at the instigation of VEP, forc-ing the major civil rights groups to work together in order to get badly needed funds. Conflicts between the participating groups were glossed over, even though there was a great deal of disagreement over methods of achieving the ends that all of the groups sought. As long as voter registration work was an effective way of organizing Mississippi African Americans, a semblance of unity was maintained in COFO. When these organizing tactics became ineffective, new ways were sought that could no longer be justifiably supported with tax-exempt funds. Nevertheless, COFO was continued in the state.

Even before VEP cut off its funding of COFO, the movement began to exam-ine ways to attack Mississippi's closed society outside of voter registration. Tim Jenkins related: "We eventually found that if we were out to register people to vote we couldn't do so without giving people reasons for voting. . . . So, we saw it was necessary to set up a candidate supporting–wing, which would oper-ate on independent type funds—non-tax-exempt funds—to give the people a purpose for voting. In time it showed such promise and such importance that it was seen it was more important to get people organized around partisan objectives . . . than it was to abstractly appeal to people to vote."[19] Encouraging people to register and then asking them to go home and suffer the penalties that it caused was inconceivable. Thus, voter registration came to be seen by the movement as a method of organizing people to gain the power they were lacking in their lives. Jesse Harris explains what happened next:

So, after a period of about six months [by the winter of 1962–63], we began to take large numbers of peoples down to register. . . . And after they went down to register, they began to start making their own decisions, without us, that they wanted to go into other things, like sit-ins. They wanted to picket; they wanted to demonstrate . . . like they made in Greenwood in '62—that they wanted a job. Then, they wanted to . . . picket the employment office for discriminating in jobs. So, people went down and picketed. They got put in jail. And so the people from the VEP came . . . and wanted us to stop people from picketing. We were simply supposed to have been, at that time, doing research. So VEP really took the position in Mississippi that mainly they were concerned about educating people around reading and writing and taking them to the courthouse, and that's it. We were concerned about people involving themselves, participating in any way, other than reading and writing and going to the courthouse. . . . And so, at a point we had to get resources from other places, other than VEP, because I think their period, in terms of their relationship with us, had run out.[20]

The Movement Attacked

On the whole, the whites of Mississippi felt that their way of life was being frontally attacked by foreign elements.[21] As late as the early summer of 1964, Mayor Allen Thompson of Jackson could say, "This is it, they are not bluffing and we are not bluffing. We're going to be ready for them . . . they won't have a chance.[22] This was the prevalent attitude in Mississippi and thereby helps explain why the movement was met with such violence, both officially and unofficially. The First Annual Report of the Voter Education Project highlights the way in which the movement's voter registration workers were attacked by the Mississippi government: "Thus, what the registration programs in these areas boil down to is this: Gallant and fantastically committed young men and women live month after month under the constant threat of physical violence from the police and thugs alike, while they coach, cajole, entreat, demand, instruct, and encourage the Negro to brace the white man's wrath at the courthouse, in pursuit of his political birthright."[23]

In the spring of 1963, the movement found it necessary to consolidate to meet the opposition. By that time it had become apparent that any federal help that was to be gained would take more time than was available and that Mississippi African Americans would have to win the hearts of the nation before they could break down the walls of Mississippi's closed society. VEP funding was available in places where African Americans could be registered; Mississippi was not such a place. It would have to become the nation's problem before Kennedy and Johnson saw fit to act. More suffering would have to be endured before Mississippi African Americans would be heard. The movement, however, had begun to come together for its confrontation with the Mississippi power structure in order to make it the "next to go."

5

The Stalemated Movement

The Civil Rights Movement has reached a stalemate in Mississippi. The State has successfully halted all direct action movements, large and small, by arresting the demonstrators and their leaders, setting huge bond fees, long-term jail sentences and extending the court cases. . . . In the wake of the demonstrations, the pressure against the Negro community is overwhelming. . . . Voter registration work has been agonizingly slow. The Negro communities are shot through with fears, from the "Metropolitan" Jackson community to the rural farm communities.

—ROBERT PARRIS MOSES, SUMMER 1963

We have seen that the near-fatal shooting of Jimmy Travis on February 28, 1963, drew voter registration workers from all of the civil rights groups in the state to Greenwood in early March in order to launch a frontal attack on the local power structure. They refused to let the enemy think the civil rights movement could be intimidated by violence, even if isolated African Americans could.

The confrontation in Greenwood let African Americans in the Delta know that they would not be deserted, and it informed the white community that the movement was serious in its attempt to smash the closed society and free its people. This holding operation lasted out the summer successfully, although Medgar Evers was murdered in Jackson. And even though violence and intimidation continued to mount, the movement was not to be stopped.[1]

When voter registration became too slow, and too dangerous, a new approach to the "Mississippi iceberg" was sought. (See chapter 6, "The Birth of Protest Politics.") The monolith began to crack during 1963, although it was not apparent to the casual observer. National concern for African Americans was mounting. It was also found that, after the initial penetration of a new area, there was normally a period of violence against the movement, which then leveled off and was replaced by tension. Nevertheless, it was not necessary for the movement to be present for violence to occur, and such violence pushed the movement to find new and creative ways to attack the closed society, although at times the violence became so rampant that it was difficult to do more than search for ways to survive White Mississippi's attack.

In 1963, the Mississippi movement operated in three primary areas: Greenwood, Clarksdale, and Jackson. The first, Greenwood, had been the principal theater of action in the state in late winter and early spring, although civil rights activity went on there throughout the year. The second, Clarksdale, would provide Dr. Aaron Henry as the candidate of the movement for the November gubernatorial "Freedom Vote." The third area, Jackson, would be the scene of mounting turmoil, leading up to the assassination of Medgar Evers in June and the subsequent riots.

Greenwood Again

Dave Dennis, CORE field secretary for Mississippi and an official in COFO, commuted between Jackson, Greenville, and Greenwood during March 1963. He reported the mounting tension in Greenwood in the following excerpted field report, which he filed with his national office in New York:

> March 19: Miss Fay Bennett, Mr. Charles Butts, and I went to Greenwood. There we had a meeting with the workers where a discussion was held on techniques of getting aid from the Federal government and putting pressure in the right places. . . .
>
> March 20: I helped in the distribution of food to over 500 people in Greenwood. On this day over 75 people attempted to register. . . .
>
> March 27: . . . Bob Moses and ten other workers from SNCC were arrested on charges of "Breach of the Peace." The night before, Mr. Greene's home was shot into by white hoods. Bob Moses, James Forman, and other workers had drawn up a resolution asking for protection from harassment and intimidations. They then, along with other citizens, went down to the Mayor's office to discuss the matter. Upon their arrival they were met by policemen and a police dog. . . . James Forman and Lawrence Guyot were arrested. The other people then proceeded to the courthouse to register. Bob and the other workers returned to the church, where distribution of food and clothing was taking place. Approximately 100 people were there. Bob and the other workers began to talk to the people about voter regis-

tration when they were approached again by the police officers. The group refused to disperse and therefore was arrested. . . . Mr. James Farmer was contacted to speak at a mass meeting on Thursday night. . . .

March 30: The registrar's office was closed, so I took Jim to Memphis via Ruleville where he met some of the people who were taking part in the home industry project.[2]

Throughout the spring and summer, the movement continued this sort of activity in Greenwood, although in most cases it was not as concentrated as in March.

Clarksdale

In early spring and summer there was a flurry of violence and intimidation in Clarksdale, the home of Dr. Aaron Henry, state president of the NAACP. On March 4, Henry's Fourth Street drugstore was broken into. He found the damage when he returned from speaking at a mass meeting in Leflore County in connection with the voter registration drive. On March 29, three white University of Iowa students—John A. Goulet, Roswell P. Donaldson, and Donald P. Flachart—were arrested on charges of running a red light and failing to give a turn signal as they left Clarksdale after delivering a truckload of food and clothing to needy African Americans.[3]

On April 2, in Washington, D.C., Senators James O. Eastland and John Stennis (both Democrats, Mississippi) stated on the floor of the Senate that African Americans had not been denied the right to register and vote in Leflore County, or anywhere else in Mississippi.[4] Then on April 12, two Clarksdale whites threw a gasoline-filled Molotov cocktail through a window of the home of Aaron Henry. Representative Charles C. Diggs (Democrat, Michigan) was visiting in Henry's home at the time. On May 4, an explosion ripped a hole in the roof of Henry's drugstore. Police said that they suspected lightning.[5] On May 8, the home of Hartman Turnbow, the first African American to try to register during a local drive in Holmes County, was firebombed. Bob Moses and three other workers were arrested on "suspicion of arson."[6] On May 30, the state highway patrol halted a busload of thirty-one African Americans who were going to Jackson to a voter registration conference sponsored by SNCC at Tougaloo Southern Christian College. The bus driver was charged with driving with an improper license plate and his bus being overloaded.

On June 8 three bullets were fired into Henry's home.[7] One was also fired into the home of Mrs. Vera Pigee, who was involved in voter registration work for the NAACP and had been beaten by a white on April 23 for trying to use a white restroom at a local service station.[8] From July 20 to August 2, ninety-five African Americans were arrested in Clarksdale while they were demonstrating over job discrimination, public accommodations, and segregation in general.

Jackson

During May and June the Jackson movement began to make progress under the leadership of the NAACP and CORE. The local reaction culminated in the murder of Medgar Evers, national field secretary for the NAACP in Mississippi, and the riots that followed his funeral.

On May 12, the NAACP got its Jackson program underway, when the Mississippi State NAACP organization met in the city and drew up its demands for progress for the African American.[9] A summary of those events is provided in Lester Sobel's *Civil Rights 1960–66:*

> The Mississippi NAACP announced May 12 its determination to end "all forms of segregation in Jackson, Miss." . . .
>
> After meeting with 75 business leaders May 13, Mayor Allen Thompson announced the rejection of the Negro demands. . . . The Negroes picked a 14-man committee May 21 to meet with Thompson. Thompson replaced 10 of the 14 committee members with his own nominees, then met with the committee May 27 and read a statement banning demonstrations, upholding school segregation, and rejecting the demand for a biracial committee. . . .
>
> A bomb explosion that night [on May 29] wrecked the home of an integrationist leader [Medgar Evers] . . . 400 Negro school children demonstrated in a Jackson schoolyard May 30. . . .
>
> Mayor Thompson and the City Commission agreed June 1 to 3 of the Negroes' demands—to hire Negroes as policemen and school crossing guards, to desegregate city facilities and to upgrade Negro employment in city jobs. The Negroes' key demand, for the establishment of a biracial committee, was rejected.[10]

After June 1 things began to calm down, but they heated up again on the night of June 11–12, when Medgar Evers was assassinated by Byron de la Beckwith, an avid member of the Greenwood Citizens' Council.

The following sequence of events was reported by Sobel concerning the events after Evers's murder in Jackson:

> Jackson Negroes reacted to Evers murder with mass demonstrations June 12 that resulted in 158 arrests. . . .
>
> A riot broke out briefly June 15 following a mourning march. Officials had granted a parade permit for the march, in which thousands of Negroes and about 50 whites participated. . . . U.S. Asst. Atty. Gen. John Doar was credited with keeping the riot from growing worse by ignoring the missiles, walking toward the crowd and appealing for calm. . . . A 2d march protesting Evers' slaying resulted June 15 in the arrest of 82 persons, including Prof. Salter.
>
> Following a suspension of demonstrations June 17 and several phone calls from Pres. Kennedy to Mayor Thompson, Thompson met with 5 Negro leaders June 18 and announced later that the city would (a) hire 6 Negro policemen and 8 Negro school-crossing guards and (b) promote 7 Negro sanitation workers to truck drivers and a Negro truck driver to crew leader, all for Negro districts. . . . The demonstrations were suspended June 20. More than 1,000 Negroes and whites had been arrested in the final 4 weeks.[11]

The Movement Stopped

While Jackson was settling down, trouble began in other places, indicating just how much the state was on edge and how the white community was reacting to movement activities in the Delta and the Jackson area.

On June 9, Mrs. Fannie Lou Hamer, of SNCC; Miss Annelle Ponder, of SCLC; June Johnson, age fifteen; James West; Euvester Simpson; Lawrence Guyot; and Milton Hancock were arrested in Winona, Montgomery County. The first four were arrested while trying to seek service at the bus-station lunch counter.[12] They were on their way to the COFO office in Greenwood after attending a citizenship education workshop in Charleston, South Carolina. They were held in jail for four days and beaten mercilessly. Guyot and Hancock were arrested when they came from Greenwood to check on the first group, which had already been in jail for two days. A federal jury later found the police not guilty of any violation of federal law after the judge had instructed the jury that these civil rights workers were outside troublemakers.

On June 18, in Itta Bena, a small town not far from Greenwood in the Delta, forty-five African Americans were arrested on charges of creating a disturbance and breach of the peace. They were walking to the home of the town marshal to ask for protection after a gas bomb was thrown into the church where they were attending a voter registration meeting. On June 20, the forty-five were sentenced to six months on the Leflore County penal farm by Itta Bena Justice of the Peace Joe Rustici. The women were fined $200 each and the men $500, in addition to the jail sentences.

They were then joined by twenty-two African Americans, most of whom were full-time volunteer SNCC staff workers.[13] The twenty-two were arrested on June 25 and 26 inside the Leflore County courthouse after an even larger group of African Americans refused to move from the registrar's office, which was closed at the time. All were sentenced to six months in jail on charges of breach of the peace. The entire group of sixty-seven was then placed in the maximum security wing of Parchman State Penitentiary. The bond money ran to $42,000, and after an appeal was sent out,[14] the National Council of Churches supplied the funds. They were released in August; among them was a seventy-five-year-old woman who, like the others, had gone down to register to vote.[15] On June 30, Joel Lovett, twenty, was shot and killed near his home in Tchula, Holmes County. A complaint was filed with the Justice Department, but nothing came of it.[16]

By late July 1963, some rethinking was necessary if the movement was to continue in Mississippi, while the March on Washington for Jobs and Freedom in August was on the horizon. In most places where voter registration work was attempted, violence had erupted. If it did not, then the people were usually arrested and the movement found itself without workers. Moreover, the State Democratic Primaries of August 6 and 27 were imminent. The question at that point was what could be done to keep the movement going.

6

The Birth of Protest Politics

Starting with the freedom rides, the ultimate target of protest and demonstration—even when ostensibly local, as in Selma—has been the federal government
itself. Protests and demonstrations have been very largely efforts to enlist greater
federal power behind the civil rights revolution.

—HAROLD FLEMING, 1966

A whole number of factors began to come together—that is, enough of a corps of
people to carry on for the first time some statewide political activity . . . plus contacts with the outside world. So that what had been a kind of desperate, almost
futile attempt to get people to register to vote, accompanied by violence, and it
seemed to run a kind of cyclical pattern. . . . And I guess there's only a certain
amount of this frustration you can take before moving on to something else. And
this something else, I feel, was the freedom ballot, which probably as soon as it
was talked about excited the imagination of everybody.

—HOWARD ZINN, 1965

M et everywhere with apparent failure in its efforts to register Mississippi African Americans, the movement began to think in terms of
a new strategy to soften up the closed society. Direct action protests
and voter registration efforts had brought little tangible success. True, Mississippi African Americans had begun to come out of their apathy to move in large
numbers in Greenwood, Clarksdale, and Jackson. Nevertheless, these and other
smaller campaigns were largely stalemated by the Mississippi power structure.
Legal harassment along with official and unofficial violence confronted the
movement at every step.

SNCC continued its campaigns, as did individual leaders of the NAACP.
CORE, represented up to this time by Dave Dennis, who traveled from project
to project throughout the state, began its own project in Canton, Madison

County, in June 1963.[1] Dennis was more attached to the local movement than to his national office. The local movement was COFO and COFO was mainly SNCC. Dennis scattered his efforts between Hattiesburg, Laurel, Cleveland, and various Delta communities, as well as being assistant program director of COFO and a member of its steering and financial committees. Little or no distinction was made between SNCC projects and CORE projects. Dennis filled in for Bob Moses at times, or Moses for Dennis, depending on who was closer to the project in need.[2]

A new strategy was sought by the movement because it appeared that the methods attempted up to that time had not borne much fruit. Little notice was taken of the Mississippi African American's plight on the national level, and it seemed senseless to continue accepting the punishment they were receiving when they had little to show for their efforts. Whether or not the movement was reaching for more visibility on a national level is not clear, but such was the result of the new method that evolved during the summer of 1963.

Up to this point very few whites were involved in the movement in Mississippi. Most protests and demonstrations had gone along lines of attempting to attain what was legally due African Americans. During the months of July to November, the movement turned from trying to enter the legal political battle, by registering new African American voters and running African American candidates in the Democratic primaries, to what were called "parallel" or "protest" politics.

The candidacies of Reverend R. L. T. Smith and Reverend Merrill W. Lindsey in June 5, 1962, were in Democratic congressional primaries that had aroused interest in the African American community. African American viewpoints had been presented to the public on radio and television, and although African American participation in the campaigns had been minimal, a statewide audience had been reached. Hindsight indicates that a similar effect was achieved by the new strategy that was born in the summer and fall of 1963. Moreover, some new elements were added to the equation: white volunteers and ongoing national concern for the plight of the state's African Americans. A national consensus for change began to appear.

The Buildup

July 1963 was the cut-off date to register and still vote in the Mississippi primary and general elections. When this date (July 5) passed, Hinds County

Circuit Clerk and Registrar H. S. Ashford closed the registration books.[3] He did this in spite of the seven hundred African Americans who had attempted to register in Jackson since the murder of Medgar Evers on June 12 and others who had not registered but still wanted to.[4] Since voter registration could no longer be used as an organizing tactic for the primaries and the general election, a new approach was necessary. Voter registration was only de-emphasized for a time; it was not eliminated as a way of organizing African Americans.

The idea of a "freedom vote" evolved in an experimental, step-by-step manner during the summer. Tim Jenkins, then a law student at Yale, described the beginning of this process:

> I was in a group of law students that had various functions to perform: liaison with Federal agencies, protection of people in their constitutional rights in criminal courts, some advice on civil legal matters, and also to direct and help deal with the problems of COFO.
>
> When we got to Mississippi, we soon discovered an old act which provided that those people who felt that they had been legally denied the right to vote could present themselves on election day, or primary day, at the polling place and sign an affidavit to the effect that they had been illegally denied the right to vote and have their votes counted if the registrar or the commissioner of elections certified that these affidavits had reasonable cause. [This particular provision was put on the statute books during Reconstruction.] It was a way to avoid the problem of the affidavits of loyalty to the Federal Government, because the commissioners of election somehow seemed to be more loyal to the local people than to the Federal Government.
>
> We attempted to dust off this statute and use it for our purpose, saying that Negroes had been illegally denied the right to vote by virtue of inequitable education and also by intimidation of a physical sort and an economic sort. . . . We then tried to get this as widely circulated in the state as we possibly could to demonstrate that Negroes could vote in large numbers if given the opportunity. We predicted that we would get something like 20,000 people to participate in this vote. And on the basis of this we set up a very elaborate program, county by county, attempting to have a central organization which would provide transportation down to the polling places, as well as a center where they could meet in the morning and a regular well-oiled political machine to get people out to the polling places.

We anticipated taking the affidavits that resulted from this protest procedure and flying them to Washington and placing them before the House
Judiciary Committee [SNCC had testified before it in May 1963] to demonstrate the number of people who believed themselves to be illegally denied
the right to vote and the people who are interested in voting. The big argument in Washington at that time by the Southerners was that anybody who
really wanted to vote could pay a poll-tax and could vote.

We were arguing on the contrary that often times the poll-tax was offered but not accepted and that registrars arbitrarily closed down their offices or discarded applications that Negroes had made to register to vote. We
thought it would be very useful if we could get a huge number of these affidavits and bring them up to the House Judiciary Committee and present
them officially to the chairman [Emanuel Celler (Democrat, New York)],
which we were able to do in 1963.[5]

The first stage in the movement's new strategy for organizing African Americans was to make use of this obscure statute in a "vote-in" to be conducted
at the Democratic Gubernatorial Primary on August 6.[6] Prior to the primary,
the NAACP's Jackson office released the COFO plans to take advantage of this
little-known Mississippi law.

On August 4, the pro-segregationist *Jackson Clarion-Ledger* quoted the State
Attorney-General Joseph Patterson as saying, "Section 3114 [the law mentioned
by Jenkins] only applies to situations wherein palpable mistakes or errors have
been made in effectuating the registration of one who has made a lawful attempt to register and was in fact lawfully registered except for error on the
part of someone transposing his name to the poll book."[7] The attorney general
further stated that any other interpretation of the statute would be unconstitutional and that anyone attempting to vote under this law would be subject
to a fine of a hundred dollars and up to one year in prison, as it was a crime
to procure registration unlawfully. The attorney general ignored a movement
leader's statement that people filing such affidavits were only trying to vote in
an election and not trying to register.

Although Patterson's pronouncements largely obviated the possibility of
having the ballots that were cast in the "vote-in" counted, the affidavits became
valuable testimony to present in Washington. On the morning of August 6,
SNCC field secretaries Curtis Hayes, of Summit, Charles McLaurin, of Jackson,

and Charles Cobb, a former student at Howard University, were arrested when they went to see Ruleville Mayor Charles Dorrough about being poll watchers in the Democratic Gubernatorial Primary that day. Dorrough, the president of the Mississippi Municipal Association, had made life difficult for civil rights workers in the past and continued to do so through the summer of 1964. When the volunteers left at the end of Freedom Summer, he said, "I don't believe they have accomplished anything, except to poison the minds of the younger Negroes [who] will now have to be taught the Democratic way of doing things."[8]

Be that as it may, the SNCC field secretaries were charged with "interfering with an election," sentenced to thirty days in jail and fined a hundred dollars each. Cobb said, "the trial took 30 seconds."[9] Dave Dennis in Canton reported a little more luck, but he said that only thirty had attempted to vote by affidavit, stating "they felt that they had been discriminated against."[10] Others in Canton sent affidavits directly to Washington.

Additional results from the "vote-in" were as follows: between 500 and 700 "voted" in Greenwood; 14 tried in Thornton but were refused, as were 10 in Tchula and 430 in Jackson. Others tried in Clarksdale, Hattiesburg, Itta Bena, and Greenville. None of the "votes" from the "vote-in" were deemed valid, but according to Jenkins, "we predicted that we could get something like 20,000 people to participate in this vote."[11] In spite of the movement's efforts, the results did not merit a continuation of this type of action after the August 27 runoff primary between Paul Johnson Jr. and James P. Coleman, a former governor of Mississippi (1956–60), both of whom were racists, the former more than the latter.

Again the movement turned within itself and came up with a new method of declaring that African Americans would vote in Mississippi if they were allowed to. A "Vote for Freedom" was conceived in which African Americans would vote on Sunday, August 25, in their churches and other conveniently located places. Under this arrangement they would not be exposed to intimidation by having to go down to the polls and would have little to fear in the way of reprisals from the white community. They were to vote by secret ballot for either Johnson or Coleman. Prior to voting they would register their names and addresses with a recorder who would be under the authority of a manager of elections. Although all member organizations in COFO participated, the campaign was directed from the Jackson office of the NAACP.[12]

The way in which the decision to try the "Vote for Freedom" was made is described by Tim Jenkins:

I think the theory was that there was too much frustration in this business of the protest affidavit and an attempt to vote because the people never could see any tangible results. You'd cast your votes; they didn't have any effect; and the people sort of felt it was a wasted enterprise. So, we thought we'd have to carry the graphic representation of what we were trying to do another step further to make its effects much more demonstrably clear to the population. We decided that we would cast these votes and then we would call the person who won under this procedure the governor, the lt. governor, and so forth. We decided then to conceive of it as a freedom vote, where the voter didn't need the credentials of the official election, because those credentials were in fact arrived at in order to discriminate against Negroes on the basis of race. And, therefore, the freedom election was con-ceived of as a complete rejection of the existing political system, a much more complete rejection than the affidavit principle. This protest election was founded in the idea of bringing home to the people the importance of voting, of running candidates, and of winning elections. Furthermore, I think that it was thought that the "Vote for Freedom" would be a more impressive way of doing it than the affidavit procedure.[13]

The results of the Vote for Freedom saw J. P. Coleman, a Mississippi mod-erate, beat Paul Johnson, the favorite of the Citizens Councils, by a margin of 26,721 to 949. To the African American, Coleman represented the better of two bad choices. In the official runoff primary on August 27, Johnson beat Coleman by a margin of 261,065 to 196,651; Coleman was unable to escape the fact that he had supported John F. Kennedy in the 1960 presidential cam-paign.[14] Nevertheless, he was later appointed by President Johnson to the U.S. Fifth Circuit Court of Appeals. Lucille Komisar, a reporter for *The Activist,* stated:

[The belief was] held by a surprising number of civil rights leaders I spoke to [that] they wanted Johnson to win, believing that the worst possible man was the best catalyst for change in Mississippi.

If Coleman were elected, he would go about fighting integration with sophistication, they said. He'd avoid the kind of open violence that brings international condemnation; he'd use his closeness to Kennedy to make deals and compromises, a tactic that the Administration had used before in Mississippi.

And a Johnson, spouting hatred and racism, would arouse more Negroes to action, they argued.[15]

Although the number of participants in the Vote for Freedom was close to 30,000, the campaign might be called a failure because it only offered a choice between a moderate racist and a racist. Allard K. Lowenstein, a liberal white with administration connections who later came under suspicion by SNCC leaders for trying to use the movement for "establishment" aims,[16] pinpointed that failure:

> In the second primary the NAACP attempted a kind of freedom vote in which they made the mistake . . . of limiting the candidates to the ones who were on the Democratic ballot in the runoff, namely Paul Johnson and Coleman. . . . But, while sure, there was some good and some validity in doing that . . . one had to have a candidate to vote for who stood for what one wanted, at least in general ways; and the NAACP didn't dissent from that. Eventually it was done that way. . . . It grew into a state convention of COFO and the nomination of Aaron Henry [on October 6], and then adding Ed King [a white Mississippian] a couple of days later to the ticket, which was an important thing also because it meant that we had not a Negro party but an interracial Democratic Party in the image of the National Democratic Party. . . . Its goals [were] similar to the national party's because we weren't being backed by a conservative Southern wing in our own midst.[17]

Whether or not the primary campaigns of August 6 and 27 were failures for the movement is debatable because these campaigns were valuable in getting an even larger number of African Americans involved in protest politics.

As usual for Mississippi, violence inevitably followed them everywhere in the period before the Freedom Vote campaign of October and November.[18] It is also possible that the March on Washington on August 28 further helped inflame and arouse Mississippi whites to violence. On August 29, an African American woman was fatally shot near the Columbus Air Force Base in Lowndes County by Technical Sergeant Rotha R. Ayers. Ayers claimed he was shooting at a stray dog and the bullet had apparently ricocheted, hitting the woman in the chest. The coroner's jury ruled the death was accidental. And on September 11, the body of an unidentified African American man was discovered by four fishermen in the Big Black River near Goodman in Holmes County in a weighted sack of stones.

The Freedom Vote Campaign

The next stage in the development of protest politics took place with the Freedom Vote campaign on October 6.[19] Dr. Aaron Henry, the state president of the NAACP, was nominated for governor by a statewide convention of COFO in Jackson. Delegates were present from SNCC, SCLC, CORE, NAACP, and various local voters' leagues and civic organizations. Two tactics of action were decided upon: to get registered voters (there were only about 28,500 registered African American voters in the state at that time) to void their ballots by writing in the name of Aaron Henry for governor in the general election on November 5; and to get unregistered African Americans (some 94 percent of the voting-age African American population) to participate on November 2, 3, and 4 in the Freedom Vote election to be conducted in community centers and staffed by special election personnel. The "freedom" ballot was to have not only Henry on it but also the regular Democratic and Republican candidates, Paul Johnson and Rubel Phillips. Over 200,000 votes were sought in order to show that African Americans would want to participate in Mississippi politics if they were given the chance.

On October 13, the day before the campaign kickoff, Reverend Edwin King, the white chaplain and dean of students at Tougaloo Southern Christian College, agreed to run for lieutenant governor on the Henry ticket. The state executive committee consisted of Bob Moses, campaign manager; Reverend R. L. T. Smith, finance chairman; Charles Evers—who had taken over for his murdered brother Medgar as state field secretary for the NAACP—speakers bureau chairman; Henry Briggs, public relations chairman; and David Dennis, policy committee chairman.[20] The objectives of the campaign were outlined by Dave Dennis in a field report he submitted to the national office of CORE:

1. To demonstrate to Mississippi, Washington, and the rest of the nation that the Negro people of Mississippi would vote if they were allowed to register free from intimidation and discrimination.
2. To form a unit by which we could unite the people throughout the state.
3. To make the people aware of the power of the ballot.
4. To communicate with the masses.
5. To focus national attention on the political system of Mississippi.
6. To encourage Negroes not to support either political party unless they both change their civil rights policies.
7. To set up a structure for a statewide political organization.[21]

The Freedom Vote platform called for desegregation, the right to vote, fair employment practices, a $1.25 an hour minimum wage, better schools which would be integrated, impartial enforcement of the law, state aid to small farmers, and numerous other planks which if achieved would bring about the full and equal participation of African Americans in Mississippi's society.

The action surrounding the campaign is well summarized in a petition that was presented to the U.S. Congress on November 25, 1963, by the Committee to Elect Aaron Henry Governor:

> Though white officials and other elements of Mississippi's white population made it abundantly clear that they were fully aware of—and violently opposed to—the "Freedom" election, the State's political leaders never publicly acknowledged the campaign. The campaign officially opened on October 14. There were no comments from the other candidates or from officials at the State Capitol. The news media never mentioned the campaign editorially, and coverage was spotty. . . .
>
> The two television stations in Jackson gave better coverage than the newspapers, possibly because of potential FCC pressure [remembering what happened during the Smith and Lindsey campaigns in 1962]. The stations covered Jackson events from the start but refused to grant anything more than one-minute spot announcements. Even these were permitted only after complaints were filed with the FCC. Near the end of the campaign one TV station conducted two 15-minute interviews with Henry and King.
>
> During the middle of the three-week effort, state and local police officers swung into full-scale statewide action against campaign workers. . . . By the end of the three-week campaign, Henry headquarters in Jackson had received reports of over fifty arrests and over sixty additional incidents of harassment.
>
> . . . Although the "Freedom" election was unofficial, the police increased the pressure against campaign workers in the final week. . . . In Jackson a policeman rapped his gun butt over the knuckles of another worker [Ivanhoe Donaldson, of SNCC], then held his cocked revolver to the head of the campaign worker and told him, "if we killed six of you niggers we'd end this whole business once and for all."[22]

The final vote in the Freedom Vote was over 83,000, a figure equal to the difference between the two official candidates. Over 80 Yale and Stanford students participated in the campaign at the invitation of COFO and Al Lowenstein, who had recruited them from their campuses in Connecticut and California. The overwhelming majority of the students were of white middle-class background and had not undergone such experiences in their past. Some of them returned to Mississippi the following summer, among them Steve Bingham, the nephew of New York Congressman Jonathan Bingham. Others also came from influential backgrounds, which provided a major new element for the movement.

Where the Mississippi African American had been passed over as not being newsworthy, this was not the case with white middle-class students. During the Freedom Vote campaign I was able to circulate news stories through the Yale *Daily News* after they had been called in from Mississippi to our newspaper. I called these stories around to the student newspapers at Harvard, Dartmouth, Cornell, the University of Pennsylvania, Princeton, the Collegiate Press Service in Philadelphia, and the *Hartford Courant*. In this way it was possible to break the almost total news blackout that had existed concerning civil rights activities in Mississippi. Apparently, white students being beaten and shot at by southern racists was not the same as African American civil rights workers and local African Americans being put in jail, murdered, and generally harassed and intimidated, which regularly happened without the nation becoming particularly aroused.[23] The movement reacted bitterly to this fact.

The Breakthrough and After

Although there have been different opinions about the significance of the Freedom Vote campaign, there is agreement it was an important event in the Mississippi civil rights movement.[24] For me, it clearly represented a breakthrough in establishing a statewide movement; it also demonstrated that Mississippi African Americans would register and vote in large numbers if they weren't physically and economically intimidated. National concern gradually began to focus on Mississippi's closed society, but it did not well up until the summer of 1964. The consequence was that the movement and the local people still had to do without federal protection. The movement, though, was able to make African Americans in the state aware of the importance of the vote and thereby spur the growth of a widespread radical grassroots movement.

The Freedom Vote became the basis of a new strategy that was later to be used in setting up the Mississippi Freedom Democratic Party in the spring and summer of 1964.[25] What had started out as nonpartisan voter registration campaigns in 1961 had become a highly partisan political strategy aimed at overthrowing the white power structure in Mississippi and substituting interracial politics in its stead. The presence of numerous Yale and Stanford students in the campaign was a departure from past practices, but it was only the number of whites on the scene and the nature of their national connections to the "establishment" that distinguished them from the few whites who had been in the Mississippi movement from the beginning in 1961.[26]

Ivanhoe Donaldson of SNCC felt that the Freedom Vote, among other things, showed "the Negro population that politics is not just 'white folks' business, but that Negroes are also capable of holding political offices. It introduced a lot of Negroes, for the first time, to the idea of marking ballots. For the first time, since Reconstruction, Negroes held a rally on the steps of the Courthouse, with their own candidates, expressing their own beliefs and ideas rather than those of the 'white folks.' There was less fear in the Negro community about taking part in civil rights activities."[27] Thus, with the Freedom Vote, Mississippi African Americans began to feel that, even though they were not able to register to vote at that time, it was possible to hope for a change.

HATTIESBURG

The transition from the Freedom Vote to Freedom Days at county courthouses throughout the state followed on the heels of the fall campaign of Aaron Henry. Although the principle had already been established in Greenwood the previous spring—large groups of African Americans lining up at the courthouse to register to vote—the two major Freedom Days conducted by the movement in the early months of 1964 had new elements. Since November 1963 COFO no longer received VEP funds for nonpartisan voter registration efforts because the Freedom Vote campaign was a form of partisan politics. Consequently, the movement did not make a pretense of being impartial in its objectives. Moreover, the experience garnered in the Freedom Vote campaign was embroidered upon. Plus large numbers of northern whites, in particular clergymen, came down to Mississippi to lend a hand and draw the attention of the nation to the state.

Whereas in the past concerted voter registration campaigns had been conducted over long periods with a few people going down to register each week, now the idea was to take large numbers of African Americans down to the county courthouse on an appointed day, supported by white ministers and other northern volunteers, thus making it more difficult for Mississippi authorities to intimidate the applicants with impunity. Most of the earlier campaigns had gone largely unnoticed by the nation; the Freedom Days of early 1964 were hit upon to change this state of invisibility and create pressure upon the federal government to do something about injustice in Mississippi.

The first of those Freedom Days took place in Hattiesburg on January 22, 1964, but like most movement actions in Mississippi this project was based on long tedious hours of work in the community prior to the public campaign.[28] Normally, such campaigns were the result of months, if not years, spent tirelessly canvassing local African Americans and were conducted on a background of conflict between the movement and the local white power structure. Such was the case with this first Freedom Day in Hattiesburg.

Civil rights work was begun there in February 1962 by two SNCC fieldworkers under the auspices of COFO, Curtis Hayes and Hollis Watkins, who had been in jail with Bob Moses in McComb in the winter of 1961. They worked in Hattiesburg, living at Vernon Dahmer's farm until September 1962, when the project was turned over to a local woman, Mrs. Victoria Gray, who was later to become the national committeewoman of the Mississippi Freedom Democratic Party (MFDP) and who would "run" for Congress from the Fifth Congressional District of Mississippi in the November 1964 Freedom Vote on the MFDP ticket.[29] She was one of the first people in the city to house the SNCC workers who came there in early 1962. A local businesswoman and former schoolteacher, she ran SCLC's citizenship program in the state and was on the national board of directors of that organization. Mrs. Gray ran the Hattiesburg program until March 1963, when it was temporarily interrupted. This project was resumed in July 1963 by John O'Neal, of Southern Illinois University, and Carl Johnson of SNCC, both working under the auspices of COFO.[30]

Mrs. Gray's attempts to register to vote were similar to those of other African Americans in the state. Although she was a graduate of Wilberforce University in Ohio, she ran up against Registrar Theron C. Lynd, whose office was located in Hattiesburg, the county seat of Forrest County. She made her first attempt in 1959, but it took a three-judge panel of the U.S. Fifth Circuit Court of Appeals and four years before she was able to successfully register in July 1963. Lynd and official Hattiesburg, according to Bob Moses, offered "the most flagrant example of the stubborn refusal of Mississippi to yield to change and the impotence of the Federal Government to force them to do so."[31]

John Doar, of the Justice Department, first took Registrar Lynd to the Federal District Court of Judge W. Harold Cox, a Kennedy appointee to the bench and a college friend of Sen. James O. Eastland. Doar had requested Lynd's registration records in August 1960 and after five months of delay went to Federal District Court in January 1961 to get them, but to no avail. Failing to get any action from Judge Cox, on July 6, 1961, the Justice Department requested an injunction against Lynd for discriminating against African Americans. This move also failed as Cox delayed while Lynd carried on his business as usual. Then, on July 15, 1963, Justices Tuttle, Brown, and Wisdom of the Fifth Circuit Court of Appeals found Lynd in civil contempt of the court and ordered him to purge himself by registering the forty-three Negroes named in the Justice Department's suit, by ceasing to require African Americans to interpret sections of the Mississippi Constitution that were more difficult than those assigned to white applicants, by halting the rejection of African American applicants for errors or omissions on their applications if they had met certain other specifications, and by allowing federal agents to inspect his records.[32]

Lynd, though, did not give in and appealed this order to the U.S. Supreme Court, which refused to review his conviction on January 6, 1964. Nevertheless, Lynd continued in his obstructionism until he was called into court again in 1965 by the Fifth Circuit Court of Appeals, and this time he was not only held in contempt for disobeying the court's previous orders but was also ordered to pay court costs as well as register 280 Negroes whom he had rejected. When questioned by one of the judges as follows, "Do you think you can do better in the future than you have in the past?" Lynd answered, "I think so, your Honor, I learn something every time I come into court."[33]

Lynd's case was only the most extreme of official obstructionism by the Mississippi power structure, but it was repeated around the state to lesser degrees. The movement felt that it was appropriate to attack such stubborn institutions. It was also apparent to movement people that the ground was fertile and ready to be sowed in Forrest County, as 3,560 of the 7,495 Negroes of voting age in the county had cast ballots in the "Freedom Vote" in November. This happened in spite of Aaron Henry having been followed through the streets by policemen during the campaign, five white students from Yale having been held in jail for five hours without being charged, and various charges such as "distributing leaflets without a permit" and "parking too far from the sidewalk" having been brought against movement workers.[34]

Prior to Freedom Day in Hattiesburg, violence and intimidation continued.[35] On December 10, Lois Chaffee, a twenty-four-year old white student at integrated Tougaloo, was charged with perjury for accusing police of brutality in using nightsticks on African American children who had participated in civil rights demonstrations. Her bail bond was set at five thousand dollars. On December 30, an African American, Romie Harris, was shot and killed in Tupelo, Lee County, by a white, Calvin Deaton, who claimed the shooting was committed in self-defense. In McComb, on January 15 and 16, four white men fired from a car into an African American café, two grocery stores, a shoe repair shop, and two African American homes.

The buildup of intimidation and harassment started with the arrest of Peter Stoner, a white SNCC voter registration worker, for "unlawful parking and obstructing traffic." When convicted of these charges he chose to remain in jail as what he called "a protest against a prostitution of justice."[36] On January 14, Oscar Chase, a white SNCC lawyer and voter registration worker who was a graduate of Yale Law School, was jailed for entering a Hattiesburg bus terminal waiting room designated for African Americans. He was charged with breach of the peace and vagrancy.[37]

On January 22, Freedom Day came to Hattiesburg.[38] Ms. Ella Baker; John Lewis, chairman of SNCC; and Jim Forman, executive secretary of SNCC, came from Atlanta. SNCC workers Mrs. Hamer; Mrs. Donna Richards Moses, Bob Moses's young wife; Lawrence Guyot, who was later to be the chairman of the MFDP; MacArthur Cotton; Jesse Harris, who ran the summer program in McComb in 1964; Mendy Samstein, a white SNCC worker from New York; Lafayette Surney; Avery Williams, from Alabama State College; Oscar Chase; and others also came from around the state. Dave Dennis, of CORE, came in from Canton, which was itself to have its Freedom Days in the near future; and about 50 white ministers and rabbis came from the North to demonstrate on behalf of over 100 African Americans who tried to register at Lynd's office in the county courthouse. In addition to the demonstrators and the voter applicants, numerous television cameramen showed up, as well as radio and newspaper reporters from all over the country. Dr. Aaron Henry, Ms. Baker, John Lewis, for SNCC; Dave Dennis, for CORE; Annelle Ponder, for SCLC; Lawrence Guyot; and John Pratt, a lawyer from the National Council of Churches (NCC), spoke to a mass meeting at the Freedom House in Hattiesburg the evening before Freedom Day.

January 22 was a rainy day, and it held many surprises for the movement. Only 2 people were arrested, Moses and Chase. Over 150 people picketed outside the county courthouse, among them some 50 local African American schoolchildren. Over 100 African Americans lined up to go in and register to vote. Very few got through the door to fill out applications, with only a handful later being declared to have passed the test. No mass arrests were made; only

Bob Moses was arrested for "obstructing traffic by standing on the sidewalk and refusing to move on when ordered by a policeman [to do so]."[39] People got wet that day from standing in the rain, but the movement took a giant step forward. A mass demonstration had been held in Mississippi without violence, intimidation, or numerous arrests.

For Oscar Chase, though, the day did not end as pleasantly.[40] He was arrested for leaving the scene of an "accident." Earlier in the day his car had bumped a parked truck, doing no damage, but the police noted the event, and he was later arrested at four o'clock in the afternoon. During the night he was severely beaten by a white prisoner while the jailer looked on but did nothing to stop it. An FBI agent duly recorded the case after Chase had been bailed out of jail in the morning. Nothing came of the investigation.

At four that afternoon the case of Robert Moses was heard in the Hattiesburg Municipal Court before Judge Mildred W. Norris.[41] Before the trial began, Howard Zinn questioned the judge's order to segregate the courtroom, saying, "The Supreme Court of the United States has ruled that segregated seating in a courtroom is unconstitutional."[42] Surprisingly enough, the judge ordered the trial to proceed even though no one had changed his place. Moses was represented by John Pratt, of the NCC, and Robert Lunney, of the Lawyers Committee for Civil Rights Under Law, a group organized at the request of President Kennedy on June 21, 1963.[43] The committee acted as counsel for the National Council of Churches during the summer of 1964 and represented the 325 ministers who went to Mississippi for the summer project. In spite of the quality of his defense counsel—movement workers had undergone considerable difficulty up to this time in finding a lawyer[44]—Moses was found guilty, fined two hundred dollars, and sentenced to sixty days in jail. A few days later he was out on bail and busy planning for Freedom Summer.

Freedom Day in Hattiesburg meant different things to different people. To Reverend Donald Register, of St. Louis, Missouri, one of the many who came down for the Freedom Day, it meant the following: "Personally I am not important in this. . . . [R]ather it's the deep over-riding fear of Negroes. . . . If they register to vote, they will lose their jobs. . . . Many of them have lost their jobs, but we are trying hard to instill courage in the townspeople."[45]

To Reverend Russell Williams, of Denver, Colorado, it meant that "We saw a great change come over the local African American community. Dick Gregory, the comedian, was there, and he told me it was the first time he had addressed an audience in Mississippi and not seen fear written on their faces."[46] And finally, Reverend Emil J. Hattoon, of Decatur, Illinois, wrote to his two sons, "I think the point is that this is much like Germany at the beginning of Hitler's rise—fear, police intimidation and summary arrests. I don't want you, or any other kids, to grow up in America in those circumstances."[47]

CANTON

The drive in Canton, Madison County,[48] started in June 1963, when Dave Dennis, George Raymond, Anne Moody,[49] who was an African American task-force worker from southwest Mississippi and a student at Tougaloo, and two other CORE workers moved into the city to set up an ongoing project. This was CORE's first beachhead in Mississippi, although Dennis had been active in the state since the spring of 1962. Canton was to be the central point for CORE's activity, which under pressure from the National CORE office was only to be located in the Fourth Congressional District of Mississippi. Financing was provided by a short-term VEP grant and the national office of CORE.

From the beginning CORE received considerable support from the local community. C. O. Chinn,[50] a prosperous African American businessman, rented them a building and continued his support of the movement even though he was twice arrested and eventually driven out of business. George Washington, a local grocer and gas station owner, was the treasurer of the local movement. His gas pumps were removed by the AMOCO representative on January 30, 1964, and wholesalers cut off his meat supply.[51]

Mrs. Annie Devine, a former teacher and debit manager for a life insurance company, worked with the movement in Canton from the summer of 1963, joined the COFO staff as a full-time worker in June 1964, and later that year ran for Congress on the MFDP ticket.[52] She was also the secretary of the MFDP delegation that went to the August 1964 Democratic National Convention in Atlantic City. Others also joined the movement and stayed in spite of the high price they had to pay for their commitment.

By the end of June 1963, 18 African Americans had been turned away from the county courthouse, but 12 had succeeded in registering to vote. Some 30 African Americans filed protest affidavits during the "vote-in" on August 6; others sent their affidavits directly to Washington; and approximately 2,800 of the 10,366 Negroes of voting age in the county "voted" in the Freedom Vote in November.[53]

In spite of both physical and economic intimidation and police harassment, Dennis made plans to set up community centers in the county and organize farm and store cooperatives. Madison County, unlike many others in Missis-sippi, had a large number of independent African American farmers who were not easily intimidated. He also hoped to have library facilities at the centers and to offer classes in vocational and citizenship training as well as African Ameri-can history. During the early period in Canton, these were only fond hopes, but by the following summer it was possible to realize them, at least in part.

During January 1964, the CORE staff and local movement people organized a boycott of twenty-one Canton retail merchants in the hope that they would put pressure on the local registrar to let African Americans vote. The town's reaction was part of a now familiar pattern. On January 21, the Canton City Council passed a law making it a crime to distribute literature without a per-mit from the mayor or the chief of police. Two additional policemen and a new police car were added to the town's force.[54] The next day George Washington was arrested for "burning trash without a permit."

On January 23, the Canton police entered the movement office and seized a list of names from a recent petition circulated by CORE workers. Then two people were arrested for making repairs on the registration office without first obtaining a building permit; bond was set for C. O. Chinn and James Collier at $350 each. Later, Theotus Hewitt was arrested for disturbing the peace and intimidating an officer. Bond was set at $500. In the late afternoon ten voter registration workers were arrested for "distributing leaflets without a permit" and other charges. The leaflets encouraged citizens to pay the poll tax. Bail was set at $800 each.[55]

The police campaign against the movement did not let up in the following days either. On January 24, Carole Merritt, a SNCC worker and a graduate of Vassar who came to help out the shorthanded CORE staff, was arrested for con-tributing to the delinquency of a minor by causing him to distribute "libelous" material. Bail was set at $500. The next day the Canton police began stopping all incoming and outgoing cars at the city limits, possibly with the idea of shutting off all help the movement might try to get. The movement, though, refused to give in to this pressure, and on January 28, between thirty and forty people went to the county courthouse to try to register. Only five were allowed inside, and voter registration worker Sylvester Lee Palmer was arrested for "disturb-ing the peace." On January 30, Henry Cooper, the owner of the Tolliver Café, where movement people sometimes met, was arrested in the presence of two SNCC workers. The nature of the charges could not be determined.[56]

The following day Louis Allen, one of the witnesses to the slaying of Herbert Lee by Mississippi State Representative E. H. Hurst in 1961, was shot and killed in his front yard the day before he was to leave the state with his family.[57] In order to protect himself he had lied at the coroner's inquest in 1961, but in February 1963 he told a SNCC worker that he had witnessed the unprovoked murder of Lee. The next month the jury at the Beckwith trial, for the murder of Medgar Evers, failed to return a verdict. Meanwhile, in Canton, the movement continued to battle with the local authorities. Seeing the futility in continuing its fight merely on a local level, an effort was made to bring federal pressure on the local registrar and at the same time encourage local African Americans. The methods of the Freedom Day were adopted, and a major effort was undertaken by COFO to focus national attention on the town.[58] The national office of CORE assigned additional field secretaries to the project; local African American ministers were convinced to participate; SNCC sent in extra help; and Charles Evers, the state field secretary of the NAACP since his brother's murder, joined about 350 Negro adults who marched to the courthouse on February 28 to try to register to vote. Observers came from the FBI, the Justice Department, the National Council of Churches, and the mass media. No arrests were made, and no repressive tactics were employed by the local power structure, but only 5 people were allowed in to register. Nevertheless, Freedom Day in Canton had a national audience, and the Justice Department filed suit against the county registrar in Federal District Court on March 2.

Following on the heels of Freedom Day, 2,600 African American teenagers staged a one-day school boycott over the overcrowded and substandard conditions of their schools. Shortly thereafter, twelve civil rights workers were arrested for their activities; the number of paid CORE workers in the state had risen to 11 in January and was to reach 18 by the summer. African Americans continued to go to register daily, and on March 13 a second Freedom Day was held, though it was less dramatic in its impact. Then, Federal District Court Judge Cox ordered the local registrar to receive at least 50 applicants on each registration day as long as his services were in demand. Nevertheless, he limited the number of potential applicants who could stand in line at one time to 25 and refused to find a "pattern or practice" of discrimination in the registrar's handling of African Americans who wished to register.

The momentum of the drive, though, proved difficult to keep up, particularly with the continuing harassment from local whites and the passage of a state law against the use of Freedom Days. Fear again mounted up in the local population, and shots were fired into the CORE office in May. On May 29, a third Freedom Day was held to try to re-ignite the local movement. James Farmer, the national director of CORE, came to address the rally, but the police turned out in large numbers and refused to let the African Americans march to the county courthouse. No national reporters were present, and 55 people were arrested.[59]

Dennis still had hope for the future. That hope was not to be broken until after the murders near Philadelphia, Neshoba County, of Michael Schwerner (a white CORE worker who was working at the community center in Meridian since January with Mat Suarez from New Orleans CORE), James Chaney (a local African American who became Schwerner's closest co-worker), and Andrew Goodman (a New York white who came with the first summer volunteers).

As violence rose all over Mississippi in anticipation of Freedom Summer, movement people began to worry about what would happen. Farmer tried in vain to meet with U.S. Attorney General Kennedy in early June, and a meeting between Lawyers Constitutional Defense Committee (LCDC) attorneys, Assistant Attorney General Burke Marshall, and FBI representatives was unproductive.[60] The murder of Schwerner, Chaney, and Goodman followed on June 21.[61]

In contrast with what was happening on the local level in towns and cities throughout Mississippi, all through the winter and spring of 1964 plans were being formulated by movement people both within the state and around the country for the long, hot summer ahead. (The State of Mississippi was getting ready for what it termed the "invasion.") No longer was the movement focused on sporadic demonstrations or individual voter registration campaigns, or even "vote-ins" and "freedom votes." The summer of 1964 was to be a time of open, pitched battle with the entire Mississippi power structure. The movement wanted to break down the walls of the closed society, melt the totalitarian iceberg, and set the Mississippi African American free.

In the nether world of Mississippi, what had started out as an attack on the legal abuses of the power structure through the use of the courts and through efforts to gain free access to public accommodations had proved unrealistic. African Americans just were not able to use these facilities or pay for the use of them even if they were so allowed. Nonpartisan voter registration activities had also proved empty because, even if African Americans could gain the vote in Mississippi, there was nobody to vote for.

Thus, the movement turned from seeking the rights of African Americans under federal law to seeking to express itself through protest, or mock devices such as the Freedom Vote. When it became obvious that, no matter what the movement did on a local level, the Mississippi power structure would not let African Americans participate, except in a passive manner, then the movement turned outside of the state to the nation as a whole and tried to create a consensus to force Mississippi to become part of the United States.

Pressures had been brought to bear on Leflore County authorities to restore federal commodities distribution in the winter of 1962–63.[62] The nation had been scandalized by the rioting at Ole Miss over the admission of James Meredith in 1962[63] and to a lesser extent over the slaying of Medgar Evers in 1963.[64]

During these years, research was done on the condition of the Mississippi African American, affidavits were gathered on the discriminatory administration of justice in the state, note was taken of racial discrimination in voter registration procedures, and generally the movement reached into the backwaters of the state and contacted thousands of rural African Americans, apprising them of their rights and giving them a glimmer of hope. No matter how much violence and intimidation movement people faced, in most instances they stayed to fight—in the case of southwest Mississippi they returned in the summer of 1964 and the winter of 1964–65[65]—and their numbers were swelled by new workers who came to shore up local African Americans against their white attackers.

After Jimmy Travis's near-fatal machine-gunning in February 1963, civil rights workers in the state converged on Greenwood, refusing to be driven out of the Delta. During the Democratic Congressional primaries of 1962 and the Gubernatorial campaigns of 1963, which culminated in the Freedom Vote, massive lists of contacts were compiled of African Americans throughout the state who wanted to see a change come to Mississippi and who were willing to risk their jobs and even their lives to bring about such a change.

Not able to bring this about through the normal channels of political democracy, the movement had been forced to adjust its strategies, turning to parallel or protest politics in mock actions. Plans along these lines were continued during the winter and spring of 1963–64. What emerged were the Mississippi Freedom Democratic Party, the Freedom Schools, and numerous other organizational devices. If the movement was not allowed to operate within the existing order of things, it was determined to operate outside that order to break open the closed society and force it to let African Americans have an equal part in it.[66] To accomplish this, a national consensus was needed to pressure the federal government into action. Such a consensus was growing but was not yet in existence in the spring of 1964. It finally came into being when the nation learned of the lynching of the three civil rights workers.

Nonetheless, it is questionable whether such a consensus would have been forged had the three civil rights workers all been Mississippi African Americans, rather than two of them having been northern whites. The movement had cynically but sorrowfully observed this fact during the Freedom Vote, when the beatings and jailings of white northern volunteers from prominent universities and families had aroused the liberal press and inadvertently provided the key element for a massive attack on Mississippi's power structure in the summer of 1964. Many civil rights people, both in SNCC and in the local Mississippi movement, preferred not to bring in hundreds of white northern college students for the summer project, but in the end they felt that there was no other choice.[67] It is my opinion that, as high as the price proved to be, nothing else would have brought about the change that took place in Mississippi and the nation during Freedom Summer.

7

Freedom Summer, Part I

They say that freedom is a constant struggle. . . .
Oh, Lord, we've struggled so long.
We must be free, we must be free.
—A MOVEMENT SONG

The strongest preservative of the closed society is the closed mind. It has been argued that in the history of the United States democracy has produced great leaders in great crises. Sad as it may be, the opposite has been true in Mississippi. As yet there is little evidence that the closed society will ever possess the moral resources to reform itself, or the capacity for self-examination, or even the tolerance of self-examination.
—JAMES W. SILVER, SPRING 1964

The Mississippi Summer Project operated on two levels. On the one hand there were programs aimed at the immediate problems within the state, and on the other there were programs that represented an attempt to dramatize those problems and win participation in the political forum for Mississippi African Americans on a national level. The first projects were voter registration activities, the Freedom Schools, community centers, research pointed at winning federal help for the African American community, and the "white folks" project. Then there was the Mississippi Freedom Democratic Party, which attempted to gain the place of the regular Mississippi Democratic Party delegation at the Democratic National Convention in August 1964 and challenged the seating of the Mississippi delegation in the U.S. House of Representatives in January 1965. All of these projects will be discussed in later chapters.

At the outset, though, it is necessary to take note of the process of getting ready for the Summer Project, along with the orientation, composition, and organization of the volunteers. In addition, the "invasion" that attempted to force open the closed society was greeted by the Mississippi power structure in ways that determined the outcome of the Summer Project.

Inasmuch as Freedom Summer was a culmination of the student-supported movement's work in the state since 1960, as well as being tied to the efforts of local African Americans since the end of World War II, and particularly after 1954, the summer of 1964 and the winter of 1964–65 represented a turning point for civil rights efforts in Mississippi. African Americans had previously been afraid to confront the white power structure, but during the summer of 1964 local African Americans participated in large numbers in the movement, especially after being violently attacked by the white population in such places as Neshoba County and southwest Mississippi. And the movement fulfilled its commitment to return to McComb during the summer after being absent from this area for two and a half years, and throughout the Delta where they had been continually harassed and attacked from the beginning. Furthermore, a substantial number of African Americans tried to register to vote, and a surprisingly large number of African American schoolchildren and adults studied in the Freedom Schools and helped movement people canvass the African American community.

The summer of 1964 was the time when Mississippi African Americans finally overcame their fear of confronting "the man" and came to the conclusion that they really had nothing to gain by staying "in their place." The Mississippi Summer Project gained attention in the national press, providing encouragement for overcoming their fears. Also, the presence of nearly one thousand summer volunteers, most of whom were white northerners, helped provide the needed push that encouraged them to abandon their pretense of happiness.

In short, the summer of 1964 represents the point at which the Mississippi civil rights movement became a national concern and the plight of Mississippi African Americans could no longer be overlooked by the federal government. During the summer, the federal policy of passivity changed, and the government turned to Mississippi with a new activism that was to shake the Mississippi power structure and encourage African Americans into open confrontation. After 1964, the movement quickly returned to being largely a local affair, and the national civil rights organizations began to withdraw from the battle.

A new spirit seemed to appear among African Americans during the summer. Not only did local African Americans take movement people into their homes; during the summer they also protected them through the long nights. Nonviolence was practiced by the movement during public activities, but weapons, which are part of African American Mississippi, just as with White Mississippi, now appeared in defense of the movement. Where African Americans had silently suffered white violence in the past, now they fired back in self-defense and guarded their homes and movement offices. The battle-hardened veterans of the movement refused to take up violent tactics and now were guarded by those who refused to let whites continue their terror tactics without opposition. Moreover, the movement did not let its staffers and volunteers arm themselves.

The movement also turned to new songs which offered up images not of love but of war:

> We are soldiers
> in the army.
> We have to fight
> although we have to die.
> We have to hold up
> the freedom banner.
> We have to hold it up
> until we die.[1]

Getting Ready

A week after the Freedom Vote campaign in November 1963, the staff of SNCC gathered in Greenville to discuss the results of their statewide action and begin planning for the following summer.[2] The most important problem broached at the meeting was whether to carry on with the idea of involving large numbers of northern whites. In and of itself, this should not have been a difficult decision to make, but in light of the direction of the movement after 1964, particularly SNCC's turning to an almost entirely African American–run effort, it is significant. The choice was in fact made to bring in large numbers of whites for the Mississippi Summer Project.

Mrs. Fannie Lou Hamer of Ruleville, one of the most important local figures in the movement, vehemently espoused making Freedom Summer truly integrated, as did many of the older locals. Lawrence Guyot, who was to become the chairman of the Mississippi Freedom Democratic Party; Dave Dennis, the CORE field secretary and the assistant director of COFO; and Bob Moses, SNCC's Mississippi project director from the beginning and the project head of COFO, all supported bringing in large numbers of white volunteers. "Black Nationalism" was delayed because of the persuasive and influential arguments of these individuals. Nevertheless, the problem of whites in the movement was a significant one because the civil rights workers' deeply held philosophy of decision-making and participatory democracy was aimed at developing local leadership as well as staffing and heading movement programs with local people. It was feared that a massive infusion of whites into the movement would retard this process. The white students who came from Yale and Stanford for the Freedom Vote campaign were indeed helpful, but they tended to inhibit local African Americans, who sometimes looked at them as they would at southern whites rather than as people who had come to learn from them and help them overcome their difficulties with the state's white power structure.

Be that as it may, when Moses initially introduced the problem to the executive committee meeting of SNCC in December, there was resistance by the SNCC and COFO staff.[3] However, by the weekend of March 27–29, which was preceded by the murder of Lewis Allen in January, the idea of the Mississippi Summer Project was approved by a general SNCC conference in Atlanta of four hundred staff members and affiliates.[4] Freedom Summer in Mississippi was no longer dreamed of as being in the distant future but was to be a reality in 1964. From there the movement hurriedly turned to the logistics of the Summer Project: finding the volunteers and selecting those best suited for the rigors of Mississippi life; finding lawyers from around the country who would volunteer their services to protect and defend movement people and local African Americans in the face of obvious legal harassment; obtaining the promise of protection from the Department of Justice and federal law enforcement agencies, who were not ready to help until after the disappearance of Schwerner, Chaney, and Goodman in Neshoba County during the night of June 21; setting up a security system to protect movement people and local African Americans; raising some $200,000 necessary to finance the project; planning the projects to be undertaken during the summer and staffing them; and numerous other problems which arose from getting such an operation underway in a very limited period of time.[5]

Additionally, during the spring of 1964 the problem of armed self-defense within the movement arose.[6] SNCC was particularly concerned with the well-being of those close to the movement and knew instinctively that little or no protection would be forthcoming from the federal government while violent attacks by lawless elements in Mississippi were a certainty. On various occasions in the past local African Americans such as Hartman Turnbow, of Mileston, had fired back on people who came to destroy their homes and kill them,[7] but the movement had not yet made any overt decision to arm itself in the fashion of Robert Williams, of Monroe, North Carolina, who conducted a shooting war with the Ku Klux Klan in the summer of 1961.[8]

The decision not to arm the movement's staffers was made because not only was it impossible to provide the necessary training and arms to the civil rights workers but also because in early 1964 it was strategically ahead of the times.[9] Even though Moses and Jim Forman sent Stokely Carmichael to the Greenwood office of SNCC to remove the arms that were there, Forman did plan and carry out a nightly armed patrol of the office, which became the national headquarters of the organization shortly before the Summer Project began. The decision, though, not to openly arm themselves was made because it was felt that at that point it would lead to open conflict with the Greenwood police and that it was tactically not the time to have such a confrontation. Nevertheless, the problem of armed self-defense had been running under the surface of events in Mississippi and throughout the entire South, and even though SNCC was no longer morally in favor of nonviolence, it held to a position of tactical nonviolence.

If the movement in Mississippi decided to continue a policy of tactical nonviolence—the COFO staff of the Summer Project consisted of seventy-six staff workers from SNCC, eighteen from CORE, and a few others from the NAACP and SCLC—it had to make plans to protect itself in other ways. And if the "invasion" force, as it was termed in the Mississippi press, was to be a nonviolent army, then this did not obviate a paramilitary security system.

Having learned early that publicity—such as a call to the Department of Justice or the FBI and the notification of the national press—was one of the best methods of protecting civil rights workers, the movement established a communication network with the world outside of Mississippi. Moses had started the ball rolling when he had placed a collect call to the Department of Justice in 1961 in southwest Mississippi, and the fact that his call was accepted might have been what saved his life.[10] This method of self-defense was used by numerous other people in the movement in various other forms, including telegrams to the U.S. Justice Department as well as appeals in person to administration officials by workers from the national offices of the civil rights organizations.

The movement conducted numerous campaigns to break the national press blackout in Mississippi. I was involved in such a campaign during the Freedom

Vote when little if any information appeared in the national press or on the wire services. Yale students called in stories daily to the Yale *Daily News*, which I then relayed by telephone to the Collegiate Press Service in Philadelphia, which sent its news stories to subscribing college newspapers. I also phoned other interested newspapers at universities and colleges. Finally, personal connections were employed to get northern newspapers to make inquiries to the wire services about events being squelched by local stringers of AP and UPI. When snatches of the stories that were being reported through movement channels appeared on the newswires, newspapers in the North began printing the stories provided to them by the movement.[11] Nevertheless, this was a hit-or-miss system of stopgap measures that had to be improved upon if civil rights workers and local African Americans were to be protected during the summer of 1964.

The security system of COFO and SNCC during the Summer Project consisted of four key elements. Notices were posted in all the project offices that called for workers to do the following things: "1) Anyone leaving town should check [in] with our WATS (Wide Area Telephone Service) operator;[12] 2) Call collect for the person you checked out with as soon as you arrive at your destination; and 3) If you are driving a car other than your own, get an authorization slip from legal department."[13] The WATS system was key to the movement's security methods. A flat monthly rate was paid to the telephone company for unlimited calls to places covered in the WATS service. The Greenwood office of SNCC had two WATS lines, one to make calls throughout the nation and the other for calls within the state. The state headquarters of COFO, which was located on Lynch Street in Jackson, also had a state WATS line. In addition, the permanent office of SNCC in Atlanta had a WATS line which covered all points east of Chicago. The Jackson office handled newsworthy stories that it called up to reporters stationed in Mississippi. The Greenwood office called the FBI and the Department of Justice if it was necessary to demand federal protection for civil rights workers, volunteers, and local African Americans or to report incidents after the fact. It also called out-of-state newspapers or parents of volunteers if required. Information and requests for support from Friends of SNCC groups east of Chicago were relayed to Atlanta rather than tying up the Greenwood line.[14]

The pressure of White Mississippi was constant during the Summer Project. During the months of June, July, and August, three workers were killed, eighty were beaten, thirty houses were bombed, thirty-five churches were burned, thirty-five shooting incidents occurred, and over a thousand arrests were made.[15] The movement kept up constant pressure on the federal government to protect its people. Rarely, though, did the FBI make arrests. Notable exceptions to the policy of observation and research by federal operatives took place when on June 26 the FBI arrested three white men on the spot in Itta Bena for interfering with the constitutional rights of civil rights workers,[16] and later in the arrest of the conspirators who killed Schwerner, Chaney, and Goodman.[17]

The final link in the security system set up by the movement was mobile communication. Some of the project offices did not have telephones, and often workers had to go to rural areas where there was little or no opportunity to communicate by phone. During the month of July a parents' committee of people who had sons and daughters in Mississippi came to the state to check out security precautions and make suggestions for improvements. Two-way radios were installed in COFO cars (the Sojourner Motor Fleet [named for Sojourner Truth]), which operated on the twenty-three-frequency Citizens' Band. Whereas normally a license from the FCC took six weeks to obtain, one was secured within twenty-four hours. By the end of August, fifty installations were operating: twenty-five radio cars and twenty-five stationary units located around the state, as well as an additional twenty walkie-talkies. Scramblers for telephones were also suggested, as most of the movement's phone lines were regularly tapped. The opposition also turned to two-way radios and walkie-talkies in Greenwood and around the state. Luckily, with all the destruction perpetrated against the movement by White Mississippi, none of the radio equipment was destroyed, although a frustrated policeman in Natchez did bend the radio antenna there.[18]

Generally, the security system functioned without mishaps, and none of the full-time staff workers was killed after the initial incident in Philadelphia, in Neshoba County. All elements of the security apparatus operated on a twenty-four-hour basis and were further supplemented by the grapevine of the local African American community, which relayed any information it had concerning threats of intended violence against movement people.[19] Finally, local African Americans mounted armed guards on project offices, Freedom Schools, and Freedom Houses in many parts of the state such as in Batesville, Mileston, Biloxi, and Harmony,[20] near Carthage, where the local community provided the land and built a Freedom School. In places such as McComb there were many African Americans who would not go to register to vote but freely came forward to stand guard over the civil rights workers without requests being made for such protection.[21]

Also important to the Summer Project were the written formulations of the rationale for planning an "invasion" of Mississippi. One such prospectus outlined the question of the project's size:

1. Projects of the size of those of the last three summers (100 to 150 workers) are rendered ineffective quickly by police threats and detention of members.

2. Previous projects have gotten no national publicity on the crucial issue of voting rights and, hence, have little national support either from public opinion or from the federal government. . . .

3. Because of the lack of numbers in the past, all workers in Mississippi have had to devote themselves to voter registration. . . .

4. Bail money cannot be provided for jailed workers; hence, a large number of people going South would prevent the project from being halted in its initial stages by immediate arrests.[22]

One suspects that the prospectus was largely the work of Bob Moses, as a great many of the movement's decisions and plans were products of his clear-headed vision and creative mind. Even though he might have been the author of this particular position paper, it was typical of Moses to leave such documents unsigned. His later actions seem to bear out his intention not to dominate the process of policy-making in the movement. In 1965 Robert Parris Moses dropped "Moses" from his name and moved out of Mississippi into neighboring Alabama in order to avoid the adulation and hero worship he had been subjected to both by movement workers and local people.[23]

Moses generally sought to train local African Americans for positions of leadership in their own communities so they might gain the self-confidence to overcome their white oppressors. He felt that people were too dependent upon him and looked to him too often to solve their problems, whereas in reality if they ever hoped to change their status in Mississippi they would have to begin to control their own lives and make decisions on matters they knew best.[24]

Prior to the summer of 1964, Mississippi African Americans were not yet used to taking charge of their own lives and battling the Mississippi power structure.[25] The movement had temporarily cut back on voter registration efforts in favor of protest politics in the hope of getting a national consensus that would force the federal government to make Mississippi stop its oppression.[26]

The prospectus from Len Holt's *The Summer That Didn't End* adds further insight into why the movement chose 1964 for a massive confrontation with the white power structure:

> Mississippi at this juncture in the movement has received too little attention—that is, attention to what the state's attitude really is—and has presented COFO with a major policy decision. Either the civil rights struggle has to continue, as it has for the past few years, with small projects in selected communities with no real progress on any fronts, or there must be a task force of such a size as to force either the state and the municipal governments to change their social and legal structures, or the federal government to intervene on behalf of the constitutional rights of its citizens. . . .
>
> . . . Major victories in Mississippi, recognized as the stronghold of racial intolerance in the South, would speed immeasurably the breaking down of legal and social discrimination in both North and South.
>
> . . . The impetus is not against Mississippi, but for the right to vote, the ability to read, the aspirations and the training to work.[27]

ORIENTATION OF NORTHERN VOLUNTEERS

The first orientation session for the summer volunteers took place at the Western College for Women in Oxford, Ohio, and was sponsored by the National Council of Churches. The first group of some three hundred volunteers began to get ready to "invade" Mississippi during the week of June 15–20.[28] Movement people came to the sessions from Mississippi to "tell it like it is," and psychiatrists, psychologists, and lawyers came to check the volunteers for suitability and help the Mississippi staff prepare them for what lay ahead.

This group was to help experienced workers on voter registration and open up new areas that the movement had been unable to reach in the past because of the lack of workers.[29] They were lectured unceasingly by movement people as to future dangers and apprised of their position in respect to the law in Mississippi. R. Jess Brown, one of the movement lawyers in Mississippi, advised them, "If you're riding down somewhere and a cop stops you and starts to put you under arrest even though you haven't committed any crime—go on to jail. Mississippi is not the place to start conducting Constitutional law classes for policemen, many of whom don't have a fifth-grade education."[30] John Doar of the Justice Department also came to answer questions. When asked what the federal government would do to help movement people survive in Mississippi, he answered, "Nothing. There is no federal police force. The responsibility for protection is that of the local police. We can only investigate."[31]

Stephen Bingham, a white Yale graduate who had been in Mississippi to help out during the Freedom Vote and who participated in Freedom Summer, described the purpose of the orientation sessions in his mimeographed "Mississippi Letter," which he sent around the country in February 1964 to explain what the Summer Project was to be like and what its purposes were:

> The three major purposes of the orientation session were: (1) to familiarize the volunteers, and some of the staff too, with the relevant historical, political, and socio-economic issues which would make us not only more effective in our work but give us a greater understanding of its meaning (2) to acquaint us with the specific jobs each of us was to do and with the specific area where we would work; and (3) to prepare us to cope with any of the multitude of problems which might arise, for example, being attacked, living with Negro families, staff/volunteer relationships, etc. . . . We were told of the murders which had occurred in the recent past, of which the press had taken no cognizance, of murderers who roamed at large, untouched by the law, and perhaps, in the society which is Mississippi, untouchable.[32]

The second orientation session was for volunteers who were to teach in the Freedom Schools and run the community centers. These volunteers, whose work was of a slightly safer nature, were women from various colleges and universities, men and women in their thirties and older, and volunteers with families they had left behind to come to Mississippi for the summer.

In all, some 650 volunteers passed through the orientation sessions held in Oxford, Ohio, from June 15 through the first week of July. These were the "shock troops" that were to participate in voter registration activities, teach in Freedom Schools, set up community centers, and help staff the project offices around the state. They were augmented by some 150 lawyers, 325 ministers, 57 doctors, and about 50 others who helped in medical and social welfare work and research around the state.[33] Additionally, the national civil rights groups built up their Mississippi staffs to nearly 100 full-time workers.[34] The first group of volunteers entered Mississippi on June 20, the second group on June 27, and other groups shortly afterwards. Mississippi authorities and citizens hoped that the "invasion" would be over by the end of August, but some 200 volunteers stayed for a further six months, and others promised to return in the spring and summer of 1965.[35]

The National Council of Churches (NCC) established the Delta Ministry on a long-term basis in August and remained active in the Delta even after other civil rights groups had left the state.[36] The volunteers brought their fears with them, but for the African Americans of Mississippi they brought the possibility of change and a feeling of better things to come.

WHO WERE THE VOLUNTEERS?

The 650 student volunteers came from thirty-seven U.S. states, England, Australia, and New Zealand. Most of them were from the North, from schools such as Howard, Yale, Harvard, the University of Illinois, Oberlin College, the University of Oregon, Cornell, Princeton, Stanford, Bryn Mawr, Skidmore, and Antioch, as well as the University of North Carolina, and were mostly of white middle-class backgrounds. Some 300 were white women, and one-third to one-half were Jewish.[37] Very few were black, and even fewer were from the South. One of the difficulties that arose during the planning stages of the Summer Project in the winter and spring of the year had been finding either African Americans who were able to pay their own way for the summer—volunteers had to bring $200 for room and board during the project as well as guarantee $500 bail money if needed—or find the money necessary to sponsor African American volunteers. By and large this problem was not overcome, and most of the volunteers who came to Mississippi were white.[38]

Some of the letters written home during the orientation sessions give an idea of what the volunteers felt and what they were trying to do by volunteering to go to Mississippi for the summer.[39] Surprisingly enough, in spite of the outward hostility many of them met with at Oxford, most who registered for the Summer Project did go to Mississippi. One of the volunteers wrote home, "Maybe we'll be able to [be accepted] at the end of the summer, but right now we don't know what it is to be a Negro and even if we did, the Negroes would not accept us. . . . Intellectually, I think many of us whites can understand the Negroes' resentment but emotionally we want to be 'accepted' at face value."[40] Another volunteer wrote, "Us white kids here are in a position we've never been in before. The direction of the whole program is under Negro leadership . . . because they've been active in the movement."[41]

In spite of the outward hostility the volunteers were subjected to at the beginning of the summer by staff people, most of them adjusted to living in the African American community. Mississippi African Americans rarely had experienced friendly whites in the past. Nevertheless, numerous families took the volunteers into their homes and shared the little they had with them, sometimes even sleeping on the floor so that the volunteer could have a bed.

In addition to the student volunteers there were numerous professional people such as lawyers, ministers, doctors, nurses, teachers, and others who went to Mississippi under the auspices of the National Council of Churches, the National Lawyers Guild, the Lawyers Committee for Civil Rights Under Law, the NAACP Legal Defense and Educational Fund, the Lawyers Constitutional Defense Committee (LCDC), the Medical Committee for Human Rights, the United Federation of Teachers, and others.

Entry into Mississippi

While plans were being made during the winter and spring of 1964 to bring in large numbers of volunteers, life in Mississippi continued as usual in the war between the movement and the white power structure. Mickey Schwerner and his wife Rita opened a community center in Meridian, Lauderdale County, in January.[42] A library was set up, and workers from the community were drawn into the movement, among them twenty-one-year-old James Chaney. Freedom Days were held in Hattiesburg in January; in Canton in February, March, and May; in Greenwood in March; and in other places around the state.[43] Mississippi—the legal one and the lawless one—also used its time to prepare for what it felt would be an "invasion" of some 30,000 or more Northern volunteers.

A MISSISSIPPI WELCOMING

In Jackson, the state capitol, Mayor Allen Thompson prepared the city by building up his police force from 390 to 450.[44] Additionally, two hundred new shotguns were purchased, tear gas was stockpiled, and gas masks were provided for every member of the force. There were also two horses and six dogs available, as well as three troop transports, two half-ton searchlight trucks, and three trailer trucks to carry demonstrators off to two big detention compounds, which the mayor claimed "can take care of 25,000" demonstrators.[45] Private citizens' groups such as the Ku Klux Klan, the Americans for the Preservation of the White Race, and the local Citizens' Councils, got ready for the impending battle.

The Mississippi legislature conducted a readiness campaign, which was all too familiar to African Americans and movement people.[46] What Professor

Lusky calls obstructionism through lawless official action was the object of most of the new legislation that had already been signed into law by the governor before June 2. Such new laws included statutes aimed at proscribing many fundamental rights guaranteed by the U.S. Constitution:[47] an anti-leafleting law; an anti-picketing law; a law to "Restrain Movements of Individuals under Certain Circumstances," which allowed police to establish curfews without declaring martial law; the "Municipal Agreement" Act, which allowed municipalities to share police personnel and firefighting equipment during "riots and civil disturbances"; the Highway Patrol Act, which enlarged the State Highway Patrol and its powers and allowed the governor to send the highway patrol into local situations; an appropriation for the State Sovereignty Commission of fifty thousand dollars to fight the 1964 Civil Rights Bill, which was still in Congress; and a bill to invalidate the Twenty-fourth Amendment of the U.S. Constitution, which appeared to comply with the banning of the poll tax in federal elections but in reality provided for a similar form of registration with the same effects as the poll tax.

Other interesting legislation that was up for consideration in the state legislature included: a bill to allow unlimited numbers of deputy sheriffs in the counties, a bill to outlaw passive resistance in civil rights demonstrations, a bill making Freedom Schools and community centers illegal, a bill to permit the segregation of schools by sexes, a bill to support private schools in the state, a bill to end the accreditation of Tougaloo Southern Christian College as well as a bill to revoke its charter, a bill to prohibit the entry of volunteers into the state for the Summer Project on the grounds that their purpose was "willful violation of the laws of the state," a bill to remove Youth Court jurisdiction for minors under twenty-one charged under laws most often used for the arrest of civil rights workers, a bill to pay the costs of county registrars and circuit clerks convicted for disobeying the Civil Rights Acts of 1957 and 1960 to register African Americans on an equal basis with whites, a bill to reduce the number of African Americans on jury lists by changing the qualifications for jury duty, and a bill providing for the mandatory sterilization of those convicted of a third felony. In short, the Mississippi state legislature proposed assaulting the movement with the law.

The second type of obstructionism mentioned by Lusky was that of official inaction which permitted lawless members of the populace to take over while law enforcement agencies sat by and watched.[48] On June 25, 1963, a charter of incorporation was filed with the secretary of state in Jackson for the Americans for the Preservation of the White Race (APWR),[49] an organization which if it did not directly participate in lawless actions certainly aroused the white population of the state to do so. The chief of police of McComb, in Pike County, was the president of the local chapter of the APWR for a time during 1964.[50] Official police harassment of movement people in southwest Mississippi was a well-known fact by the time of the Summer Project.[51]

It is impossible to know exactly what organizations like the Ku Klux Klan planned for civil rights workers during the summer of 1964, but the news media in the state continued to issue numerous inflammatory statements calling on whites to defend Mississippi's honor,[52] and only a day after the first group of summer volunteers arrived in the state on June 21, two white workers and a Negro co-worker disappeared from the county jail during the night in Philadelphia, Neshoba County. Furthermore, after President Johnson signed the 1964 Civil Rights Bill into law on July 2, Governor Paul Johnson was cited in the *Hattiesburg American* on July 3 advising Mississippians not to comply with the law until it had been tested in the courts.[53] The *Clarksdale Press Register* quoted him on August 3 as saying, "Mississippi must outmaneuver those who would destroy us and our way of life."[54]

The *Jackson Clarion-Ledger* continued the inflammatory bombardment when it quoted the governor as saying on August 10 at the Neshoba County Fair, "Integration is like prohibition. If people don't want it a whole army can't enforce it."[55] Moreover, he made this statement after the bodies of Schwerner, Chaney, and Goodman had already been uncovered within view of the spot where he spoke to some of the murderers. If this wasn't enough, he added to the same crowd of six thousand, "the delinquency of adults who ignore their children, like those delinquent adults who allowed their children to invade Mississippi this summer [was one of the nation's problems]. . . . The people of Neshoba County are law-abiding people. Some news media have tried hard to run down this section of our state."[56] Barry Goldwater Jr. and Alabama Governor George Wallace were to be the main speakers at the Neshoba County Fair, but they canceled their appearances at the last minute. Johnson filled in for them.[57]

In light of the governor's open encouragement of noncompliance with federal and state criminal law and tacit support of lynch law, it is not surprising that terror tactics were employed throughout the state against movement workers and local African Americans. It is only surprising that more havoc was not done and more people were not killed. Part of the explanation for this may rest in the federal presence in the state after the disappearance of the three civil rights workers, even though their exact fate was not known until after their bodies were found on August 4.

When J. Edgar Hoover visited on July 10–11 to open an office of the FBI in Jackson,[58] it was not important what he said ("no protection" would be given to civil rights workers beyond reports based on complaints and directions for investigation from the Civil Rights Division of the Department of Justice;[59] and "in the southern part of the state, in the swamp country, the only inhabitants seem to be rattlesnakes, water moccasins, and redneck sheriffs")[60] but what he represented, the presence of the federal government in the person of over 150 FBI agents in Mississippi. Nevertheless, in spite of the few arrests made by federal law enforcement officers and the widespread investigatory actions and public education campaigns they conducted throughout the state, including their claimed penetration of the Klan, it was still a known truism that it was difficult if not impossible to find a judge and a jury who were willing to take action against the lawless elements in Mississippi.

The only immediate result of President Johnson's increasing of the numbers of FBI agents in the state and the use of four hundred troops from the Naval Air Station in Meridian in searching for Schwerner, Chaney, and Goodman seems to have been that no other white civil rights workers were killed during the Summer Project. This, though, did not prevent Mississippians from attempting murder on numerous occasions, particularly in southwest Mississippi.[61]

THE TRIPLE LYNCHING AND AFTER

Two of the Mississippi Three arrived in the state from New York City; the third was from Mississippi.[62] The first, Michael Henry Schwerner, twenty-four, and the second, Andrew Goodman, twenty, were white. The third, James Earl Chaney, twenty-one, was an African American from Meridian. Schwerner was a college graduate and a social worker in New York who joined Downtown CORE with his wife and then decided to go to Mississippi in the winter of 1963–64.[63] He entered the state in January 1964 and began the process of involving local African Americans in the movement. One of the first people who came to work with him and his wife was James Chaney, a high-school dropout who had already logged a year with the movement. They became fast friends. Goodman arrived in the state on June 20, driving down from the Oxford orientation sessions with Schwerner and Chaney, who had gone to Ohio to instruct the volunteers in what lay ahead. All three had their reasons for being involved in the civil rights movement.[64] Both Schwerner and Chaney were full-time task-force workers for CORE and COFO.

Goodman's interest in Mississippi and the movement apparently grew out of a talk that Louis E. Lomax, the prominent African American writer, gave at Queens College in 1963.[65] Goodman left behind a poem, which he had submitted to a writing course at Queens College, in New York, in the spring of 1964, which was a corollary to a poem by A. E. Housman's "To an Athlete Dying Young." That poem quoted in part reveals the depths reached by his feelings on the race problem in the United States:

> How dismally the day
> Screams out and blasts the night.
> What disaster you will say,
> To start another fight.[66]

Schwerner, Chaney, and Goodman's lives were sacrificed to a cause called civil rights on the night of June 21. It was not the first such lynching in Mississippi, or in the South, or in the nation, but it was probably the most significant one because it finally did wake up the American public and the federal government to their responsibility for the savage and sadistic abominations being perpetrated in Mississippi in the name of white supremacy and southern justice.

No official autopsy report on the Mississippi Three was ever filed with the court in Neshoba County, where they were murdered and where their bodies remained hidden in an earthen dam for forty-four days after the murder was committed.[67] The Coroner's Jury of Neshoba County declared that the cause or causes of death could not be officially determined.[68] The examination of the bodies was conducted by a private pathologist, ostensibly appointed by the county coroner. The report he filed was submitted jointly by him, the University of Mississippi Pathology Department, in Jackson, and the FBI. It stated that the bodies were badly decomposed, that Schwerner and Goodman had been shot once and that Chaney had been shot three times, one bullet fracturing his wrist. Furthermore, it stated that no other evidence of mutilation or bodily injury could be found.[69]

The movement knew what to expect and made a very serious effort to conduct its own autopsy. However, permission could only be obtained to examine the body of James Chaney, as Goodman's was flown out of the state shortly after it was found and Mississippi would not allow the Schwerner family to give consent over the telephone.[70] Mrs. Chaney, though, was a braver soul than white Mississippians had bargained for. She not only consented but also said to John Pratt, the legal representative of the National Council of Churches: "I want everyone to know everything possible about what has happened. I know he could die only once, but if they did these awful things to him, this ought to be no secret. It is even more important now that the guilty ones be brought to trial and justice and be punished. God must forgive them; it is very difficult for me to do so."[71] Three weeks after she signed the consent form for the second autopsy, her home was bombed and shot into. She was a widow with young children at that time.[72]

Despite White Mississippi's desire not to have the specific fate of the three civil rights workers made public, the movement wanted exactly that. The fact that the causes of death were not officially determined by the Coroner's Jury made it possible for that body not to ask the district attorney to seek an indictment from the grand jury.

Chaney's second autopsy was conducted on August 7 by Dr. David M. Spain, a clinical professor of pathology at the Downstate Medical Center in New York City, who was called to Mississippi by the Medical Committee for Human Rights (MCHR). Contrary to what White Mississippi found, he stated:

> In lay terminology—the jaw was shattered, the left shoulder and upper arm was reduced to a pulp; the right forearm was broken completely across at several points, and the skull bones were broken and pushed in toward the brain. Under the circumstances, these injuries could only be the result of an extremely severe beating with either a blunt instrument or chain. The other fractures of the skull were the result of bullet wounds. . . . In my experience of 25 years as a Pathologist and as a Medical Examiner [of Westchester County, New York], I have never witnessed bones so severely shattered except in tremendously high speed accidents such as aeroplane crashes.[73]

Dr. Spain was not able to determine what internal injuries Chaney sustained, as the internal organs had been removed from the body during the first autopsy. And the examination of Chaney's wrist failed to reveal a bullet wound.[74]

If one still thought that the FBI represented the federal government and the nation in Mississippi, then why was the report from the first autopsy, which was conducted in part under the FBI's auspices, so full of errors and so misleading? The general facts on how the three were murdered are well known. For all intents and purposes, the lynching was committed by White Mississippi in the persons of twenty-one white men acting against the civil rights movement in a concerted action to make sure that African Americans would remain "in their place" in Neshoba County. Movement people have indicated that they knew that they could find out exactly what happened if they were willing to pay enough. The black comedian Dick Gregory helped the investigation along by offering $25,000 for information leading to the discovery of the bodies and the identities of the murderers. He felt that if he could have offered $100,000, it would not have taken forty-four days to find the bodies.[75]

Apparently, a white Mississippian wanted the money badly enough because the names of the conspirators and those of the murderers were finally revealed, and the FBI knew just where to look for the bodies on August 4. Nevertheless, the written confession of Horace Doyle Barnette, one of the ten men who had played a role in the actual murders, was found inadmissible by U.S. Commissioner Esther Carter at the preliminary hearing in Meridian in December because she said it was presented by an FBI agent who had transcribed it and was thus hearsay evidence since Barnette was not present at the hearing.[76] The result of this farce was that Miss Carter released most of the arrested men on December 12, and the others subsequently, and ruled that "no real evidence had been presented to hold them for federal grand jury action."[77]

An official of the Department of Justice stated, "In the experience of the department, the refusal by a U.S. Commissioner to accept a law enforcement officer's report of a signed confession in a preliminary hearing is totally without precedent."[78] Among those who were arrested by the FBI on December 4 on federal conspiracy charges were Neshoba County Sheriff Lawrence Rainey, forty-one; Deputy Sheriff Cecil Price, twenty-six; Otha Neal Burkes, seventy-one, a former Philadelphia policeman; the Reverend Edgar Ray Killen, thirty-nine, a fundamentalist Baptist minister, and several leaders of the White Knights of the Ku Klux Klan of Mississippi.[79] Of the four mentioned by name, only Deputy Sheriff Price directly participated in the murders, which were committed in the name of Neshoba County and White Mississippi by state officials. The men were never convicted of murder, even though Sheriff Rainey did admit to FBI agents on one occasion that he had killed two Negroes in the past in what he called "self-defense."[80]

Reconstruction of the events leading up to the lynching has revealed that the three civil rights workers' progress to and from the Mount Zion Methodist

Church in the Longdale Community in Neshoba County was closely reported over the "Citizens Short Wave Band," used by the Ku Klux Klan and the Citizens' Council. Apparently, Price reported the information over the two-way radio while following the workers, who had gone to investigate the burning of the African American church near Philadelphia in the Longdale Community; the church had been pledged by the community as a Freedom School site for the summer. Price arrested Schwerner, Chaney, and Goodman—Chaney for speeding and Schwerner and Goodman for suspicion of arson, even though all three were in Oxford, Ohio, at the time the church burned down on June 16. Sometime during the night, the three were released from jail and murdered.

If the three were arrested at around 4:30 in the afternoon, and Price had admitted to arresting them at this time, how was it that they voluntarily left jail during the night? All civil rights workers knew that it was extremely dangerous to get oneself released from jail at night. In any event, they apparently fell into the hands of the mob outside of Philadelphia. One of the available eyewitness accounts to the lynching indicates that Schwerner and Goodman were still alive when Chaney was beaten and that only after they tried to intervene and stop the beating were they shot and killed. Much of what transpired can only be taken as supposition, although the available accounts seem to be trustworthy.[81]

Unidentified sources state that the murders of the Mississippi Three were the ninth, tenth, and eleventh civil rights murders of 1964 in Mississippi and that the twelfth and thirteenth were represented by the dismembered, decomposed bodies of African Americans Charles Moore, nineteen, and Henry Dee; the former was a student at Alcorn A&M College who had participated in civil rights activities there which led to the summary dismissal of seven hundred Negro students in April. "Moore's body was found severed at the waist, the legs bound at the ankles. Dee's was a headless torso. Only after medical examination was it possible to determine their sex or race."[82]

It is pointless to go on citing the endless acts of terror, beatings, shootings, bombings, arrests, harassments, and murders that took place during the summer and fall of 1964, as they were only a continuation of an already well-established pattern of violence and intimidation. The point to be made is that even White Mississippi was shocked by the triple lynching, although it was found impossible to bury Schwerner and Chaney side by side in a Mississippi graveyard.[83]

If White Mississippi was shocked then, White America was more so, and for possibly the first time constant pressure was exerted upon President Johnson to do something to change the nature of the closed society. The programs undertaken by the Mississippi Summer Project gained at least part of their significance because they were carried out in the shadow of the murder of the three civil rights workers and at a time when a national consensus for change had finally emerged. The results of this consensus were felt at the Democratic National Convention in Atlantic City in August. (See chapter 9, below).

The programs conducted during the Summer Project were in many ways an expression of just how sick and tired African American Mississippi had become of suffering under white oppression. Dave Dennis, who directed CORE's project for COFO in the Fourth Congressional District—Neshoba County is located there—expressed the anger that had welled up in the hearts of Mississippi African Americans during Freedom Summer and then spilled over in an attitude of impatience in waiting for things to change and bitterness and hostility toward White Mississippi. At Chaney's memorial service on August 7 in Meridian, Dennis could no longer hold back his feelings. It is easy to believe that he spoke for the movement and the African American community as he addressed a crowd of seven hundred: "I'm sick and tired of going to the funerals of black men who have been murdered by white men. . . . I'm not going to stand here and ask anyone not to be angry, not to be bitter tonight. We've defended our country. To do what? To live like slaves. . . . Don't just look at me and go back and tell folks you've been to a nice service. Your work is just beginning. And I'm going to tell you deep down in my heart what I feel right now. If you go back home and sit down and take what these white men in Mississippi are doing to us . . . if you take it and don't do something about it . . . then God damn your souls!"[84]

Voter Registration

It is relevant to ask how these frightful standards of legalized injustice could have persisted for so long in a state which ostensibly is integral to the American community and shares its principle of democratic justice. Last summer the existing corruption of law and order in Mississippi was accentuated by the white oligarchy's knowledge that the registration of Negroes portended the end of its arbitrary rule.

—REINHOLD NIEBUHR, 1965

The violence of Philadelphia was repeated around the state throughout the summer, but usually to a lesser degree and mostly without the blatant connivance and obvious participation of local law enforcement officers. [85] Almost all voter registration work had to be conducted in an atmosphere of terror and intimidation, and the movement's work must be understood within this eerie framework. Mississippi was just not the same as other states, even though it was allegedly part of the United States. Except where federal pressure was directly applied, little if any concrete results in registering new African American voters were achieved. Voter registration drives, Freedom Days, Freedom Votes, and other forms of protest politics did not achieve substantive results.

Any and all acts of identification with the movement brought violent reprisal. One did not even have to be in touch with the civil rights cause to achieve martyrdom; one just had to be African American and in the way when White Mississippi went on a rampage. You did not have to be a civil rights worker; it was enough if you were not from Mississippi, even if you were a lawyer, doctor, or minister come to help the movement out, even if your name was Franklin Delano Roosevelt III (who was arrested in Clarksdale on August 17 for "speeding" while going 25 in a 35-miles-per-hour zone). [86]

Continuing in its policy of running candidates for public office who offered an alternative to Mississippi African Americans and a reason to register and vote, the movement entered its own candidates in the Democratic Party Primary elections on June 2. Mrs. Hamer ran in the Second Congressional District against the incumbent Jamie Whitten; Mrs. Victoria Gray faced Senator John Stennis for the seat once held by Theodore Bilbo; the Reverend John Cameron, of Hattiesburg, ran in the Fifth Congressional District against William Colmer; and James W. Houston, of Vicksburg, faced John Bell Williams in the Third Congressional District. Early in the primary campaign, the State Election Commission—composed of Governor Paul Johnson, Attorney General Joe Patterson, and Secretary of State Heber Ladner—stated that neither Mrs. Hamer nor Mrs. Gray could participate in both the primary and the general election. All of the candidates were enjoined by the state from taking part in the Freedom Democratic Party, which was established during the summer. [87]

The significance of running African American candidates in the Democratic Primary for the second time—the first occasion was in 1962—can be seen as part of the movement's overall strategy in getting Mississippi African Americans involved in the political intricacies of national, state, and local politics. This process of involving African Americans in politics at the grassroots level was carried a step further in the establishment of the Mississippi Freedom Democratic Party during the spring and summer of 1964. (See chapter 9, below.)

The Summer Project plans were under the direction of COFO; the president was Aaron Henry, the field director was Bob Moses, and the assistant program director was Dave Dennis. They called for a massive effort to get Mississippi African Americans to go to county courthouses throughout the state and attempt to register to vote. The tangible results during the summer were paltry, except in Panola County. There Robert J. Miles and his wife were very active in the Voters League, which was founded in 1955.[88] By the summer the county registrar had been ordered by the Fifth Circuit Court of Appeals (*United States v. Duke,* 332 F.2d 759 [1961]) to register African Americans who were twenty-one years of age without paying the poll tax and without the registrar or deputy registrar being present if they were not able to be there in person. Furthermore, the registrar was ordered to take as many applicants as physical space permitted. Over 800 African Americans successfully registered to vote at the county seat in Batesville during the summer, but this still was only 12.1 percent of voting-age African Americans in the county.[89] As for the rest of the state, results were not as promising. According to Aaron Henry, some 17,250 African Americans filled out registration forms but only about 1,300 more were added to the rolls in the other counties.[90]

In organizing the voter registration program, the state was divided up by congressional districts: SNCC staffed the First, Second, Third, and Fifth districts, and CORE staffed the Fourth. Both organizations contributed personnel to the state COFO office in Jackson. In the First Congressional District, projects were set up in Aberdeen, Columbus, Starkville, and Tupelo; in the Second, in Batesville, Belzoni, Charleston, Clarksdale, Cleveland, Greenville, Greenwood, Holly Springs, Indianola, Itta Bena, Mayersville, Ruleville, Shaw, and Tchula; in the Third, in Jackson, McComb, Natchez, and Vicksburg; in the Fourth, in Canton, Carthage, Flora, Meridian, and Philadelphia; and in the Fifth, in Biloxi, Gulfport, Hattiesburg, Laurel, Moss Point, and Pascagoula.[91]

The techniques for fieldwork in voter registration were outlined to the volunteers in the COFO handbook by the following four areas:[92] (1) safety, (2) canvassing, (3) workshops, and (4) taking people to the courthouse. Safety measures included the following salient steps: know all roads in and out of town, know location of sanctuaries and safe homes in the county, keep in constant contact with the Jackson or county office, and decide whether to work at night or during the day depending on suitability and safety. The major points to be made in canvassing for potential registrants were patience, letting the people know you had a lot of time to listen to them and their problems, gathering information on activities in the community, and getting people to come to workshops and mass meetings where they would be able to overcome their fears by joining with their neighbors.

In running workshops, they were to be supplied in advance with the necessary materials for training people in voter education and getting them ready to go to register; sessions were to be run at a slow-enough pace that everyone would be able to follow; and the workshops probably should be opened and closed with a song or a prayer.

The confrontation of taking people to the county courthouse called for arranging transportation in advance, getting people to go in groups of at least two, and trying to accompany the registrants up to the registrar's door if permitted by the local authorities.

Additionally, local people with leadership potential were to be encouraged to attend the biweekly citizenship-training sessions at Dorchester, Georgia, which were run by SCLC—with travel expenses paid by that organization. The handbook also offered the following advice to all registration workers: "You will find in time that the simple process of delivering small groups of Negroes to the courthouse is not enough. The people become frustrated, discouraged. Weekly mass meetings pale when the community can see no absolute progress in registration—what's the use? The entire community must somehow be involved, a feeling of real movement must be restored. Calling a 'Freedom Day' may revitalize the town as well as providing a probable basis for a Federal suit."[93] Finally, the worker was advised to maintain a "feeling of motion, of purpose."[94] When the community sang "We Shall Overcome," it should "mean it and believe it."[95]

As the Summer Project got underway toward the end of June, the movement quickly accelerated its drive toward freedom. Staffed with the most personnel it ever had gathered in the state for a concerted drive against the Mississippi power structure—in the past it was only possible to move effectively in one place at a time—confrontations were forced throughout the state. Signs that the monolithic order of Mississippi was beginning to crack appeared during the summer, although the price was terribly high.

Even though Freedom Days were outlawed by the state legislature in the spring of 1964[96]—in response to those held in Hattiesburg in January, in Canton in February, March, and May, and in Greenwood in March—the movement continued to hold them throughout Freedom Summer with varying degrees of success. The campaigns leading up to the Freedom Days were generally met with ever-increasing violence, but the marches to county courthouses were for the most part orderly affairs with a minimum of violence and intimidation and surprisingly few arrests. It seemed as if the white power structure had learned the lesson that it was better not to confront the movement on such public occasions when the national news media and federal agents might be present. Some mass arrests did take place, however, and mobs did gather to threaten and intimidate African Americans and civil rights workers, if not to attack them.[97]

In almost all cases the Freedom Days that were held were conducted in the hardcore areas of the Delta where the number of registered African American voters was at a minimum.[98] Sometimes campaigns were conducted for a Freedom Day only to find that the county registrar had decided that he was too busy to keep the office open; for example, in Clarksdale, Coahoma County (7.3 percent of the voting-age African American population was registered), on July 13 because the registrar claimed that with court in session he was too preoccupied to deal with the African American community, or in Aberdeen, Monroe County (0.2 percent of the voting-age African American population was registered), on August 12 because the registrar claimed to be ill. The problem of absenteeism was only gradually addressed by the movement because it meant turning to the courts, as in the case of Panola County, and it generally took two or three years for the Fifth Circuit Court of Appeals to hand down a decision ordering the registration of African American applicants.[99] Furthermore, at times the registrar's voting records had a tendency to disappear for long periods.[100]

Nonetheless, the movement persevered in its attempts to register African American voters, and the white power structure continued in its efforts to stave off the onslaught. On July 14, members of the State Sovereignty Commission visited the Hattiesburg COFO office.[101] On July 15 at a voter registration rally in Drew, Sunflower County (the home county of Senator Eastland, where 1.4 percent of voting-age African Americans were registered voters), 25 people were arrested and put in jail. The local Citizens' Council had met at 9:00 that morning.

On July 16, though, Freedom Days were held in three Delta communities, Greenwood, Greenville, and Cleveland.[102] The first, in Greenwood, in Leflore County (2.1 percent of the voting-age African Americans were registered), had been the scene of unceasing confrontations between the movement and the white power structure, but only 281 African Americans had managed to register to vote by the time the 1965 Voting Rights Act was passed. During the Freedom Day there—one was also held on March 25—the police arrested 111 people,

13 of whom were juveniles, 9 of whom were SNCC staff, and 13 of whom were volunteers. The following day the cases of those arrested in Drew and Greenwood were removed to Federal District Court, with the bond being reduced to $200 for those from out of state and $100 for residents. Nevertheless, on July 19 all of them were still in jail and were not allowed to receive visitors. Finally, on July 20, the arrestees were tried in the local court in Greenwood, in spite of the removal order. The defendants chose to stand mute, basing their action on being tried in violation of their constitutional rights. They were convicted on a charge of violating the anti-picketing law, sentenced to thirty days in jail, and fined $100 each.

The second Freedom Day was held in Greenville, in Washington County (8.5 percent of the African American population of voting age was registered), a town known for its quiet law-enforcement practices. Here, there were no arrests, and 101 African Americans were allowed to take the test. Nevertheless, 100 other potential registrants were found to be too late in coming and were not allowed to enter the registrar's office to fill out the forms.

The third Freedom Day conducted on July 16 took place in Cleveland, in Bolivar County (with 3.8 percent of voting-age African Americans registered), the home of Amzie Moore, who had convinced Bob Moses to work in the Delta in 1962.[103] As in Greenville, there were no incidents, but only registrants and picketers were allowed near the courthouse. Some 75 African Americans came to register, and 20 of the 25 from Shaw registered, while 30 of the 50 from other parts of the county were able to do so. The police came out in force to supervise the activities—10 regular policemen and 45 auxiliary policemen. A further 50 African Americans lined up at the county courthouse in Cleveland on August 4 and were admitted one by one at 45-minute intervals. Leaflets were passed out without incident until some civil rights workers decided to move across the street and distribute pamphlets among the pedestrians. All 13 of the workers were then arrested on an anti-littering ordinance, and bond was set at $300 each.

Following the first Freedom Day in Cleveland, one was held in Holly Springs, in Marshall County (2.5 percent of the African Americans of voting age were registered), on July 24. The white power structure in the town was not so lenient with the demonstrators, apparently because Holly Springs had been the scene of constant civil rights activities on the campus of Rust College, a coed African American institution established in 1866. Some 55 helmeted state highway patrolmen and 35 local police were present. Integrated picketing was canceled in light of the circumstances, and some 40 to 50 African American registrants were ordered to walk to the courthouse steps one by one at intervals of eight feet and had a police escort from the courthouse steps to the registrar's office. Nevertheless, no violence took place, even though intimidation was highly visible, and only one volunteer was arrested for "disturbing the public peace." Bond for him was set at $500. A second Freedom Day was held in Holly Springs on August 15, this time for African Americans from all over the county.

During this period other towns were trying to make life difficult for movement workers in other ways.[104] In Canton, in Madison County (with 2.1 percent of voting-age African Americans registered), all civil rights workers were ordered on June 26 to register with the local police. In Shaw, on August 7, workers were notified of a similar procedure. In Canton, a main base of CORE activities, a civil rights worker's car was shot up on June 24, but luckily no one was hurt. On August 2, white CORE worker George Johnson was shot at three times on his way to the Canton Freedom House. On August 11, the Freedom House had a firebomb thrown at it from a passing car, but no damage was done. Subsequently, shots were fired at the building on August 14 and a bomb which did not go off was found there on August 20.

Other movement offices were also shot at and bombed, sometimes with damage done, sometimes not. Shots were fired at the national office of SNCC in Greenwood on August 2 and at one of the movement cars there on August 20. Tear gas bombs were thrown into the project offices in Batesville on July 26 and in Aberdeen on August 9. The tavern next to the project office in Natchez, in Adams County, was bombed on August 14. After the bombing a policeman came to investigate and was heard to mutter in disgust that the wrong building had been destroyed. In frustration apparently, he bent the radio antenna located at the COFO office.[105] And on August 23, the COFO project office in Tupelo, Lee County, was bombed.

Churches, community centers, and Freedom Schools were also burned and bombed: the Williams Chapel in Ruleville, Sunflower County, was firebombed on June 26; the Bovina Community Center in Vicksburg, Warren County, was burned on July 7, even though it had no connection with the movement;[106] an attempt was made to bomb the well-guarded community center in Mileston, Holmes County, on August 9, after a SNCC car had been burned there on July 26; and the Freedom School in Gluckstadt (near Canton), in Madison County, was gutted by fire on August 11. Additionally, the Reverend R. L. T. Smith's home in Jackson was shot into on June 23, and nine shots were fired at civil rights workers going to a mass meeting in Greenville on July 20. Other communities suffered similar violence during the long, hot summer.[107]

Even though these sorts of blatant intimidation and violence continued, the movement persevered in its registration activities. Local African Americans were no longer frightened away from the movement; rather, they joined forces with it and continued to confront their white oppressors. Sometimes they had a little help from the federal government, as in Tallahatchie County (0.3 percent of the voting-age African Americans were registered), where the registrar was enjoined not to discriminate in registering African American applicants and not to use the interpretation test, and the sheriff was enjoined not to intimidate African Americans who wanted to register.[108] Nevertheless, when 24 African Americans braved the consequences of a trip to the county courthouse in Charleston on August 12, they were met outside the office by a group of about 93 armed whites who stood around threateningly during the day.

When African Americans held a precinct meeting of the Freedom Democratic Party at the Moon Lake Baptist Church on July 27 in Mayersville, Issaquena County (with 0.5 percent of voting-age African Americans registered), they were told by the owner of the plantation across the street from the church that, if they held any more such meetings, the church would be burned down. And Marks, the county seat of Quitman County (7.7 percent of the voting-age African Americans were registered), was not much better. When an LCDC attorney went on August 4 to check on the detention of a voter registration worker there, he stopped alongside a car filled with other registration workers which had been stopped by the town marshal. He was subsequently beaten by this law enforcement officer, receiving head injuries, among them a large gash over one eye. After this, the lawyer was arrested for "obstructing an officer in the performance of his duties" and was held on $200 bail.[109]

In places like Rolling Fork, the county seat of Sharkey County (0.1 percent of the voting-age African Americans were registered), registration efforts were generally stopped before they could get started. Two local African Americans who tried to hand out leaflets in Anguilla announcing a Freedom Day in Rolling Fork were arrested on August 11 on an anti-littering charge, and bond was set at $200. Similarly, other rural counties in the Delta presented a face of hostility and adamancy in their confrontations with the movement.

Other places, like Tunica County (0.7 percent of the voting-age African Americans were registered), were largely passed over by the movement.[110] And when it was named by a federal agency as "the most poverty-stricken area of the nation," the editor of the *Tunica Times-Democrat* defended his county (median family income in 1969: whites, $6,670; African Americans, $2,093) by saying African Americans there receive free rent and a government check, have cars and television sets, and "aren't working and don't want to work."[111] He added that, if the plantation owners "would turn these African American families out[,] . . . you would really see poverty."[112] Be this as it may, it was no idle threat. Tens of thousands of African Americans were thrown out of work by the mechanization of cotton production in the Delta in the 1960s and were subsequently thrown off the plantations where they had lived for years.[113]

The threat posed by the movement to the white power structure in these hardcore Delta counties was indeed real. (See table 2 for population percentages of African Americans in Delta counties in 1960 and 1970.) Bolivar County's African American population was 67.8 percent of the county in 1960. In Coahoma County the figure was 68.3 percent; in Holmes, 72.0 percent; in Humphreys, 69.8 percent; in Issaquena, 67.1 percent; in Leflore, 64.6 percent; in Madison, 71.8 percent; in Marshall, 70.4 percent; in Panola, 56.4 percent; in Quitman, 63.3 percent; in Sharkey, 69.8 percent; in Sunflower, 67.8 percent; in Tallahatchie, 64.4 percent; in Washington, 55.2 percent; and in Tunica County the figure was an overwhelming 79.2 percent, the highest of any county in Mississippi. If the African Americans were to win the franchise in any of these counties, it was likely that the local white power structure would lose the stranglehold that had enabled the white community from time immemorial to do as it wished with its African American citizens.

Other places such as Moss Point, in Jackson County (27.4 percent of voting-age African Americans in the county were registered, but only 19.6 percent of its citizens were African American),[114] did not have so many African American inhabitants but still did not like them to move out "of their place." On June 23, a hall used for voter registration activities was slightly damaged in an arson attempt. And when the movement persisted, a voter rally was shot up by whites on July 6.[115] An African American woman was shot twice while singing "We Shall Overcome," and three African Americans were arrested by the police when they tried to follow the car they thought the shots came from. The white car was not checked. If this was not enough, when the community was holding a voter registration meeting on the front lawn of the SNCC office on August 4, the police came into the meeting which had just gotten underway and gave the people fifteen minutes to disperse. When no one moved, 18 helmeted policemen with guns, bayonets, and clubs surrounded the group, and fifteen minutes later a prison bus drove up. A total of 40 officers in ten police cars and two motorcycles congregated nearby. Finally, 62 people were arrested, 5 of whom were civil rights workers, the rest being local African American citizens. Everyone was charged with "breach of the peace," and bail was set at $300 cash or $600 property bond.[116]

McComb, in the southwestern part of the state, was important symbolically to the movement because local African Americans there had been left to suffer the abuses of their white terrorizers ever since the civil rights workers had pulled out in the winter of 1961. By the time the 1965 Voting Rights Act was passed, only 3 percent of the voting-age African Americans in Pike County, where McComb is located, were registered to vote—207 of 6,936. When the movement decided to return to the southwest, it was strictly on a volunteer basis, as everyone knew the chances of coming out alive were low. Eight full-time SNCC and CORE staffers went in at the beginning of July to stay: Curtis Hayes, twenty-two, of Summit; Dennis Sweeney, twenty-one, of Portland, Oregon; George Greene, twenty, and his sister Fredeye, nineteen, both of Greenwood; Julius "Mendy" Samstein, twenty-five, of New York City; Jesse Harris, twenty-two, of Jackson, the project's director; Sherry Everitt, nineteen, of Pittsburgh, Pennsylvania; Pat Walker, a CORE worker from New York City; and two Summer Project volunteers, Reverend Don McCord, twenty-six, of Stafford, Kansas, and Clinton Hopson, twenty-six, of Asbury Park, New Jersey. Samstein, Sweeney, McCord, and Walker were white.[117] They were followed by others who decided to make the commitment later in the summer and during the winter. SNCC and the movement had made its decision to return.

White McComb was just as united in its decision to drive the movement out for a second time. Even before the civil rights workers arrived, elements of the McComb community started its own summer project—havoc and terror. On June 22, the homes of two local people who had decided to house the workers were bombed. One of them was damaged extensively. Seven sticks of dynamite were left on the lawn of a third home, whose owner had no connections with the movement.

On July 8, after the workers had settled into the tense community and had held a rally attended by 150 local African Americans, terror struck. The Freedom House was severely damaged by bombs during the night, and Curtis Hayes was cut by flying glass while Dennis Sweeney suffered a mild concussion.[118] Seeing that these acts did not deter the civil rights workers, the terror was continued.

On July 17, the Mount Zion Hill Baptist Church in Pike County was bombed, or burned, to the ground. The pastor of the church had let the movement use his McComb church, St. Mary's. On July 22, the Mt. Vernon Missionary Baptist Church, which was not connected with the movement, was also burned to the ground. And on July 24, the home of Curtis C. Bryant, the head of the Pike County NAACP and one of the two people who had invited Bob Moses to come to McComb in 1961, was shot into. It was not the first time. Two days later two bombs were thrown at the home of Charles Bryant, who was later a Freedom Democratic Party delegate to the Democratic National Convention. Bryant's wife shot back at the terrorists, and when the terrorists returned, Bryant himself ran out to get a better look at his attackers but was knocked down by the second explosion, which caused extensive damage to the house.[119] A voter registration meeting of 50 people had been conducted at his home earlier in the day. Another church, the Mt. Canaan Baptist Church, was burned to the ground on August 6.

One might imagine that the movement would retreat under such pressures, but it did not. On July 15, some 35 young people enrolled in the McComb Freedom School. The enrollment grew to 75 by July 21, and by the end of the summer it had reached 108.[120] Also, the Free Southern Theater performed Martin Duberman's *In White America* at the Freedom School on August 1, and Pete Seeger, working with the Mississippi Caravan of Music, gave a concert in the African American community on the night of August 3 and conducted workshops on folk music at the Freedom School on August 4.

The violence, like the civil rights activity, did not let up, as the movement aroused the community for the Freedom Day that was to be held on August 18, the day before three busloads of delegates from the Freedom Democratic Party were to leave for Atlantic City and the Democratic National Convention. On the night of August 4, the Burglund supermarket, across the street from the McComb Freedom School, was almost completely destroyed by a bomb. The blast left a large hole in the ground, and a voter registration worker in the Freedom House two blocks away was almost knocked down by shock waves from the explosion. Mendy Samstein jumped into his car and followed two white men who were leaving the scene. He found that their license number was one of those on SNCC's "suspicious car" list. Law student Clinton Hopson was arrested for interfering with an officer as he tried to get through the crowd to the scene of the bombing. A local registration worker, Roy Lee, was arrested when he returned to the scene of the bombing and was charged with inciting to riot, threatening the life of a policeman, profanity, and disorderly conduct. He was held on bond of $900, and although a SNCC spokesman said he was arrested for no apparent reason, it is possible to imagine that this time a Mississippi African American had been arrested on charges that were in part true. McComb African Americans were really angry and no longer tried to hide it.

The McComb police, though, seemed to feel that the movement workers had not been harassed enough. Therefore, on August 16, at 1:30 in the morning, 24 policemen in five cars, representing the McComb City Police, the sheriff of Pike County, and the State Highway Patrol, raided the project office, armed with warrants to search for illegal liquor. None was found, but this did not stop the officers from reading letters and civil rights material found in the office. On the evening of August 17, a mass meeting of over 200 local African Americans was held in the city to protest the terrorism. At 1:30 in the morning of August 18, Mrs. Vera Brown, a local African American who was planning to register later in the day, was awakened by the smell of smoke. Under her house she found a smoking gasoline-filled jar, which she smothered before damage could be done. Her daughter was active in the movement.[121]

Finally, on August 18, Freedom Day came to Pike County, where McComb is located.[122] After all the buildup, the day proved to be a peaceful one, as 25 potential African American registrants went to the county courthouse in Magnolia. The registrar processed 23 of them at a rate of one every forty-five minutes. Police and FBI agents were present throughout the day. After the Freedom Day, workers continued to receive beatings and be harassed by the police, houses continued to be bombed and shot at, and numerous other attacks were made on the African American community, but southwest Mississippi was no longer the same.

McComb might be taken as a symbol of the rest of Mississippi, as African Americans during the summer of 1964 refused to be intimidated any longer, even if they were terribly frightened, as they proved to be in Philadelphia. Many African American communities, though, were in open revolt against the local white power structure, shooting back when attacked in the night and turning out in massive numbers at county courthouses throughout the state. They had come to embrace the movement.

8

Freedom Summer, Part II

Freedom Schools and Community Centers

[I]t was unlawful, as well as unsafe, to teach a slave to read. . . . Learning would spoil the best nigger in the world. Now, if you teach that nigger (speaking of myself) how to read, there would be no keeping him. . . . From that moment, I understood the pathway from slavery to freedom.

—FREDERICK DOUGLASS, 1845

Douglass's words, although written in 1845, penetrate to the heart of the modern "slavery" endured by Mississippi African Americans, a slavery of ignorance.[1] Throughout the early years of the student-supported civil rights movement's work in Mississippi, efforts had been made to arouse these benighted African American citizens from their "apathy" and spur them on their way to freedom. From the beginning, young people had been among the first to embrace the movement. Whereas African American adults in Mississippi had everything to lose—their homes, their jobs, and even their lives—young people instinctively knew that they really had nothing to lose but their ignorance, their invisible chains, and their poverty. The movement held out to them a promise for the future, a glimmer of freedom, a ray of hope that things would no longer be the same. So they flocked to the piper who played a different tune, one of revolt, one of Freedom Now, not in the next world.[2]

The "Nonviolent High," opened by Moses and SNCC in McComb in the middle of October 1961 for the students who had walked out of Burgland High School after the school authorities refused to readmit Brenda Travis and Isaac Lewis, sought to guarantee those students the education denied them by the white power structure in McComb, and possibly even a little more. SNCC workers Bob Moses, Chuck McDew, and Dion Diamond, an African American Freedom Rider who left Howard University to work for SNCC in the South, taught the McComb youths until they were admitted a few weeks later to Campbell

Junior College in Jackson.[3] Those 103 African American students, who had boy-
cotted their segregated high school and had defied the school authorities' demand that they either sign a pledge not to participate in future civil rights demonstrations or be expelled from school, issued a statement on October 4, 1961:

> We feel that as a member of Burgland High School they [Travis and Lewis]
> have fought this battle for us. To prove that we appreciate them for doing
> this, we will suffer whatever punishment they have to take with them.
>
> In school we are taught democracy, but the rights that democracy has
> to offer have been denied to us by our oppressor: we have not had the right
> to vote; we have not had a balanced school system; we have not had an op-
> portunity to participate in any of the branches of our local, state, and federal
> government.[4]

Freedom Schools sought to redress these wrongs committed in the name
of white supremacy, not just to teach the normal curriculum that was offered
to African American students in Mississippi but also to instill in them a spirit
of freedom and thus build for the future.

Initially, one must accept the fact that the public school system in Mississippi was and remained for many years after Freedom Summer an instrument
used by the power structure to maintain the status quo of African Americans.
Mississippi in 1964 had no law of compulsory education, and schools were
closed during the times when labor was needed to chop and pick the cotton
crop. Even for those who attended school the hope held out for them was bleak,
as African American teachers in the state were generally not registered to vote
and were afraid of losing their jobs if they dared to teach or say anything to
their pupils that might be construed by white authorities to be detrimental to
the "natural" order of the "Southern, or Mississippi, way of life."

What did this mean in hard facts?[5] In 1970, the school-age population of
Mississippi was 50.8 percent African American, the highest in the Deep South.
Only 26.4 percent of the African American school population attended schools
where they comprised less than 50 percent of the total enrollment, which was
the lowest in the Deep South. Furthermore, the median number of school years
completed by an African American over twenty-five years of age in Mississippi
failed in most, if not all, cases to even approach the level of attainment reached
in the other Deep South states. Across the South, the median number of years
of schooling completed by African Americans over twenty-five was 9.1 years.

For African Americans living in a metropolitan area, the figure was 9.9 years; for nonfarm areas, it was 8.2 years; and for farm areas, 7.1 years. (These figures represent the median years of education for African American males and females together.) The breakdown by Mississippi counties in 1970 presents an even bleaker picture than that of the Deep South as a whole.

First of all it should be noted that only the city of Jackson, the state capital, can in any way be called a metropolitan area—its population in 1970 was 153,968. No other city in Mississippi had a population over 50,000, although five others had more than 30,000 residents (Biloxi, 48,486; Meridian, 45,083; Gulfport, 40,971; Greenville, 39,648; and Hattiesburg, 38,274). Most of the other cities were in reality nothing more than large towns.[6] This atmosphere of small-town mentality and provincialism was, in part, what made it so difficult for the movement to achieve anything at all in the state.

African American educational achievements in the closed society were minimal:[7] the median number of school years completed by African Americans over twenty-five years of age in 1970 in Bolivar County was 5.3 for males and 6.6 for females; in Coahoma County, the figures were 4.8 and 6.6; in Hinds County, they were 8.3 and 9.0; in Holmes County, 5.7 and 7.9; in Humphreys County, 5.8 and 6.9; in Issaquena County, 5.2 and 6.2; in Leake County, 7.4 and 8.9; in Leflore County, 5.4 and 7.0; in Madison County, 6.4 and 8.1; in Marshall County, 6.3 and 7.6; in Quitman County, 4.4 and 6.2; in Sharkey County, 4.7 and 6.8; in Sunflower County, 5.4 and 6.5; in Tallahatchie County, 4.2 and 6.3; in Tunica County, 4.3 and 6.2; in Warren County, 7.0 and 8.4; in Washington County, 5.9 and 7.2; and in Yazoo County, 5.4 and 7.5. These statistics, though, represent only part of the story, as the real picture was to be revealed in the state of education in Mississippi which was definitely separate and unequal in 1964, as well as in 1970 and after.

The Freedom Schools, then, were in part an effort to rectify the deplorable condition of the education available to the state's African Americans. School facilities were substandard; curriculum deficiencies were ever present; freedom of thought and speech were constantly stifled; and opportunities to advance in life were generally curtailed by the white power structure. As in the sphere of political action, so also in the realm of education, the movement tried to gain access to the future for African Americans. Denied this, civil rights workers established an independent but parallel network of institutions that would be both a protest against the inherent inequality of educational opportunities available to African American schoolchildren and an effort to fill that gap with a meaningful education that would prepare them to live in the twentieth century and to fight for their freedom.

During the summer of 1964, some forty-seven Freedom Schools were established in twenty or more communities around the state with over 2,500 students enrolled in classes covering subjects such as African American history, citizenship education, creative writing, drama—through reenacting real-life situations familiar to all African Americans in the South—and other subjects not offered to them in Mississippi schools, such as foreign languages, advanced mathematics, and typing. Additionally, students were taught to doubt and were encouraged to ask questions and generally not to accept things at face value but to penetrate the surface and delve into popular beliefs about the southern way of life and African Americans' part in it.

According to Staughton Lynd, who directed the Freedom Schools during the summer but returned to academic life in the fall, twenty or so Freedom Schools with about 1,000 pupils had been planned.[8] By the end of the Summer Project, this number had been far exceeded and a full-time staff of 175 teachers was supplemented with an additional 50 to 100 staff members, many of whom were drawn from local communities after being trained by Freedom School teachers.

In places such as Hattiesburg the anticipated enrollment at the Freedom Schools was far lower than the final total of enrollees—on July 6, five schools were opened in the city with a total enrollment of over 600, and two more schools were opened at nearby Palmers Crossing. The McComb Freedom School had 108 pupils; 300 studied in Vicksburg; 250 in Gulfport; 200 in Moss Point; 100 in Valley View; 100 in Sharon; 100 in Camden; 75 in Indianola; 60 in Canton; 60 in Greenville; 50 in Greenwood; 30 in Mileston; 30 in Ruleville; 30 in Clarksdale; 14 in Gluckstadt (the Freedom School was destroyed by fire on August 11, but the classes continued outdoors), and others in Shaw, Holly Springs, Harmony, Biloxi, and Cleveland. Two one-month sessions were planned for July and August, but in the end the program was continued through the fall and winter.[9]

Although the idea for the Freedom School program was essentially Charlie Cobb's, a former Howard student who dropped out of college in the early years of the movement and went to work with SNCC in Mississippi, most of the COFO staff played a part in creating the curriculum and teaching from time to time in the schools themselves.[10] When the idea was first conceived, it was felt that the Freedom Schools would be a good supplement to the education of

Mississippi African Americans. By the end of the summer, it became apparent that this program was not just a place for African American high school students to enrich their education but moreover a place where future movement leaders could be trained.

The establishment of the Mississippi Student Union (MSU) at the Freedom School Convention in Meridian on August 7–9, which was attended by some 150 students, provided the African American community with a group of 1,500 high-school students from around the state who were able to express themselves on problems that were basic to the African American community. Civil rights workers had tried to organize such a group in the past, but the time apparently had not been ripe for it. The Freedom School program made the possibility of such an organization a reality.

The experience of the Freedom Schools often led to other things in the African American community. Shaw, a small town located in the cotton fields on the border of Bolivar and Sunflower counties, had a total population of 2,062 in 1960 and 2,513 in 1970. There were only about 130 African Americans who went to high school there in 1964, but 35 of them attended the Freedom School during the summer. (On August 4, 75 percent of the Shaw schoolchildren under the leadership of the Mississippi Student Union had called for a school boycott. The school authorities had then closed the African American schools.)

By August 19, the effects of the freedom school began to be felt in the adult African American community. Some 100 African American farmers attended a meeting of the Bolivar Improvement Association on the evening of the nineteenth and drew up plans to: (1) organize the African American farmers in the county in order to win federal aid that might help solve problems of unemployment and poverty; (2) plan for the establishment of local industry to employ African Americans; and (3) take the initial steps in planning a school boycott aimed at winning a place in local white schools for African American students.[11]

The experience in the Harmony community (near Carthage), in Leake County, was in some ways similar.[12] This African American community of 300–400 was the first in Mississippi to file for integration of its school system. In 1964 the children of the Harmony community had no place to go to school as its schools had been closed in 1961 by the Leake County authorities. When the Summer Project volunteers arrived at the beginning of July, they were greeted by 40 members of the community, fed, and taken in. Then, daily, 20 adults, as well as teenagers and smaller children, came to help clean up one of the three abandoned school buildings located in the community. After they had finished cleaning one of the buildings, the county sheriff came and told them they could not use it as it was county property. After the community took the case to court and lost, they began putting up a building for the Freedom School that was finished at the beginning of August.

After the thirty-by-sixty-foot frame structure was opened and made available to the entire community, and a board of trustees had been elected, the Leake County authorities announced that the three African American schools in the county would open on August 10. Apparently this was done to get the Freedom Schools in the county to close two weeks ahead of time, as well as to prevent the integration of the first grade in the county's white schools. The parents and students of Harmony countered with a school boycott and demanded, among other things, an equal student-teacher ratio, heat in winter, better buses, no firing of African American teachers for registering to vote, and no "hand-me-down" school books, desks, and buses from the white schools. When school finally opened in Leake County, one African American first-grade child attended a white school.[13]

The establishment of twenty-six community centers around the state was complementary to the Freedom School program. In Mileston a community center was built through the help of two white Californians, Abe Asheroff and Jim Boebel, who raised $10,000 and then came to help in putting up the building.[14] Similar centers were established in already existing structures owned by the African American community, or in rented quarters, in places such as Meridian, Indianola, Palmers Crossing, Hattiesburg, Ruleville (in the home of Mrs. Hamer), Greenville, Batesville, Shaw, Greenwood, and other towns.

Community centers generally included a library, a meeting hall, facilities for conducting Freedom School classes, and a place where children and adults could come to read and relax. The programs conducted were largely for adults, but open to all, in areas such as literacy, citizenship training and political organization, sewing, home crafts, hygiene, prenatal and child care, and other subjects. The community-center workers also attempted to get federal aid from the Farmers' Home Administration and the Office of Manpower, Automation and Training to investigate abuses of the Area Redevelopment Act and the Manpower Development and Training Act, and straighten out problems with Social Security, unemployment insurance, and welfare.[15] This aspect of the movement's activities was, in effect, a continuation of the work done in Greenwood in connection with the cutting off of federal surplus commodities by Leflore County officials during the winter of 1962–63.[16]

Finally, Mickey and Rita Schwerner's early successes were achieved in part in the establishment of a community center in Meridian in January 1964. When the Schwerners attended the June orientation sessions in Oxford, Ohio, one of their jobs was to instruct volunteers in how to set up a community center and involve local people in its programs.[17]

One of the things they learned during 1964 was that community-center programs had to be tailored to fit the needs of the African American community. They learned that African Americans in Mississippi had to be drawn out of their protective shells by establishing a bond of commitment and trust. This done, the African American community was not only capable of learning from movement workers and Summer Project volunteers but also of teaching them. Many of the volunteers, like the full-time civil rights workers before them, claim that this was in fact the case. The numbers of African Americans who joined hands with the movement, as well as those who emerged as viable leaders, during the summer of 1964 and after seems to justify such a conclusion. Illiteracy and initial ignorance did not mean a lack of intelligence; instead, these were marks of oppression that the movement helped the Mississippi African American remove. Given freedom of thought and self-expression, the Mississippi African American learned at an astonishing rate.

Supporting Organizations and Their Work

Just as any military organization needs its support troops, so did the Mississippi movement during the Summer Project. A major part of the white power structure's attack on the movement and Mississippi African Americans consisted of legal harassment and obstructionism as well as persecution by means of lawless official action. Additionally, the threat of official inaction, which opened the movement to lawless private action, was with the civil rights workers throughout the summer, particularly after the lynching of Schwerner, Chaney, and Goodman and during the ongoing terrorism of the Ku Klux Klan in southwest Mississippi. Some 150 northern lawyers volunteered their professional services as the legal corps of the Summer Project. A medical corps was also organized under the name of the Medical Committee for Human Rights (MCHR), and 57 doctors as well as 50 nurses and other medical workers spent at least part of the summer in the state. Apart from the legal and medical needs of movement workers, Summer Project volunteers and Mississippi African Americans had needs of a spiritual and cultural nature that were not overlooked.

Some 325 ministers under the auspices of the National Council of Churches (NCC) came to do whatever they could to help out. Finally, two groups toured the Freedom Schools—the Free Southern Theater and the Mississippi Caravan of Music. A photographic team was also outfitted and trained to document the Summer Project.

The legal corps of the Summer Project came into being under the shadow of doubt cast by the 1950s McCarthy Era. Red baiting and attacks on alleged communists played at least a minor part in the decisions made by civil rights organizations to ask legal groups for help in Mississippi. SNCC staff, however, chose to ignore such matters and welcomed anyone and everyone who was willing to help out on the condition that those who chose to participate followed the leadership and direction of movement people.[18] CORE was less open in its acceptance of help, as were the NAACP and SCLC.[19]

SNCC's position on freedom of association was not just civil libertarian in nature. All those who had worked with the movement in Mississippi from the beginning in 1960–61 knew that there had been little legal assistance for civil rights workers and local African Americans in the past, with the notable exception of the NAACP Legal Defense and Educational Fund's (the Ink Fund's) assumption of the cases arising out of the Freedom Rides in 1961. The Ink Fund took over the caseload from CORE in November only after considerable outside pressure was exerted and because CORE was threatened with bankruptcy.[20]

During 1962–63, SNCC, COFO, and the movement in general in Mississippi suffered from a lack of legal aid, even though the Ink Fund was involved in James Meredith's admission to Ole Miss.[21] Only three African American lawyers in the state—Carsie Hall, R. Jess Brown, and Jack Young—and one white lawyer—Leonard Rosenthal—would handle civil rights cases.[22] A second white lawyer, William L. Higgs, was run out of Mississippi in February 1963 for working with the movement.[23] Since any lawyer from outside of the state needed to be sponsored by a local attorney, the problem for a civil rights person retaining legal counsel was compounded. Furthermore, during the Freedom Vote campaign it became urgent for the movement to overcome the legal problem, since much of the white power structure's obstructionism was channeled through the courts and would continue to be so during the Summer Project.

During the latter part of the summer of 1962, the National Lawyers Guild made just such an offer of massive help at a SNCC conference; representatives of the Department of Justice were invited but did not show up. When the problem of legal aid was raised again during the planning stages of the Summer

Project, SNCC and COFO people remembered the guild's offer and decided to invite them to come to Mississippi.[24] Dave Dennis, of CORE, was also aware of the urgent need for outside legal help, and he pressured his national office to do something about it.

The Ink Fund, which had been directed by Thurgood Marshall and was directed by Jack Greenberg in 1964, refused to help out in Mississippi if SNCC went through with its threat to invite the National Lawyers Guild. CORE was also extremely upset by the possible participation of what it felt was a communist-connected organization (i.e., the guild).[25]

Nevertheless, the movement's need for outside lawyers was so vital that SNCC chose to disregard the warnings of the "liberal establishment," and more than 60 lawyers from the guild worked in Mississippi on a rotating basis during the Summer Project in June, July, and August.[26] The guild's plan was set up on a twelve-week schedule for the five congressional districts. Sixty "lawyer weeks" were filled by five lawyers each week, one in each of the districts. When one group of five lawyers was finished, five others took their places. Thus, during the Summer Project the National Lawyers Guild tried to ensure that legal counsel would always be available. The organization also established a reserve system of 90 lawyers who spent at least forty hours during the summer writing briefs and legal memoranda and doing other work that did not require lawyers to be present. The guild's operation was coordinated by George Crockett, of Detroit, who worked out of Jackson. Its other offices in the state were located in Hattiesburg, Meridian, and Greenwood; these offices were supported by the organization's larger one in New Orleans.

The second major legal support group was the Lawyers Constitutional Defense Committee (LCDC), which was set up in the spring of 1964 to provide legal counsel for the movement in Mississippi, as well as possibly to counter the guild's work.[27] Among its founders were Dean Robert P. Drinan of Boston College Law School, Melvin L. Wulf and John de J. Pemberton of the American Civil Liberties Union (ACLU), Edwin Lukas of the American Jewish Committee, Leo Pfeffer of the American Jewish Congress, John Pratt of the National Council of Churches (NCC), Howard Moore of SNCC, Carl Rachlin of CORE, and Jack Greenberg of the Ink Fund. Henry Schwarzschild was appointed executive secretary of the organization, and offices were established in Jackson, Memphis, and New Orleans. Some 40 of its lawyers worked in the state on a rotating basis, and another 20 worked out of Memphis and New Orleans. All lawyers working with the LCDC did so on a volunteer basis, as did those who worked under the auspices of the National Lawyers Guild. Only in April 1965 did the LCDC hire a full-time attorney for its Jackson office; he was assisted by three volunteer attorneys. Even later, the organization became an official part of the ACLU.

In spite of its threats to leave the state if SNCC used lawyers from the guild, the third major legal organization operating during the Summer Project was the Ink Fund.[28] The Ink Fund maintained an office in Jackson with only one full-time staff member, but it worked with the LCDC, which it had helped set up, and took over the handling of a hundred cases arising out of the Summer Project. In addition to these three groups, the Lawyers Committee for Civil Rights Under Law acted as counsel for the National Council of Churches, which sponsored the presence of some 325 ministers who participated in the Summer Project.[29] Also, William Kunstler and Mel Wulf were members of COFO's unofficial Legal Advisory Committee. A number of other distinguished lawyers came to Mississippi to help out on an individual basis.

All of these legal groups were invaluably assisted by 15 law students who went to Mississippi for two months under the Law Students Civil Rights Research Council (LSCRRC), which operated out of New York City in close conjunction with the New York Civil Liberties Union.[30] Howard Slater, a graduate of Yale Law School, coordinated the LSCRRC's efforts out of the New York office that sent Clinton Hopson to McComb; George Johnson to Canton; Mike Starr to Hattiesburg; and William Robinson, Sherwin Kaplan, Alan M. Lerner, Lowell Johnston, Dan Perlman, Miss Cornelia McDougal, Mike Smith, Bob Watkins, Richard Wheelock, Larry Hansen, Bennett Gershman, and Leonard Edwards, whose father, W. Donlan Edwards, was a Democratic Congressman from California, to other projects around the state.[31] These students helped provide the necessary transition and coordination between the ever-changing lawyers who came to volunteer their services and who were unable to spend the time the students did preparing legal briefs and running down the necessary facts to defend movement and local people. From time to time I also did volunteer work in Slater's New York office.

The legal work was coordinated from the Jackson COFO office by Hunter Morey, a SNCC field secretary who had finished his first year and a half at law school.[32] His work was particularly hectic, as lawyers from the different law groups had to be sent all over the state on short notice to make sure that what happened to Schwerner, Chaney, and Goodman did not happen to others. The lawyers, in fact, were only able to practice their profession on rare occasions.[33]

Their main work was concerned with bailing or bonding volunteers and local African Americans out of jail; both the guild and the LCDC maintained their own bail funds, getting cases removed from state courts to Federal District Court, acting as observers or advisers, and generally helping prevent local law enforcement officials from turning civil rights workers over to the mob in the middle of the night.

Generally, the charges brought against Summer Project volunteers and movement workers were misdemeanors—some one thousand arrests were made during the summer involving movement-affiliated people. Not only were Summer Project volunteers, full-time staff, and local African Americans harassed, attacked, intimidated, and arrested, but lawyers were on occasion subjected to the same treatment. An LCDC lawyer was beaten and arrested in Marks, Quitman County, on August 4, and another LCDC lawyer was arrested on charges of reckless driving in Columbus, Lowndes County, on August 14, after a pickup truck ran into the back of his parked car.[34]

The Medical Committee for Human Rights was organized on June 27, 1964.[35] Its chairman was Dr. Aaron Wells, an African American who was an assistant professor at Cornell Medical School in New York City.[36] The committee was made up of doctors who chose to volunteer their services in Mississippi for limited periods of time rather than just contribute money. They had the enthusiastic support of the African American doctors' group, the National Medical Association. The approximately 100 doctors, registered nurses, and other medical personnel could not practice medicine in Mississippi, but they set up liaison with many of the 57 Mississippi African American doctors, and some of the 37 African American dentists and 376 professional nurses. Among the committee's sponsors were Drs. Benjamin Spock, Paul Dudley White, Alan Guttmacher, Albert Szent-Gyorgyl, Robert Coles, and Joseph Brenner.[37]

The Medical Committee's stated aim was to establish a "medical presence" for the civil rights movement in Mississippi. The committee functioned primarily as a medical body to check and advise civil rights workers in the state, although at times doctors found themselves subject to harassment and arrests. Committee doctors also attended the orientation sessions in Oxford, Ohio, and worked through the Freedom Schools and community centers to teach local African Americans. Additionally, doctors went into the local communities to see what they could do to help in the future.

On August 16, the committee issued its statement on what it had found during the Summer Project: "We have found there to be many programs, inadequate though they may be, that Mississippi provides on paper to maintain the health of its people. These range from the prenatal clinic, to the checking of school children's eyesight and hearing, to the pittance in medical assistance for the aged on welfare. But even these programs barely reach out to the rural Negro."[38]

The Medical Committee chose not to leave Mississippi at the end of the summer. It drew up a list of areas in which it intended to operate: a group health plan, health education, health research, professional training, and rest and recreation.[39] By 1965, it had fourteen chapters around the country, a medical director, Dr. Alvin Poussaint, who had completed his residency in psychiatry at Cornell Medical School, and five nurses trained in public health who were working in Mississippi, as well as a group of nine medical, nursing, and social science students who were to work in Mississippi during the summer of 1965.[40] COFO workers and volunteers who had been subjected to "battle fatigue" were able to gain help from within the movement itself, and the promise of valuable research that would lead to a better life for Mississippi African Americans became more than a dream.

The chaplain corps also played an important role both during and after the Summer Project.[41] Some 325 ministers and rabbis came to Mississippi to be advisers and give counsel. The ministers came under the auspices of the National Council of Churches (NCC), which had participated in Freedom Day in Hattiesburg in January 1964. Their activities and placement around the state were supervised by the Reverend Warren McKenna from the Jackson office of the NCC. The ministers occasionally preached in Negro churches and visited under the darkness of night in white ministers' homes, but they mainly drove cars, canvassed in voter registration drives, mopped floors, received beatings (e.g., Rabbi Arthur Lelyveld, of Cleveland, Ohio, in Hattiesburg on July 10),[42] were arrested (e.g., Reverend Robert Beech in Hattiesburg on July 8 and Reverend Edward K. Heiniger in Carthage on July 31 after he had been beaten in the office of a local doctor he had taken a summer volunteer to see),[43] taught at Freedom Schools, led singing and other activities.

Like the student volunteers, lawyers, and doctors, the ministers also chose to stay on in Mississippi, and the NCC's Commission on Religion and Race set up the Delta Ministry in August to work with African Americans who had been thrown out of work by the mechanization of cotton production on a large scale.[44] The NCC's presence in Mississippi was particularly galling to the white power structure.[45] In spite of the white community's professed religiosity, forty-one African American churches were destroyed by fire or bombs during the summer of 1964.[46]

The last group of supporting organizations was the cultural corps of the Summer Project.[47] Their work was closely connected with the Freedom Schools and the community centers because, even though the African American community produced a rich folk culture, Mississippi African Americans were largely cut off from mainstream America. The Free Southern Theater and the Mississippi Caravan of Music toured throughout the state during the Summer Project.

The first of these, the Free Southern Theater, was created early in 1964 through the efforts of SNCC workers Doris Derby, Gilbert Moses, and John O'Neal, as well as Tougaloo drama instructor William Hutchinson. The repertory company was sponsored by Harry Belafonte, James Baldwin, Langston Hughes, Ossie Davis, Ruby Dee, Theodore Bikel, and Lincoln Kirstein, the general director of the New York City Ballet.

One of the basic aims of the group was to acquaint Mississippi African Americans with values other than those of the closed society. The company toured Mississippi from August 1 to 17, giving performances of Martin Duberman's *In White America* and holding workshops in conjunction with the performances in McComb, Hattiesburg, Gulfport, Meridian, Canton, Lexington, Greenwood, Ruleville, and Indianola. On the evening of August 8, the company's production was presented at the Freedom School Convention in Meridian together with an original drama that portrayed the life and death of Medgar Evers written and produced by the Holly Springs Freedom School. The short piece was called "Seeds of Freedom." The Free Southern Theater continued to work out of its home base in New Orleans after the summer of 1964.

The second organization, the Mississippi Caravan of Music,[48] was created in spite of the Mississippi African American community having given the nation such important musicians as Mississippi John Hurt, Huddie "Leadbelly" Ledbetter, Big Bill Bronzy, and many others. African Americans, though, had been taught to hate these musicians because they were both African American and Mississippians. The caravan tried to restore these musicians' status in African American communities across the state. Workshops were held in numerous Freedom Schools, and performances were given in the evening at community centers and at mass meetings in African American churches.

A large element of the caravan's success was in the groundwork and planning of Bob and Susan Cohen, who arranged for the following artists to appear in Mississippi during the Summer Project: Len Chandler, Bob Cohen, Judy Collins, Jim Crockett, Barbara Dane, Dick Davey, Alix Dobkin, the Eastgate Singers (Adam and Paul Cochran, James Mason, and Jim Christy), Jim and Jean Glover, Carolyn Hester, Greg Hildebrand, Roger Johnson, Peter La Farge, Julius Lester, Phil Ochs, Cordell Reagan (of the Freedom Singers, a SNCC group which originated in southwest Georgia), Pete Seeger, David Segal, Ricky Sherover, Gil Turner, Jackie Washington (who also worked with the Free Southern Theater), and Don Winkleman. They brought Mississippi African Americans into intimate contact with an American culture from which they had been isolated.

The final supporting group that worked in the Summer Project was not a group but a few individuals who recorded the Summer Project photographically on motion-picture film and in still shots. SNCC Field Secretary Willie Blue was trained in New York by Peter Smollet and Hortense Beveridge of Calpenny Studios and equipped to shoot with 16-millimeter and 8-millimeter cameras. Matt Herron ran the Southern Documentary Project in Mississippi and was assisted by three other photographers in taking still shots. Another SNCC field secretary, Cliff Vaughs, continued the work he had begun with COFO the previous year.[49]

In all, the work done by the supporting organizations made it possible to enlarge the movement's scope of activities as never before. Many of those who made up the support groups originally planned to come to Mississippi for a short period. What they found when they arrived inspired many of them to make their commitment more permanent. And if, as individuals, they left the state at the end of August, the support organizations did not.

"White Folks" Project

It must not be imagined that all the white people in Alabama and Mississippi support the George Wallaces, the Ross Barnetts, the Lawrence Raineys and the Cecil Prices. When Wallace ran for Governor in 1962, my home county voted two to one against him. In the urban counties of Alabama Wallace was badly beaten. He became Governor only with the massive support in our backward counties where few or no Negroes voted. There is nothing wrong with Alabama or Mississippi that 300,000 Negro votes in each state can't help cure.

—WILLIAM BRADFORD HUIE, SPRING 1965

I have seen avowed segregationists—some of them unstable individuals in addition—submit quietly to the most radical kinds of integrated society because

they worked on a federal air force base. American laws and jobs seemed curiously
more influential than "deeprooted" attitudes.

—DR. ROBERT COLES, 1967

During the summer of 1964, an interesting experiment was undertaken by the
movement. A pilot program called the white community project, or more ap-
propriately the "white folks" project, was initiated in the belief that poverty
was a unifying force for African Americans and whites and that the race issue
had been used by the white power structure to keep poverty-stricken African
Americans and whites apart.[50] A deep faith in the basic good of humanity was
necessary to attempt such a program, but a true reading of economic realities
clearly indicated that Mississippi African Americans could never achieve real
freedom alone. Their bondage was also the economic slavery of the poor white.
Divided in poverty, united the "uncomfortables" of Mississippi would be able
to overthrow the "comfortables" of the white power structure.[51]

In the first week in July, twenty-five volunteers went into five white communities in four of the state's five congressional districts—eighteen entered
the Biloxi and Gulfport communities, and the other seven were assigned to
Jackson, Greenville, Meridian, and Vicksburg. During the first month in Biloxi,
over thirty white ministers and business and professional people were contacted. The results of the contacts promised little for the future. In the other
four cities the volunteers worked mainly on mailing literature to the business
and professional groups that explained the Summer Project and encouraged
the white power structure to keep the schools open in the fall and tried to
convince people of the necessity of avoiding violence in connection with the
fall integration of schools in Jackson, Biloxi, and Leake County. Some of the
volunteers also went secretly to visit people who were "suspected" of having
"liberal" inclinations.

The program was directed by Sam Shirah, a twenty-two-year-old white Al-
abamian, who was the co-director with Bob Zellner of the recently formed
Southern Student Organizing Committee (SSOC). Both Shirah and Zellner were
rarities in the southern civil rights movement, but both were an indication
of the possibility of organizing southern whites to fight white supremacy.[52]
During the summer Zellner worked in the African American community of
Greenwood, as he was well known in the state;[53] Shirah directed the "white
folks" project, which included Ed Hamlett and Sue Thrasher, two of the founding members of SSOC. Shirah, however, was the only one in the project who
had had any previous organizing experience.

Bayard Rustin, the deputy director of the March on Washington, and Anne Braden, of the Southern Conference Education Fund (SCEF) and the editor of the *Southern Patriot,* encouraged the formation of SSOC. The volunteers were mostly white and from the South. Advice and encouragement for the volunteers also came from SCEF, which had experience in organizing poor whites in eastern Tennessee and Kentucky.

At the end of the first month, the volunteers held a retreat at the Highlander Folk School in Monteagle, Tennessee, where they were advised by Myles Horton, the director of the school. Horton asked them many questions that were essential in analyzing the first month's experience. Those who felt that valuable work was to be done in contacting white ministers and professional people and in writing to influential members of the white community returned to this type of work. The other ten volunteers, though, felt it was more important to penetrate and work in the poor white community.

In the end the second group's work proved more significant than the first's. During the first three weeks in August, this integrated group of volunteers visited the homes of poor whites in the Biloxi community, discussing the Mississippi Freedom Democratic Party and trying to convince people to fill out freedom registration forms. These forms called for a person's name, age, residence, and length of residence in the community and the state. Only twenty people were persuaded to fill out this form, but these twenty increased the number of registered white Freedom Democrats in the state to twenty-two; the other two were the Reverend Edwin King and his wife, Jeanette, of Tougaloo Southern Christian College. Furthermore, two of these twenty chose to make their decision as public as one could in Mississippi. Robert W. Williams, supported by his wife, Lois, became one of the sixty-eight delegates of the Freedom Democratic Party who went to Atlantic City on August 19. When one of the Biloxi city officials questioned him about how he would feel if his head were blown off, Williams answered, "About the same you'll feel when my buddies get the bastard who did it."[54]

In addition to registering a small group of white Freedom Democrats, it was proven that integrated teams of canvassers could be used to work in the white community in Mississippi and that in many cases this kind of group was even more effective than all-white groups. The dialogues that arose between African American canvassers and prospective white registrants seemed to indicate that the real issue was poverty and not race. It also became apparent to a few people in the white community that poor whites and poor African Americans shared the same basic problems in wanting better educational opportunities, more jobs, better health facilities, stronger unions, and economic cooperatives that would afford them a way of successfully breaking the white power structure's economic stranglehold over poverty-stricken people in the state.

Finally, it became apparent that the movement was fighting the same enemy that the poor white community was—the white power structure—and that the movement's programs, which were aimed at providing the African American community with voter and citizenship education, Freedom Schools, and community centers with programs and facilities, were also desired by the poor white community. Poverty was the common enemy of the two groups (28 percent of the African American families in the state in 1960 earned less than $2,000 a year, while 12.7 percent of the white families also earned less than that figure). If the issue of race could be overcome, a joint effort by these groups really did hold promise for the future.

The disappointments of the "white folks" project were few but were important to learn from if success was to be achieved in such programs in the future. The publicity that accompanied all of the civil rights workers and Summer Project volunteers wherever they went made it difficult, if not impossible, for clandestine contacts to be made in the white community. In 1964 it was important that certain aspects of the white community project be conducted in a less open manner.[55]

The challenge of continuing such programs after the end of the Summer Project in August led SNCC to expand these activities into the poor white communities of five Mississippi counties in September, and plans were made to expand into an additional fifteen counties during the summer of 1965. The projects in the poor white communities made little if any effort to disguise their connections with SNCC and COFO, and the apparent success made by the civil rights workers seemed to have been in the fact that Mississippi whites who saw a future in associating with the movement and who made little effort to hide their feelings were also subjected to the same kinds of pressure and intimidation that were so common for African Americans who stepped out of "their place."

Mrs. Hamer, who spoke for the movement in talking about the "uncomfortables" (i.e., all poor people, African American and white) and the "comfortables" (i.e., those whites in power), answered the question of whether her goal was equality with the white man: "No. What would I look like fighting for equality with the white man? I don't want to go down that low. I want the *true democracy* that'll raise me and that white man up."[56] Len Holt, an African American lawyer who volunteered his services during the Mississippi Summer Project and later wrote *The Summer That Didn't End,* further crystallized the meaning of Mrs. Hamer's words concerning the challenge held out by the white community project: "There is a realization in Mississippi—by even the most naïve—that if the poor whites of the state (at least one-third of the abjectly poor in the state are white) and the poor Negroes of the state, who have far more in common than it is safe to enunciate, join hands around, through, and in spite of the veil of color, the present power arrangement will be changed. This is precisely what must be done to resolve the pressing matters of poverty, health and education in Mississippi—indeed, in the nation."[57]

That challenge—overthrowing the white power structure—had already been taken up by the African American community in Mississippi. Large numbers of African Americans had committed themselves as never before, but in reality they were only a minority in the state, even if they were a large minority. The ultimate success of the Mississippi civil rights movement lay in welding together a strong coalition with poor whites, a thing that the Populist and Labor movements had failed to do in the past.

Finally, the spirit that invested the Mississippi Summer Project with light was personified in the actions of the McGhee family of Greenwood, Silas and Jake, their half-brother Clarence Robinson, and their mother, Mrs. Laura McGhee.[58] Other Mississippi families dedicated their lives entirely to the movement, such as the Greene family, also of Greenwood, but few families showed such a militant and complete commitment in physically and spiritually confronting the state's power structure no matter what the danger, no matter what the price. Individual African Americans and whites had devoted their lives to the Freedom Revolution, and some had paid the ultimate price even though they had sensed what lay in store for them. Few families, though, were so visibly defiant of "the man" in pursuing what they felt was rightfully due African Americans, even in Mississippi.

Shortly after President Johnson signed the 1964 Civil Rights Act into law on July 2, Mississippi African Americans began to take matters into their own hands. Selective buying campaigns, or economic boycotts, were conducted in various cities around the state where African Americans refused to buy from merchants who discriminated against them. They also began to test Title III of the recently passed law, which called for the desegregation of public accommodations.[59] These actions were locally inspired and not part of the Summer Project, as the movement had already learned in the past that little could be accomplished by such protests and that the price that had to be paid for such actions was prohibitive.

The case of Silas McGhee and his family was only one of many such efforts to seek what the law states as the rights of African Americans and whites alike. Unaccompanied, he sought to sit in the white section of a Greenwood movie theater on July 15 and 16. On the evening of July 16, three whites forced him to enter their pickup truck at gunpoint and then brutally beat him with a pipe and a board. Later that night McGhee filed a report at the local FBI office in Greenwood that led to the arrest on July 23 of the three whites on charges of conspiring to deprive him of his right to sit in an integrated movie house. On July 25 a shot was fired into his home, but McGhee refused to give up his personal battle against White Greenwood.

On the evening of July 26, Silas returned to the theater with his brother Jake. This time they were mobbed by a group of some 150–200 whites while leaving the theater to go to their car. Both received body and head injuries and went to be treated at the Leflore County Hospital. They were joined at the hospital by other SNCC workers and their half-brother Clarence Robinson. When they tried to leave the building, they found that the exits were blocked and the roads back to Greenwood were filled with carloads of armed whites that were waiting for them. During their three-hour wait, Robinson, who was on leave from the army, suggested shooting their way out, but he was dissuaded after speaking on the phone to Jim Forman in the Greenwood SNCC office. The FBI, local police, State Highway Patrol, and county sheriff all refused to protect them if they left the hospital. Finally, at one o'clock in the morning the sheriff agreed to follow the SNCC car back to the city. Then on July 31, Silas McGhee was arrested for driving with an improper vehicle license, even though he had valid seven-day Tennessee license plates.

As the pressure began to build up in the city of Greenwood, local African Americans decided to boycott the store of a local police officer who had brutally dragged and beaten Mrs. Annie Lee Turner, a pregnant fifteen-year-old Greenwood African American, during Freedom Day on July 16. More arrests followed during the boycott, and then on August 15 Silas McGhee was shot in the face while sitting in his car outside an African American restaurant waiting for the rain to stop. Two SNCC staff then took McGhee to the Leflore County Hospital, where the two workers were refused admittance because they had no shirts on—they had used their shirts in trying to stop the bleeding. The hospital staff claimed they were unable to remove the bullet that had entered

McGhee's head through the temple and had lodged itself in his neck, and it was only removed later that month.

On August 16, several hundred people gathered at a Greenwood church to protest the shooting. Afterwards some one hundred local African Americans who had been at the meeting went to the SNCC office, where they were met by police in full riot gear and armed with tear gas and guns. The police blocked off both ends of the street until the angry group was dispersed by Jesse Harris of SNCC. With Silas McGhee in the hospital, Jake was arrested on a traffic violation on the morning of August 18. Later in the day George Greene and Ed Rudd, both of SNCC, accompanied Mrs. Laura McGhee to the police station to pay Jake's fine and get him out of jail. At the station house, Mrs. McGhee was hit in the chest by the desk sergeant. She hit him back in the nose, and the police officer in turn tried to take his gun out but was restrained by the two SNCC workers until another policeman came and calmed the first officer down. Jake was then fined one hundred dollars for having an improper license—he had a valid temporary license as he had lost his permanent one—and for impersonating his brother Silas because his brother's wallet and license were in Jake's possession. Later, a warrant was sworn out against Mrs. McGhee for assaulting an officer. By the fall, Silas McGhee had returned to Greenwood and was again active in the movement.

The McGhee family's spirit of active resistance to white terror and open protest of denial of civil rights was repeated throughout the state during the summer of 1964. Where in the past civil rights workers had to look for people who were willing to fight for freedom, by 1964 Mississippi African Americans began to look for the movement. Not only did they actively participate in the programs initiated under the Summer Project, they also undertook actions on their own. The Freedom Revolution, which was sparked by the activities of SNCC and CORE workers who came into Mississippi from other parts of the South, inspired local civil rights workers to continue their fight and prodded Mississippi African Americans to move against the white power structure under a banner of "Freedom Now!" That revolution was a revolt in the minds of Mississippi African Americans who had learned that they had nothing to lose—except their poverty-stricken lives and their bondage—by fighting for their freedom and everything to lose by waiting. By the summer of 1964 the time for waiting was over, and the time for doing had come. The Mississippi Freedom Democratic Party was the embodiment of the people's impatience with White Mississippi and a protest to the people of the nation to let them go.

9

The Political Organization
of Protest Politics, Part I

Midway

I've come this far to freedom

And I won't turn back. . . .

You've slashed me and you've treed me

And you've everything but freed me,

But in time you'll know you need me

And it won't be long.

—FROM "MIDWAY," BY NAOMI MADGET

Seek ye first the political kingdom and all other things shall be added.

—PRESIDENT KWAME NKRUMAH OF GHANA

There's no question about it that the formation of the Freedom Democratic Party and the [Convention] Challenge at Atlantic City was a type of confrontation, as well as the Congressional Challenge.

—JAMES FORMAN, WINTER 1965

The other programs created within the framework of the Summer Project of 1964 were those which focused on the creation of the Mississippi Freedom Democratic Party (MFDP) in early 1964, as well as such offshoots as the Mississippi Freedom Labor Union (MFLU) in January 1965 and the Poor People's Corporation (PPC) in August 1965. Both the political programs of the MFDP from 1964 on and the economic programs of the MFLU and the PPC in 1965 and after were aimed at organizing Mississippi African Americans for action within and outside the closed society, and all three were forms of parallel protest organizations established to challenge the white power structure. In reality, the latter two were the natural extension of the former, which attempted to gain a national audience for Mississippi African Americans who had been unable to break down the white power structure from within.

The movement's inability to create a voice for local African Americans within the existing structure of Mississippi politics drove it into the realm of radical protest, or parallel, politics and then on to a presentation of Mississippi African Americans' case at the Democratic National Convention in August 1964 and in the U.S. Congress in 1965. In both cases a surprising amount of support for ameliorating the Mississippi African American's plight was achieved. Alongside this support came the downfall of radical protest politics within the State of Mississippi, the withdrawal of SNCC and CORE from the local scene, and the gradual weakening of the MFDP, which temporarily continued to maintain an extreme posture within the state but gradually moved toward politics that required compromise and participation in support of the national Democratic Party.

Moreover, with the withdrawal of SNCC and CORE activists from the state in 1964 and 1965, local MFDP members gradually moved away from the radical stances of SNCC and CORE and began to adopt positions closer to those of liberal and labor groups as well as the whites in Mississippi who were willing to work with them toward future goals of political participation in Democratic politics. This, moreover, was after local and national elements of the NAACP and SCLC, as well as liberal elements in the Democratic National Party, had moved on to more conventional forms of political activity in Mississippi.

During this period the Mississippi power structure escalated the violent war against the movement until it reached its most extreme form of confrontation —in McComb. Thereafter, White Mississippi began to gradually adjust itself to twentieth-century America. This though was only after vigorous pressure had been mounted against it by the federal government and the Democratic National Party, as well as on a local level by the economic realities within the state.

By the middle of 1965 it was readily apparent that White Mississippi had begun to move in new and different ways to minimize the African American's participation in the closed society,[1] while at the same time trying to reduce the outside pressures exerted upon the state by national political and governmental elements. Thus the white power structure sought to accommodate the nation's demands and at the same time ensure that African Americans would not be able to frustrate white supremacy in Mississippi in the future.

The Birth of the Mississippi Freedom Democratic Party

The origins of the Mississippi Freedom Democratic Party lie within the evolving structure of the civil rights movement within the state and the civil rights workers' constant efforts to draw African Americans into the political process there.[2] The movement was encouraged by Reverend R. L. T. Smith's and Reverend Merrill W. Lindsey's runs against the regular Democratic nominees in the June 5, 1962, congressional primaries. Mississippi African Americans regained interest in registering to vote, as they were given an alternative to white-supremacy slogans and hope of a future change in the white power structure. The beginnings of the movement's political program in Mississippi were thus laid in a hopeless campaign—if one only examines the immediate substantive results of the primaries—but when it is analyzed within the spectrum of protest politics, one sees the opening act of the MFDP and the basis for real future substantive political action.

Later, in the summer of 1963, the movement returned to the idea of protest politics by conducting a "vote-in" on August 6 and a "Vote for Freedom" on August 25, where on the latter date the movement held its first "parallel" election in the state (see chapter 6, above). The occasion was the state gubernatorial primary in which former Governor James P. Coleman ran against Paul Johnson, who campaigned on his having stood up against the federal government at Ole Miss when Governor Barnett failed to arrive in person. Some 30,000 people participated in the Vote for Freedom.

Following this apparent "success," one step further led to the launching of Aaron Henry for governor and Reverend Edwin King for lieutenant governor in November 1963 in a three-day Freedom Vote. This form of protest included: a nominating convention in Jackson on October 6; a campaign platform similar to the Democratic National Party's; and appearances throughout the state aimed at getting the 28,500 registered African Americans to void their ballots on election day—November 5—by writing Henry's and King's names in and at getting 200,000 unregistered African Americans to vote in the Freedom Vote on November 2, 3, and 4; there Henry's and King's names appeared on the ballot with those of the Democrat Paul Johnson and Republican Rubel Phillips.[3]

The Freedom Vote was a true watershed in protest politics in Mississippi, as over 83,000 people "voted" in this parallel election, even though it had no apparent affect on the official one. Mississippi African Americans emphatically demonstrated that they would vote in Mississippi elections if they were allowed to register. Valuable lists were compiled during this "mock" election, and they were used again in the process of "freedom registration" throughout the Summer Project in 1964 and after.

The next step was the establishment of a parallel political party to represent disfranchised African Americans. It is not clear who exactly was responsible for the idea, but it is certain that SNCC and Bob Moses were prime movers in the drawing up of the plans for the Mississippi Freedom Democratic Party, which were presented to a SNCC staff meeting in Atlanta on February 1, 1964.[4] The name itself was put forward by George Ballis, the editor of a labor newspaper in Fresno, California, and a participant in the Freedom Day demonstrations in Hattiesburg on January 22, 1964.[5] Later, during the meetings of the California Democratic Council (on February 21–23 in Long Beach), Ballis; Mrs. Beverly Axelrod, a San Francisco civil rights lawyer; and Claude Hurst, of Fresno, introduced a resolution calling for the seating of the MFDP delegates at the 1964 Democratic National Convention. This first resolution in support of the MFDP was unanimously passed by the council on February 23.[6]

During spring 1964, the idea of the MFDP began to take shape as a group of Mississippi African Americans that wished to broadcast its protest to the nation. The group said that, since the Mississippi power structure would not allow African Americans to participate in the political workings of the State Democratic Party, then it would challenge the right of the regular Mississippi Democrats to represent Mississippi citizens in the national party councils and at the Democratic National Convention in Atlantic City in August. This necessitated the creation of a parallel but identical—as much as that was possible —political party that would present itself to the Credentials Committee of the Democratic National Party as the only true and legal representative of Mississippi Democrats.[7]

This challenge required unity of action among the national civil rights groups if this bold stroke were to succeed. SNCC led the way in organizing both on the national level as well as the local one but was without funds—a normal occurrence—and the convention, as well as the Summer Project, was near at hand. The only other real support that was forthcoming was from CORE, which hesitantly offered the services of Norman Hill, of its national office.[8] Hill, though, was politically aligned with the liberal labor elements of the Democratic Party and was a close friend of Bayard Rustin, the deputy director of the March on Washington (Rustin later wanted the MFDP to accept a compromise proposal at the Convention).[9]

On a national level the NAACP was not involved in the MFDP's challenge effort other than in calling for the same compromise that was pushed by Rustin and Martin Luther King Jr.; the MFDP rejected that offer in pollings of the delegates. Ms. Ella Jo Baker—a former board member of SCLC and a central figure in the founding of SNCC, as well as its adviser[10]—offered her services when SNCC asked for help in setting up the MFDP.[11]

On the local level these differences lost their importance, and COFO successfully functioned as the joint representative of the national civil rights groups. Furthermore, local representatives of SNCC, CORE, the NAACP, and SCLC all worked together in setting up the local party branches of the MFDP.

National support, though, was the key to unseating the regular Mississippi delegation at the Democratic National Convention. With this in mind, Bob Moses traveled to Washington in early spring to meet with liberals and outline plans for the Summer Project and the Convention Challenge.[12] Joseph L. Rauh—vice-president of the Americans for Democratic Action (ADA), general counsel for Walter Reuther's United Automobile Workers (UAW), leader of the Democratic Party in the District of Columbia, and a close confidant of Hubert Humphrey—was present at one of those meetings. He made the following statement: "If there's a challenge; if there's anybody at the Democratic Convention challenging the seating of the outlaw Mississippi Democrats [the traditional Mississippi Democrats], I'll help make sure that the challengers are seated."[13] After the meeting, Rauh reiterated his willingness to help to Moses and Jack Pratt, of the Commission on Religion and Race of the National Council of Churches. Nevertheless, a great deal of money was necessary, as well as an enormous amount of legwork in contacting other state party delegations that would be at the convention.

In order to take advantage of Rauh's services, a tentative meeting was hinted at, but it was first necessary to consolidate plans within the movement. Ms. Baker was contacted, and she agreed to help out. CORE was then approached, and the help of Norman Hill was secured.[14] From there, Moses, Baker, and Hill went on to the UAW National Convention—March 20–26—to see Walter Reuther about securing moral and financial support. Mrs. Mildred Jefferies, a Michigan Democratic State Committeewoman and a UAW member, arranged a luncheon for Reuther and Moses of SNCC, as well as representatives of Students for a Democratic Society (SDS) and the Northern Student Movement (NSM). Reuther, however, saw fit to talk about the poverty program and not the challenge.[15]

In spite of this setback, Moses returned to Washington to meet with Rauh, who agreed to be the legal counsel for the MFDP, even though there was no money to pay his fees. At the conference, Rauh stated that in order for the challenge to succeed it would be necessary for the MFDP to participate in precinct, county, and state conventions of the Mississippi Democratic Party; if these attempts were frustrated it would then be necessary to follow procedures as closely as possible to those of the regular Mississippi Democrats.[16]

Furthermore, Rauh indicated that a legal brief would have to be prepared for presentation to the Credentials Committee at the convention, and research personnel would be needed. Miss Eleanor Holmes (later Mrs. Norton) volunteered her services, but not until May when she had passed her bar examinations. Her help was to be extremely important to the MFDP during the challenge and after. Not only was she black, but she also received her license to appear before the U.S. Supreme Court before she was thirty years old.[17] Under the circumstances temporary help was needed, and H. Miles Jaffe, who worked under William Higgs at the Washington Human Rights Project, offered his services.[18] Shortly afterwards, the full-time volunteer services of a sociologist, Dr. Danny Foss, were also secured.[19]

By the end of April, with the Democratic National Convention only four months away, the MFDP was still experiencing birth pangs. Bayard Rustin, who had promised to organize massive demonstrations outside the convention hall, was involved in trying to solidify a broad coalition of the UAW, CORE, SNCC, and SCLC but apparently had not yet succeeded in doing so.[20]

At this point Ms. Baker and SNCC took the initiative and decided to separate the demonstrations from the organizational steps of the challenge. On April 24, an office of the MFDP was set up in Washington, using borrowed money and ten-dollar-a-week SNCC personnel. Ms. Baker took on the job of coordinating the office, which was staffed by Walter Tillow, Bernard Conn, Reggie Robinson, Alex Stein, Charles Sherrod, Leslie McLemore, Miss Barbara Jones, and Frank Smith, all of SNCC. Then Ms. Baker and the staff wrote letters, made speeches at state party conventions, where money permitted, and hounded senators and congressmen in Washington.[21] Nevertheless, the importance of the demonstrations outside the convention hall continued to be a pressing problem. CORE withdrew its personal participation in the MFDP at the beginning of May.[22] Later, in August, Hill resigned from National CORE after most of his main supporters had been purged from the national office's staff.[23]

In spite of the apparent difficulties that troubled the MFDP on a national level, plans proceeded apace on a local level; a state office was established in Jackson in March, and Dave Dennis arranged for his fellow CORE worker Richard Jewett, of New York, to work there.[24] On April 26, the MFDP was formally established as the Mississippi Freedom Democratic Party at a state convention in Jackson.[25] And even though only two hundred representatives of the Mississippi African American community attended this convention, SNCC and the MFDP were not discouraged, as apathy and fear had constantly surrounded the Mississippi movement in the past and inauspicious beginnings had had a way of changing radically. The important thing was that a state chairman, Lawrence Guyot, was elected, and the COFO staff—largely SNCC and CORE workers—began to move ahead.

In May, four candidates of the MFDP—Mrs. Gray, of Hattiesburg; Mrs. Hamer, of Ruleville; Reverend Cameron, also of Hattiesburg; and Mr. Houston, a seventy-four-year-old retired machinist of Vicksburg—began their campaigns for the June 2 Democratic primaries. During the campaign the process of "freedom registering" was begun, and the names that were gathered were added to those that had been compiled during the 1963 Freedom Vote campaign. The file of incidents of intimidation and violence against freedom workers and local people was also added to and microfilmed for the SNCC office in Atlanta. This was done in order to protect against police confiscations and fires which had caused the loss of valuable records in the past.[26]

On a national level the pace also began to pick up in June. A subcommittee of the Democratic National Committee ruled that party loyalty was a prerequisite for the seating of delegations at the convention. (This committee dealt with the allocation of delegates to the National Convention.)[27] On June 13, Americans for Democratic Action passed what was an encouraging resolution from the MFDP's point of view. It called for the "rejection of the racist Mississippi Democratic Delegation [and the seating of the] integrated Freedom Democratic Party."[28] Then on June 14, the state Democratic convention in Michigan called for the seating of the MFDP;[29] and on June 15, the New York State delegation passed a similar motion.[30]

June 16 in Mississippi was a significant day in the history of the MFDP. The 1,884 voting precincts around the state were to have precinct meetings to elect delegates to the eighty-two county conventions. Apparently only one-fourth of these meetings was ever held. Where precinct meetings were held, either African Americans were locked out or, as in the case of one meeting in Meridian, they were allowed inside but could not vote on the selection of delegates.[31]

In accordance with the procedures suggested by attorney Rauh, the MFDP then proceeded to hold its own precinct meetings and county conventions.[32] In all, precinct meetings of this sort were conducted in twenty-six counties, and county conventions were held in thirty-five counties. (Due to harassment, precinct meetings were postponed in nine counties.)[33] Some three hundred delegates were chosen to attend the state convention of the MFDP in Jackson on August 6. On June 23, African Americans also tried to attend various Democratic Party county conventions but were similarly frustrated in their efforts.[34]

Plans for the MFDP's confrontation with the power structure were in hand by the time of the official date for the precinct meetings of the Mississippi Democratic Party, but the manpower was lacking; the volunteers for the Summer Project only began arriving in Mississippi at the end of June. Consequently, the majority of organizational work was held up until July. "Freedom registration," which was possible for all those who were state residents for two years and county residents for one year, was open to people over twenty-one. It made no difference whether a person was literate if his or her registration was duly witnessed.[35] This wearying job was largely undertaken by the summer volunteers from the middle of July.[36] Furthermore, even if the Mississippi authorities did not recognize the legality of these tactics, official harassment, violence, and intimidation, as well as the unofficial kind, were constant reminders to the civil rights workers that they were making progress against the white power structure.[37]

From July 19 through August 2, constant political activity characterized Freedom Summer throughout the state. Precinct meetings were held in the following places: On July 21, 160 people attended two precinct meetings in Clarksdale; on July 24 in Jackson and Meridian; on July 27 in Batesville, Holly Springs, Mayersville, and Gulfport; on July 28 in Vicksburg; on July 29 in Greenville; on July 30 in Laurel; and on July 31 in Ruleville.[38]

During the same period, county conventions were held in the following places: On July 25, 300 people—102 of whom were voting precinct delegates— attended the county convention in Canton (Madison County), and county meetings followed on July 27 in Batesville (Panola County) and Holly Springs (Marshall County); on July 28 in Clarksdale (Coahoma County); on July 29 in Gulfport (Harrison County); on July 30 in Meridian (Lauderdale County) and Laurel (Jones County); on August 1 in the county courthouse in Vicksburg (Warren County), in Ruleville (Sunflower County], Moss Point (Jackson County), and Jackson (Hinds County); and the last one on August 2 in Greenville (Washington County).[39] Some county conventions were also held in Jackson because it was impossible to hold them safely under local conditions of hostility and violence.[40]

Finally, on August 6, at the Masonic Temple in Jackson, the state convention of the Mississippi Freedom Democratic Party convened to select its delegates to the Democratic National Convention, which was to take place August 25–26 in Atlantic City, New Jersey. Some 240 delegates and 700 alternates and observers attended the state convention, and 68 delegates and alternates were elected to represent the MFDP.[41] Over 60,000 Mississippians signed "freedom registration" forms by August 24—the cutoff date for registration—less than what was hoped for but still a considerable number considering the shortness of time and the lack of adequate manpower working with the movement.[42]

Nevertheless, the convention was overshadowed at least in part by the discovery of the bodies of Schwerner, Chaney, and Goodman on August 4 in Philadelphia, Neshoba County, and the memorial service that was held for them in Meridian on August 7. (See chapter 7, above.)

While violence and intimidation swept through Mississippi and the MFDP was organizing itself to attend the Democratic National Convention in Atlantic City, national support for the MFDP began to coalesce and confront the Democratic National Party and President Johnson. On June 19, at an orientation session for the Mississippi Summer Project in Oxford, Ohio, William Kunstler (a white civil rights lawyer from New York City who was later to represent the MFDP in its Congressional Challenge in 1965) announced that he had filed suit in Federal District Court that attacked section 3107 of the Mississippi Code. This statute enabled the Mississippi State Democratic Party to select its Democratic presidential electors after the Democratic National Convention had been held.[43]

Under this law, then, how was it possible for the Mississippi Democratic Party to pledge its loyalty to the Democratic National Party? It was not even possible to promise that the candidates of the national party would appear on the ballot in November. Be that as it may, on June 30, the Mississippi State Democratic Party released its official platform, which was against civil rights, the poll-tax amendment to the U.S. Constitution, the United Nations, and various other things, and further stated, "We reject and oppose the platforms of both national parties and their candidates."[44] By then it had adjourned its convention—on June 28—until after the Democratic National Convention had finished in Atlantic City and presidential electors could be chosen in the September primary.[45]

Whether Mississippi liked it or not, support for the MFDP began to mount as Oregon on July 5 and the District of Columbia on July 6 joined New York, California, and Michigan in pledging their support for the seating of the MFDP.[46] Even though another five delegations—Massachusetts, Minnesota, Wisconsin, Washington, and Colorado—voted by August 7 to back the MFDP, the choice of Barry Goldwater as the Republican presidential candidate in early July seemed to presage a waning of support thereafter, and President Johnson apparently began to move in an effort to ensure that he would not lose the South to his Republican rival in the fall.[47]

Shortly after Goldwater's nomination, the movement invited Martin Luther King Jr., to conduct a five-day speaking tour in Mississippi in late July.[48] A conference was also set up in Jackson, and James Farmer, the national director of CORE; Bayard Rustin; Ms. Baker; James Forman; and Bob Moses sat down with King to discuss plans for the Atlantic City challenge. At this time it became apparent that SNCC and the Mississippi movement would have to handle the demonstrations outside the convention hall, as Rustin expressed marked reservations about their conduct.[49]

At the same time as the end of King's speaking engagements in Mississippi, Senator Paul Douglas, of Illinois, projected the idea on national television—on July 24—that both the regular Democratic Party and the MFDP delegations be seated at the Convention.[50] With sentiments rising in Mississippi that the challenge was not so impossible, Jim Forman consulted with Bob Moses and decided to make a sweep through the state, stopping in Hattiesburg, Biloxi, Gulfport, Natchez, Vicksburg, and Batesville to prepare the African American community for what was felt would be the ultimate sellout of the MFDP.[51] Forman expressed those feelings:

I was both elated and yet disturbed about the challenge. I was elated because it seemed that at last we were building the type of organization that I had long hoped for. It had a broad base among black people and a clear structure that fed into counties and then into precincts. But I was concerned about the aftermath: the challenge had to be made, but we couldn't win at Atlantic City—how would people accept their defeat? Would they see their attempt as a resistance effort in a long struggle or would they be discouraged and give up? . . . I wanted to alert people at the various county conventions and mass meetings of the MFDP to the fact that we might not win but that it was absolutely vital for the party to continue its grass-roots organizing effort.[52]

Forman's fears about the future success of the MFDP and its challenge were of importance, as the white power structure of Mississippi began taking official notice of the MFDP. On July 24, Mississippi Secretary of State Heber Ladner refused the MFDP's request for a charter,[53] and then on August 13 Attorney General Patterson requested and received a court order from Chancery Court Judge Stokes Robertson banning the MFDP and enjoining its officers to stop functioning forthwith.[54] The state attorney general charged that the party "would cause irreparable damage to the public" and claimed that it was a "conspiracy," a "sham," and a "fraud."[55] This was followed up with an official statement by the State Government on August 22 that the MFDP was a communist organization.[56] The MFDP's delegates, though, had already left for Atlantic City to present their case to the nation. The MFDP chairman, however, remained in a Hattiesburg jail, where he was confined on a charge from the Freedom Day demonstrations in January.[57] Additionally, Mississippi promised to jail those delegates who went to Atlantic City upon their return to the state.[58]

In spite of the threats, COFO held a three-and-half-day conference at Tougaloo Southern Christian College, which ended on August 19, in order to smooth over the transition for the period after the convention. At the end of the staff meeting, plans were announced for two hundred volunteers to stay on in the state, together with sixty-five SNCC and thirty CORE staff. Other support groups also voiced their plans to remain in Mississippi and expanded voter registration activities—in conjunction with Robert Miles and the Voters League— for Panola and Tallahatchie counties.[59]

The three busloads of delegates and supporters who left for Atlantic City on August 19 knew that, even though they were going off to fight the president and the Southern Democrats, the MFDP's challenge was based on strong legal grounds. They also knew that support was forthcoming from ten party delegations and twenty-five Democratic congressmen, as well as numerous other supporters who would be scattered throughout the convention.[60] The MFDP's legal position was based on the following points:

1. Negro voters in Mississippi (and most of the white [voters]) had been illegally denied access to the delegate-selection machinery of the Democratic Party in Mississippi and all other political processes of the state. . . .

2. The traditional Democrats had systematically and consistently prevented Negro voter registration by every statute, custom and lynch rope available.

3. Under no circumstances would the traditional Democrats support the
National Party or the national candidates.[61]

Thus the MFDP delegation went off to Atlantic City with the knowledge
that: it was the only truly open and integrated political party in Mississippi;
it would support the platform and the candidates of the Democratic National
Party in the November elections; and its delegates would sign the party loyalty
oath. None of this was true for the regular Mississippi Democratic Party. But
apparently this was not enough, as the results of the challenge were to show.
Under these circumstances, the question to be decided at the convention was
whether the MFDP was a protest organization or a political one that dealt with
the possible while sacrificing the moral imperatives of the movement.

At the Democratic National Convention and After

For most of the nation, the Democratic National Convention started on Tuesday
evening, August 25, but for the MFDP it began on Saturday afternoon, August
22. At that time the MFDP presented its case to the 108-member Credentials
Committee of the Democratic National Party as to why it should be seated in
place of the regular Mississippi Democrats.[62] From Saturday noon until Tuesday
noon it appeared that the MFDP would have its way and that the Democratic
National Party would give the party what it had been denied by the white power
structure of Mississippi: a voice in the councils of the Democratic National Party.

The story of that challenge is a tortuous one that is marked throughout by
Mississippi African Americans' refusal to compromise its moral mission and
White America's insistence that politics is the art of the possible. The MFDP's
demands—although they stirred the hearts of the nation and hardened them
against White Mississippi—were impossible demands. The political machine
that Lyndon Baines Johnson built in 1964 refused to give in to the pressures
of justice and right, possibly because it meant the loss of the South in the upcoming elections, possibly because southern senators and congressmen were
too powerful in the halls of Congress, or possibly because the threat of Barry
Goldwater was too frightening. Thus, from the time of the appearance of witnesses for the MFDP before the Credentials Committee that Saturday, President Johnson ran scared.[63]

After Joseph Rauh, a member of the Credentials Committee, had finished
presenting his legal brief for the MFDP to that committee, the witnesses for

African American Mississippi began to speak.[64] First, Aaron Henry spoke, then Reverend Ed King, all on national television at a time when nothing else of importance was happening. Finally, Mrs. Fannie Lou Hamer began her tale, the tale of dead Mississippians, dead from injustice; of living Mississippians, those who beat her in the Winona jail, and those like herself who had suffered silently while White America went about its business. The White House listened and panicked and frantically arranged for President Johnson to also go on national television; it made little difference that Mrs. Hamer and Mrs. Rita Schwerner were cut off by the president's remarks. Later that night the proceedings of the Credentials Committee were replayed to the nation.[65]

If the committee was not stampeded by the legal arguments of attorney Rauh to seat the MFDP, then they were most certainly persuaded by Mrs. Hamer and the other witnesses. If their testimony was not enough to convince the committee members, then possibly the thousands of letters, telegrams, and calls that poured in were.[66] The seven African American members of the Credentials Committee were moved to anger and were joined in that anger by Congresswoman Edith Green of Oregon, Congressman Robert W. Kastenmeier of Wisconsin, Joseph Rauh, and others.[67] Martin Luther King Jr., James Farmer, Bayard Rustin, Jack Pratt of the National Council of Churches, other civil rights leaders, Congressman Charles C. Diggs Jr. of Michigan, Congressman William L. Dawson of Illinois, and others all pushed for seating the MFDP delegates.[68]

Meanwhile, President Johnson had apparently retreated from his initial position of not seating the MFDP delegates at all and proposed that two of the delegates be seated at-large. Rumors were also released suggesting that, if Hubert Humphrey wanted to be his vice-president, Humphrey would have to settle the MFDP matter.[69]

By this time it was known that the MFDP would not be seated in place of the regular Mississippi Democrats—there were not enough votes for it—but there was still hope that a minority report would be presented by the Credentials Committee when it reported to the convention on August 25. Only eleven members (or 10 percent) of the committee were needed for such a report.[70] Such a minority report calling for the seating of the MFDP would then be presented, and if eight delegations voted for a roll-call vote on the seating, the entire convention would decide the matter.

When the administration forces polled their supporters, they found there were enough delegations to get a roll-call vote. Consequently, contact was made with Georgia Governor Carl Sanders, who had the Rules Committee pass a regulation stating that only state delegations could demand a roll-call vote.[71] Of the state delegations, only Oregon was definitely for seating the MFDP delegation instead of the regular Mississippi Democrats, while Michigan was a very likely supporter, Wisconsin and Colorado were probable supporters, New York and Massachusetts were possible supporters, and California was unsure. The District of Columbia and a number of the territories, though, were definite supporters.[72] To make doubly sure that the MFDP efforts were frustrated, pressure was then exerted on Credentials Committee members known to support a minority report. Using heavy pressure and distorting his intentions, Congressman Diggs got Bob Moses to give him the names of those Credentials Committee members who would sign a minority report if the full committee did not vote to seat the MFDP.[73]

In the end, Rauh backed out, as did Diggs and others. The pressures applied were various. A woman committee member from California was apparently warned that if she did not back down her husband would not get the federal judgeship that he had been promised.[74] It is also known that Walter Reuther told Rauh he would lose his job as general counsel for the UAW if there were a floor fight.[75] Congresswoman Edith Green later made a public statement to the MFDP delegation that "she never knew Johnson would stoop to some of the things he did."[76]

Be that as it may, up until Tuesday noon the so-called "Green Compromise" still had considerable support among the committee members.[77] This proposal called for the public administration of an oath of loyalty to the Democratic nominees and platform to be given individually to the members of the regular Mississippi Democrats and the Freedom Democrats. Those who assented to the oath were to be seated, and those who refused were to be sent home. The delegates who swore their loyalty were then to split the state delegation's votes between them.[78]

During the afternoon of August 25, the administration beat a retreat under the threat of a possible stampede of the convention by the MFDP and its supporters, who refused to let up the pressure inside the convention and outside.[79] During the deliberations in the various committees prior to the opening of the convention, a constant vigil was conducted on the boardwalk by SNCC and CORE and their supporters.[80] Also, the presence of Mrs. Hamer and other MFDP delegates and supporters at the sessions of the Credentials Committee made it extremely difficult to put off the MFDP's demands.[81] Additionally, the southern delegations threatened to walk out of the convention if the MFDP were seated.

A compromise proposal was put forward by the administration and adopted by the Credentials Committee for presentation to the convention that Tuesday evening:

1. We recommend the seating as the delegates and alternates from Mississippi those members of the regular Democratic Party of Mississippi who subscribe to the following assurance:

    We, the undersigned members of the Mississippi delegation to the 1964 Democratic National Convention hereby each formally assure the convention of our intention to support the convention's nominees in the forthcoming general election.

2. We recommend that the convention instruct the Democratic National Committee that it shall include in the call for the 1968 Democratic National Convention the following amended first paragraph:

    It is the understanding that a State Democratic Party, in selecting and certifying delegates to the Democratic National Convention, thereby undertakes to assure that voters in the state, regardless of race, color, creed or national origin, will have the opportunity to participate fully in Party affairs, and to cast their election ballots for the presidential and vice presidential nominees selected by said convention, and for electors pledged formally and in good conscience to the election of these presidential and vice presidential nominees, under the Democratic Party label and designation.

3. We recommend that the convention adopt the following resolution:

    Resolved: That the chairman of the Democratic National Committee shall establish a special committee to aid the state Democratic parties in fully meeting the responsibilities and assurances required for inclusion in the call for the 1968 Democratic National Convention, said committee to report to the Democratic National Committee concerning its efforts and findings and said report to be available to the 1968 convention and the committees thereof.

4. We recommend that the members of the delegation of the Freedom Democratic Party, like the Democrats proposed, but not seated, as members of the Oregon, Puerto Rico and Virgin Islands delegations, be welcomed as honored guests of this convention.

5. Wholly apart from the question of the contest as to the delegates from Mississippi and in recognition of the unusual circumstances presented

at the hearing, and without setting any precedent for the future, it is recommended that Dr. Aaron Henry, chairman, and the Reverend Edwin King, national committeeman-designate, of the Freedom Democratic Party, be accorded full delegate status, in a special category of delegates-at-large of this convention, to be seated as the chairman of the convention may direct.[82]

If there was any doubt concerning the presentation of a minority report before the administration submitted its compromise proposal, there was none afterwards. This proposal, which in effect was the same as that presented to the convention by the Credentials Committee, caused the following results, according to Arthur I. Waskow, who was present at the convention: "[It] won the grudging acceptance of most of the South, although most of the Mississippi regulars refused to take the oath." Only three did.[83] To Waskow it also appeared to resolve the rest of the administration's problems concerning the MFDP and its challenge, as well as the results of such a confrontation, as he states: "To most of the supporters of the Green Compromise on the Credentials Committee, the new offer seemed a reasonable solution. It would end any danger of embarrassment to Senator Humphrey, it would end any danger that the whole South might bolt the convention and so hurt the party's chances in November, and it would end the danger of an open fight and possible defeat for President Johnson on the floor of the convention. Enough of the Freedom Party's allies on the Credentials Committee accepted the proposal to make it impossible under the rules for the fight to be carried to the floor."[84]

Even if the administration may have thought its compromise proposal was a just and worthy one, the movement was not convinced of its value. And the movement at the convention was not Martin Luther King Jr., Bayard Rustin, Roy Wilkins, James Farmer, or other nationally prominent civil rights leaders, but Mississippi African Americans backed by Bob Moses, his fellow workers in SNCC, and Dave Dennis and the Mississippi CORE staff. Thus, when the compromise proposal was put to a voice vote by the MFDP delegation on Tuesday afternoon, it was unanimously rejected.[85]

It is possible that members of the MFDP saw in the proposal a triumph of right over wrong, but for the most part the delegates and alternates felt that too little had been offered to them and, if there was to be any compromise at all, it would have to be along the lines of the Green Compromise. Considerable pressure was mounted on Bob Moses to get the MFDP to accept the offer,[86] but if one holds in mind his character, one can only conclude that he would not have tried to convince the Mississippians one way or the other. After the convention he stated: "The FDP delegates were the only people at that whole convention who were free in any meaningful use of the term. The President told everyone else . . . what to do. All I cared about was the insides of those 68 delegates and the future of the FDP in Mississippi. It wasn't my responsibility to care about Humphrey or the backlash. We couldn't let others single out two people and appoint them our spokesmen. *The whole point of the FDP is to teach the lowest sharecropper that he knows better than the biggest leader what is required to make a decent life for himself*" (my emphasis).[87]

Moses's refusal to compromise what he felt were Mississippi African Americans' best interests, though, was only part of the story behind the rejection of the convention's proposal. To many delegates it appeared that the proposal was only another form of "tokenism" that the African American community had long endured at the hands of whites. Furthermore, the fact that the MFDP's two delegates-at-large were chosen by the Credentials Committee and that the MFDP had nothing to say in the matter, smacked of the same sort of patronizing attitude that African Americans had suffered with for so long in the South. Additionally, the MFDP felt that morally, if not legally, it rightfully deserved to be seated at the convention as Mississippi's representatives, not as at-large delegates. These reasons, and probably other unstated ones, led the MFDP to flatly reject the administration's offer.[88]

Under the circumstances, Johnson and his liberal supporters were probably uneasy about what would happen when the convention formally opened at 8:30 on Tuesday evening. According to Jim Forman, who spoke to the Michigan delegation and was close to a number of its members, the delegation was ready to fight Congressman Diggs—who had refused to sign the minority report of the Credentials Committee calling for the seating of the MFDP[89]—and the administration. This could have reopened the issue to the floor of the convention that night, but word was quietly passed to certain delegations, including Michigan, that the MFDP had in fact accepted the compromise proposal—a blatant untruth that smoothed over the acceptance of the Credentials Committee's report by the convention.[90]

With the demonstrations going on outside on the boardwalk, Moses suggested and the MFDP delegates decided to take further action to guarantee their visibility across the nation by staging a sit-in on the convention floor. There is some indication that, if Moses had not taken matters into his own hands at this point, the demonstrations outside the convention would have gotten out of hand. Bitterness and a sense of having been betrayed certainly were expressed by many of the MFDP delegates and civil rights workers. Thus, on the evening of the formal opening of the convention, Moses organized a sit-in for which friendly delegates from Michigan, Oregon, Wisconsin, California, and other states and territories loaned their passes to the members of the MFDP delegation, thereby enabling them to enter the convention hall and take the unfilled seats of the regular Mississippi Democrats who had refused to take the required loyalty oath. For a period of about twenty minutes, convention officials tried to remove the sit-inners by force, but after an order was received—supposedly from the White House—the MFDP delegation was left in possession of the Mississippi seats. Meanwhile, the nation watched this ultimate expression of protest on national television.[91]

The following day a further attack was mounted by the administration's allies to get the MFDP to reconsider its decision on the compromise proposal. Apparently, Aaron Henry and Ed King had been convinced to take the seats that were designated for them by Senator Humphrey, but such a decision had to be taken by the entire MFDP delegation. Therefore, a meeting was called for the afternoon of August 26 at which pro-compromise people tried to win the day for the administration.[92]

Aaron Henry, as chairman of the MFDP delegation, introduced the speakers. Jack Pratt, of the National Council of Churches, urged the delegates to accept the offer, calling it "the greatest thing that has happened for the Negro since the Emancipation Proclamation."[93] Bayard Rustin, who had promised so much, stated "Yes . . . there is a difference between protest and politics. The former is based on morality and the latter is based on reality and compromise. If you are going to engage in politics then you must give up protest. . . . You must be willing to compromise, to win victories and go home and come back and win some more."[94]

Martin Luther King Jr. then spoke in favor of accepting the compromise, stating that even though there were some segregationists in the Democratic Party it was the only party that had helped African Americans. Moreover, he said that he had spoken with Humphrey, who had promised him "there would be a new day in Mississippi if you [the MFDP] accept[ed] this proposal."[95] He also added that Humphrey had promised that the U.S. Commission on Civil Rights would hold hearings in Mississippi and that the president would meet with representatives of the MFDP.[96]

Next, Robert W. Spike, director of the Commission on Religion and Race of the National Council of Churches, objected to the way the decision had been made and said that more time should have been spent deliberating on what to do.[97] James Farmer, though, took the most honest position of the national civil rights leaders. He said that there was a difference between protest and politics but that the MFDP was neither one nor the other. He then indicated that no matter what decision the MFDP made CORE would give it its backing.[98] Wayne Morse also spoke, even though he seemed out of place at such a forum, and stated that the two seats should be accepted.[99] Joseph Rauh indicated that he felt the two seats were a victory for the party and added, "I am with you and want you to know we're going to work to make the resolution work."[100] After Rauh, Bob Moses spoke of the necessity of bringing morality into politics.[101]

Finally, Jim Forman rose to rebut the administration's arguments and present SNCC's position on the compromise proposal:

I am not a part of the delegation. I was not a party to the decision made last night to reject the compromise, although I agree with it. I have been asked to speak for SNCC, but I cannot speak as though I am not one of you, for I am. . . . The Credentials Committee resolution welcomes you, the Freedom Democratic Party, as honored guests of the convention. . . . To accept the status of guests is to deny the legitimacy, the rightness of your position. The regular or traditional Mississippi Democratic Party is clearly illegal and violates the rules of the convention. . . .

Those of you who are here as delegates represent many people in the state of Mississippi. . . . What effect wills a decision to accept the honored guest status and the two seats-at-large, with the delegates named for you? It seems you have no other choice but to reject support of this resolution.[102]

With the speeches over, the MFDP delegation retired alone to poll its members. For the second time the MFDP flatly rejected the compromise proposal, as Mrs. Hamer, Mrs. Devine, and Mrs. Gray spoke out against the compromise, this time by a vote of sixty to four, with four abstentions.[103] Howard Zinn, the historian of SNCC, said: "The SNCC mood was dominant in the Freedom Democratic Party, not only because SNCC workers were by far the most numerous among all civil rights groups working in Mississippi, but also because SNCC, more than any other organization, remained close to its soil, to the poverty-stricken, rural, black countryside, reflecting the temper of the people living there."[104]

After rejecting the compromise proposal for a second time, the MFDP del-egates prepared to penetrate the convention that evening. In the meantime, President Johnson had received word of the rejection and hastily prepared to come to Atlantic City and confront the Democratic Party.[105] Len Holt indicates that Johnson's motivation for coming was that "[t]he Freedom Democratic Party could not be permitted an evening of prime time of nationally televised interviews, during which they might tell all why the 'at-large' status was un-worthy of acceptance."[106]

When the MFDP delegates entered the convention hall, they found the three traditional Mississippi Democrats surrounded by a protective shield of suit-wearing men—by some reports from the FBI and the Secret Service. Nevertheless, the MFDP delegates stood there—the seats that had been left unoccupied by the regular Democrats had been removed—for the rest of the evening.[107] Later, after the proceedings of nominating Johnson and Humphrey were over, Bayard Rustin went outside to the boardwalk to apologize to the people who had counted on him. He told the crowd, "I opposed a lot that went on here that you wanted. But when I think of those big, black, ugly and beau-tiful asses in the seats of those nice, lily-white, dainty, traditional Mississippi delegates, I'm happy!"[108]

The Mississippi Freedom Democratic Party, though, represented much more than just a challenge to the regular Mississippi Democrats. It was also a chal-lenge to the integrity and honesty of the entire Democratic Party. The fear that possessed the administration and drove it to do what it did was not just that the southern delegations would walk out of the Democratic National Conven-tion. It was more. It was what Dick Gregory expressed, that if the Freedom Democratic Party were not seated at the convention, then African Americans in the North would "go fishing" on election day in November. It was a fear that, if the true story of what happened at the convention got out to the public, the liberal white community would also be disgusted, even if they did not vote for Goldwater.[109] Moreover, it was possible that this could lead to a radical democ-ratization of the Democratic Party structure in the future by doing just what the MFDP hoped for, by introducing an element of morality into the inner workings of the party.

The MFDP, however, learned many lessons at the Democratic National Con-vention. According to Howard Zinn, "The FDP never made sufficiently clear to itself or to the nation that its chief reason for demanding seats at the Conven-tion was not its greater loyalty to the national Democratic Party, but its position as true representative of the 45 per cent of Mississippi's population which was Negro."[110] By the time the convention was over, or shortly thereafter, the MFDP did know what it was fighting for—if it had ever forgotten, even temporarily. Nonetheless, the liberal-labor elements of the Democratic Party were not long in reminding them of their reasons for coming into existence.

One of the most important things the MFDP, and SNCC, learned at the convention was the close connection between what Jim Forman termed the "liberal-labor syndrome" and the national civil rights leaders—Roy Wilkins, Martin Luther King Jr., Bayard Rustin, and James Farmer. If this connection was only partially clear to the movement prior to Atlantic City, it was readily apparent by Tuesday, August 25, when the above-mentioned civil rights leaders joined Joseph Rauh, Jack Pratt and Art Thomas of the National Council of Churches, and Senator Wayne Morse in trying to convince the MFDP delegation to accept the administration-backed compromise proposal. When they were unable to get the MFDP to change its decision, it became obvious that different tactics were called for to control the MFDP, SNCC, and its new allies on the national scene.[111]

However, it is necessary to go back a little before discussing that new strategy, which Jim Forman calls "profiles in treachery."[112] It will be remembered that as early as 1961 the movement had discussed the possibility of concentrating on voter registration work in Mississippi (see chapter 2, above), and that at that time officials in the Kennedy Administration and the Democratic National Committee had promised financial support and Justice Department protection for movement workers and Mississippi African Americans if such a step were taken. After SNCC and the other civil rights groups agreed to concentrate on voter registration work in Mississippi, the Voter Education Project (VEP; see chapter 4, above) and the Council of Federated Organizations (COFO; see chapter 3 above) were set up. From its inception COFO was seen as an umbrella group to coordinate the activities of SNCC, CORE, the NAACP, and SCLC in Mississippi. It was also the recipient of VEP funds until they were cut off in the fall of 1963.

COFO, though, was fraught with organizational difficulties from the beginning. Initially, it was seen as a conduit of national civil rights groups operating in Mississippi. In fact, this was not the case at all. Bob Moses, the state field director of COFO, worked in conjunction with SNCC, but as the latter organization's Mississippi project director he had a great deal of freedom to decide what was done in the state. Additionally, Dave Dennis, CORE's sole representative in the state from the spring of 1962 until the summer of 1963 and the assistant program director of COFO, often acted independently of his national office. Furthermore, SCLC's only worker in Mississippi from 1960 to 1964 was Ms. Annelle Ponder, whose sole function there was to send local African Americans to SCLC's leadership training and citizenship courses.

This, though, was not the whole problem, since both SCLC and the NAACP had its local representatives in the state. Mrs. Victoria Gray, of Hattiesburg, was SCLC's state supervisor, but until 1964 her work was largely confined to her hometown, Hattiesburg. Only in 1964 did she get deeply involved in the MFDP's political program in other parts of the state, when she ran against Senator John Stennis in the June 2 Democratic primary. Nevertheless, she worked in close contact with SNCC, housing and assisting COFO workers—they were really SNCC staffers working with COFO—from 1962 onward (see chapter 3 above). In 1964, both Mrs. Gray and her husband, Anthony Gray, became deeply involved in the MFDP, and in June of that year he was fired from his job at the Hattiesburg Department of Water Works.

Compared to SCLC's limited involvement in the state, local branches of the NAACP had a long history of civil rights action in Mississippi. This activity, though, was mainly the work of local NAACP chapters and was not undertaken through the offices of the state field secretary, who was directly connected with the national office of the NAACP. Even though Medgar Evers, and later his brother Charles Evers, did represent the NAACP's national office in Mississippi, the most important NAACP work done in the state was initiated and carried out by local leaders such as Curtis C. Bryant in McComb, E. W. Steptoe in Amite County, Amzie Moore in Cleveland, and Dr. Aaron Henry in Clarksdale, and then sometimes at cross-purposes with the national office. Aaron Henry, as state president of the NAACP, was the most important of the four local leaders of that organization. Their work, unlike that of Reverend R. L. T. Smith in Jackson, who worked closely with the Evers brothers, was done in the rural sections of Mississippi. Furthermore, these four were in closer contact with SNCC and COFO than with their national organization and its field representative.

SNCC, under Bob Moses's leadership, went into the trouble spots and in most cases stayed to weather violence inflicted upon the movement and local African Americans. In these acts of personal bravery SNCC won Mississippi African Americans over to its side, as was quite clear at the Democratic National Convention when the MFDP delegation chose to listen to the words of Bob Moses, Jim Forman, and other SNCC people rather than to those of Aaron

Henry, who wanted to accept the compromise proposal of two at-large seats on the convention floor.[113]

According to Jim Forman, when it became apparent to the liberal allies of the administration and the major national civil rights leaders that the radical spirit of SNCC was dominant in the MFDP delegation, then those same "leaders" made an effort to neutralize SNCC's position of power in Mississippi and the nation.[114] SCLC, which received a large part of its funds from the UAW, moved decisively into the camp of the liberal-labor establishment at the convention, if it was not already there.[115] Bayard Rustin, who had long-standing ties with the House of Labor, also defaulted on his promises to the MFDP, even though he did express his apologies to the pro-MFDP crowd outside the convention hall on August 26. James Farmer, who had his problems with Dave Dennis in maintaining the independence of CORE in Mississippi, refused to advise the MFDP one way or the other on the compromise proposal, apparently trying to keep his organization on the fence. This halfway position typified CORE's position, even though it was not as damaging to the Mississippi movement as stances taken by the NAACP.

It is quite possible, though, that the NAACP had the most to lose by going against the administration's wishes, as it was not only the wealthiest of the civil rights organizations and the oldest, but it was also the most conservative. In the past it had generally entered the southern civil rights movement through its legal wing, the NAACP Legal Defense and Educational Fund (the Ink Fund). In Mississippi it picked up the bill for the Freedom Rides after CORE was close to bankruptcy in the fall of 1961 and organized the legal battle to get James Meredith admitted to Ole Miss in 1962. Nevertheless, the NAACP's day-to-day involvement in the statewide Mississippi movement was kept at a minimum.[116]

Thus, by the end of the Democratic National Convention in August 1964, it was apparent the liberal-labor group would make some effort to lessen SNCC's influence in the MFDP and COFO. The first step in this assault on SNCC came in September, when Bob Moses, Jim Forman, eight other SNCC officers and staff, and Mrs. Hamer were in Africa.

On September 18, a meeting was called by the National Council of Churches (NCC) in New York, for what Jim Forman feels "clearly revealed a campaign to undermine . . . SNCC by the liberal-labor establishment and its brokers."[117] SNCC was represented at the meeting by Courtland Cox, who as program director was left in charge when the other leaders went to Africa.

Also present was Mendy Samstein, a white SNCC worker from New York with extensive experience in Mississippi. The other people present included: James Farmer, of CORE; Jack Greenberg, director of the Ink Fund; Gloster Current, director of branches of the NAACP; Bruce Hansen, of the NCC; Allard Lowenstein; John Morsell, assistant executive secretary of the NAACP; Jack Pratt, formerly of the NCC but from the summer of 1964 connected with the Democratic National Party; Joseph Rauh, of the ADA and general counsel for the UAW; Robert W. Spike, director of the Commission on Religion and Race of the NCC; Art Thomas, a fieldworker for the Delta Ministry of the NCC; and Andy Young, executive director of SCLC.[118] There were no representatives of COFO and the MFDP present, and only Mendy Samstein had had any field experience in the Mississippi.

That meeting, which had been called to discuss the future of the movement in Mississippi, was not attended by Mississippi African Americans at all. Furthermore, the leaders who did attend were prominent among those who had encouraged the MFDP delegates to accept the administration's compromise proposal at the convention. Samstein's notes taken at the proceedings make apparent why the meeting was called:

> Spike: Meeting has been called to discuss ways of cooperating in Mississippi in the future.
>
> Young: Must develop structure of cooperation—MFDP or COFO or some other ad hoc organization for funneling projects into Mississippi [SCLC had taken very little part in the "Freedom Summer" Mississippi Summer Project]. . . . [W]e must work to reestablish the coalition we had on Saturday and Sunday in Atlantic City.
>
> Spike: Mississippi is no longer a local problem. It exerts leverage on the national scene. *Tension has been created between those who are moved by local considerations and those who must heed national considerations* [my emphasis].
>
> Young: We must re-establish national pressure for the right to vote in Mississippi.
>
> Greenberg: We must assault the state, county by county. Have people go to the courthouse, follow that up with legal action. . . .
>
> Rauh: What is needed is federal legislation that says: where less than one-third of the Negro population is registered, federal registrars will be sent in. . . .

Current: We should concentrate on urban areas like Atlanta. *The Freedom Democratic Party is a delusion* [my emphasis].[119]

Farmer: Decision-making in COFO is the nub of the problem. . . . We must agree on decision-making structure.

Cox: . . . The structure of MFDP and COFO is one in which decisions are made by the people of Mississippi and those who must face the consequences of any action taken. . . . This whole meeting has been aimed against SNCC. . . .

Young: COFO was originally formed as a structure to receive Voter Education Project money. . . . After VEP, appeals for resources were made to the various organizations. SNCC gave the most, then CORE. NAACP gave to its branches and SCLC to its citizenship program. *The idea in COFO has been that those who don't pay the piper don't call the tune* [my emphasis].

Lowenstein: The past is done. Now the question is, how to maximize cooperation and not drive anyone out?

Rauh: *But I would like to drive out the Lawyers Guild. I think it is immoral to take help from Communists* [emphasis in original source].

Lowenstein: . . . SNCC was the main source of funds and resources, but this is no longer the case. Now students, labor, other groups are involved, so these must have a say. . . .

Farmer: I agree with Al, but wouldn't you agree that not all who contribute should have a role in decision-making—only those who are part of the action?

Lowenstein: Yes, that's what I meant.

Spike: With Bob Moses and Jim Forman not here, we can't make any decision. We obviously can't decide for COFO or SNCC.

Morsell: We have a commitment to Mississippi, whether in COFO or not. . . . In the event of decisions injurious to our national interests, . . . we must have a way out.

Lowenstein: . . . We can't leave Mississippi . . . though we might talk about it.

Morsell: Precisely the point. We're caught.[120]

———

Cox: We have begged and asked for help for COFO. . . . People on the scene make the decisions . . . so SNCC plays a major role in decisions. But at Atlantic City it was the people, the MFDP, who rejected the compromise—

Mrs. Hamer, Devine, and Miles. It is only democratic that we have the right to present our position.

Pratt: I would disagree with your reading of history. . . .

Cox: We asked for help but it was not given. . . . I question whether groups are really prepared to come in now.

Lowenstein: There was no cooperation before because there lacked a structure to cooperate through.

Thomas: It is unreal, as far as Mississippi is concerned, for an ad hoc group to meet in New York and determine what should go on.

Morsell: . . . This is a national question and so national interests are involved.

Thomas: Last summer we proposed to the NAACP a common training school for volunteers but there was no interest.

Current: We didn't know about the Summer Project and the Oxford training program . . . until we read about it in the newspaper and we saw that we were not involved. The NAACP is a disciplined army. No decision is made on lower levels without authorization from the top. *Aaron Henry has got to get in line* [my emphasis].

Morsell: In our organization, things take time to get done. . . .

Spike: It's not just bureaucratic delay. I talked to Roy [Wilkins] and he has grave doubts about the whole thing. . . .[121]

Current: The whole program must be reviewed. We need a summit meeting. . . .

Cox: The need is for a low-level meeting. Next meeting should be in Mississippi with people of Mississippi and based on interpretations from them.

Current: The more I listen to Cox, the more I know we need a top-level meeting. *I have been listening to people from Mississippi cry for seventeen years* [emphasis in original source]. I don't want to listen to Steptoe. *We need a high-level meeting so we can cut away the underbrush* [my emphasis]. . . .

Spike: Both are essential. We see here represented some basic differences in ideological outlook. We need a high-level meeting but also must recognize the psychological importance of a low-level meeting. . . .

Current: We have to decide what to do in 1965. Budget considerations. These are top-level decisions, not to be made by the man in the field.

Morsell: We do have a national budget and constituents across the country. A knowledge of local situation is necessary but not alone sufficient. *Can acquire vital knowledge without living in Mississippi.* . . . [my emphasis] I would like another high-level meeting with Moses and Forman.

Lowenstein: At some point, we need to think of the volunteers, who are not being represented. . . .

Morsell: *We don't have to caucus with Negroes in Mississippi. You want us to listen to people in Mississippi; we don't want to be attacked* [my emphasis].

Current: 1. Mississippi projection [*sic*] must be continued in 1965 under a coordinated agency. 2. We must think organizationally, that is, with budget considerations. These are realistic problems [!]. *Can't listen to grass roots* [my emphasis]. 3. We can go alone or be involved in broader commitment but we will have to decide at top-level meeting.

Spike: I will try to get in touch with Bob [Moses] and Jim [Forman] and try to set up a meeting for as soon as they get back into the country.[122]

After this, other meetings were held with more or less the same groups represented. These took place between December 1964 and mid-January 1965, but SNCC was not represented at any of them and was not invited to the sessions. According to sources Jim Forman was in contact with, the issues discussed were approximately the same as those raised at the September 18 meeting. Furthermore, with SNCC not present, more discussions were conducted concerning the necessity of finding a way to work around SNCC, which was felt to be too much in control of COFO's decision-making procedures.[123] At a session held on December 29, where Summer Project volunteers and representatives of the U.S. National Student Association were present, Allard Lowenstein and others again raised the idea of a national board that would include representatives of all the organizations putting resources into Mississippi, as well as middle-class elements of the African American community who had been excluded from COFO. Lowenstein's idea never got off the ground.[124]

Quite apart from the machinations of the liberal-labor groups and the national civil rights leaders, the MFDP returned from the Democratic National Convention and continued its work with COFO and SNCC in Mississippi. SNCC also began to make plans for the future, and a second Freedom Vote was scheduled to be conducted in conjunction with the presidential and congressional elections in November. But even before that, Mississippi set out a warm welcome for the returning MFDP delegation. The center of that storm was McComb, and there violence overflowed as never before.

Explosion in McComb

During 1964 the movement returned to McComb to take up the work that it had begun there in 1961, and during the Summer Project, McComb became a symbol of African American resistance to white violence.[125] But even though McComb was a center of white violence and Ku Klux Klan activity prior to the Democratic National Convention, from August 28 to September 23 official and unofficial lawlessness was unleashed upon the African American community as never before: nine bombings were committed against African American property in and around the city.[126] Nevertheless, the unrest in McComb in 1961 and African American anger expressed prior to the Democratic National Convention are mild in comparison with the open resistance and hostility demonstrated by the African American community in September 1964.

The story of that change in spirit comes through in the poem of a Freedom School youth who witnessed the difficulties the movement encountered in finding a site where McComb youths could study the doctrines of Freedom. (In 1961, McComb schoolchildren and youths were among the first to join SNCC in its voter registration campaign there.)[127] According to William McCord, the following poem and the registration of 108 children on July 16 at the Freedom School stirred the adult community to action. Joyce Brown's statement to African American parents reads:

> I asked for your churches, and you
>   turned me down
> But I'll do my work if I have to do it
>   on the ground,
> You will not speak for fear of being heard
> So crawl in your shell and say, "Do not disturb."
> You think because you've turned me away
> You've protected yourself for another day.[128]

During July, many of the African American business people from the city met secretly to organize themselves in support of the movement. At that time Joyce Brown's poem was read to them, and it might be a reason why they donated land for a community center later in the summer. Their group, the Citizens' League,[129] was only one of the McComb community's expressions of help. African Americans also came forward individually to help out, and they, too, felt the anger of the white community. On August 28, the home of

Mr. and Mrs. Willie Dillon was bombed, but only the detonator cap exploded. When they called the police to the scene, they found themselves subjected to an investigation not connected with the bombing. Mrs. Dillon had joined the NAACP in 1963 and let her children attend the McComb Freedom School. COFO workers had frequented her home in the past, and on the night of the bombing her husband had been repairing a movement car. The result of the police investigation was that Mr. Dillon was charged with operating a garage without a permit and stealing electricity. (During the summer he had installed floodlights outside of his house because cars had been circling his property at night.) Three weeks later, he was still in jail.[130]

On September 7, three more bombings took place, but in each case the victims had no connection with the movement.[131] On September 9, another bombing was perpetrated, this time against the home of an African American minister, the Reverend James Baker. According to information presented at the February 1965 U.S. Commission on Civil Rights' hearings in Jackson, there had been rumors that the minister was active in civil rights, but in fact Reverend Baker felt that "membership in a civil rights organization was inconsistent with membership in either of his churches."[132]

If these four bombings were warnings to the movement, the next two were frontal attacks. On the evening of September 20, the Society Hill Baptist Church was bombed, causing the entire center portion of the roof to cave in and the walls to collapse. The church was a total loss. Even though the congregation did not let COFO hold meetings there during the summer, mass meetings of the NAACP and weekly voter-registration classes were held in the building. Furthermore, the 275-member congregation included Curtis C. Bryant. An eleven-thousand-dollar insurance claim was paid, but no arrests were made.[133]

The same night the home of Mrs. Aylene Quin was bombed while she was at work; her cafe was a constant meeting place of movement workers during the summer. Two of Mrs. Quin's four children were home with a babysitter. The youngest, Anthony, who was four years old, was pinned to his bed by the fallen ceiling but was not injured. Nine-year-old Jacqueline suffered injuries to her ears as a result of the explosion. It is quite probable that the Quin home was bombed because Mrs. Quin, a member of the Citizens' League, had successfully registered to vote in Harrison County in 1952 and had on several occasions tried unsuccessfully to register in Pike County. Additionally, her oldest daughter had been involved in the school walkout in 1961.[134]

Unlike the previous bombings, the attack on Mrs. Quin's home stirred up the McComb community and touched off a riot.[135] On the night of September 22, some 150 people attended a rally at the site of the Society Hill Baptist Church. Afterwards, about 2,000 African Americans gathered and threw bottles and bricks at a police patrol car. Twenty-four African Americans were arrested on charges of "criminal syndicalism." On September 23, two more African American homes were bombed. The first belonged to Mr. Matthew Jackson, who had not registered to vote but was a member of the local NAACP.[136] The second was rented by Artis Garner, who was hired at the beginning of the summer as a policeman. Prior to the bombing, Garner, an African American, had suffered considerable harassment. While on duty on July 8, he was shot at—he finally left the police force around August 20. On August 26, Vernel Felder, another African American policeman, warned him to leave McComb. Then, on the nights of September 16, 17, and 18, two white McComb policemen drove around his house, shining their headlights in the windows. Finally, on the night of September 19 he was arrested and held at the county jail in Magnolia until the next day, when he was released without being charged. Just prior to the bombing of his home, he had sent his wife and children to Jackson to live. He himself was also preparing to leave the city and testify at a Greenville hearing of the Mississippi State Advisory Committee to the U.S. Commission on Civil Rights about Klan influence in the McComb police force and a number of incidents involving the police themselves. Garner and his family never returned to live in McComb.[137]

The Garner bombing was the last of sixteen such attacks during the summer and fall, possibly because Mrs. Quin, Mrs. Charles Bryant (whose home was bombed on July 26, and she and her husband moved to California in September), and Mrs. Willie Dillon met with President Johnson on September 24 in Washington to inform him of the terrorism and racial violence in McComb.[138] As a result of that meeting, Johnson ordered the FBI to investigate Klan activities in southwest Mississippi. On October 1, three men were arrested in connection with the bombings; on October 4, another man was detained; and on October 6, an additional seven men were taken into custody by the police.[139] During this period Governor Paul Johnson also ordered an investigation of the bombings but indicated that some of the bombings "were plants set by COFO people," while "some were bombings by white people."[140]

Prior to the trial of nine of the defendants, Circuit Judge W. H. Watkins was quoted in the *McComb Enterprise-Journal* as saying, "We should protect our state from invasion and maintain segregation of the races to the full extent that our federal laws will permit, and in the meantime, to live with it peaceably as law-abiding citizens."[141] When Judge Watkins tried and sentenced the nine on October 23, he suspended their sentences but warned them that, if there were any further violence in the area he would revoke the suspensions and put them in jail. According to the *Enterprise-Journal,* the judge informed the men that he was doing what he did because: "1—They are 'mostly young men, just starting out [their ages, in fact, ran from 30 to 44]. 2—All came from 'good families,' who were perhaps 'more surprised than anyone else at the implication' of the men in the acts of violence. 3—'You were unduly provoked, and were ill advised.'"[142]

Governor Johnson's reaction to the suspended sentences was Mississippi understatement: "I certainly believe that these words of Judge Watkins constitute a strong and determined stand against the repetition of the type of action which has occurred in this area."[143] When FBI Director J. Edgar Hoover finally spoke about the suspended sentences in December, he cited the court's action as an example of "blindness and indifference to outrageous acts of violence which encourage others to defy the law."[144]

In spite of the mildness of the McComb court in dealing with the bombers, the city began to settle down after the arrests; by November 17, some 650 McComb citizens had signed a public statement calling for an end to acts of terrorism and the reestablishment of law and order in the city. The editor of the *McComb Enterprise-Journal,* Oliver Emmerich, led the campaign against racial violence, but his newspaper had not always been as helpful in the past in trying to calm the storm. (See chapter 1, above.)

Emmerich's words on the editorial page of his paper on October 30 seemed to usher in a new phase of the struggle for civil rights in Mississippi, even though they were still atypical of public statements in the Mississippi press: "Responsible men know that we cannot have a dual system of justice—one set of rules to apply to white people and another set of rules for Negro people."

Thus, by the time of the November elections, blatant terrorism and racial violence had begun to wane due to pressure mounted against the white power structure by the federal government. Although outright violence had begun to slacken, harassment and intimidation, as well as economic threats and reprisals, continued. Meanwhile COFO and the MFDP were getting ready for the presidential and congressional elections and the second Freedom Vote.[145]

10

The Political Organization
of Protest Politics, Part II
The Second Freedom Vote and the Breakup of COFO

The second Freedom Vote was in many ways different from the first. Outwardly, they were both protest, parallel elections held to demonstrate to the nation that Mississippi African Americans would vote if given the opportunity. Both were conducted prior to the regular elections in the state, and both provided all Mississippians, white and African American, registered or not, the opportunity to vote for the regular nominees as well as Freedom candidates. Furthermore, in both elections voting booths were set up in movement offices and other places not directly subject to white intimidation and violence. Here, though, the similarity between the two Freedom Votes ended.

The second "Freedom Vote" was conducted in the shadow of the Democratic National Convention and was a way station between the convention and the Congressional Challenge in January 1965. Unlike the Freedom candidates in the first election, the nominees in the second contest were part of a statewide party organization that reached down to the precinct level. Moreover, their party, the Mississippi Freedom Democratic Party, adopted the platform of the Democratic National Party and campaigned for Lyndon Johnson and Hubert Humphrey in the November elections—unlike the Mississippi State Democratic Party.[1]

Finally, the second Freedom Vote was less a political campaign than an overt effort to gather documentary proof that the MFDP was the only truly open and democratic political party in Mississippi, as well as the only party that supported the national Democratic Party, and that the entire political apparatus of the State of Mississippi was illegal because it denied the vote to 94 percent of its African American citizens. Therefore, according to the MFDP, the candidates of the traditional Democratic Party had no legal right to be seated in the U.S. Senate and House of Representatives.

In September, the MFDP received some help from the Mississippi white power structure in establishing its claim as Governor Paul Johnson announced, "Mississippi's debt to the national Democratic Party is now paid in full and we are absolutely free to act in the best interests of our people."[2] The MFDP, though, got its campaign for President Johnson off the ground throughout the state.

When Mrs. Hamer ran in the June 2 Democratic primaries against Representative Jamie Whitten and Mrs. Gray ran against Senator John Stennis, they had been informed by the State Election Commission that they could not run in both the primary and general elections. Moreover, the MFDP had been denied a state charter by Secretary of State Heber Ladner on July 24, and the party and its officers had been enjoined by Judge Robertson on August 13 from functioning in the state. Nevertheless, COFO and the MFDP, having pledged to support the Democratic National Party at the convention, began their campaign shortly after the MFDP delegation returned from Atlantic City.[3]

That campaign centered on the candidacy of Mrs. Hamer, Dr. Aaron Henry, and Mrs. Annie Devine, who circulated petitions to get on the November 3 ballot in the Second Congressional District, the U.S. Senate contest, and the Fourth Congressional District, respectively (Mrs. Gray only ran in the "Freedom Vote"). On October 6, Secretary of State Ladner said that the three did not have the required number of signatures of registered voters on their petitions and that those petitions were "ridiculous."[4] He did not mention that the petitions contained more than the required number of signatures but that many county registrars refused to certify them because the signatures were those of people who had refused to pay the poll tax. This was in spite of the Twenty-fourth Amendment to the U.S. Constitution, which went into effect on February 5, 1964—outlawing the poll tax as a bar to voting in federal elections for president, vice-president, senator, and representative.[5]

With the way blocked to running candidates in the regular elections, the movement focused all of its efforts on the Freedom Vote, which was to take place on October 30 and 31, and November 1 and 2. The regular election was held on November 3. The 65 SNCC and 35 CORE staff in the state were joined by some 200 Summer Project volunteers who had stayed on after the convention and 100 other northern volunteers who came down for the period of October 20 to November 4 to help out. This last group of volunteers was predominantly white students from Princeton, Stanford, Brandeis, Tulane, Southern Illinois, Oberlin, Dartmouth, Sarah Lawrence, and St. Elizabeth's College.[6]

Mrs. Fannie Lou Hamer ran against Jamie L. Whitten—chairman of the Subcommittee on Agricultural Appropriations—in the Second Congressional

District; Mrs. Annie Devine ran against Arthur Winstead (Democrat) and Prentiss Walker (Republican) in the Fourth Congressional District; Mrs. Victoria Gray ran against William M. Colmer—chairman of the House Rules Committee —in the Fifth Congressional District; and Aaron Henry ran against Senator John Stennis, the second-ranking member of the Senate Armed Services Committee and its chairman from 1971. The ballot in the Freedom Vote was headed by the Democratic and Republican slates of Lyndon Johnson and Hubert Humphrey and Barry Goldwater and William Miller.

At a meeting in Jackson, Lawrence Guyot, the state chairman of the MFDP, stated that since Mrs. Hamer, Devine, Gray, and Aaron Henry had been barred from the regular ballot, the MFDP had decided to conduct the Freedom Vote. Guyot also stated that the Freedom Vote would "give local African Americans and whites a choice between the segregationist candidates of the closed regular Mississippi Democratic Party and a slate of MFDP candidates."[7] He further announced that the voting would be conducted "in churches, schools, community centers, barbershops, cotton fields, in fact, anywhere that people are."[8]

At a meeting in Mileston, Holmes County, on October 18, the MFDP passed a resolution concerning the October 6 exclusion of Mrs. Hamer, Mrs. Devine, and Aaron Henry from the regular election ballot. It was resolved that these three, as well as Mrs. Gray, would challenge the winners of the November 3 election and try to win those congressional seats for the representatives of the MFDP.[9]

The treatment of movement workers during the campaign followed the already established pattern of intimidation, violence, and arrests, as shown by this list of incidents:

BELZONI: Oct. 1: Six campaign workers arrested on charges of "criminal syndicalism" while distributing registration leaflets.

TCHULA: Oct. 24: Home of Hartman Turnbow, FDP delegate to Atlantic City in August 1964, shot into.

MCCOMB: Oct. 23: Campaigning clergymen arrested for "distributing leaflets without a permit." 13 campaign workers arrested. . . .

RULEVILLE: Oct. 29: Shots fired through window riddling pictures of Johnson, Humphrey, and local candidate.[10]

When the votes were finally tabulated for the November 3rd presidential election, White Mississippi had demonstrated its dislike for the man they called "the Counterfeit Confederate"[11] by giving 359,693 votes to Goldwater and only 53,063 to Johnson.[12] The only surprise of the election was that Prentiss

Walker was the first Republican elected to Congress from Mississippi since Reconstruction.[13]

The results of the "Freedom Vote" were not encouraging to the MFDP, either. Some 68,000 people participated in this parallel protest election,[14] even though it was only necessary to be a resident of the state for two years and be over twenty-one years old. The previous Freedom Vote had drawn more than 83,000 voters under similar circumstances of intimidation and violence and with less of an organizational base.

The immediate reason for this poor turnout is possibly the disappointment resulting from the Democratic National Convention. Mississippi African Americans had gone there knowing that they were more loyal to the president and the publicly stated objectives of the Democratic National Party than the Mississippi Democratic Party ever was, or possibly would ever be. Furthermore, the MFDP delegation had good reason to believe that on legal grounds it had the right to be seated in place of regular Mississippi Democrats. Additionally, the Freedom Vote was held after the MFDP's candidates had been blocked from appearing on the regular election ballot. Finally, it is quite possible that some of the MFDP members might have felt that their parallel election could not have any direct influence on the November elections and that its only value lay in its efficacy as a demonstration of denial of the right to vote in Mississippi and its future use in the upcoming Congressional Challenge.

All of these reasons, then, may have been cause for the weak participation in this Freedom Vote. Nevertheless, one has the feeling that other reasons were more important, and that those reasons are to be found in the disintegration of the COFO coalition that began at the Democratic National Convention. In September, Dave Dennis left the state after working there for two years without a break and under considerable strain because he felt partially responsible for the deaths of Schwerner, Chaney, and Goodman.[15] The fact that he was not there during the Freedom Vote may have caused the poor response in Canton, even though Mrs. Devine was from that city and James Farmer flew in for the campaign.

If Dennis's absence is compounded with the gradual withdrawal of Bob Moses from decision-making in the movement, it is possible to see that COFO was falling apart.[16] Moreover, after the convention Aaron Henry moved more in line with his national office's policies, and with him the NAACP began to cut itself off from COFO, formally severing ties in April 1965. Both the NAACP and National CORE, as well as the Lawyers Constitutional Defense Committee

(LCDC), continued to express complaints about being left out of the decision-making process at COFO.[17] Finally, during the winter, Moses withdrew completely from Mississippi and changed his name to Bob Parris. When talking about this change, he indicated that he wanted to unload the burden of charisma and influence he had acquired as Bob Moses.[18]

Moses's decision to leave Mississippi was apparently connected with the series of staff meetings SNCC held during the late fall and winter of 1964–65.[19] The first of these staff conferences was a direct result of the September 18 meeting at the National Council of Churches in New York. Courtland Cox scheduled it for mid-October and contacted the SNCC leaders and staff who were still in Africa. Moses, Mrs. Hamer, Forman, Julian Bond, Ruby Doris Smith Robinson, Bill Hansen, Prathia Hall, Matthew Jones, and Donna Moses all quickly returned to Atlanta. John Lewis and Don Harris remained in Africa.[20]

Nevertheless, the major leaders of SNCC found themselves unprepared for the five-day conference, which was held shortly after their return.[21] Cox had already established an agenda for the sessions—contrary to the established SNCC practice of leaving the agenda open—and Forman felt that adequate preparations had not yet been made concerning the coming summer. Inasmuch as Forman and the southern field staff wanted to continue the successes and eliminate the failures of the Mississippi Summer Project in what was called the Black Belt Project—to include all of the Black Belt counties from Virginia to Texas and was planned "to consolidate bases in a regional structure with national potential"—Forman felt that further detailed planning was necessary before calling the staff together.

He was never to get the chance to discuss those detailed plans at a full staff meeting because it became apparent at the October meeting that SNCC was divided into two camps: one—the southern field staff—that wanted strong leadership from SNCC and its leaders; and the other—Bob Moses and many of the African American and white college students, who came from northern middle-class backgrounds—which held an extreme belief in participatory democracy and denigrated the concept of leadership from above. (Forman called this malady "local peopleitis.")

By the fourth day of the conference, the Black Belt Project had been tabled "forever," the southern field staff had walked out of the conference to return home—Lawrence Guyot had left even earlier because he felt the Black Belt Project, if adopted, would destroy the strength of the Mississippi Project—and finally the meeting had been adjourned until November. All this took place prior to holding the Freedom Vote, and it probably had a serious impact on the internal cohesiveness of the Mississippi movement.[22]

When the SNCC staff met again in November at Waveland, Mississippi,[23] Moses continued to hold back his support for the Black Belt Project, even though he, Forman, and other staff members had done considerable work in preparing plans to be presented at the conference. As in the previous meeting, as well as the September 18 conference of liberal and national civil rights leaders, northern African Americans and whites of middle-class background continued to disrupt the sessions—thereby delaying discussion of the Black Belt Project—by pressing for a discussion of just how decisions should be made. According to Forman, "Since it was SNCC's practice to make decisions by consensus rather than by voting, that liberalism opened the door for meetings to be tyrannized by a minority."[24] Furthermore, that minority, "[i]nstead of finding ways that people with natural leadership qualities could make their contribution and help to develop leadership qualities in others, this attitude simply said, Curb your leadership."[25]

That philosophy, which came to be known as "freedom high," help split SNCC into two camps.[26] In addition to this problem, the question of how SNCC was to be run also weighed heavily on the organization. The spring 1964 conference had tabled the matter until the October meeting, where it had not been resolved either. In the meantime, SNCC's national staff, which was already large—70 members—in December 1963, had grown to more than 150 during the Summer Project, and even the expanded Executive Committee did not have more than day-to-day decision-making power. Important decisions continued to be made by the entire Coordinating Committee—all of the SNCC staff meeting as a committee of the whole.[27] According to Forman, "many of the new people felt no strong ties to the South or to the idea of southern African American people having a strong national organization at their command."[28] This worried Forman considerably about the future of the Mississippi movement, as well as the general movement in the South.

The problems of decision-making and organizational structure also went unanswered at the seven-day Waveland conference. The southern field staff again left early out of a feeling of disgust as Bob Moses continued to withhold himself from the discussions. Moses's apparent alignment with the "freedom high" group from the time of the October conference retarded progress toward a resolution of these problems, and talk began to grow in SNCC about a "Moses" faction and a "Forman" faction.

Shortly after the Waveland meeting, Moses refused to attend the first gathering of the Mississippi Summer Project volunteers that was to be held after the summer. He told Forman, "if he [Moses] went, discussion would be cut off and the ordinary workers wouldn't feel free to talk."[29] Not only did he fail to attend the meeting, but he also did not send a letter or note of explanation. The problems of internal structure in SNCC and of how decisions were made went unresolved until the following February. The cost of this internal disorder was high: the eventual and gradual loss of power in the Mississippi movement.

In addition to the gradual withdrawal of CORE from Mississippi, the withdrawal of the NAACP from COFO, and the hesitancy of Bob Moses to remain in a position of power in the movement, a conflict developed between the MFDP and SNCC. Many members of SNCC found Lawrence Guyot's position of officially supporting Johnson in the November election objectionable—Guyot had been in jail during the Democratic National Convention and was unaware of many of the goings-on there. On the other hand, the internal chaos in SNCC led to strained relations between that organization and the MFDP. Furthermore, the MFDP was in many ways the child of SNCC, and when SNCC made little effort to prevent the MFDP from becoming just another reform political institution, many of the party members felt embittered and estranged, particularly after SNCC people had encouraged the party toward a radical politics in not accepting the compromise proposal at the Democratic National Convention.[30]

Thus the overt failure of the Freedom Vote was a manifestation of the internal conflicts within the Mississippi movement that were both inter- and intra-organizational. August Meier states that, by the end of 1964, "The [COFO] staff failed to do serious political organizing and instead expended time in meetings to discuss endlessly such matters as internal democracy, personality conflicts, and COFO's proper role in helping indigenous leaders make decisions for their communities."[31] Additionally, black-white staff relations began to break down, causing the Jackson COFO office to close for a week in November.[32] If the liberal-labor establishment had been looking in September for a way to break up the Mississippi movement and weaken SNCC's position of power there, it could not have hoped for more. Additionally, attacks began to be launched by local people against MFDP leadership as being unable to understand their problems and relate to them.[33]

In spite of these difficulties, the Mississippi movement continued to function after the second Freedom Vote, and it even began to lay plans for the

Congressional Challenge in January 1965. COFO continued to operate in the state, not, though, as a smooth well-oiled machine but in fits and spurts.

The Congressional Challenge and
the Voting Rights Act of 1965

Three major events affected the Mississippi movement on a national level in 1965: the Mississippi Freedom Democratic Party challenged the seating of the regular Mississippi congressmen on January 4; the U.S. Commission on Civil Rights finally held hearings in Mississippi, from February 16 to 20; and the Voting Rights Act of 1965 passed the U.S. Congress and was signed into law by President Johnson on August 6. All three were closely interconnected, and although they ostensibly took place under the shadow of the federal government, they were largely by-products of the pressures exerted upon federal authorities and the Democratic National Party by the Mississippi movement.

The success of that movement in the legal sphere can be seen in these events. Nevertheless, the movement's revolution in civil rights was not completed until the signing of the Civil Rights Act of 1968 on April 11 and the seating of the Loyal Democrats of Mississippi in place of the regular Mississippi Democratic Party at the Democratic National Convention in Chicago in 1968.[34]

The mushrooming participation of African Americans in the Mississippi political sphere was largely based on the triumphs of the movement that were accomplished in 1965 and earlier. Nevertheless, the actual winning of positions in the political, social, and economic spheres took many years after 1965 to achieve. These then were victories that enabled the African American community to participate in the democratic process and win elective office in the closed society. How did this come to pass, particularly in the face of the massive resistance thrown up against the movement by the Mississippi power structure?

On October 18, the Mississippi Freedom Democratic Party resolved to challenge the seating of the Mississippians who would be elected to Congress on November 3. This resolution was passed by a meeting of the MFDP because Secretary of State Heber Ladner had denied the petitions of Mrs. Hamer and Mrs. Devine to appear on the regular election ballot and had also previously blocked Mrs. Gray's right to do so. A further meeting was called by the MFDP on November 28, in Washington, D.C., to gather supporters for the Congressional Challenge from around the nation. (The MFDP had Michael Thelwell set up an office there.) Present at the meeting were representatives of SNCC, the

MFDP, Jesse Gray of the Harlem rent-strike group, Al Raby of the Freedom Democrat clubs of Chicago, Cleveland SDS, and Noel Day of Boston. Conspicuously absent were representatives of the NAACP, SCLC, the Urban League, and CORE, although these groups eventually did support the challenge. Lawyers Ben Smith, of New Orleans, and Arthur Kinoy, of New York, presented the challenge idea at that meeting.[35]

On December 4, 1964, Mrs. Hamer, Mrs. Devine, and Mrs. Gray, with the law offices of Kunstler, Kunstler and Kinoy, formally filed petitions of challenge with Congressmen-elect Whitten, Walker, and Colmer, outlining the reasons why these three did not deserve to represent the Second, Fourth, and Fifth Congressional Districts of Mississippi in the U.S. House of Representatives. All of these petitions were heavily documented with citations of intimidation, murder, and official restraint against the adult populations of the respective districts.[36] The challenges were filed under the provisions of Title 2, U.S. Code, Sections 201–6. Section 201 reads: "Whenever any person intends to contest an election of any Member of the House of Representatives of the United States, he shall, within thirty days after the result of such election shall have been determined by the officer or board of canvassers authorized by law to determine the same, give notice, in writing, to the Member whose seat he designs to contest, of his intention to contest the same, and, in such notice, shall specify particularly the grounds upon which he relies in the contest."[37]

The next step in the challenge took place on January 4, 1965, when hundreds of Mississippi African Americans lined both sides of the tunnel leading into the House of Representatives and through which congressmen-elect had to pass in order to take their seats. There the representatives were met with silent stares as they moved forward toward the House.[38] Then Mrs. Hamer, Mrs. Devine, and Mrs. Gray sought to enter the House, "not declaring their right to replace the Mississippi congressmen-elect in the seats which are being contested, but as contestants who wish to avail themselves of the business of Congress during the period of contest so that in the event that contest is decided in their favor they will have sufficient background about the current session of Congress so that they might function effectively."[39] This action was taken under House Rule 32, which governs access to the floor of the House during the period in which cases are pending before it.[40] Nevertheless, the three African American women were denied admittance.[41]

After the congressmen-elect had entered the House and the oaths of office were about to be administered, Representative William Fitts Ryan (Democrat,

New York) stood up and objected to the seating of all five congressmen from Mississippi. Some fifty other congressmen stood up with him. Then Speaker of the House John McCormack (Democrat, Massachusetts) administered the oath to all of the other members so that the members who had been sworn in could decide what to do about the Mississippi delegation.[42] At this point Ryan rose again, hoping to be recognized in order to introduce his "Fairness Resolution" that delineated why the Mississippi congressmen-elect had no right to be seated at this session of the Eighty-ninth Congress and stated that the matter should be held in abeyance until "the House shall finally decide the question of the right of each said Messrs. to be seated."[43] This resolution further stated that "this Challenge is separate from, but not in derogation of, whatever rights flow from the Challenge of the Mississippi Freedom Democratic Party."[44] It was supported by a long list of liberal and civil rights organizations.

Representative Ryan, however, was not recognized by the Speaker of the House at this time, and Democratic House Majority Leader Carl Albert, of Oklahoma, was called upon. Albert moved to seat the regular Mississippi delegation until the dispute was finally resolved by the House Committee on Administration's Subcommittee on Elections and Privileges, which would hear both parties to the contest. He then asked the Speaker to close debate on his resolution, but Mrs. Edith Green, of Oregon, requested a roll-call vote on his motion. Under the circumstances, if the motion to close debate on Albert's motion had been defeated, the possibility of airing the entire matter might have made it difficult for northern congressmen to support the seating of the regular Mississippi group. Again, the administration got its way;[45] the representatives voted to close debate, but 149 of them, a surprisingly large number, voted to keep debate open.[46]

Even though the Mississippi congressmen were seated, the three challengers had 40 days to take testimony under federal subpoena power in support of their arguments. The Mississippi congressmen were then given the subsequent 40 days. A final 10 days were provided for rebuttal, after which the House Subcommittee on Elections and Privileges was to weigh the evidence and make a decision. The whole process was to take no longer than 260 days from its inception.

During its period, the MFDP spread out through Mississippi, issuing subpoenas to former Governor Ross Barnett, Secretary of State Heber Ladner, Director of Public Safety Colonel T. B. Birdsong, and State Sovereignty Commission Director Earl Johnston as well as questioning sheriffs and registrars in the presence of some 130 volunteer lawyers who took depositions concerning the elections as well as statements by African Americans concerning terror, intimidation, and illegal practices connected with their attempts to register to vote. Attorney General Joe Patterson and former Governor and Attorney General J. P. Coleman were deposed in federal buildings rather than in state buildings, and Patterson even admitted membership in the Citizens' Council. Forrest County Registrar Theron Lynd when deposed could not answer how many voters there were in his county and did not know anything about the Congressional Challenge. These state officials took every opportunity to dodge the questions asked of them. Moreover, the regular Mississippi congressmen did not use their 40 days, as they had decided not to recognize the challenge.[47]

Unlike white Mississippians, the African American community came forward to be deposed. Those depositions, however, led to expected retributions from the white power structure. Credit was revoked for local people, student organizers were arrested on trumped up charges, threats were voiced, churches were burned down, local adult activists were arrested, houses were fired into, and groups of people trying to register to vote were arrested for charges such as "parading without a permit." However, according to MFDP Chairman Guyot there was much more restraint than normal on the part of Mississippi authorities, possibly because they did not want an unfavorable picture to be passed on to the House of Representatives Subcommittee on Elections and Privileges.

In July, the challenge was to go to the House Committee on Administration for consideration and referral back to the full House of Representatives, which would then make a final decision on the validity of the challenge. Attorneys William Kunstler and Arthur Kinoy, both of New York City, and Morton Stavis, of New Jersey, organized some eight hundred depositions—they ran to three thousand single-spaced pages—and presented the MFDP's brief to the House subcommittee before discussion in the full committee.[48]

Concurrent with these actions, SNCC organized demonstrations in Washington. On June 14, one hundred college students and SNCC staff arrived in the Capitol, and the next day they demonstrated in front of the Department of Justice. Then, on June 19, twelve Mississippi African Americans were arrested for refusing to leave the office of the clerk of the House of Representatives.[49] The group was trying to get House Clerk Ralph R. Roberts to print the depositions—which had been submitted to him on May 17—and send them on to the House Subcommittee on Elections and Privileges. (Those depositions were printed by the Government Printing Office in July, after considerable pressures and protests by Kunstler, the MFDP, and its supporters around the country.)[50]

The depositions were then forwarded to House Speaker McCormack at the end of July, and they were put before the House subcommittee for consideration. The challenge was finally brought before the House of Representatives on September 17, 1965, in House Resolution 585. The MFDP challengers were defeated on a roll-call vote of 240 to 155.[51] In the meantime, though, the Voting Rights Act had been signed into law on August 6, implying an administration decision that, if Mississippi African Americans wished to have their own representatives in Congress, they would have to mobilize the necessary voters to get their candidates elected to public office.

This being the case, the MFDP Congressional Challenge was taking place concurrently with the process through which the Voting Rights Bill was moving through Congress. Moreover, the challenge, with its three thousand pages of subpoenaed depositions, served as proof of the necessity to rectify the denial of the vote to Mississippi African Americans. The events in Selma, Alabama, also contributed significantly to the passage of the Voting Rights Act of 1965. (Even with the passage of the Voting Rights Act of 1965, it took until 1986 for an African American to be elected from the reconstituted Second Congressional District of the Delta.)

The problem of the new voting legislation started much earlier in the year in connection with the Mississippi hearings of the U.S. Commission on Civil Rights. In spite the federal commission having been asked to hold public hearings in Mississippi as early as 1962, none were held until early 1965. The commission first scheduled hearings for October 1962, but numerous requests from U.S. Attorney General Robert F. Kennedy led to their postponement. Contrary to movement charges that the commission was responsible for the delay in holding the hearings, it is clear that both the Kennedy and Johnson administrations caused the delay. Furthermore, throughout this period the commission issued reports filed by the interracial Mississippi State Advisory Committee to the U.S. Commission on Civil Rights. That body held six open meetings in Jackson, Greenville, Clarksdale, and Meridian between October 1, 1961, and December 31, 1962, and an additional nine open meetings in Jackson, Natchez, Greenville, Biloxi, Meridian, and Vicksburg in 1963 and 1964. Nevertheless, the Mississippi committee was no substitute for the federal group, which was empowered under the Civil Rights Act of 1957 to investigate denials of civil rights and make recommendations for appropriate federal remedies.

Thus, to the Mississippi movement it was not enough that the Mississippi State Advisory Committee had held periodic hearings. These were only unofficial reports and recommendations of a local group, and if anything were to be done on a national level, it was imperative that the federal commission hold its own hearings in Mississippi. Consequently, when Martin Luther King Jr. relayed Hubert Humphrey's promise to hold the hearings if the MFDP accepted the administration's compromise proposal at the Democratic National Convention, the movement was further disenchanted with President Johnson and the national Democratic Party. The explosion of racial violence in McComb, Johnson's decision to have the FBI investigate the Ku Klux Klan's activities in southwest Mississippi, the violence surrounding the second Freedom Vote, and the MFDP's Congressional Challenge in January 1965 all helped bring about the holding of federal hearings in the state in 1965.

The U.S. Commission on Civil Rights met in Jackson, Mississippi, from February 16 to 20, at which time it investigated both the voting process and the administration of justice in the state.[52] Various local and state officials were asked, or subpoenaed, to give evidence, as well as local African Americans who had been subject to threats, intimidation, violence, and other denials of their civil rights. Wiley A. Branton, the director of the Voter Education Project (VEP), testified, as did Charles Evers and Aaron Henry of the NAACP, but significantly absent were SNCC, CORE, and MFDP representatives.[53] Nevertheless, those hearings clearly testify to the monolithic nature of white supremacy in Mississippi.

Whether the findings and recommendations of the U.S. Commission on Civil Rights were available in time to be used by the House and Senate Judiciary Committees in drawing up voting rights legislation in 1965 is not important, because by the end of 1964 it was readily apparent to the American public that Mississippi was by far the most brutally efficient of the southern states in denying its African American citizens their constitutional rights. Moreover, the buildup of racial violence in Selma, Alabama, from mid-January probably provided the final impetus needed for President Johnson to address the nation on March 15, in Baltimore, with the words, "We Shall Overcome."[54] Two days later he sent his draft version of the voting rights bill to Capitol Hill.[55]

On the same day, Emanuel Celler (Democrat, New York), the chairman of the House Judiciary Committee, introduced the draft bill in the House. The next day, March 18, it was cosponsored in the Senate by 66 Senators. At the same time, the House Judiciary Committee began to call witnesses.[56] Movement people and supporters found these hearings extremely valuable, as numerous individuals came forward to present their case for a strong voting-rights bill and others conducted write-in campaigns to their various Congressmen. Nevertheless, matters dragged on slowly in the Senate. Then, on May 21, Senate Majority Leader Mike Mansfield (Democrat, Montana) and Senate Minority Leader Everett Dirksen (Republican, Illinois) filed a cloture petition. On the twenty-fourth day of debate on the Senate bill—May 25—cloture was invoked by a vote of 70–30. The next day the bill was passed by the Senate by a vote of 77–19. The House debate on the bill began on July 6, and on July 9 the House passed its version by 333–85. It was then sent to the Senate-House Conference Committee, where a final version was completed by July 29. Both houses of Congress then approved the measure speedily: on August 3, the House passed the bill by a vote of 328–74, and on August 4, the Senate approved the measure by 79–18.[57]

Finally, on August 6, President Johnson went before the nation to announce the signing of the Voting Rights Act of 1965. Among other things he stated, "Today the Negro story and the American story fuse and blend. . . . This good Congress acted swiftly in passing this act. I intend to act with equal dispatch in enforcing it. . . . If any county anywhere in this nation does not want federal intervention, it need only, open its polling places to all of its people."[58] After addressing the country from the Lincoln Memorial, Johnson signed the bill into law in the "President's Room" of the Senate, where Lincoln had issued the Emancipation Proclamation in 1863.[59]

The provisions of the new law were most forcefully felt in the appointment of federal voting examiners to southern counties where less than 50 percent of the total voting-age population was registered or actually voted in the 1964 presidential election and where a test or device (e.g., the poll tax) was maintained as a prerequisite to registration or voting as of November 1, 1964.[60] In spite of all eighty-two Mississippi counties being eligible to receive federal examiners who would register all African American residents of the state over twenty-one—whether literate or not—by December 20, there were only nineteen such examiner counties in Mississippi: Leflore and Madison, from August 9; Jefferson Davis and Jones, from August 18; Benton, Bolivar, Clay, Coahoma, and Humphreys, from September 24; DeSoto, Hinds, Holmes, Jefferson, Neshoba, and Walthall, from October 29; and Carroll, Newton, Simpson, and Warren, from December 20.[61] By September 30, 1967, the number of federal examiner counties had grown to thirty-one, but at no time during this period was an examiner appointed to Senator Eastland's home county, Sunflower (the senator was chairman of the Senate Judiciary Committee), or to Pike and Adams counties, where there had been so much Klan violence in 1964.[62] Furthermore, by 1967 the voter registration figures for nonwhites (i.e., African Americans) in examiner counties had reached a full 70.9 percent, while in non-examiner counties it was only 50.3 percent. The president's promise to move quickly in enforcing the Voting Rights Act apparently broke down, but White Mississippi enlarged its number of registered white voters from 76.7 percent to 93.5 percent in non-examiner counties and from 83.7 percent to 90.8 percent in examiner counties.[63]

Thus, during 1965 the promised revolution in civil rights moved forward considerably on a national level, as pressures were mounted against the Johnson administration by the Mississippi movement. Given no alternative, Congress responded with a strong voting-rights act. Nevertheless, U.S. Attorney General Nicholas Katzenbach and the Department of Justice did not move as quickly as they might have after the act was signed into law in August. Additionally, the Mississippi power structure also began to organize itself for the continuing struggle to maintain white supremacy.

The Mississippi Movement in 1965

In 1965 the Mississippi movement tried to maintain the momentum it had created during Freedom Summer, and the Mississippi power structure attempted to regain the upper hand. The violence and intimidation that surrounded the 1964 Summer Project had led to national pressures against the continuation of white supremacy and its use of violence as state officials and leaders began to back off from their extreme stance by the end of 1964. Was this retreat a tactical one only, or was the closed society beginning to become an open community?

In 1965, White Mississippi was in fact trying to lessen the pressures exerted on the state from outside and at the same time trying to reorganize its forces for the continuing struggle with its African American citizens. Thus, if public statements of local Mississippi leaders are examined in light of what was happening on a national level, it will be easier to understand what was taking place on a local level.

By the end of 1964 the Mississippi movement had begun to lose its internal cohesion and the disparate elements of COFO had started to operate separately within the state. By April 1965, the NAACP formally withdrew from COFO, and during the summer it joined with the state AFL-CIO to form the Mississippi Democratic Conference at the instigation of the national Democratic Party.

This action excluded the remaining groups in COFO and the MFDP from its programs.[64] CORE gradually withdrew from Mississippi during the year, leaving Meridian at midyear and Canton by the fall. CORE Task Force worker George Raymond remained after the summer, but Richard Jewett, who headed the CORE staff in Mississippi, left in September.[65]

Furthermore, SNCC had lost its momentum during the staff meetings in October and November 1964, and most of its staff had left the state, many going to Washington, D.C., to work on the Congressional Challenge and others going to the Black Belt counties in Alabama, particularly Lowndes County. Nevertheless, some of the organization's earlier drive was recovered at the February staff conference, where the "field machine" (i.e., the southern field staff) regained the upper hand and the "freedom high" elements lost much of their influence in SNCC.

Even though the Black Belt Project was never reformulated, a series of spring "people's conferences" were decided upon at which local movements would come together and draw up plans for the summer of 1965. The new executive committee of SNCC was heavily weighted toward southern African Americans of lower-class background, and mechanisms for armed self-defense were finally agreed upon. It was also decided to organize demonstrations in support of the Congressional Challenge in Washington and to recruit summer volunteers for the Mississippi movement at the direction of the MFDP.[66] At the same time a new group, the Delta Ministry, tried to take up some of the slack left by the dissolution of COFO.[67]

Nevertheless, the movement in 1965 was not what it had been in 1964, and the Mississippi power structure had used its time well during the winter in attempting to modify its national image and lessen the pressures on the state from outside. Citizens in McComb had begun to speak up against violence, terror, and intimidation during October and November. Additionally, in the beginning of 1965, the official Mississippi community began to be heard on the side of racial tolerance for the first time. It was also joined by members of the economic community who had begun to feel the pressures exerted upon them by national business concerns.

During January and February 1965, strange voices of moderation began to surface on the local scene in Mississippi. Nevertheless, they must be understood within the framework of events that were occurring on a national level. The MFDP's Congressional Challenge in January, the impending February hearings of the U.S. Commission on Civil Rights in Jackson, and the rumors of new voting-rights legislation all combined to keep Mississippi in the national spotlight.

During January the Mississippi courts exhibited the first glimmerings of a change of heart in the white power structure. On January 15, a federal grand jury in Jackson indicted eighteen men in connection with the murders of Schwerner, Chaney, and Goodman,[68] after murder and conspiracy charges against them had been dismissed in December 1964 by U.S. Commissioner Esther Carter at the preliminary hearing in Meridian. This time the men were indicted on a one-count felony of conspiring to deprive the three of their civil rights and a four-count misdemeanor based on another federal statute of participating in a conspiracy in which law enforcement officials inflicted "summary punishments" "without due process of law." The presiding judge was W. Harold Cox of the Federal District Court (Southern District, Mississippi), Sen. Eastland's law-school friend from Ole Miss. On February 25, Cox seemed unbothered by the FBI's evidence when he dismissed the felony indictment against seventeen of the defendants—the trial of the eighteenth participant in the murder conspiracy had been transferred to the jurisdiction of the Federal District Court in Atlanta. At the trial Cox stated that the indictment specified a "heinous crime against the state of Mississippi but not a crime against the United States."[69] The following day Judge Cox upheld one count of the misdemeanor indictment and dismissed the three others, which charged fourteen of the seventeen with actual violation of the law. Neshoba County Sheriff Lawrence Rainey, Deputy Sheriff Cecil Price, and Richard Willis, a Philadelphia policeman, remained charged with three counts of acting "under color of the law" against Schwerner, Chaney, and Goodman.[70]

On January 22, however, Allie W. Shelby, an eighteen-year-old Flora Negro, was shot to death by police in the Hinds County Jailhouse in Jackson, after having been sentenced to six months in jail for making indecent gestures at a white woman. The same day a coroner's jury ruled the death "justifiable homicide." Later, in connection with the shooting, state judges barred an African American protest demonstration set for January 29 at the Hinds County Courthouse, and local African American leaders called off the protest on advice from NAACP lawyers.[71]

In spite of the continuing difficulty in receiving justice at the hands of Mississippi courts, on January 25 the Mississippi Supreme Court reversed the conviction of William B. Harper, an African American, and ordered a new trial because African Americans had been effectively excluded from the juries that had indicted and convicted him of attempted rape of a sixteen-year-old white girl near Forest, in Scott County. The court ruled that "token summoning of Negroes for jury service" was not enough.[72]

On February 3, with the Civil Rights Commission hearings near at hand, the one-hundred-member board of directors of the Mississippi Economic Council issued a statement in Jackson calling for racial peace and compliance with the Civil Rights Act of 1964. In the same announcement it also proposed the follow-ing program: "(1) Order and respect for the law must be maintained. Lawless activities in the state by individuals and organizations cannot be tolerated. (2) Communications must be maintained between the races in the state. (3) Reg-istration and voting laws should be fairly and impartially administered for all. (4) Support of public education must be maintained and strengthened."[73]

The same week Governor Paul Johnson told a meeting of sheriffs in Jack-son, "The day for doing a lot of bull-shooting is over. We've got to meet the challenges of the coming years. A lot of people have made the mistake of turn-ing their heads to the problems and saying they probably are going away. They are not going away."[74] Attorney General Patterson followed the governor. He also showed an apparent change of heart in saying, "We must put our heads together and recognize that we are part of the Union and we're going to stay as such, and that we are bound by the laws of the United States and the decisions of the U.S. Supreme Court."[75]

When the Civil Rights Commission's public hearings finally opened in Jack-son on February 16, Governor Johnson continued to speak in the same vein:

The Civil Rights Act of 1964 as passed by the Congress is the law of the land, and Mississippi knows it. . . .

Violence against any person or any group will not—I repeat, will not be tolerated.

. . . I am joined and supported by the statewide association of local law enforcement officials.[76]

This atmosphere of outward compliance with federal law continued through February and March, as the Mississippi Board of Education agreed on Febru-ary 24 to comply with federal requirements in order to continue receiving $23 million per year from the federal government for state schools.[77] Previously, on January 15, Greenville had drafted desegregation plans for its schools, which stood to lose $272,000 in federal aid, and in May the city began its program of voluntary compliance.[78] Nevertheless, not every city was as willing, and the state government was not as open in its compliance as it at first appeared to be. Thus, on October 1, the Department of Justice found it necessary to file suit under the Civil Rights Act of 1964 to bar enforcement of the state law requiring tuition payments in public schools for students with parents who lived out of state.[79]

Moreover, Greenville was atypical of Mississippi, and the Department of Justice found it necessary to intervene on June 14 in private suits to speed up the integration of schools in Canton, Meridian, Biloxi, and Leake County, where the federal courts had ordered it the previous summer.[80] Other counties like Forrest—whose county seat is in Hattiesburg—tried suing U.S. Attorney General Katzenbach and Secretary of Health, Education, and Welfare John Gardner to force the release of federal education funds that had been withheld for noncompliance with Department of Health, Education, and Welfare guidelines. Forrest County's suit of October 8 was met by a Department of Justice counter suit on December 13, which asked for an injunction forbidding the county to operate a segregated school system.[81] Thus, in spite of public promises of compliance, White Mississippi generally continued in its intransigent ways by using the court system to delay any progress it could get away with.

Governor Johnson's promises of racial tolerance and law enforcement were also ambivalent. On the one hand, during 1965 there were no significant incidents of lynch law perpetrated against northern whites or African Americans with northern connections. On the other hand, the local movement and African Americans were still subjected to occurrences of racial violence, harassment, and intimidation. It appears almost as if White Mississippi had learned its lesson during Freedom Summer and, when the nation was looking, comported itself on its best behavior. Sometimes, though, even this minimal amount of restraint was missing.

Thus, in early March the Freedom House in Laurel was burned to the ground.[82] Shortly thereafter, on March 5, the Indianola Freedom School and its two-thousand-volume library were also destroyed by fire. Following the fire, eight civil rights workers were arrested by local police for interfering with the investigation of possible arson suspects.[83] When the nation was looking on, though, as in the case the CORE-conducted Freedom Day in Canton on March 30, the results were different. CORE worker George Raymond was able to lead fifty-four Negroes down to register, few police were on hand, and no attempts at intimidation were made.[84]

Similarly, when CORE conducted a well-publicized march on May 28–29 from Fannin to Brandon, the county seat of Rankin County, in protest over the burning of five African American churches between November 1964 and April 1965, the marchers were met by Brandon Mayor C. J. Harvey and county officials who had received orders from the governor to maintain racial calm. When they arrived at the county courthouse, 50 of the 278 marchers were taken to the registrar's office. (The Department of Justice had filed suit against the registrar in April.) The other marchers were led upstairs and allowed to sit in the courtroom, and after the first group had finished registering, James Farmer addressed a rally in front of the courthouse.[85] For the movement this outward show of compliance was of some significance, as Rankin County was one of the Ku Klux Klan's strongholds in the state and the marchers had followed their fifteen-mile route while being protected by a county police escort.

Nonetheless, it appears as if the specter of another invasion by the federal government—like the one that had recently taken place in Selma, Alabama —was too much for the Mississippi power structure to allow. Moreover, the MFDP's Congressional Challenge was still pending during the summer of 1965, and the prospects of a tough Voting Rights Act were good.

In spite of its organizational difficulties and the breakdown in communications between the various civil rights groups, the Mississippi movement continued to operate throughout the state in 1965 as three hundred northern white students and ministers came down for the summer. Even though some of its momentum was lost during the winter and early spring of 1965, the national actions of the MFDP largely filled the vacuum left on the local level, and the presence of the students in the summer helped keep the local movement going.

During the spring the movement was able to get a program of attack off the ground that added a new dimension to its work. That program tied the political elements of the movement to economic ones, which in turn were the outward manifestations of the Mississippi African American's lack of freedom and were in many ways the real reason for fighting the state's power structure.

African Americans' lack of political freedom in Mississippi was based to a large extent on their impoverishment, their low standard of education, and on their physical subjugation by the white power structure. The early movement had tried to ameliorate their condition by helping them gain the vote. However, by the end of 1963 it was apparent that this could only be achieved by federal intervention through the courts, as well as by involving economic and political groups on the national scene.

Furthermore, it was readily seen by civil rights workers that the Civil Rights Act of 1964 had little or no meaning for poverty-stricken Mississippi African Americans. The early movement felt that the answer to these problems was in attaining the vote and consequently focused its activities on voter registration and political action. Up to the end of 1964 it was felt that, if African Americans could win the vote, then they would be able to correct the economic injustices that locked them out of mainstream America.

Even though various efforts were made as early as the winter of 1962–63 to force Greenwood and Leflore County authorities to restore federal surplus commodities to Delta African Americans, the focus of the movement's programs was elsewhere. Again, during the summer of 1964, research was done by movement people with the idea of involving the federal government in helping the Mississippi African American in the economic sphere. Moreover, the fieldwork done by the Medical Committee for Human Rights revealed the appalling state of health and deprivation suffered by the community.

Nevertheless, positive action to correct these conditions was largely left in abeyance until 1965, even though SNCC and other civil rights groups did a great deal of groundwork in documenting the plight of the Mississippi African American. Those conditions of economic deprivation and educational benightedness in the Delta, and the rest of the state, became a major target of the Mississippi movement in 1965. The organization that moved into the Delta, and in doing so tried to fill the vacuum left by the fragmentation of the COFO coalition, was the Delta Ministry (DM) of the National Council of Churches (NCC).[86]

Even though the Delta Ministry was not formally created until September 1, 1964, the NCC made exploratory trips into the state as early as 1963, and some 40,000 white church people took part in the March on Washington. The NCC's Commission on Religion and Race (CORR) then sponsored a ministers' project in Hattiesburg in early 1964, and the NCC lobbied vigorously for the passage of the 1964 Civil Rights Act.[87] The NCC also financed the orientation sessions of the Mississippi Summer Project at Oxford, Ohio. During Freedom Summer, the Reverend Warren McKenna coordinated the volunteer work of 325 ministers and rabbis from the Jackson office of the NCC.[88] Nevertheless, Robert W. Spike, the director of CORR; Jack Pratt, a lawyer for the NCC; and Arthur Thomas, who became the field director of the Delta Ministry, all spoke for accepting the administration's compromise proposal at the Democratic National Convention and were later present at the September 18, 1964, meeting called by the NCC, where an effort was made to neutralize SNCC's power in the movement.[89]

While the churchmen took a liberal stance in 1964, the Delta Ministry quickly became more radical in its outlook. From an initial staff of five white ministers and an African American secretary who opened the ministry's office in Greenville in the fall of 1964, the group grew in 1967 to a staff of 7 whites and 27 African Americans, 25 of whom were Mississippi African Americans. Moreover, only 5 of the 34 were ministers; the rest were county directors of Freedom Corps groups and office personnel. (Curtis Hayes, who had been active with SNCC since 1961, was the Freedom Corps director.) As the staff drew closer to the local African American community—it was largely shut out of the white community—the Delta Ministry's position became more and more radical.[90]

Difficulties arose, however, because the ministers' group was financed by a representative of the NCC. The Delta Ministry many times found itself constrained by the conservative character of the national church body, but this effect was neutralized in part by contributions from the World Council of Churches.[91] Nevertheless, the Delta Ministry's ties with such a large and powerful organization enabled it to exert pressures in Washington where the civil rights groups had been unable to.

According to Bruce Hilton, the efficacy of the church group on a local level was largely based on the staff's personal commitment in trying to ameliorate the brutal living conditions of the Delta African American.[92] Hilton further states that the Delta Ministry "has also managed to stay nearly anonymous outside Mississippi, largely through its practice of working alongside—and giving public credit to—the local indigenous organizations. . . . [T]he Delta Ministry has been a model for . . . the church-funded mission agency that draws both its leadership and its agenda from the people themselves."[93]

Thus, the Delta Ministry in reality became synonymous with the movement. This in itself was an important step because the larger Mississippi movement was predicated upon the same philosophy, that the local people knew their own problems best and that, if they were to really achieve their freedom, it was imperative that they lead the struggle themselves. The help that groups like SNCC and COFO had provided in the past had been both in discovering and developing local leadership and in connecting that leadership with national political elements. The Delta Ministry continued SNCC and COFO's work in the state by giving its support to the MFDP and other local groups where it was needed.[94]

Any discussion of the Delta Ministry's activities in 1965 must naturally focus on the groups and programs it supported, even though it did do significant work on both the national and local levels in pressuring into action nine of eighteen Mississippi counties that had refused to distribute free federal surplus commodities in the past. Art Thomas, the field director of the Delta Ministry, helped accomplish this by arranging with the U.S. Department of Agriculture for his group to distribute the free food. When the county supervisors of the food programs discovered that the Delta Ministry was taking this program over, they petitioned the federal government to do the job themselves. Consequently, some 64,000 people were able to receive badly needed food that had never been available to them before. (Added pressures by the ministry on the federal government caused the program's expansion by the end of July 1965 to eighty of Mississippi's eighty-two counties, and by March 1966 it reached 500,000 people.)[95]

The Delta Ministry also became involved in the Head Start program of the Office of Economic Opportunity (OEO),[96] and the movement set up the Child Development Group of Mississippi (CDGM) with funding from OEO. This group provided jobs for 1,300 adults—mostly poor and African American—during the summer of 1965 in a pre-school program for some 6,000 schoolchildren in twenty-eight communities.[97]

The success of the program can be measured in the effort made by Senator Stennis in the fall of 1965 to block its refunding as a year-round project. Even though funds were held up until February 1966, CDGM pre-schools continued to operate, as the teachers and other workers volunteered their services without charge. Then, a budget of close to one million dollars per month was granted, providing for 2,000 poor African Americans to teach, feed, transport, and clean up after 12,000 children in 125 centers located in twenty-eight counties.[98] By this time, though, the white power structure had learned that there was no way to keep the OEO programs out of Mississippi; consequently, various counties made requests for similar programs in order to preempt movement-affiliated groups.

Apart from the Delta Ministry's specific involvement in CDGM—its headquarters was located in Edwards, Hinds County, at the Mt. Beulah Conference Center which the DM had leased—it was also the distribution center for federal surplus commodities. Part of the church group's staff also worked closely with the Mississippi Freedom Labor Union (MFLU). The MFLU was formally established on April 9, 1965, with George Shelton, of Shaw, as the state president.[99] It apparently grew out of discussions on how to meet the serious threat of eviction from Delta cotton plantations that were quickly adopting mechanical cotton pickers and chemical defoliants and therefore no longer needed massive numbers of farm laborers. (By the end of the 1960s, almost 95 percent of the cotton production was picked by machine, and stalks were cleaned away by chemicals.)

Thereafter, on May 31, twelve tractor drivers struck the A. L. Andrews plantation near Tribbett, in Washington County. They demanded $1.25 per hour instead of the $6.00 per day they were receiving. The twelve men and their families—eighty people—were then evicted; they set up tents on the land of Roosevelt Adams, the only independent African American farm owner in the Leland area (also in Washington County).[100] During the spring, the quarters of the strikers came to be generally known as Strike City. On June 3, the strike spread to the E. G. Thomas plantation in Duncan, Bolivar County. Unlike the first group of strikers, the Duncan group was made up of day laborers from Cleveland, the county seat of Bolivar County.[101] With support provided by COFO, the Delta Ministry, the National Council of Churches, and the MFDP, the strikes spread to Bolivar, Sunflower, Washington, Issaquena, Sharkey, and Holmes counties, involving 268 workers by September. Membership rose to well over 1,000.[102]

Even though the strikers knew they would never be allowed to return to work on these plantations, they probably felt they had nothing left to lose and that the strikes would serve as a further dramatization of the African American's economic plight. Moreover, during the summer Curtis Hayes, who had transferred from SNCC to the Delta Ministry, tried to raise $500,000 to buy land for the evicted farmers.[103] He was unable to raise the necessary money, but in 1966 both land and money were found to establish what came to be known as Freedom City, in Washington County. In 1967 the group, which had organized itself as the Poor People's Conference, received further funds, this time from OEO through a Delta Ministry project called the Delta Opportunities Corporation.[104]

The success of the MFLU led to further efforts in the economic sphere. The Freedom Now Brick Company, Inc., was established by Frank Smith, a former SNCC staff member;[105] an okra cooperative was set up near Batesville;[106] and sewing firms were founded in Canton and Indianola.[107] Then, on August 29, Jesse Morris, also of SNCC, called the first meeting of the Poor People's Corporation, which he had been building up to since the spring. By 1966 there were fifteen different cooperatives and groups that had become members of the organization.[108]

In its efforts to help various movement groups, the Delta Ministry opened up its facilities at the Mt. Beulah Conference Center to groups of evicted strikers affiliated with the MFLU, the cooperatives and businesses of the Poor People's Corporation, the CDGM (whose offices were located there in 1965, but before being refunded in 1966 it was forced to move to Jackson),[109] and other local and national civil rights groups.[110] The MFDP also worked closely with the Delta Ministry and from time to time used the Mt. Beulah facilities for meetings and state conventions.

Nevertheless, the campus at Mt. Beulah had been leased primarily as a retreat for Delta Ministry staff and as a training center for its prospective Freedom Corps county directors. The work of the latter individuals is described as follows: "This is responsible and specialized work involving direction of the program of the Delta Ministry Project in a specific county or similar area in Mississippi [and includes] relief, economic development, education, health, citizenship, culture, community centers, and farm program[s]."[111]

None of the county directors for the Delta Ministry, though, undertook all of the above programs. In Issaquena County work was done on the Head Start program, whereas in Washington County more attention was paid to welfare services, and so forth.

Sunflower County, which had a highly motivated political program under Mrs. Fannie Lou Hamer and the MFDP, continued to work in the political sphere.[112] On April 8, in Greenville, Federal District Court Judge Claude P. Clayton Jr. (Northern District, Mississippi), handed down a sweeping one-year injunction against Sunflower County Registrar Cecil C. Campbell that ordered him to register all those over twenty-one who met the state and local residency requirements. Furthermore, the registrar was ordered to reexamine past applications, file a monthly report with the Department of Justice and the court, give specific reasons for all rejections, make no distinctions based on race in registering voters, and process no less than four applicants at a time.[113]

Judge Clayton's injunction led to impressive results in the two-week period that followed: over three hundred people registered at a rate of thirty to forty per day. Thus, it was not surprising that on May 1 firebombs were thrown at a Sunflower County Freedom House as well as the homes of three people associated with the movement, two of which were completely destroyed.[114] During April, MFDP lawyers also filed a petition with Judge Clayton asking him to postpone municipal elections in Drew, Rome, Doddsville, Sunflower City, Iverness, Ruleville, and Moorhead in order to give Sunflower County African

Americans time to register and thus participate in those elections. Even though the request was denied, the court stated, "if the suit were filed again under less hurried circumstances, it had the right to throw out the elections and call for new ones."[115] On March 11, 1966, just such a decision was handed down by the U.S. Fifth Circuit Court of Appeals in *Mrs. Fannie Lou Hamer v. Cecil C. Campbell, Circuit Clerk and Registrar of Sunflower County.*[116]

Political programs aimed at becoming part of the established political institutions of Mississippi were also conducted in other towns in conjunction with municipal elections. One of three women succeeded in getting on the ballot in Greenwood, one African American entered the special election for city selectman in McComb, two men failed to get on the ballot in Moss Point and Shaw respectively, and one woman attempted to qualify for a place on the city council in Meridian.[117]

In addition to these political programs, African American farmers also nominated candidates in the Agricultural Stabilization and Conservation Service (ASCS) committee elections in December 1964 and December 1965. These particular elections are conducted yearly throughout the South under the auspices of the U.S. Department of Agriculture's crop restriction program. They determine how much land a farmer can cultivate for cotton, corn, and other federally controlled crops, and they are open to all farmers who own their own land. Even though African American farmers ran for ASCS posts in fourteen counties in 1964, their success was minimal due to a great deal of intimidation before the elections and at the polls. This was particularly so in Madison County—with 40 percent of the land owned by small black farmers—where National CORE Community Relations Director Marvin Rich was insulted by former Governor Ross Barnett and later had his nose broken by whites.[118]

After the ASCS elections in 1964, movement people and supporters filed complaints with the Department of Agriculture, the Department of Justice, and the U.S. Commission on Civil Rights.[119] As a result, the 1965 elections were conducted through the mails rather than in person. Consequently, in 1965 African Americans put up 243 candidates in fifty-three communities in twenty different counties. Incidents of vote fraud, however, were reported, as were economic pressures.[120]

In fact, though, the movement in 1965 had moved away from protest politics and into the realm of real politics, the world of compromise, as had been demonstrated by Aaron Henry at the Democratic National Convention in 1964. Local people had supported the National Democratic platform and ticket in

November 1964, and they took the same steps in 1965 and afterward to gain a place in the Mississippi political establishment.

The major political campaign that was conducted by the movement in 1965 centered on the special session of the Mississippi State Legislature in June, which was called to revise the voter registration laws before Congress could pass the Voting Rights Bill.[121] In a matter of weeks the following legislation was rammed through:

1. a bill allowing counties to choose their five supervisors at large;
2. a constitutional amendment empowering the legislature, by a two-thirds vote, to merge any two counties;
3. the Delta Congressional district was divided into three pieces [to make] each piece . . . overwhelmingly white in population;
4. machinery set up to make the office of county superintendent of schools appointive;
5. a law disqualifying anyone who votes in the June primary from running as an independent in the fall general election;
6. qualifying fees and number of certified signatures needed to become a candidate raised;
7. a law moving the date for qualification to forty-eight hours after the law was passed—and stiffening the requirements for qualification.[122]

In addition to the above-mentioned legislation, voter registration forms were shortened to include only nine simple questions dealing with name, address, age, length of residence in state, county, and municipality, possible commission of felonies, as well as an oath.[123] White Mississippi knew, as the movement did, that even though the new legislation would permit thousands of African Americans to register to vote, it was the only possible way to cut down on the number of federal examiners who would probably be sent to the state after the passage of the new federal voting-rights bill. Furthermore, if federal examiners were appointed in large numbers to the state—every Mississippi county was eligible under the bill then in Congress—a very large percentage of the African American population would probably be able to register quickly. Federal examiners would not check any literacy qualifications whatsoever, whereas even the most simplified Mississippi requirements would require African Americans to fill out their applications without help.

Thus, the movement timed its political action program of protest demon-

TABLE 4

Voting-Age Population for Congressional Districts, by Race, 1960

CONGRESSIONAL DISTRICTS PRIOR TO REDISTRICTING IN 1966

Congressional District	Voting-Age Population (1960)	White Voting-Age Population (1960)	Nonwhite Voting-Age Population (1960)	% Nonwhite of Voting-Age Population
1st C.D.	204,244	150,434	53,810	26.3
2nd C.D.	306,463	147,031	159,432	52.0
3rd C.D.	251,022	149,322	101,700	40.5
4th C.D.	163,838	107,509	56,329	34.4
5th C.D.	244,955	193,970	50,985	20.8
Total	1,170,522	748,266	422,256	36.1

CONGRESSIONAL DISTRICTS AFTER REDISTRICTING IN 1966

Congressional District	Voting-Age Population (1960)	White Voting-Age Population (1960)	Nonwhite Voting-Age Population (1960)	% Nonwhite of Voting-Age Population
1st C.D.	233,981	130,271	103,710	44.3
2nd C.D.	228,948	146,750	82,198	35.9
3rd C.D.	234,705	141,724	92,981	39.6
4th C.D.	227,933	135,551	92,382	40.5
5th C.D.	244,955	193,970	50,985	20.8
Total	1,170,522	748,266	422,256	36.1

Sources: U.S. Commission on Civil Rights, Political Participation (Washington, D.C., 1968); computations based on table 9, pp. 244–47.

Note: The Mississippi Freedom Democratic Party and several Black plaintiffs filed a complaint before a three-judge Federal District Court, which they later amended when the Mississippi State Legislature changed its redistricting plan in 1966 (Connor v. Johnson, 11 Race Rel. L. Rep. 1859 [S.D. Miss. 1966]). Their complaint challenged the validity of the new legislation on the grounds that it was racially motivated and that the redistricting failed to follow the boundaries of the economic, geological, and geographic regions of the state. Furthermore, even though nonwhites made up 42.3 percent of the state's population, by the redistricting plan they would not be able to send their own representative to the U.S. House of Representatives, which according to the prior district lines had been a possibility. The old Second Congressional District was 52 percent nonwhite by voting population, but it was divided among the First, Second, and Fourth congressional districts under the new plan. Nevertheless, when the plaintiffs appealed to the U.S. Supreme Court (Appellants' Jurisdictional Statement at 4, Connor v. Johnson, 386 U.S. 483 [1967]), the lower-court judgment was affirmed summarily, without hearing oral argument and without opinion. Mr. Justice Douglas was the lone dissenter. The Delta and its adjacent counties (see table 1) had a voting age population of 293,021, of which 161,517 (55.1 percent) were nonwhite and only 131,504 (44.9 percent) were white in 1960. These twenty counties included thirteen Delta counties and seven counties whose demographic, agricultural, economic, and geographic circumstances were similar to the Delta's.

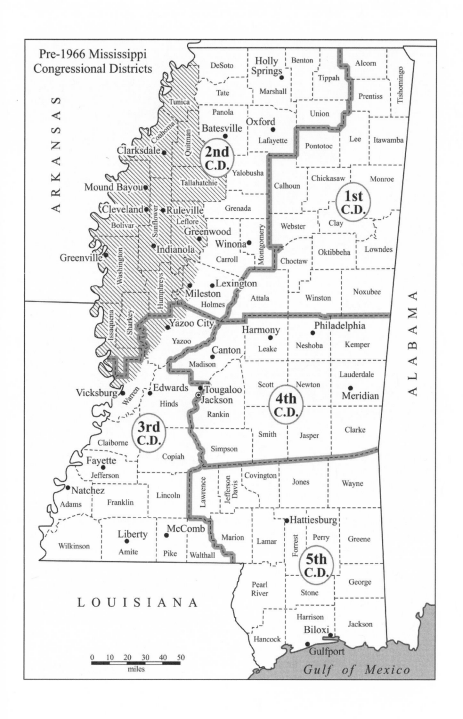

Pre-1966 Mississippi
Congressional Districts

ARKANSAS

ALABAMA

LOUISIANA

Gulf of Mexico

DeSoto · Holly Springs · Benton · Alcorn · Tishomingo

Tunica · Tate · Marshall · Tippah · Prentiss

Panola · Union

Coahoma · Quitman · Batesville · Oxford · Lee · Itawamba

Clarksdale · Lafayette · Pontotoc

2nd C.D.

Yalobusha · Chickasaw · Monroe

Mound Bayou · Tallahatchie · Calhoun

Cleveland · Ruleville · Grenada · Clay

Bolivar · Leflore · Webster · 1st C.D.

Sunflower · Greenwood · Oktibbeha · Lowndes

Greenville · Indianola · Winona · Carroll · Choctaw

Washington · Humphreys · Lexington · Attala · Winston · Noxubee

Mileston · Holmes

Issaquena · Sharkey · Yazoo City · Harmony · Philadelphia

Yazoo · Leake · Neshoba · Kemper

Canton · Madison

Lauderdale

Vicksburg · Edwards · Tougaloo Jackson · Scott · Newton · Meridian

Warren · Hinds · Rankin · 4th C.D.

3rd C.D.

Claiborne · Smith · Jasper · Clarke

Copiah · Simpson

Fayette · Jefferson

Natchez · Lincoln · Covington · Jones · Wayne

Adams · Franklin · Lawrence · Jefferson Davis

Hattiesburg

Liberty · McComb · Marion · Lamar · Perry · Greene

Wilkinson · Amite · Pike · Walthall · Forrest

5th C.D.

Pearl River · Stone · George

Harrison · Jackson

Hancock · Biloxi · Gulfport

0 10 20 30 40 50
miles

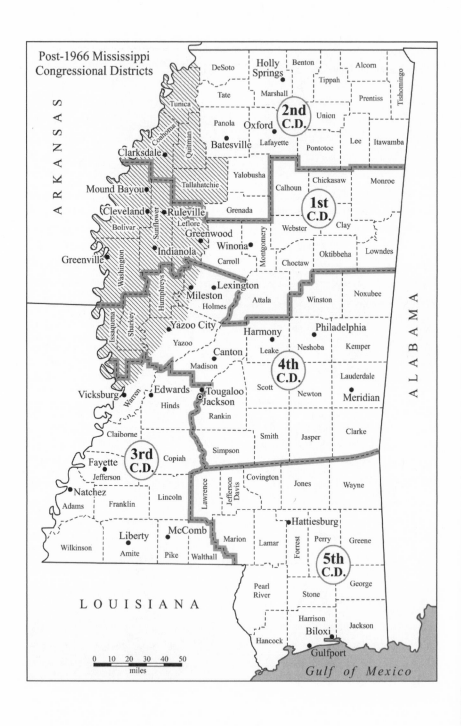

Post-1966 Mississippi Congressional Districts

strations to coincide with the opening of the special session of the state legislature on June 14.[124] The protest action was conducted simultaneously with similar demonstrations in Washington, charging that, since the state representatives had been elected by an overwhelmingly white electorate, the special session was illegal. The MFDP organized the Jackson demonstrations with the support of some of the 200 summer volunteers SNCC had sent to Mississippi, as well as the help provided by the Delta Ministry.[125] Between June 14 and 18, 856 demonstrators were arrested on charges of parading without a permit and distributing leaflets without a permit. The 100 arrested juveniles were released quickly, but the others were locked up at the Jackson state fairgrounds.[126]

On June 22, three members of CORR of the NCC filed charges against the police for brutality, as did Dr. David M. French of the Medical Committee for Human Rights.[127] Some 60 of the internees also signed statements charging police brutality. By June 24, the Lawyers Constitutional Defense Committee (LCDC) had put up enough bail to release all but those who wished to remain in jail—about 224 of the demonstrators. The same day, 70 demonstrators were arrested on charges of breach of the peace after publicly protesting against police brutality.[128]

Then on June 30, a three-judge Federal District Court in New Orleans issued a temporary restraining order barring Jackson officials from arresting voting-rights demonstrators under the city parade and leafleting ordinances. Three days of peaceful protest marches followed on July 1–3. The last day of the marches was observed closely by local and federal officers, as the demonstrators marched two abreast for two hours past the state capitol, the governor's mansion, and through downtown Jackson. Only one arrest was made on July 3, when a white attacked one of the march leaders.[129]

On August 6, President Johnson signed the Voting Rights Bill of 1965 into law. The following day the Justice Department filed suit in Federal District Court in Jackson against the use of the two-dollar poll tax in state and local elections. (This device was judged and outlawed in *U.S. v. Mississippi* in 1966.)[130] Then on August 17, White Mississippi moved to protect itself against the impending onslaught of African American voters by overwhelmingly supporting a referendum that gave formal approval to a constitutional amendment enabling the state legislature to combine any two counties, thus assuring a white majority in most if not all districts.[131] Thereafter, African American registration rose quickly throughout the state, but not fast enough to seriously affect the 1966 Democratic primaries.[132]

Apart from the political and economic campaigns of the MFDP, the Delta Ministry, the MFLU, the Poor People's Conference, and the Poor People's Corporation, the Mississippi movement conducted one other sustained campaign of significance during 1965. It began after August 27, when the car of George Metcalfe, the local head of the Natchez NAACP, was bombed and Metcalfe critically injured. Shortly thereafter, Governor Johnson sent 650 National Guardsmen into the city to maintain order. Then, on September 7, Johnson felt sure enough about the situation to begin withdrawing the troops. Protest marches followed quickly after that, and on September 30 the Chancery Court issued an injunction against street protests attacking segregated public facilities and other discriminatory practices.[133]

Taking the challenge in hand, Charles Evers, the Mississippi state field secretary of the NAACP, led a series of protests from October 1 to 7, during which 544 demonstrators were arrested for violating the injunction. Some 265 of them were sent to Parchman State Penitentiary—two hundred miles north of Natchez —including Evers. After spending five days in jail, the demonstrators were then released on two hundred dollars' bail each. On October 7, Evers called a temporary halt to the demonstrations in order to allow time for negotiations with city officials. Nevertheless, an economic boycott of the downtown shopping district—which had started earlier—was continued. By October 12, Mayor John Nosser indicated that business was down between 25 and 50 percent.[134]

On October 13, African American leaders began to negotiate with the city, but when a statement of the terms that had been agreed upon during the talks was read at an African American rally, the mayor quickly issued a denial. Consequently, on October 16, Evers made a show of strength by conducting a march of some 600 protestors. He then suspended all further marches during the remainder of October but continued the economic boycott.[135]

Finally, on December 3, the boycott was also suspended as the city agreed to meet the African American community's demands. The points agreed upon included provision for African American policemen, an African American school board member, a biracial housing commission, integration at the local hospital, and that city employees were to address adult African Americans by the courtesy titles of "Mr.," "Miss," and "Mrs." Nevertheless, when a fight broke out between a white man and seven African American picketers on December 22 and was stopped by the police, Evers called for a resumption of the economic boycott because of alleged police brutality.[136]

Charles Evers's economic campaign in Natchez was only the beginning of his serious and sustained civil rights and political activities in the state. But, even though he had taken over for his murdered brother Medgar Evers in 1963 as state field secretary for the NAACP, Charles Evers did not really emerge as a militant and active leader in Mississippi until 1965. Up until then he had been forced to operate within the shadow of COFO and the MFDP. After 1965, he and Aaron Henry began to fill the political vacuum left by the demise of COFO and the withdrawal of SNCC and CORE from the state. Furthermore, unlike the people connected with the MFDP, Evers and Henry were prone to operate within the realm of politics and compromise rather than conduct campaigns of protest politics based mainly on issues that were aimed at achieving moral victories.[137]

Thus, even though the movement had not won the war by the end of 1965, the closed society of Mississippi had begun to show cracks in its monolithic structure. The iceberg had begun to melt, and the light of freedom began to shine in. The incessant attack of the movement and the mounting pressures exerted by the federal government and the national liberal community finally combined in 1965 to force White Mississippi to retreat somewhat and reorganize in the face of the enemy, which was freedom.

Nevertheless, at that very moment, the movement paused before its final victory drive. The attacking forces fragmented and weakened while on the threshold of achieving what they sought to do in Mississippi: pry open the closed society and force it to become part of twentieth-century America. White Mississippi was given time to regroup. The national liberal establishment had decided it had too much to lose by giving the radical forces of the freedom movement free reign in the nether land of Mississippi.

The Freedom Revolution would have to be a revolution of law, of civil rights, not a quick overthrowing of the white power structure. And the African American people would have to create their place in Mississippi by operating within the framework of the law. It was not to be a routing of the white power structure using moral protest shored up by federal law. There would be no Second Reconstruction and invasion of the South by the federal government. No military occupation. The U.S. Congress and the Johnson administration wrote the new rules of the war: evolution, not revolution. Mississippi was given time to breathe.

The delay in delivering the final blow to the closed society gave White Mississippi just enough time to reorganize itself and thus create an image of apparent conformity with the demands of the federal government and the nation.

Voter registration laws were rewritten to "allow" Mississippi African Americans to register to vote, but district lines were redrawn to nullify that vote.[138] Time had been gained. The white power structure was able to make provisions for a new African American electorate. When the federal poverty programs came, White Mississippi quickly learned that it had either to co-opt those programs or let them be run by the movement. By late 1965 it had learned its lesson well; the power structure chose to co-opt them and thereby lessen their ameliorative effects on African Americans.

Thus, it might be said that in 1965 Mississippi was in a state of ferment that would determine the war of the future. The white power structure made a tactical retreat in order to get the nation off its back and at the same time to make sure that African American Mississippi would not have too much of a say in that future. The movement continued its war, but largely alone.[139] By the end of 1965, the nation had passed it by and had gone on to worry about other matters like the war in Vietnam. The Freedom Revolution was left to work within Mississippi law, and White Mississippi had time and the law on its side.

Conclusions

Lord, we ain't what we wanna be—we ain't what we gonna be—but, thank God, we ain't what we was.

—SAYING ON THE WALL OF THE COFO OFFICE IN JACKSON

Their cause must become our cause too. Because it is not just Negroes, but really it is all of us, who must overcome the crippling legacy of bigotry and injustice.

And we shall overcome. . . .

But we will not accept the pace of stifled rights, the order imposed by fear, or the unity that stifles protest. For peace cannot be purchased at the cost of liberty. . . .

Because all Americans must have the right to vote. And we are going to give them that right.

All Americans must have the privileges of citizenship regardless of race. And they are going to have those privileges of citizenship regardless of race.

—LYNDON BAINES JOHNSON TO A JOINT SESSION
OF CONGRESS, MARCH 15, 1965

By 1965 the movement's fight seemed to be the nation's. This condition passed quickly, however, as the country and the student-supported movement became caught up in the controversy over the meaning of Black Power,[1] the allocation of funds for the War on Poverty, and the moral issues of the Vietnam War. The Mississippi movement was given its brief moment in the national spotlight, but its time was too short to mount enough pressure against the Mississippi power structure to overthrow it. After 1965 the Mississippi movement returned to being a local affair—as it had been before 1960. Nevertheless, the years 1960–65 mark a watershed in African American history, both on a national level and on the local level in Mississippi. During that period Mississippi was revealed to the country and the world as an example of southern white intransigency and totalitarian suppression of minority rights. Mississippi's African American struggle was briefly revealed to the nation, and hope for change welled up in hearts thought to be apathetic and uncaring. People overcame fears and confronted their oppressors, and cracks appeared in the monolithic, closed society called Mississippi. In reality, however, this was only a beginning to the weakening of white supremacist rule in the state.[2]

After 1965, African American Mississippians were largely left alone to translate the gains of 1960–65 into real progress toward becoming full Mississippians. That story, important as it is, has been left untold because it is essentially the period after the civil rights movement's concerted efforts in the state. By 1965 the legal battle for civil rights legislation on a national level had largely been won, even though the Civil Rights Act of 1968 did include a long-delayed protection clause for civil rights workers involved in voter registration.

The Mississippi civil rights movement quickly became a local struggle to overcome poverty, educational inferiority, and the lack of political power within the state. Counties where the movement had developed extensively and where it was locally based remained the strongest locations of African American community activity, with rare exceptions. According Kenneth T. Andrews, there is a close correlation between the amount of movement activity in Mississippi counties and the degree of continued activity after 1965. Andrews points us to the conclusion that, where an active local movement developed before 1965, then even after COFO broke up and SNCC and CORE ceased activity in the state, local people continued to look after their own needs. In many cases they were joined by middle-class African Americans who had not previously been involved in the movement, and together they developed their own leadership cadres. This was certainly true in Holmes Country, which in 1967 sent the first African American, Robert Clark, to the state legislature since Reconstruction.[3]

Throughout this study of the Mississippi movement I have striven to substantiate the problems that confronted African Americans in Mississippi in their battle to become first-class citizens in a closed society. That battle was a slow and dangerous struggle against the Mississippi power structure that obdurately refused to give up its stranglehold over local African Americans. Furthermore, the federal government dragged its feet during 1960–65 until a national consensus pressured it into passing the 1964 Civil Rights Act and the 1965 Voting Rights Act. Nevertheless, even after the passage of these laws and the creation of the War on Poverty, the Mississippi power structure was able to reorganize and successfully block efforts by the local movement to elect African American representatives to city, county, state, and national office well into the 1980s as well as regain and keep control of federal economic programs.

A possible reason for this was that, up until the summer of 1964, the problems of African Americans in Mississippi were considered local ones to be dealt with on a local level rather than matters of national concern. Thus, the southern student-supported civil rights movement stood between southern white resistance and federal passivity. The movement's job, in many ways, was a straightforward one: to force the federal government to recognize that the African American's fight for freedom was a national problem and that that problem was essentially the winning of the American Dream for southern African Americans. After 1965, Mississippi's African Americans' problem was no longer one of civil rights within the framework of the U.S. Constitution and federal law, but one of poverty, ignorance, and power on the local level.

African American Mississippians' objectives changed from "Freedom Now" to local "Black Empowerment." That realigning of goals after 1965 represents the essential result of the Freedom Revolution, not because Mississippi African Americans had solved their problems of freedom but because they had undergone a spiritual transformation that enabled them to stand before the nation at the Democratic National Convention in August 1964 and the U.S. Congress in 1965 and demand what was rightfully due them under the U.S. Constitution.

Many lines of development were inextricably intertwined in the Mississippi movement. Any examination of that movement had to first of all compare the outward spiritual state of the African American community at the beginning of the period in 1960, and then again at the end, in 1965. Thereafter, one must visualize the interaction of the following elements: (1) the organic development of the movement leading up to the establishment of parallel, protest institutions that enabled African American Mississippi to verbalize its longing to be free; (2) the position of the federal government vis-à-vis the movement and the Mississippi power structure; (3) the building of a national consensus for change in the South; (4) the involvement of large numbers of northern whites in the southern civil rights movement; and (5) the strategies, priorities, and processes of decision-making within the general civil rights movement as well as the Mississippi movement. Additionally, the interaction of these disparate and, in many cases, counterproductive elements led to a basic change in Mississippi African Americans themselves. And even though that change only became truly visible to the observer when African Americans were finally able to register to vote in massive numbers—after August 1965—the years 1960–65 reveal more than adequate proof of the spiritual awakening of African American Mississippians and their resolve to stand up to the white power structure and demand their rights under law.

Thus, when Bob Moses went to Mississippi in 1960 and 1961 and disappeared into the rural areas, he began the process of bringing the United States to Mississippi African Americans.[4] That process was a long, drawn-out one because rural African Americans were basically isolated and benighted figures who during the years after the Civil War and the end of Reconstruction never managed to fully throw off the fetters of slavery, even though their freedom had been promised them under the Fourteenth and Fifteenth amendments to the U.S. Constitution. Together with rural African Americans' state of ignorance, oppression, and poverty was the added problem of their fear of moving out of "their place."[5]

The movement tried to break the white power structure's hold over the African American community; the southern power structure attempted to maintain that stranglehold. One of the movement's many victories in the South was that it was able to free the southern African American spiritually, if not materially.

Bob Moses's philosophy of going to the people and losing himself among them was one of the basic elements of strategy of the struggle for "Freedom Now." However, because such a strategy involved getting local African Americans to understand and then voice their discontent, the battle was a long process of unchaining the African American community and getting it to join forces with the movement in confronting the white power structure.

During the years 1960–65 the movement was driven out of the conventional channels of American democracy and slowly found its way into a network of parallel political institutions that were set up to give voice to African American protest. That process was a step-by-step organic evolution of strategies from the direct action of sit-ins and freedom rides to voter registration campaigns aimed at winning direct participation for Mississippi African Americans in their state's political machinery to the establishment of parallel, protest structures aimed at pressuring White Mississippi into allowing African American Mississippi its rightful place in the state community.[6]

During those years it became adequately clear to the movement—if not to the nation—that "the Opposition" was not just White Mississippi but also the federal government, which when it moved to help African American Mississippi did so only after considerable pressures had been mounted against it by the movement. The appendix (see below) indicates that there was more than adequate statutory power to force the Mississippi power structure into guaranteeing the African American community its freedom. Nevertheless, Congress and the Democratic administrations of Kennedy and Johnson moved very slowly in passing the 1964 Civil Rights Act. And the movement was forced to press its battle through the slow-moving local, state, and federal courts.[7]

Furthermore, the U.S. Commission on Civil Rights, which was established in 1957 to investigate denials of civil rights and make recommendations to the president and Congress for possible remedial legislation, had its Mississippi hearings postponed from 1962 to 1965. This was in spite of the extreme urgency for the hearings to be held. It is impossible to know what their restraining effect would have been on the Mississippi power structure if they had been held earlier, but Mississippi Governor Paul Johnson's words to the commission in February 1965 seem to indicate that, if the hearings had been held when they were first called for, a great deal of bloodshed would have been prevented.[8]

Additionally, the promises made by Democratic National Committee representatives and the Department of Justice—in unofficial meetings with movement representatives in 1961—convinced the Mississippi movement that the most effective course of action would be through voter registration activities. Nevertheless, by the fall of 1963 foundation funds for nonpartisan political action—voter registration work—had been cut off and it had proved largely impossible to register new African American voters. Furthermore, the protection promised by the Department of Justice for voter registration workers for the most part failed to materialize.

Thus, by late summer 1963 the movement began to put into practice its first steps in the field of parallel, protest politics. Those steps were primarily aimed at two audiences: the local African American community, in getting it to symbolically participate in the political process and give that participation significance for them; and the nation, in building up pressure on the federal government to direct action against the Mississippi power structure.

African American Mississippi was successfully reached and drawn into direct support of the movement during the fall of 1963 in the first Freedom Vote, during the Freedom Summer of 1964, and in the protest actions of the Mississippi Freedom Democratic Party (MFDP) in 1964 and 1965. And the mounting of a national consensus in support of the Mississippi and general southern civil rights movements is visible in President Johnson's "We Shall Overcome" speech in March 1965 and the passage of the 1964 Civil Rights Act and the 1965 Voting Rights Act.

The forging of that national consensus, which forced the federal government to act on the demands of African American Mississippi and the movement, is to be seen within the evolving strategies of the movement. The evolution of those strategies was closely connected with such external factors as the nature and actions of the white power structure and the promises of federal protection and support, as well as the promises of various national political groups.

A complete picture of how and why the movement changed its tactics from direct action and voter registration to protest, parallel politics must ultimately be seen in the movement's desire to advertise to the nation and the world the deplorable state of Mississippi African Americans. Being unable to force the existing political machine of Mississippi to let the African American community take part in the closed society, the student-supported movement turned to establishing parallel, or "mock," political institutions to demonstrate that Mississippi African Americans were vitally interested in participating in political life, and furthermore, that they were being prohibited from doing so by methods of violence, legal obstructionism, and physical as well as economic intimidation.

In spite of the justice in the African American community's demands, if whites had not become involved in large numbers in the Mississippi movement, then national public opinion would not have been aroused enough to create the necessary pressures on the federal government. The place of whites in the movement, though, is problematic at best, particularly after the movement turned to Black Power slogans and programs of Black Nationalism. For me, it goes without saying that the presence of over eighty white Yale and Stanford students in Mississippi during the first Freedom Vote and the participation of large numbers of white volunteers and white-dominated support groups in the Mississippi Summer Project in 1964 both created the necessary pressures on the federal government and the liberal elements in the national news media and public to bring about the Freedom Revolution.

Nevertheless, that revolution, if it can be called such, largely had to take place in the hearts and minds of southern African Americans if it were to prove efficacious. Here, then, lies the problematic nature of the relationship between African Americans and whites in the movement. One can easily believe that the struggle for freedom in the South is not just an African American problem but also a white one, and not just a southern problem but a national one. What then was the African American's place in that battle, and what was the white's place?

Obviously, rural African Americans' part in the movement was that of oppressed people trying to throw off their oppressor. Nevertheless, when Bob Moses and other movement workers entered Mississippi in 1960 and 1961, it quickly became apparent that the overwhelming majority of African American Mississippi was in such a state of repression that the first stage of any civil rights campaign there would have to be an effort to reach the community and give it a reason to fight for its freedom. Furthermore, local African Americans generally acted as if any and all whites were their superiors and masters in order to survive in this closed society.

Thus, during the years 1960–63 the place of the white man in the Mississippi movement was at best marginal. This initial period, then, was in fact a time of drawing African Americans out of their shell of apparent apathy—in reality, fear of the white man—and giving them a reason to openly fight the white power structure, no matter the cost.

Most probably a crucial breakthrough for the African American community was made in Greenwood after James Travis was critically injured on February 28, 1963. During the winter preceding the shooting, the movement had mounted a successful food-and-clothing drive that brought many African Americans in the Delta to the SNCC office in Greenwood after the local white power structure had cut off federal surplus commodities. The movement's decision to send in workers from all over the state after the shooting represented a change in policy—the movement having left southwest Mississippi in the fall of 1961 after facing harassment and considerable violence—a change that was symbolic of the decision to move in and weather white terror tactics.

This movement decision to become one with the people thereafter led to a swelling of the numbers of African Americans in the Delta who decided to go to county courthouses and confront "the man" at the seat of his power. Nevertheless, in spite of the movement's obdurate confrontation with the local power structure, little or no progress was made in registering new voters.

At this point the idea of "vote-ins," "votes for Freedom," and "Freedom Votes" was put forward and adopted. Being unable to crack the closed society on a local level, the movement probably decided to try to bring national pressure upon the Mississippi establishment. Whatever the case, the decision to hold parallel, protest elections during the late summer and early fall of 1963 did create the beginnings of national concern for the plight of Mississippi African Americans. The key to arousing this concern, though, had more to do with the harassment and attack of the white volunteers who came to help in the Freedom Vote than with the already well-established pattern of intimidation and violence against African Americans and civil rights workers.

When plans for the Mississippi Summer Project were debated during the winter of 1963 and spring of 1964, the fact of the national liberal community's concern for northern white college students working with the southern movement under conditions of violence and intimidation was not forgotten. This, then, was African American Mississippi's means of contact with the outside world. Even if this might be considered a cynical exploitation of white faces and influence, the fact remains that the triple lynching of Schwerner, Chaney, and Goodman aroused a firestorm in the national news media and the northern liberal community, whereas the murders of Herbert Lee, Medgar Evers, Louis Allen, and countless other Mississippi African Americans had not.

The position of the white man in the Mississippi movement after the summer of 1964 can be seen on two levels: (1) as psychologically inhibiting local African Americans from rising to positions of leadership and decision-making in their communities by the fact of whites' far superior education and training; and (2) as no longer being essential as organizers in the Mississippi movement, as well as being against strong leadership from non-Mississippi African Americans (e.g., Jim Forman) and as being for an ineffectual and mystical philosophy of "freedom high" and extreme participatory democracy. In addition, it should be remembered that because of the long years of being led by the white community and directed in religion by a conservative African American clergy, the rural Mississippi African American was little prone to move against the white power structure without strong outside leadership. Moreover, even though a considerable body of local African American leaders did develop comparatively quickly, the main source of funds for the Mississippi movement was a northern liberal community that was little able to understand the rural African American's plight until after it had been primed in its understanding by such figures as James Farmer and Martin Luther King Jr.

The question of strong outside and nationally oriented leadership of the southern civil rights movement—as opposed to locally oriented leadership—raised another problem that created serious conflicts. That problem was strategy: whether a civil rights group should quietly and effectively move into a rural community and slowly build a widely based grassroots organization or whether massive demonstrations should be used to dramatize the southern African American's plight to the nation. The Mississippi movement, which was overwhelmingly influenced by the guerrilla-warfare infiltration tactics of SNCC, grew slowly but surely into a statewide phenomenon in 1965. Although the tactics of Martin Luther King's SCLC were much more dramatic, they never did lead to the establishment of a statewide civil rights movement in Alabama.

Nevertheless, it is difficult to question the efficacy of either of these types of strategy when examining their place in the general civil rights movement. The tactics of a Martin Luther King or a James Farmer led to massive infusions of money into the southern movement that enabled the Mississippi movement to finance the Freedom Summer of 1964, the challenge at the Democratic National Convention in 1964, and the Congressional Challenge on the opening day of the U.S. Congress in 1965.

Furthermore, even though the strategies and decision-making processes of such groups as the NAACP and SCLC tended to be more conservative and more attuned to the liberal-labor community than those of SNCC and CORE, the NAACP's Legal Defense and Educational Fund played an important role in the legal battle fought by the general civil rights movement, and the mass demonstrations of SCLC in Birmingham and Selma—supported by the other civil rights groups—were certainly important in creating the necessary atmosphere for forcing through civil rights legislation. If civil rights groups like SCLC and the NAACP were largely out of contact with the rural African American communities of the Black Belt South, it is of little import. The grassroots-based groups like SNCC and CORE filled this important gap.

Moreover, it is difficult to imagine that figures such as Mrs. Fannie Lou Hamer would have had such a powerful impact on the nation if groups such as Martin Luther King's had not presented the general message of the southern African American's plight to the country. Additionally, even though there were intra-movement conflicts over how to divide up the funds donated to the movement and as to which strategies were most appropriate in specific cases, there was definite agreement on what the goals of the civil rights movement were during the years 1960–65.

After 1965, this agreement over objectives began to break down, the movement began to fragment and divide into radical and moderate wings, and the momentum of 1960–65 was irretrievably lost. This foundering of the movement was at least in part connected with the search for new goals after the passage of the 1964 Civil Rights Act and the 1965 Voting Rights Act; the controversy over the definition of what exactly Black Power meant; and the definition of what type of course the movement was to take, whether it was to be a gradual legalistic approach or a radical revolutionary one aimed at confronting the southern white power structure both morally and physically and overthrowing it.

It has been seen that this conflict over strategy split the Mississippi movement in 1965, as the NAACP and SCLC left COFO, and SNCC and CORE gradually withdrew from the state and left the MFDP to continue its efforts alone. And when the Delta Ministry's work in Mississippi slackened after 1966, it gradually became apparent to the MFDP that it could not fight the Mississippi power structure alone. Thus, by 1968 the radical strategies of SNCC and CORE, as well as the MFDP, had passed from the scene, as the latter group saw that it had no choice but to join the more moderate civil rights, labor, fraternal, social, and political groups in forming the Loyal Democrats of Mississippi to challenge and successfully unseat the regular Mississippi Democratic Party at the 1968 Democratic National Convention in Chicago.[9]

Another possible reason for the dissipation of the movement's momentum after 1965—aside from the changing tactics of the Mississippi power structure—can be seen in the necessity for the movement to operate on a strictly local level in trying to win a place for African Americans in the local power structure. This battle, by its very nature, was of considerably less interest to a national audience. Furthermore, such a battle was based on small and barely visible gains on the local front that went largely unnoticed by the outsider, even though the number of elected African American officials in Mississippi did grow rapidly after 1965.

In contrast with the years after 1965, those that preceded it were fraught with dramatic representations to the nation of the southern African American's inequalities. And finally, African American Mississippi's struggle after 1965 was no longer much different from the one fought by African Americans throughout the United States, inasmuch as it was pointed at overcoming conditions of unequal education and poverty and aimed at winning a place for itself as a minority group in a white-oriented but pluralistic society.

In conclusion, what I have termed "protest politics in the closed society" was a step-by-step process of organizing African American Mississippi and making audible the cries of a people to be free. Moreover, it should be clear that the Mississippi power structure and the federal government played major roles in that struggle. The building of a national consensus for change in Mississippi and in the South generally brought the necessary pressures to bear on the federal government, thus forcing it out of a stance of passivity into a position of civil rights activism.

By the end of 1965, a spiritual revolution had taken place in the minds and hearts of African American Mississippians. The years that came after were years of trying to translate that revolution of rising expectations into concrete gains at the ballot box and gradual improvement in the economic, educational, and social condition of the African American community in Mississippi.[10]

Afterword

The years after 1965 were truly years of change for Mississippi's African Americans. Change came slowly, but it came through ongoing legal battles throughout the 1960s, 1970s, and 1980s. It came on the backs of local movement people who fought the white power structure's constant efforts in rewriting state laws through redistricting, gerrymandering, pairing white majorities with African American counties, changing positions from elective to appointive, and generally instituting legal mechanisms that inhibited the empowerment of African American public officials. In the end the white power structure's efforts failed as they were overturned in the state and federal courts. However, this process took many years, and only in 1986 did Mississippians finally elect an African American to the reconstituted Second Congressional District in the Delta.

This continuing fight has led to the election and appointment of more African American officials than in any other state. The local movement has remained active, and such people as Hollis Watkins, Lawrence Guyot, Leslie McLemore, Charles McLauren, Dorie and Joyce Ladner, Owen Brooks, Brenda Travis, Reverend Willie Blue, Ben Chaney, L. C. Dorsey, Euvester Simpson, Jesse Harris, George Greene, Bobby Talbert and Lafayette Surney, along with many others, are still working for change. Mrs. Fannie Lou Hamer stayed active until her death in 1977, and other activists have also worked toward economic progress for many years. Even outside SNCC and CORE, activists such as Bob Moses and Dave Dennis, who were the project director and assistant project director for COFO, returned to the state to create projects to improve the condition of African Americans.

The substantive change brought about by the civil rights movement did not happen during the years of my study, 1960–65, but that change happened in the years afterward and continues today. Civil rights history is taught in Mississippi schools as of 2009. A law was passed in 2006 mandating its inclusion in schools throughout the state. The pilot programs have begun in McComb, the home of an extreme amount of violence against local people, and in Neshoba County, where Michael Schwerner, James Chaney, and Andrew Goodman were lynched in 1964. Byron de la Beckwith was finally convicted in 1994 for his assassination of Medgar Evers in 1963 while other cases of lynching have been reopened where whites had never been convicted for the murder of African Americans.

Yearly conferences are held to memorialize former civil rights activists, and school children have written about their parents and their efforts to bring about change in the closed society. There is a Fannie Lou Hamer Institute at Jackson State University and a memorial park for her in Ruleville in the Delta. The efforts to bring about positive change and economic improvement are as important as ever, and the struggle to attain a better quality of life for African Americans continues.

APPENDIX

The Power of Protection: The Federal Government

I want to know: Which side is the Federal Government on?

—JOHN LEWIS at the March on Washington, 1963

For those who were in Mississippi with the civil rights movement, or for those who were African American Mississippians and ventured from "their place," the paramount question in their minds was survival. It was not a question of civil rights, but a question of what "the man" would do to them. The air was laden with fear which could border on extreme paranoia or could subside into mild tension. W. Haywood Burns said of these people that:

> under the Constitution of the United States they are possessed of certain First Amendment rights to speak freely, to assemble peacefully and distribute literature; that they are possessed of certain Fifteenth Amendment rights that guarantee the right to vote; that under the Fourteenth Amendment no state official may deprive them of these rights or discriminate against them because of their race. These constitutional provisions are the "supreme law of the land" (Article VI) and, in the final analysis, it is the duty of the President of the United States to see that the laws be "faithfully executed." (Article II)[1]

In spite constitutional and federal legal guarantees, local African Americans and civil rights workers experienced repeated denials of their rights at the hands of both private citizens and state and local officials. Moreover, the movement experienced a lack of support and protection from the federal government even though under law it should have been supplied.

The federal government has generally resisted intervention in state affairs; in the field of individual civil rights there has been little protection offered to the southern African American if it would mean a direct confrontation between federal and state government. Since 1965 Congress has moved away from this position, but in 1960–65 there seemed to be little, if any, desire on the part of Presidents Kennedy and Johnson to act decisively to protect the civil rights of African Americans in Mississippi, with the exception of upholding the 1954 Supreme Court decision of *Brown v. the Board of Education* at Ole Miss in 1962 and in searching for the bodies and murderers of Michael Schwerner, James Chaney, and Andrew Goodman in 1964.

A case in point is the murder of Louis Allen on his front lawn in Liberty on January 31, 1964, the day he was to move away from Mississippi. Allen had witnessed the murder of Herbert Lee in Liberty on September 25, 1961, at the hands of State Representative E. H. Hurst, and he was afraid to testify against Hurst. When he finally asked for federal protection in order to testify, he was murdered. Moreover, just prior to Lee's murder, E. W. Steptoe had told John Doar of the Justice Department that he feared for his and Lee's lives.

Probably the most crucial issue of debate was whether the federal government really had the legal power to intervene in upholding the rights of African Americans guaranteed by the United States or if there were other reasons for the lack of federal action. The issue was avoided whenever possible because Mississippi Senators James Oliver Eastland, chairman of the Judiciary Committee, and John Stennis, chairman of the Appropriations Committee, held stranglehold positions over federal judicial appointments and monetary allocations, and Delta Congressman Jamie Whitten was chairman of the House Appropriations Subcommittee on Agriculture. In addition, the president might not have felt that public opinion was behind such action at the time.

The request for federal protection was called for by Mississippi African Americans and civil rights workers but to little avail. President Kennedy, however, did use U.S. marshals at the Oxford riots that started on the Ole Miss campus on September 30, 1962, and Professor James W. Silver, of the University of Mississippi, was conscience-stricken enough to write *Mississippi: The Closed Society*. Far more important is Russell H. Barrett's *Integration at Ole Miss*, which deals with the abdication of responsibility by the faculty at the University of Mississippi and blames this abdication in part on the behavior of Ole Miss students and the public. Professor Barrett feels that the Oxford riots could have been avoided if there had been a responsible public attitude on integration and the supremacy of federal law.

Presidential Power

The most powerful federal instrument available for protection of constitutional rights is Title 10, Section 333, of the U.S. Codes, which is entitled "Interference with State and Federal Law":

> The President, by using the militia or the armed forces, or both, or *by any other means* [my emphasis], shall take such measures as he considers necessary to suppress, in a State, any insurrection, domestic violence, unlawful combination, or conspiracy, if it—
>
> (1) so hinders the execution of the laws of that State, and of the United States within the State, that any part or class of its people is deprived of a right, privilege, immunity, or protection named in the Constitution and secured by law, and the constituted authorities of that State are unable, fail, or refuse to protect that right, privilege, or immunity, or to give that protection; or
>
> (2) opposes or obstructs the execution of the laws of the United States or impedes the course of justice under those laws.
>
> In any situation covered by clause (1), the State shall be considered to have denied the equal protection of the laws secured by the Constitution.

This statute is unquestionably powerful, if a president wishes to exercise it. This then is the crux of the matter. It has only been in the most glaring instances of public denial of civil rights that a president has exercised this power. Except in the Meredith case at Ole Miss, no other federal action under the power of this statute was forthcoming from 1960 to 1965 in Mississippi.

Federal Law

Federal action, when taken, was under lesser statutory powers. The first of these laws is Title 18, Section 242, of the U.S. Codes:

> Whoever, under color of any law, statute, ordinance, regulation, or custom, willfully subjects any inhabitant of any State, Territory, or District to the deprivation of any rights, privileges, or immunities secured or protected by the Constitution or laws of the United States . . . shall be fined not more than $1,000 or imprisoned not more than one year, or both.

The basic problem with this law has been the U.S. Supreme Court's interpretation of it in *Screws v. United States*[2] in 1945, which made it necessary to prove "willful" deprivation of a person's rights. Robert Hall was beaten while he was handcuffed. The Supreme Court found Hall to be willfully deprived of "rights, privileges, or immunities secured or protected" to him by the Fourteenth Amendment.

Another important civil rights law is Title 18, Section 594, of the U.S. Codes, which deals with interference with the right to vote:

> Whoever intimidates, threatens, coerces, or attempts to intimidate, threaten or coerce, any other person for the purpose of interfering with the right of such other person to vote or to vote as he may choose, or of causing such other person to vote for, or not vote for, any candidate for the office of President, Vice President, Presidential elector, Member of the Senate, or Member of the House of Representatives, Delegates or Commissioners of the Territories or Possessions, at any election held solely or in part for the purpose of electing such candidate, shall be fined not more than $1,000 or imprisoned not more than one year or both.

The power of this law lies in mitigating tampering with federal elections and in securing the opportunity for the Mississippi African American to gain a share of the available power in the state.

In addition to the laws mentioned, Title 18, Section 241, of the U.S. Codes, makes it a crime for

> two or more persons to conspire to injure, oppress, threaten, or intimidate any citizen in the free exercise or enjoyment of any right or privilege secured to him by the Constitution or laws of the United States, or because of his having so exercised the same.

According to Burns, "The background of this statute shows that it was directed mainly at *private* acts of violence which were being used as a means of keeping the African American from voting. The statute was drafted during Reconstruction with the Ku Klux Klan specifically in mind. Though potentially an extremely powerful weapon, the federal government had virtually ignored it in recent times until the FBI arrested three men on the spot in Itta Bena, Mississippi, on June 26, 1964, when they were interfering with voter registration workers."[3] Further statutes which provide the potential power to protect constitutional rights are Title 18, Section 1509, which makes it a federal crime to interfere with the "due exercise of rights or performance of duties under any order, judgment, or decree of a court of the United States"; Title 18, Section 837, which covers the illegal use of explosives and threats to damage or destroy "real or personal property by fire or explosives"; and Title 18, Section 1074, which makes "flight to avoid prosecution for damaging or destroying any building or other real or personal property" a federal crime.

Throughout the period of 1960–65 it was the policy of the Justice Department to declare that such powers did not exist. But in addition to the statutes already cited, under Title 18, Section 3052,

> The Director, Associate Director, Assistant to the Director, Assistant Directors, Inspectors, and agents of the Federal Bureau of Investigation of the Department of Justice may carry firearms, serve warrants and subpoena issued under the authority of the United States and make arrests without warrant for any offense against the United States committed in their presence, or for any felony cognizable under the laws of the United States if they have reasonable grounds to believe that the person to be arrested has committed or is committing such felony.

Furthermore, under Title 18, Section 3053, U.S. marshals and their deputies have the same powers as are stated above, and under Title 18, Section 549, a United States marshal and his deputies, in executing the laws of the United States within a state, may exercise the same powers which a sheriff of such state may exercise in executing the laws thereof. The main obstacle to Federal exercise of these powers has been the Federal Government's desire not to interfere with the police power of the states.

Federal Intervention

There are two cases in which federal power to intervene in local affairs has been clearly declared. Justice Bradley, writing for the U.S. Supreme Court in the case of *Ex parte Siebold*[4] in 1879, said:

> We hold it to be an incontrovertible principle that the government of the United States may, by means of physical force exercised through its official

agents, execute on every foot of American soil the powers to command obedience to its laws and hence the power to keep the peace to that extent.

The second case occurred when the government secured an injunction against a strike by the American Railway Union in 1895. The Supreme Court said in this case, *In re Debs*,[5] that

> Every government, entrusted by the very terms of its being with powers and duties to be exercised and discharged for the general welfare, has a right to apply to its own courts for any proper assistance . . . whenever the wrongs complained of . . . are in respect of matters which by the Constitution are entrusted to the care of the nation.

The U.S. Supreme Court granted this injunction even though Congress had not passed any statute giving it the right to issue such an order. This decision could have opened the way for government injunctions against Mississippi registrars who were racially biased in registering voters. Even though the precedent was not used to override the existing bias by Mississippi registrars, the Voting Rights Act of 1965 rectified the problem.

Professor Howard Zinn of Boston University suggested, in *SNCC: The New Abolitionists*, that a force of federal agents be created by the president to deal specifically with the protection of the constitutional rights of any person against private or official action.[6] Such a force would remove the pressure which the FBI operates under in investigating denials of civil rights to African Americans. FBI agents have generally been drawn from the area in which they work, and the nature of their work requires them to cooperate with local law enforcement agencies. If a force of "E-Men" (or Emancipation-Men) were created, it could operate independently of local prejudices and pressures.

Concluding this discussion on federal power to intervene on a local level, Burns says:

> The mandate for Federal action in this area (protection of civil rights) comes from a failure of a state to protect its citizens and live up to its responsibilities under the Constitution. As long as these responsibilities are being fulfilled, there are no grounds for wide-scale Federal action, but when they are being disregarded, the Federal government must step in to fill the vacuum. . . . The basis for wider Federal action in Mississippi is apparent. The catalog

of violence and lawlessness in that state is a matter of record, and for every deed of cruelty and crime of violence in Mississippi, there are others that never come to light.[7]

James Forman of Chicago, the former executive secretary of the Student Nonviolent Coordinating Committee (SNCC), outlined the plight of the civil rights workers:

> It is hard to describe the irony of the situation. Voting is a Constitutional right. We take the time out of school, take all sorts of risks and try to register folks. . . . Take Mississippi. The government has filed suits. O.K. But people are still scared. They tell us, "All right, I'll go down to register, but what are you going to do for me when I lose my job and they beat my head?" And we can't do anything. The local folks are beginning to doubt that it's worth the risk.[8]

Mr. Forman's words present one of the most painful dilemmas the civil rights movement in Mississippi had to overcome. Life for African Americans in the "closed society" was so difficult that their fear to speak out many times overcame their desire to do so. The federal government took notes on what was happening in Mississippi for future court cases. The people continued to endure their hell.

NOTES ON SOURCES

I nitially I answered the question of how and in what manner the civil rights movement developed in Mississippi by reading sources that gave only the general outlines of events. The problem I had to confront was that much of the material was provided in journalistic accounts that were sketchy and incomplete. In order to confirm the historical judgment that the movement was a gradual, evolutionary chain of events critically influenced by the nature of the society in which it worked and developed, I had to use unpublished documents, movement documents and mimeographs, U.S. Commission on Civil Rights reports, U.S. Census reports, private diaries, personal interviews, and my own personal recollection of those events events in which I was personally involved.

The basic problem of writing such a book was not simple because the situation in Mississippi was such that heavy censorship slanted information that was published inside and outside the state during the period of my initial research in 1965–66. The traditional form of spreading local news stories in the United States, except in the case of serious national events, was through the local bureaus of the national newswires; in Mississippi, local reporters were whites who were part of the local patterns and traditions of southern life.

Only stories such as those of James Meredith, Emmett Till, Medgar Evers, and the triple lynching of the summer of 1964 carried enough national interest to counteract the force of this unofficial censorship. The day-to-day actions of the civil rights movement mostly went unnoticed by the American public. Even though the Civil Rights Division of the Department of Justice did begin work in the state by filing suits in federal court to guarantee the rights of African Americans to vote, very little of this was apparent until the fall of 1963 and the spring and summer of 1964 when white civil rights volunteers joined efforts with the movement and brought national attention to the events taking place in Mississippi.

The Sources

The extent of national news coverage in the state was largely limited until the summer of 1964 when President Johnson sent in federal troops and the FBI to look for the bodies of Schwerner, Chaney, and Goodman.[1] The limited press coverage, except in rare instances, made it very difficult to research the historical facts of the movement in Mississippi. Heavy reliance had to be placed on movement newspapers and documentation that African Americans, civil rights lawyers, and the U.S. government put together in their research for appeals of convictions of civil rights workers and general studies made by the movement to present its case to the public as well as to the federal government.[2] The U.S. Commission on Civil Rights also made a number of detailed studies in an effort to confirm whether the movement's judgments were justified and correct in their content, but the commission did not hold hearings in Mississippi until early 1965, even though they had been called for in 1962.[3]

Secondary sources were valuable as an instrument through which it was possible to establish a general framework for the events that took place in the entire civil rights movement during the period. Such sources as Howard Zinn's *SNCC: The New Abolitionists* (2nd ed., 1968), Michael Dorman's *We Shall Overcome* (1964), articles in *The New Republic* and *The Nation,* Pat Watters and Reese Cleghorn's *Climbing Jacob's Ladder: The Arrival of Negroes in Southern Politics* (1967), August Meier and Elliott Rudwick's *CORE: A Study in the Civil Rights Movement, 1942–1968* (1973), James Forman's *The Making of Black Revolutionaries: A Personal Account* (1972), Bruce Hilton's *The Delta Ministry* (1969), and numerous books on the summer of 1964 provided general factual material for the more specific study I undertook in 1965–66 and revised and updated in 1974–75.

More importantly, though, my study went deeply into the primary sources I gathered and the interviews I conducted in the field because I was able to take advantage of my closeness to the events that had taken place in Mississippi before they were reviewed and redacted by later scholars. This proximity to events has given me a unique perspective on and understanding of the Mississippi movement during 1960–65. Consequently, I have been able to place the later studies that have been written within the picture of the events I have written about.

Important studies that have been published since I wrote my expanded study in 1975 include: Eric Burner's *And Gently He Shall Lead Them: Robert Parris Moses and Civil Rights in Mississippi* (1994), John Dittmer's *Local People: The Struggle for Civil Rights in Mississippi* (1994), Charles Payne's *I've Got the Light of Freedom: The Organizing Tradition and the Mississippi Freedom Struggle* (1995), Wesley C. Hogan's *Many Minds, One Heart: SNCC's Dream for a New America* (2007), Barbara Ransby's *Ella Baker and the Black Freedom Movement: A Radical Democratic Vision* (2003), Danny Lyon's *Memories of the Southern Civil Rights Movement* (1992), Doug McAdam's *Political Process and the Development of Black Insurgency, 1930–1970* (1982), Kenneth T. Andrews *Freedom Is a Constant Struggle: The Mississippi Civil Rights Movement and Its Legacy* (2004), Frank R. Parker's *Black Votes Count: Political Empowerment in Mississippi after 1965* (1990), Mark Newman's *Divine Agitators: The Delta Ministry and Civil Rights in Mississippi* (2003), and Fred Powledge's *Free at Last? The Civil Rights Movement and the People Who Made It* (1991).

These studies, published since my unpublished work in 1975, have made it possible for me to fill in gaps in my research, but I feel they have passed over critical materials I gathered through my personal interviews in 1965–66 and documents I obtained in 1965 and 1966 directly from SNCC and National CORE files to which I was given access. My closeness to the events of the period provided an important perspective in writing about the events in Mississippi. I also feel that the later studies have provided me with clarifications for my conclusions rather than changing them because they made use of materials that went to archive after my early access to many of these same documents. And these archival materials used by other researchers have actually strengthened my conclusions based on the primary materials I had used. Additionally, my recent examination of the University of Southern Mississippi's online materials and my visit to the King Center in Atlanta and examination of the SNCC Papers there have provided further confirmation of my conclusions.

Even though there are other studies and memoirs that deal with the Mississippi movement in part, the analyses that I posit are the results of my own particular interpretations of what I feel have been glossed over or mentioned only tangentially.

Additionally, there have been a few studies written about local movements in Mississippi since 2004. They include: Emilye Crosby's *A Little Taste of Freedom: The Black Freedom Struggle in Claiborne County, Mississippi* (2005), J. Todd Moye's *Let the People Decide: Black Freedom and White Resistance Movements in Sunflower County, Mississippi, 1945–1986* (2004), and Chris Myers Asch's *The Senator and the Sharecropper: The Freedom Struggles of James O. Eastland and Fannie Lou Hamer* (2008). Asch's work on Senator Eastland is particularly piercing in his point-by-point elucidation of Eastland's use of his position in the U.S.

Senate to stymie the civil rights movement in any way he could in blocking liberal federal judicial appointments and in red-baiting the student movement by using his Senate Internal Security Subcommittee, records of the FBI, the Citizens' Councils, and the Mississippi State Sovereignty Commission. Asch also examines Eastland's continuing fight to maintain segregation and control of cotton production and white land ownership in the state as long as he could.

All three of these studies devote a significant part of their work to defining what life was like under Jim Crow and the systems that were used to hold African Americans in "their place."[4] I have chosen not to devote my work to proving the existence and description of the systems employed by the white power structure and instead have devoted extensive space to delineating the efforts of the civil rights movement to overcome Mississippi's power structure. Nevertheless, a close reading of Gordon A. Martin Jr.'s Count Them One by One: Black Mississippians Fighting for the Right to Vote (2010) presents a lucid picture of Registrar Theron Lynd's denial of the right to vote in Hattiesburg, Forrest County, and the support he received in his legal obstructionism in the Federal District Court of W. Harold Cox. A valuable study of segregationism in its different aspects in Mississippi is Joseph Crespino's In Search of Another Country: Mississippi and the Conservative Counterrevolution (2007).[5]

Moreover, although these studies extend the period of civil rights activity in Mississippi beyond 1965, I feel that the real battle for African American political empowerment after 1965 was fought in the courts against the Mississippi power structure's nullifying voting rights by rewriting state voting and office-holding laws. That battle continued into the 1980s and is ably examined by Jere Nash and Andy Taggart's Mississippi Politics: The Struggle for Power, 1976–2006 (2006), as are Gordon Martin's and Crespino's monographs, mentioned above. Nevertheless, Crosby's and Moye's works do provide well-documented portraits of the civil rights movements in Claiborne and Sunflower counties after Freedom Summer.[6]

In short, my early efforts involved gathering basic facts as to the events that took place during the years 1960–65—I did my initial field research in 1965–66 in Mississippi; Atlanta; Washington, D.C.; and New York City—where I looked for the various individuals who were involved and questioned them as to the sequence and nature of the events that had taken place. (Unfortunately, most of the later sources concerned with the Mississippi movement have relied on interviews from later dates than mine and either failed to reach the same people I did or failed to ask the questions I feel were important, or failed to note when participants' memories or judgments had changed.)

Additionally, the evolution of the movement in Mississippi was not a straightforward chain of events. The conflicts between the different organizations slowed the development of the organizations and their strategies. Since there were various groups that carried out this attack on the white establishment, the materials necessary to piece together the study were scattered throughout the various organizations' files, with numerous individuals in many places and local people who continued their work after the SNCC and CORE organizers had left Mississippi, as well as with middle-class African Americans who became involved in the movement only after 1965.[7]

Furthermore, documentation was not a simple matter because a number of people who lived in the state and were also active had done civil rights work in Mississippi prior to the organized efforts of the student-supported groups. Medgar Evers, the national NAACP field secretary in Jackson; Amzie Moore, the head of the NAACP in Cleveland in the Delta; and many other local people had started direct action and voter registration movements. Additional local NAACP leaders such as Dr. Aaron Henry, who was the state president of the NAACP and the Freedom Vote candidate for governor in 1963, also had to be reached.

Bob Moses (at the invitation of Curtis C. Bryant, the head of the Pike County NAACP, and E. W. Steptoe, the head of Amite County NAACP) had started a voter registration drive in southwest Mississippi in the summer of 1961, and I was able to interview him at length in 1990. Additionally, Tim Jenkins had been the liaison between the U.S. Department of Justice and the civil rights movement when the Department of Justice was called upon to protect harassed workers and local people who wanted to register to vote. The Federal Government in the person of individual representatives of the Justice Department and the Democratic National Committee encouraged the civil rights workers to go into voter registration work because it would not only be easier to finance their activities but, they said, it would also be easier to legally protect workers and African Americans who desired to vote from physical abuse.[8]

I made further verification of this in personal interviews with Tim Jenkins and with William Higgs, a white Mississippi lawyer who helped the civil rights movement during the 1961 Freedom Rides and continued to offer his services as a civil rights lawyer in Washington, D.C., after he had been driven out of Mississippi for his actions.[9] By the fall of 1963 the funds for voter registration work in Mississippi had dried up because no efficacious work was being done from the Democratic Party's point of view. Previously funds had been supplied by the Taconic and Field Foundations—which were linked with the party—for non-partisan voter registration work under the auspices of COFO.[10]

An essential understanding of the decision to go into voter registration work could only come from numerous interviews with civil rights workers in order to eliminate discrepancies in information, and checking these facts and ideas against the existing published materials on this period. This process has been continued in the current update by reviewing published sources and studies since 1975 along with additional interviews I have conducted with movement figures. Such research was also necessary for understanding the process of developing protest political actions in the state.

In order to rely upon such source material, it was necessary to use secondary materials to confirm facts garnered from the movement's records and from personal interviews. I initially gained a general background from secondary materials and then turned to the movement itself to ask the questions that the material presented as to the nature of the growth of the movement over the period of 1960–65.

The next stage was to try to confirm the answers that were provided by checking further into newspaper articles, as well as magazine and journal articles. One can generally accept source materials such as the *New York Times*, and I was able to do so with events such as the riots at Ole Miss. However, what was published prior to 1963 and the breaking of the press blackout I was involved in while I was a student at Yale College can only be considered as unreliable concerning the State of Mississippi and its efforts to continue the oppression of its African American population. Since this was the case, I was forced to establish as fact the monolithic nature of Mississippi society and the failure of the federal government to uphold its obligations and then turn to original sources within the movement.

On the whole I found it compulsory to place disproportionate weight on original research drawn from movement sources and confirmed through secondary materials. Moreover, the nature of my research was largely forced to this extreme because of the make-up of the topic. The one-sided nature of the Mississippi establishment dictated such methods.

Recent sources have failed to examine the Mississippi movement with questions of how and why the movement developed along lines I have delineated. They do tell the story and do stress the importance of local people in the movement in two important studies,[11] but they do not generally analyze it as I have: moving from direct action and voter registration efforts, to protest politics, to local participation within the established political processes and economic actions in establishing federally funded poverty programs and cooperative farming and industrial organizations.

NOTES

Foreword

1. Qtd. in Charles M. Payne, *I've Got the Light of Freedom: The Organizing Tradition and the Mississippi Freedom Struggle* (Berkeley, Calif., 1995), 297.

2. Ibid., 473n21.

3. Staff meeting minutes, June 9–11, 1964, SNCC Papers, roll 3, frames 975–92. I wish to thank Wesley Hogan for making these minutes available to me. I was invited to one session of this meeting but not to the session from the proceedings of which I quote above.

4. Casey Hayden, "Fields of Blue," in Constance Curry et al., *Deep in Our Hearts: Nine White Women in the Freedom Movement* (Athens, Ga., 2000), 357. I believe that such maneuvering took a toll. By the time of the Waveland conference in November 1964, Casey felt "uninterested in electoral politics" ("Fields of Blue," 367).

5. Quoted in *Letters from Mississippi*, edited and with a new preface by Elizabeth Sutherland Martinez (Brookline, Mass., 2002), 250–51.

6. Nelson Lichtenstein, *The Most Dangerous Man in Detroit: Walter Reuther and the Fate of American Labor* (New York, 1995), 394–95; Taylor Branch, *Pillar of Fire: America in the King Years, 1963–1965* (New York, 1998), 469–75.

7. Hasan Kwame Jeffries, *Bloody Lowndes: Civil Rights and Black Power in Alabama's Black Belt* (New York, 2009), 243.

8. Boycotts "became the focal point of movement activity in Greenwood in the middle and late sixties. . . . Most Greenwood activists feel strongly that the immediate cause of real change, change that they could feel in their daily lives, came in response to economic pressure. It is a point worth noting, because most histories of the movement . . . pay little attention to economic pressure." Payne, *I've Got the Light of Freedom*, 323, 328. What appears to have been the most successful boycott was in the city of Natchez and surrounding Claiborne County, led by Charles Evers of the NAACP (Emilye Crosby, *A Little Taste of Freedom: The Black Freedom Struggle in Claiborne County, Mississippi* [Chapel Hill, N.C., 2005]).

9. Payne, *I've Got the Light of Freedom*, 339–48.

10. Qtd. in Wesley C. Hogan, *Many Minds, One Heart: SNCC's Dream for a New America* (Chapel Hill, N.C., 2007), 221, 375n8.

11. Jeffries, *Bloody Lowndes*, 213.

Introduction

Epigraph 1: Qtd. in Jack Newfield, *A Prophetic Minority* (New York, 1967), 48.

Epigraph 2: James W. Silver, *Mississippi: The Closed Society* (New York, 1966), 151; see also Kim Lacy Rogers, *Life and Death in the Delta: African American Narratives of Violence, Resilience, and Social Change* (New York, 2006), for life of fear and oppression in the Delta.

1. Michael Dorman, *We Shall Overcome: A Reporter's Eyewitness Account of the Year of Racial Strife and Triumph* (New York, 1964).

2. Interviews with James Farmer and Marvin Rich, 1965; National CORE files.

3. COFO, "Mississippi: Handbook for Political Programs," Jackson, Miss., 1964.

4. Howard Zinn, *SNCC: The New Abolitionists* (Boston, 1968); Moses, taped talk, June 20, 1963; see Doug McAdam, *Political Process and the Development of Black Insurgency, 1930–1970* (Chicago, 1982), 146–80.

5. Marion Barry Jr. interview with author, December 18, 1965.

6. Zinn, *SNCC*; interviews with Bob Moses by author, 1990; Tim Jenkins interview with author, December 18, 1965; Barry interview.

Chapter One

Epigraph: Lowenstein interview.

1. See V. O. Key, *Southern Politics in State and Nation* (New York, 1949); C. Vann Woodward, *The Strange Career of Jim Crow* (New York, 1962); Silver, *Mississippi;* Patricia Moseley, " A Reminiscence," in Susie Erenrich, ed., *Freedom Is a Constant Struggle: An Anthology of the Mississippi Civil Rights Movement* (Montgomery, Ala., 1999), 9–11.

2. See W. Haywood Burns, *The Voices of Negro Protest in America* (London, 1963); James Forman, *The Making of Black Revolutionaries: A Personal Account* (New York, 1972); see introduction, note 3.

3. See Louis E. Lomax, *The Negro Revolt* (New York, 1962).

4. See Zinn, *SNCC*; U.S. Commission on Civil Rights, *Law Enforcement* (Washington, D.C., 1965).

5. See Avery Leiserson, ed., *The American South in the 1960s* (New York, 1964); Silver, *Mississippi;* Walter Lord, *The Past That Would Not Die* (New York, 1965); Payne, *I've Got the Light of Freedom,* 29–66, for civil rights activities in Mississippi in the 1950s and White Mississippi's violent response. John Dittmer, *Local People: The Struggle for Civil Rights in Mississippi* (Urbana, Ill., 1994), talks about the early civil rights work around voter registration by the NAACP and other groups such as the Regional Council of Negro Leadership (RCNL) under the leadership of T. R. M. Howard, Amzie Moore, Aaron Henry, Medgar Evers, and others who all became role models for young activists such as Sam Block, Willie Peacock, the McGhee and Greene families, Hollis Watkins, Curtis Hayes (Muhammad), and Dorie and Joyce Ladner; see Vicki L. Crawford, Jacqueline Anne Rouse, and Barbara Woods, eds., *Women in the Civil Rights Movement: Trailblazers and Torchbearers, 1941–1965* (Brooklyn, N.Y., 1990), 1–50, for an examination of the role of women in the movement in Mississippi.

6. Anthony Lewis and the New York Times, *Portrait of a Decade* (New York, 1964), 204–37; Russell H. Barrett, *Integration at Ole Miss* (Chicago, 1965); Silver, *Mississippi;* Robert Canzoneri,

"I Do So Politely": A Voice from the South (Boston, 1965); Lord, *The Past That Would Not Die;* see also David R. Davies, ed., *The Press and Race: Mississippi Journalists Confront the Movement* (Jackson, Miss., 2001); Ira B. Harkey Jr., *The Smell of Burning Crosses: An Autobiography of a Mississippi Newspaperman* (Jacksonville, Ill.,1967); and Paul Hendrickson, *Sons of Mississippi: A Story of Race and Its Legacy* (New York, 2003) for pictures of the Mississippi press's handling of movement actions in the state; see also Leiserson, *The American South;* Silver, *Mississippi;* Newfield, *A Prophetic Minority;* Neil R. McMillen, *The Citizens' Council: Organized Resistance to the Second Reconstruction* (Urbana, Ill., 1971) and Hodding Carter III, *The South Strikes Back* (Garden City, N.Y., 1959) for a white Mississippi newspaperman's reaction to the establishment of the Citizens' Councils.

7. See Silver, *Mississippi,* 8n2.

8. Ibid.

9. Lester Sobel, ed., *Civil Rights: 1960–66* (New York, 1967), 58.

10. U.S. Commission on Civil Rights, *Law Enforcement,* 15.

11. Robert Coles, M.D., *Children of Crisis: A Study of Courage and Fear* (Boston, 1964), 315.

12. U.S. Commission on Civil Rights, *Law Enforcement,* 15n3.

13. Newfield, *A Prophetic Minority,* 44–45; Sobel, *Civil Rights,* 15; see Barbara Ransby, *Ella Baker & the Black Freedom Movement: A Radical Democratic Vision* (Chapel Hill, 2003), for a biography of Ms. Ella Josephine Baker and in-depth analysis of her political philosophy, her close connection with the foundation of the Student Nonviolent Coordinating Committee, and her ongoing connection with SNCC throughout its existence; see Payne, *I've Got the Light of Freedom,* 77–102, for an analysis and commentary of Ms. Baker's ideas on organizing and her part in the early student movement, particularly in the development of women and young people as local leaders and her comment, "STRONG PEOPLE DON'T NEED STRONG LEADERS" [caps in original], 77; see Andrew B. Lewis, *The Shadows of Youth: The Remarkable Journey of the Civil Rights Generation* (New York, 2009), 3–13; see also Crawford, Rouse, and Woods, eds., *Women in the Civil Rights Movement.*

14. Newfield, *A Prophetic Minority,* 44–45.

15. Ibid., 44–5.

16. Ibid., 45.

17. Ibid., 46; see Ransby, *Ella Baker,* chap. 8, "Mentoring a New Generation of Activists: The Birth of the Student Nonviolent Coordinating Committee," 239–72; Clayborne Carson, *In Struggle: SNCC and the Black Awakening of the 1960s* (Cambridge, Mass., 1981), 25–27; see also Payne, *I've Got the Light of Freedom,* 29–47, for a picture of Moore and his involvement in the movement in the 1950s and after.

18. Zinn, *SNCC,* 62–66; see also Carson, *In Struggle,* 26, 46; see Forman, *The Making of Black Revolutionaries,* 278–82, for a personal statement by Amzie Moore of his life in the armed forces and in Mississippi.

19. My interview with Moses in 1990. See SNCC, *The General Condition of the Mississippi Negro,* 1963.

20. Tom Hayden, *Revolution in Mississippi* (New York, 1962), 8; see also Joanne Grant, *Black Protest: History, Documents, and Analyses, 1619 to the Present* (New York, 1968), 303–8.

21. Newfield, *A Prophetic Minority,* 47.

22. Staughton Lynd, *Nonviolence in America* (New York, 1966), 398–99.

23. Louis Lusky, "Racial Discrimination and the Federal Law: A Problem in Nullification," rpt. in Leon Friedman, ed., *Southern Justice* (New York, 1965), 255–80.

24. Ibid., 260.

25. Ibid., 263.

26. Sobel, *Civil Rights*, 82–83.

27. Ibid.; Zinn, *SNCC*, 25; U.S. Commission on Civil Rights, *Law Enforcement*, 65–66; see Dittmer, *Local People*, 87–89, 116–17; see also John R. Salter Jr., *Jackson, Mississippi: An American Chronicle of Struggle and Schism* (Hicksville, N.Y., 1979).

28. Sobel, *Civil Rights*, 82–83.

29. Lusky, "Racial Discrimination and the Federal Law," 266.

30. Ibid., 267–68.

31. See Silver, *Mississippi*; Barrett, *Integration at Ole Miss*; Lord, *The Past That Would Not Die*; Canzoneri, *I Do So Politely*; Lewis, *Shadows of Youth*; Dorman, *We Shall Overcome*; Sobel, *Civil Rights*, 56.

32. Sobel, *Civil Rights*, 56.

33. Ibid.

34. Ibid., 56–57.

35. U.S. Commission on Civil Rights, *Hearings Held in Jackson, Mississippi, February 16–20, 1965* (Washington, D.C., 1965), vol. 2: 449–60.

36. Ibid., 450; for a brief personal history of Curtis C. Bryant, see Pat Watters and Reese Cleghorn, *Climbing Jacob's Ladder: The Arrival of Negroes in Southern Politics* (New York, 1967), 103–4.

37. U.S. Commission on Civil Rights, *Law Enforcement*, 39, 42.

38. See Silver, *Mississippi*; William McCord, *Mississippi: The Long, Hot Summer* (New York, 1965).

39. Lord, *The Past That Would Not Die*.

40. See Raymond Arsenault, *Freedom Riders: 1961 and the Struggle for Racial Justice* (New York, 2006), for the most thoroughgoing documentation of the Freedom Rides, with lists of participants and the individual freedom rides from their beginnings in the 1940s through the 1960s; for individual personal accounts of freedom riders, see James Farmer, *Freedom—When?* (New York, 1966); for Lewis's personal account of the Freedom Rides, see John Lewis with Michael D'Orso, *Walking with the Wind: A Memoir of the Movement* (San Diego, 1998), 115–72; see also James Farmer, *Lay Bare the Heart: An Autobiography of the Civil Rights Movement* (New York, 1985), 1–32, 195–204; James Peck, *Freedom Ride* (New York, 1962); for oral testimony by Freedom Ride participants, see Henry Hampton and Steve Fayer with Sarah Flynn, eds., *Voices of Freedom: An Oral History of the Civil Rights Movement from the 1950s through the 1980s* (New York, 1991), 73–96; Lewis, *Shadows of Youth*, 91–111; August Meier and Elliott Rudwick, *CORE: A Study in the Civil Rights Movement, 1942–1968* (New York, 1973); for more general studies, see Taylor Branch, *Parting of the Waters: America in the King Years 1954–63* (New York, 1988), 412–91; Sobel, *Civil Rights*; Zinn, *SNCC*, 40–61; see also Mark Lane, "Southern Journey," in Erenrich, ed., *Freedom is a Constant Struggle*, 21–26, for his personal Freedom Ride from Atlanta to Jackson, Mississippi; see also Bob Zellner with Constance Curry, *The Wrong Side of Murder Creek: A White Southerner in the Freedom Movement* (Montgomery, Ala., 2008), 89–100; also Hogan, *Many Minds, One Heart*, 45–55, 57–66, for the emotional significance of the Freedom Rides and early action in southwest Mississippi and their importance in showing the South and the Federal Government that the movement refused to be stopped by violence and intimidation; Carson, *In Struggle*, 31–44; see also Terry H. Anderson, *The Movement and the Sixties: Protest in America from Greensboro to Wounded Knee* (New York, 1995), 3–86, for a brief examination of the concept of "The Movement" as it developed in the 1960s separate from the Old Left and distinctly a student phenomenon that sought new answers to racial discrimination in both the South and the North; see also Lynd, *Nonviolence*; William Brink and Louis Harris, *The Negro Revolution in America* (New York, 1963); Leiserson, *The American South*; Burns, *Voices of Negro Protest*.

41. 364 U.S. 454 (1960).

42. See Meier and Rudwick, *CORE*, 135–43, for brief summary of various Freedom Rides.

43. See Lusky, "Racial Discrimination and the Federal Law," 271–77, for the legal battle the movement fought with the Mississippi courts; see also Meier and Rudwick, *CORE*.

44. Meier and Rudwick, *CORE*, 296–304; see also Sobel, *Civil Rights*, 68–69, 72–73.

45. Information on McComb in 1961 is taken from Tom Hayden, *Revolution in Mississippi*. Robert P. Moses and Charles E. Cobb Jr., *Radical Equations: Math Literacy and Civil Rights* (Boston, 2001), 23–57; Moses relates his initial organizing efforts in southwest Mississippi in 1961 and how he used grassroots methods to become one with local leaders rather than an "outsider." Lewis, *Shadows of Youth*, 112–20. Lewis, *Walking with the Wind*, 181–85. Zinn, *SNCC*, 62–78. Branch, *Parting of the Waters*, 492–523. Jack Minnis, *A Chronology of Violence and Intimidation in Mississippi Since 1961* (Atlanta, 1964). Mary King, *Freedom Song: A Personal Story of the 1960s Civil Rights Movement* (New York, 1987), 146–51. Lynd, *Nonviolence*, 428–41. See Clayborne Carson, David J. Garrow, Vincent Harding, and Darlene Clark Hine, eds., *Eyes on the Prize: America's Civil Rights Years, A Reader and Guide* (New York, 1987), 128–33, for Bob Moses's recounting of the movement's early work in southwest Mississippi. Carson, *In Struggle*, 45–55.

46. See Payne, *I've Got the Light of Freedom*, 111–31, for recap of SNCC work in southwest Mississippi in fall of 1961; according to Payne, even though McComb was looked upon as "a defeat for SNCC, which is true in a narrow sense . . . but it overlooks the fact that SNCC learned in McComb that merely the process of trying to organize a town would attract young people, a few of whom were willing to identify completely with the organization's work. The Mississippi movement would be built around these home-grown organizers" (119).

47. Documentation of John Hardy case in Lynd, *Nonviolence*, 429–34; see Grant, *Black Protest*, 308–11, for Hardy's part in *U.S. v. John Q. Wood*, 295 F. 2d. 772 (1961); Zinn, *SNCC*, 70–71; Forman, *The Making of Black Revolutionaries*, 225–26, 230–31.

48. Information on murder of Herbert Lee can be found in *Mississippi Black Paper: Statements and Notarized Affidavits* (New York, 1965), 32; Zinn, *SNCC*, 72–74; Forman, *The Making of Black Revolutionaries*, 231; Bob Moses, taped talk; and various unpublished materials of SNCC.

49. Bob Moses, taped talk.

50. *Mississippi Black Paper*, 30–37; Jack Newfield, *A Prophetic Minority*, 57–58.

51. Zinn, *SNCC*, 68–70, 74–76; Sobel, *Civil Rights*, 69; see also Bob Zellner, "McComb, Mississippi," in Erenrich, *Freedom Is a Constant Struggle*, 13–20, and Zellner, *The Wrong Side of Murder Creek*, 150–72.

52. Lynd, *Nonviolence*, 436–40; Zinn, *SNCC*, 76.

53. Unita Blackwell with JoAnne Prichard Morris, *Barefootin': Life Lessons from the Road to Freedom* (New York, 2006), 93.

Chapter Two

Epigraph: Marion Barry Jr., interview with author, 1965.

1. On the leadership of Bob Moses, see chapter 1, above. See Ransby, *Ella Baker*, 170–209, for organizing techniques Baker used in setting up SCLC's Crusade for Citizenship in the South in 1958 and its similarity to what the voter registration wing of SNCC did when Bob Moses went to McComb, Mississippi, in 1961; see Emily Stoper, *The Student Nonviolent Coordinating Committee: The*

Growth of Radicalism in a Civil Rights Organization (Brooklyn, N.Y., 1989), 9. Nash married James Bevel during the winter of 1961-62.

2. For a fuller discussion of decision-making in the movement, see chapter 3, below. Barry interview; see also interview with Charles Jones in Stoper, *Student Nonviolent Coordinating Committee*, 173-81, on the decision to work on voter registration.

3. Meier and Rudwick, *CORE*, 172-75; Zinn, *SNCC*, 58-59; Lomax, *The Negro Revolt*, 247-49; see also Stephan and Abigail Thernstrom, *America in Black and White: One Nation, Indivisible* (New York, 1997), 127-9.

4. Meier and Rudwick, *CORE*, 172-3; see Payne, *I've Got the Light of Freedom*, 108-11, for a recap of the Kennedy Administration's issue with the Freedom Rides and desire for a "cooling off period" and for the movement to do voter registration work as a safer alternative and source for funds for that work; see McAdam, *Political Process*, 169-80, for federal government's position vis-à-vis the civil rights movement. The Potomac Institute was funded by the Taconic Foundation, which Stephen Currier had created.

5. Tim Jenkins interview with author; see Stoper, *Student Nonviolent Coordinating Committee*, 173-81, for the Jones interview.

6. Meier and Rudwick, *CORE*, 173.

7. Ibid., 174.

8. Ibid., 174.

9. Zinn, *SNCC*, 58; see Aldon D. Morris, *The Origins of the Civil Rights Movement: Black Communities Organizing for Change* (New York, 1984), 139-57, for an examination of Highlander Folk School and its role in the movement, particularly as an integrated meeting place for SNCC staff to work out ideas for future action, not just in Mississippi but throughout South. (See highlandercenter. org for a history of the still-active center.)

10. Jenkins interview.

11. Ibid.

12. Zinn, *SNCC*, 58-59; Ransby, *Ella Baker*, 267-70; Jenkins and William L. Higgs interviews; John Lewis, *Walking with the Wind*, 178-81.

13. My impressions from personal meetings with Bob Moses in winter 1963-64 and interviews in 1990; see also Payne, *I've Got the Light of Freedom*, 103-18.

14. Barry interview.

15. Information on Moses's part in the R. L. T. Smith campaign comes from interviews with Bill Higgs and Rev. R. L. T. Smith, Jackson, Miss., December 30, 1965; see also Crosby, *A Little Taste of Freedom*, 79-90, for the Rev. Smith campaign in 1962 and its effects on Claiborne County and voter registration there; 1990 Moses interviews. For more on Moses's activities, see chapter 4, below.

16. Jack Newfield, *A Prophetic Minority*, 56-59; see also Thernstrom, *America in Black and White*, 129.

17. Newfield, *A Prophetic Minority* , 59-70.

18. Lynd, *Nonviolence*, 440-41; Zinn, *SNCC*, 76; Forman, *The Making of Black Revolutionaries*, 233.

Chapter Three

Epigraph: Moses memo.

1. Information on planning in winter 1961-62, the poll-tax campaign, and congressional primary campaigns of Rev. R. L. T. Smith, Rev. Theodore Trammell, and Rev. Merrill W. Lindsey is from

recorded interviews in 1965 I conducted with Aaron Henry, Rev. Smith, Jim Forman, Jesse Harris, Bill Higgs, and Tim Jenkins; see also Hampton, *Voices of Freedom,* 139–57, for oral testimony for 1961–63 in Mississippi; see also Forman, *The Making of Black Revolutionaries,* 262–69; Aaron Henry with Constance Curry, *Aaron Henry: The Fire Ever Burning* (Jackson, 2000); Hogan, *Many Minds, One Heart,* 77–79.

2. Forman, *The Making of Black Revolutionaries,* 277–82; Lord, *The Past That Would Not Die,* 31–97, offers a narrative on the period after World War II up to time of the movement in Mississippi in the early 1960s; also see J. Todd Moye, *Let the People Decide: Black Freedom and White Resistance Movements in Sunflower County, Mississippi, 1945–1986* (Chapel Hill, N.C., 2004), 40–63.

3. See Ransby, *Ella Baker,* 310, who quotes Carol Mueller, "Ella Baker and the Origins of 'Participatory Democracy,'" in *Women in the Civil Rights Movement*, 51–70; see also Joanne Grant, *Ella Baker: Freedom Bound* (New York, 1998) for an account of Ms. Baker's life as an organizer in battle for civil rights.

4. Students for a Democratic Society, *The Port Huron Statement* (New York, 1964), 7–8; see James Miller, *"Democracy Is in the Streets": From Port Huron to the Siege of Chicago* (Cambridge, Mass., 1994); see also Hogan, *Many Minds, One Heart,* 140, for the limited success of participatory democracy within SDS; see note 7 below for Ms. Baker's views on decision-making.

5. Blackwell, *Barefootin',* 90.

6. Coles, *Children of Crisis,* 322.

7. Jack Newfield, "The Student Left," *The Nation,* May 10, 1965, 493; see Payne, *I've Got the Light of Freedom,* 68–102, for roles of Mrs. Septima Clark in establishing literacy programs in the rural South, Myles Horton of Highlander Folk School and his part in labor movement and then in civil rights movement, and Ms. Ella Josephine Baker in her development and promotion of leadership by local people as representations of ideas of participatory democracy later espoused by Students for a Democratic Society; see Ransby, *Ella Baker,* 291–98, on "Gender Politics and Grassroots Organizing," 170–95: "Baker was a militant egalitarian"; thus, her belief in "most oppressed sectors of society" as being ones who needed to lead themselves out of their oppression, i.e., the sharecroppers, tenant farmers, manual laborers, not the middle class of the teachers and ministers who were dependent for positions on white people who in fact were their oppressors. According to Ransby, Ms. Baker's idea of movement organization was that an "inclination toward inclusion and a genuinely participatory democracy militated against the tendency to replicate the dominant society's concept of proper gender roles, which most black southern colleges actively encouraged." (309); see also Ransby, *Ella Baker,* 368–70, for "Baker's emphasis on grassroots participatory democracy." See Staughton Lynd, *From Here to There: The Staughton Lynd Reader* (Oakland, Calif., 2010), 85–95; Lynd states: "One aspect of participatory democracy is the idea of parallel structures. The [Freedom Democratic Party] is a parallel political party, prompted by the conclusion that registration of Negroes in the regular Democratic Party of Mississippi is presently impossible. Freedom Schools were parallel schools, although delegates to the Freedom School Convention decided they would return to the public schools and seek to transform them rather than continue into the winter a parallel school system. . . . The intent of these structures is still unclear, even to those involved in organizing them. There is a spectrum of possibilities. At one end of the spectrum is the concept of using parallel institutions to transform their Establishment counterparts. Thus it would follow that when Mississippi Negroes can register and vote, the FDP would wither away. At the spectrum's end is the conviction that in an America whose Establishment is inherently and inevitably hostile, existing institutions cannot be transformed, participation will always mean cooptation and merely token success, hence parallel institutions must survive and grow into an anti-Establishment net-

work, a new society. For the moment participatory democracy cherishes the practice of parallelism as a way of saying No to organized America, and of initiating the unorganized into the experience of self-government. The SNCC or SDS worker does not build a parallel institution to impose an ideology on it. He views himself as a catalyst, helping to create an environment which will help the local people to decide what they want." (88–89).

8. Recorded talk with William Mahoney of SNCC, December 17, 1965; see also Stoper, *Student Nonviolent Coordinating Committee*, 69–70, 105–19 ("The Mind of SNCC"), 121–33.

9. Coles, *Children of Crisis*, 322.

10. See note 1, above.

11. Higgs interview; see Crosby, *A Little Taste of Freedom*, 79–90, for Smith 1962 campaign and affects on voter registration in Claiborne County; Crosby says conservative administration at Alcorn A&M led to suppression of all civil rights activity on campus, and little was done to promote the movement in Claiborne from 1962 to 1965, and the NAACP was active only underground in spite of the Freedom Vote in 1963 and the Summer Project in 1964; Crosby also states, "Claiborne County blacks remained on the sidelines from 1963 through late 1965" (84); see Payne, *I've Got the Light of Freedom*, 47–56, for information on Medgar Evers.

12. Lewis, *Shadows of Youth*, 127.

13. Higgs interview.

14. Interview with Aaron Henry, Clarksdale, Miss., December 28, 1965.

15. Brief mention of Rev. Lindsey in Frank Smith, *Congressman from Mississippi* (New York, 1964), 298–99; Henry interview; see also Eric Bruner, *And Gently He Shall Lead Them: Robert Paris Moses and Civil Rights in Mississippi* (New York, 1994), 67–68.

16. "First" and "Second Annual Reports of the Voter Education Project of the Southern Regional Council." See chapter 4, below, for more on COFO.

17. See Minnis, *Chronology*.

18. *Mississippi Black Paper*, 6; Zinn, *SNCC*, 80.

19. Zinn, *SNCC*, 79–83; *Mississippi Black Paper*, 4–6.

20. Zinn, *SNCC*, 79–83.

21. Federal Writers' Project of the WPA, *Mississippi: A Guide to the Magnolia State* (New York, 1938), 3–4, and Rogers, *Life and Death in the Delta*, 13; see Stokely Carmichael with Ekwueme Michael Thelwell, *Ready for Revolution: The Life and Struggles of Stokely Carmichael (Kwame Ture)* (New York, 2003), 277–96, for his organizing work in the Delta and stories connected with local people; see Nicholas Lemann, *The Promised Land: The Great Black Migration and How It Changed America* (New York, 1991), 1–59, for background on the Delta, sharecropping, blacks who lived under this oppressive system, and how the Delta was affected by the mechanization of cotton production.

22. Leon Howell, *Freedom City: The Substance of Things Hoped For* (Richmond, Va., 1969), 16–17.

23. Ibid; see Rogers, *Life and Death in the Delta*, for a close examination of Delta residents in Washington, Coahoma, Bolivar, and Sunflower counties. Work is based on interviews with residents who lived through the civil rights movement and continue to live there. Interviewees come from two major groups: poor and oppressed tenants and sharecroppers from Sunflower County and those who were better off economically, including independent landowners from Bolivar County, and able to take advantage of what the movement brought in organizing for progress and change in their lives; see Kenneth T. Andrews, *Freedom Is a Constant Struggle: The Mississippi Civil Rights Movement and Its Legacy* (Chicago, 2004), for the long-term significance of the movement in Bolivar County and its African American infrastructure as compared to Holmes and Madison counties;

see also Jeffrey Blackmon and Youth of the Rural Organizing and Cultural Center, *Minds Stayed on Freedom: The Civil Rights Struggle in the Rural South, an Oral History* (Boulder, Colo., 1991), for interviews by eighth- and ninth-graders from Holmes County, Miss.; see also Winson Hudson and Constance Curry, *Mississippi Harmony: Memoirs of a Freedom Fighter* (New York, 2002).

24. Zinn, *SNCC*, 82–90; *The Student Voice*, April 1963; see also "First Annual Report of the Voter Education Project"; Watters and Cleghorn, *Climbing Jacob's Ladder*; see Forman, *The Making of Black Revolutionaries*, 282–91, for statements by Sam Block, Luvaughn Brown, and Willie Peacock about movement experiences in the Delta; see Dittmer, *Local People*, 117–57; Carson, *In Struggle*, 77–81, 96–97; see also Fred Powledge, *Free At Last? The Civil Rights Movement and the People Who Made It* (Boston, 1991), 474–79 for information about the Voter Education Project (VEP), Wiley Branton, its head and great-grandson of Greenwood Leflore, Jimmy Travis's shooting, and the call to concentrate the movement there after the shooting.

25. Watters and Cleghorn, *Climbing Jacob's Ladder*, 64; Forman, *The Making of Black Revolutionaries*, 288–90.

26. Zinn, *SNCC*, 86–89; Forman, *The Making of Black Revolutionaries*, 296; Sobel, *Civil Rights*, 192–93; John Lewis, *Walking with the Wind*, speaks about Mrs. Hamer in the following words: "Without her [Mrs. Hamer] and hundreds of women like her, we would never have been able to achieve what we did" (187–88); Dittmer, *Local People*, 143–57; see Chana Kai Lee, *For Freedom's Sake: The Life of Fannie Lou Hamer* (Urbana, Ill., 1999), 23–44, for Mrs. Hamer's involvement and development as local leader for SNCC; see Endesha Ida Mae Holland, *From the Mississippi Delta: A Memoir* (New York, 1997); see Moye, *Let the People Decide*, 87–118, for civil rights organizing by Charles McLaurin, Charles Cobb Jr., and Lafayette Surney in Ruleville and Indianola; see "First Annual Report of the Voter Education Project."

27. See my Conclusions, where the Delta Ministry's continuation of this program was expanded to eighty of Mississippi's eighty-two counties. Minnis, *Chronology*; Zinn, *SNCC*, 89–92; see Forman, *The Making of Black Revolutionaries*, 294–307, for Greenwood and the movement during this period; see Payne, *I've Got the Light of Freedom*, 132–41, for early 1950s through 1962 on older civil rights leaders, 141–79 for the student-supported movement in 1962–63 and its buildup, and 180–283 for the flowering of the Greenwood movement in years afterward.

28. See Minnis, *Chronology*, by date.

29. Barrett, *Integration at Ole Miss*.

30. Silver, *Mississippi*; see Hendrickson, *Sons of Mississippi*, for Mississippi lawmen at Ole Miss in 1962 when James Meredith was admitted and riots ensued.

31. See also, Lord, *The Past That Would Not Die*, 94–112, 139–232; Lewis and the New York Times, *Portrait of A Decade*, 214–24; Sobel, *Civil Rights*, 110–24, 220–21, 334; see Kay Mills, *This Little Light of Mine: The Life of Fannie Lou Hamer* (New York, 1993), 29–33, on the lynching of James Eastland's uncle and on Sen. James O. Eastland who served in the U.S. Senate from 1941 to 1978 and was the chairman of the Senate Judiciary Committee as well as an extreme opponent of the civil rights movement and who was believed to have used prison labor from Parchman Penitentiary to harvest his cotton; see Moye, *Let the People Decide*, 3–21.

32. Forman, *The Making of Black Revolutionaries*, 294–95; Dittmer, *Local People*, 147–57; *Mississippi Black Paper*, 8–9; Sobel, *Civil Rights*, 192; U.S. Commission on Civil Rights, *Law Enforcement*, 54; *The Student Voice*, April 1963; Branch, *Pillar of Fire*, 712–17; see also Zellner, *The Wrong Side of Murder Creek*, 253–67.

33. U.S. Commission on Civil Rights, *Law Enforcement*, 54.

34. Ibid., 54–55.

35. Zinn, *SNCC*, 89–92; Watters and Cleghorn, *Climbing Jacob's Ladder*, 59–63; see Forman, *The Making of Black Revolutionaries*, 296–307, for events in Greenwood in 1963 by Charles Cobb, James Forman, and Bob Moses; see also Branch, *Pillar of Fire*, 66–74; see Lee, *For Freedom's Sake*, 61–84, on Mrs. Hamer's work with COFO and SNCC in the Delta in voter registration, as well as her run for Congress in the June 1964 Democratic Primary and its connection with gathering and distributing food and clothing.

36. According to Payne, in *I've Got the Light of Freedom*, "the story of Greenwood in 1962–63 is . . . about a young activist tradition building . . . on an older one. . . . [L]ocal people and the younger COFO activists made a way where there had appeared to be no way" (179); see Hogan, *Many Minds, One Heart*, 80–92; "First Annual Report of the Voter Education Project," 39; see Steven F. Lawson and Charles Payne, *Debating the Civil Rights Movement, 1945–1968* (Lanham, Md., 2006), 115–209, for the importance of local people in the Mississippi movement and the connection between leaders of the 1950s and the development of local leaders in the 1960s.

Chapter Four

1. See CORE, "Mississippi: The Civil Rights Commission versus The Civil Rights Movement" (Washington, D.C., 1963), Chronology of Events.

2. Joint testimony of Aaron Henry and Charles Evers before the U.S. Commission on Civil Rights, Jackson, Miss., as qtd. from U.S. Commission on Civil Rights, *Hearings Held in Jackson* 1: 153–76.

3. The depositions gathered by the Mississippi Freedom Democratic Party—some 3,000 single-spaced pages—for its Congressional Challenge of the regular Mississippi Congressmen in 1965 are superior and more representative of the state of affairs in Mississippi during the period under discussion.

4. Higgs interview.

5. U.S. Commission on Civil Rights, *Law Enforcement*, 143.

6. Ibid., 54; see also, Sobel, *Civil Rights*, 190–92, 247.

7. Sobel, *Civil Rights*, 192–93; Zinn, *SNCC*, 91–92; Forman, *The Making of Black Revolutionaries*, 296–307.

8. Harris interview.

9. A good summary of the proceedings against Registrar Lynd is found in Lord, *The Past That Would Not Die*, 120–32; see also Gordon A. Martin Jr., *Count Them One by One: Black Mississippians Fighting for the Right to Vote* (Jackson, Miss., 2010) for a review of *United States v. Lynd*.

10. See chapter 1, above.

11. Barry interview.

12. Harris interview.

13. Higgs interview.

14. Henry interview.

15. See chapter 2, above. See Watters and Cleghorn, *Climbing Jacob's Ladder*, on the Voter Education Project; Meier and Rudwick, *CORE*.

16. "Second Annual Report of the Voter Education Project," 9–10.

17. Jack Minnis, "Diary Notes."

18. Higgs interview.

19. Jenkins interview.

20. Harris interview.

21. Charles J. Lapidary, "Ol' Massa Jim Eastland," *The Nation* 184 (February 9, 1957): 121.

22. McCord, *Long, Hot Summer*, 18.

23. The "First Annual Report of the Voter Education Project," 12–13.

Chapter Five

Epigraph: Moses memo, summer 1963.

1. On January 2, 1963, in *Moses et al v. Robert F. Kennedy and J. Edgar Hoover,* the movement brought suit in Federal District Court to gain protection for its workers; see Dittmer, *Local People,* 143–69.

2. Dave Dennis, field report for March 1–31, 1963, to the national office of CORE; see Dittmer, *Local People,* 143–57; see Payne, *I've Got the Light of Freedom,* chapter 3, notes 23 and 32, for the movement's work in Greenwood with a recap of its socio-economic history and place in the Delta; see also Zinn, *SNCC,* 91–92; see also Zellner, *The Wrong Side of Murder Creek,* 253–67; Branch, *Pillar of Fire,* 718–25.

3. See Minnis, *Chronology,* by date.

4. Ibid.; see also, Sobel, *Civil Rights,* 193.

5. Minnis, *Chronology.*

6. See Forman, *The Making of Black Revolutionaries,* 376; see also often-cited case of firebombing of Hartman Turnbow's home in Holmes County in the Delta and his armed response in Simon Wendt, *The Spirit and the Shotgun: Armed Resistance and the Struggle for Civil Rights* (Gainesville, Fla., 2007), 100–101, 107–8, 118; see also Andrews, *Freedom Is a Constant Struggle,* 80, 115–17 for discussion of the firing on Turnbow's home in Mileston with a citation of documents from the author's analysis of civil rights activity in Holmes County in the Delta.

7. Minnis, *Chronology;* see Dittmer, *Local* People, 176–77, for events in Clarksdale; see also *Mississippi Black Paper,* 14.

8. Thomas Gaither, field report for July 20–27, 1963, on Clarksdale, to the national office of CORE; see also, Minnis, *Chronology.*

9. For the situation leading to death of Medgar Evers, see Dorman, *We Shall Overcome,* 233–77. See Salter, *Jackson,* for recording of events of Jackson movement in 1962–63 involving local blacks from Jackson and students from Tougaloo and their fight against the Mississippi establishment, 27–35; for the Jackson sit-ins, 36–52. See also Dittmer, *Local People,* 157–69; see also Maryanne Vollers, *Ghosts of Mississippi: The Murder of Medgar Evers, the Trials of Byron De La Beckwith, and the Haunting of the New South* (Boston, 1995); see also Gene Roberts and Hank Klibanoff, *The Race Beat: The Press, the Civil Rights Struggle, and the Awakening of a Nation* (New York, 2006), 334–52, for a behind-the-scenes look at the reporting of Evers's murder in Jackson; see also Branch, *Pillar of Fire,* 813–16, 817–18, 826–27, 831–33.

10. Sobel, *Civil Rights,* 189–90; National CORE press release, dated May 29, 1963, from Jackson; Dorman, *We Shall Overcome,* 245.

11. Sobel, *Civil Rights,* 191–92; Salter, *Jackson;* also Vollers, *Ghosts of Mississippi.*

12. See *Mississippi Black Paper,* 17–24, for depositions of Mrs. Fannie Lou Hamer, Annelle Ponder, and June E. Johnson; see Mills, *This Little Light of Mine,* 56–77; see Lee, *For Freedom's Sake,* 45–60, for another look at the Winona incident and its place as a metaphor of Mississippi violence and the sexual overtones of white violence toward African American women as well as the way in which SNCC, COFO, and the MFDP and Mrs. Hamer used the incident to reveal Mississippi's true racial character to the nation; this action against Mrs. Hamer in particular led to her revealing her sterilization at the hands of a Mississippi Delta hospital and the fact that Mississippi was trying to codify this process legally after the fact of having done this to her (21–22, 80–81); see Dittmer, *Local People,* 170–77; see also Watters and Cleghorn, *Climbing Jacob's Ladder,* 363–75; see also Branch, *Pillar of Fire,* 819–21, 825–26.

13. SNCC press release, July 30, 1963.

14. Ibid.

15. See Zinn, *SNCC,* 96–98.

16. Minnis, *Chronology.*

Chapter Six

Epigraph 1: Harold Fleming, Session IV of the American Academy Conference on the Negro American, May 14–15, 1965, transcript in *The Negro American, Daedalus,* II (Winter, 1966), 386.

Epigraph 2: Interview with Prof. Howard Zinn.

1. See Meier and Rudwick, *CORE.*

2. Dave Dennis letter to National CORE, November 18, 1963.

3. Jenkins interview; Joseph A. Loftus, *New York Times,* August 7, 1963, 20.

4. For further information on the registration drive in Jackson after Evers's murder, see *New York Times,* July 10, 1963.

5. Jenkins interview; Lewis, *Shadows of Youth,* 144–47; Forman, *The Making of Black Revolutionaries,* 354–61; see also Branch, *Pillar of Fire,* 118–23, 156–59.

6. Watters and Cleghorn, *Climbing Jacob's Ladder,* 65–67; see also Lucille Komisar, "Mississippi: Story of an Election," *The Activist* 3 (Fall 1963): 6–8; see Richard Cummings, *The Pied Piper: Allard K. Lowenstein and the Liberal Dream* (New York, 1985), 229–45; see also Curry, *Aaron Henry,* 156–61.

7. See August 6, 1963, NAACP press release.

8. Silver, *Mississippi,* 250; see Shirley Tucker, *Mississippi from Within* (New York, 1965), 107.

9. SNCC press release, August 8, 1963.

10. Dave Dennis, field report, October 19, 1963, to National CORE office.

11. Jenkins interview; see Watters and Cleghorn, *Climbing Jacob's Ladder,* 66–67; see also Forman, *The Making of Black Revolutionaries,* 354.

12. COFO, Vote for Freedom directives No. l (August 14), No. 2 (August 16), and No. 3 (August 21); Ransby, *Ella Baker,* 311–14; Payne, *I've Got the Light of Freedom,* 291–94.

13. Jenkins interview.

14. Komisar, "Mississippi," 7; *Mississippi Free Press,* August 31, 1963.

15. Komisar, "Mississippi," 7.

16. See Forman, *The Making of Black Revolutionaries.*

17. Lowenstein interview; Cummings, *The Pied Piper,* 229–45; see Doug McAdam, *Freedom Summer* (New York, 1988), 36–38; see Payne, *I've Got the Light of Freedom,* 56–66, for a picture of Aaron Henry.

18. See Minnis, *Chronology*, by date, for incidents cited in text.

19. Information corroborating the facts of the Freedom Vote campaign was gathered from (1) SNCC Papers, Series XV, Box 98, Folders 11–12: COFO, Overview of the Political Program, Jackson, October 1963, and Statement of Purpose of the Freedom Ballot for Governor, including budget, and events in Mississippi on November 1 and 2, 1963; (2) Robert Gore, field report for October 31–November 5, 1963, to the national office of CORE; (3) Ivanhoe Donaldson, field report for October 30–November 5,1963, to the Atlanta office of SNCC; (4) Dave Dennis, field report for October 21–November 7, 1963, to the national office of CORE; (5) Minnis, *Chronology*; (6) Affidavits of Robert Ferris, Richard Van Wagenen, Bruce Payne, John Anthony Speh, Robert Haverfield, Nelson Soltman, Gary Saxonhouse, and Jon M. Van Dyke, all of whom were Yale students who participated in the Freedom Vote campaign; (7) Ronnie Dugger, *Washington Post,* November 3, 1963; (8) *Mississippi Free Press,* October 26, 1963; (9) *Mississippi Free Press,* November 2, 1963; (10) Bruce Payne, "The Quiet War," *The Activist* 4, no. 2 (1964): 75–80; (11) *Mississippi Black Paper,* 38–39; (12) Yale *Daily News,* October 17–18, 21–25, 28–31, November 1, 4–8, and 11, 1963; (13) Forman, *The Making of Black Revolutionaries,* 354–61; (14) U.S. Commission on Civil Rights, *Hearings Held in Jackson* 2: 70–76; (15) Watters and Cleghorn, *Climbing Jacob's Ladder,* 67; (16) COFO. "A Petition Requesting Congress to Investigate State-Supported Denial of Constitutional Rights in Mississippi, presented to: United States Congress, Washington, D.C., November 25, 1963, by the Committee to Elect Aaron Henry Governor." Jackson, Miss., 1963. See also Burner, *Gently He Shall Lead Them*; Dittmer, *Local People,* 195–214; Payne, *I've Got the Light of Freedom,* 294–97; Hogan, *Many Minds, One Heart,* 143–54; Mills, *This Little Light of Mine,* 78–83.

20. Joan Bowman, field report, October 23, 1963, to the Atlanta office of SNCC; Dave Dennis, letter to National CORE, November 18, 1963.

21. Dave Dennis, "An Abortion for a Pregnant State," field report to the National Action Committee of CORE.

22. See note 19 above; See Mills, *This Little Light of Mine,* 82–93, for transition from Freedom Vote to Mrs. Hamer's and Mrs. Victoria Gray's run in the congressional primary on June 2, 1964.

23. I gathered information on the national news media and the wire services and their treatment of the events during the Freedom Vote campaign while coordinating news stories relayed back to Yale by students who went to Mississippi for the campaign. Yale students phoned in their news stories to the Yale *Daily News,* and I gave them to college newspapers such as the Cornell *Daily Sun,* the Harvard *Crimson,* the Dartmouth and Princeton papers, to Dean Gotterer at the Collegiate Press Service in Philadelphia, and United Press International (UPI) at the *Hartford Current* in Connecticut. It was thus possible to break the news blackout by bypassing the local bureaus of the Associated Press (AP) and UPI; see Payne, *I've Got the Light of Freedom,* 396: "Much of SNCC's organizing was a response to their assumption that national institutions, including the press, were more interested in what happened to whites than to Blacks. . . . That surprised no one in SNCC, but it was nonetheless embittering because it reflected the same underlying disregard for Black people that had made it possible for the nation to ignore the murders of Hebert Lee and Louis Allen."

24. Jeannine Herron, "Underground Election," *The Nation* 197 (December 7, 1963): 387–89.

25. See chapters 9 and 10, below.

26. Based on information given to me in numerous unrecorded interviews and private talks after the Freedom Vote with Yale students and movement people.

27. Qtd. in Forman, *The Making of Black Revolutionaries,* 356.

28. The most complete account of the events in Hattiesburg is to be found in Zinn, *SNCC,* 102–22; see also Dittmer, *Local People,* 179–84, 219–41; Ransby, *Ella Baker,* 317–19; Mark Newman,

Divine Agitators: The Delta Ministry and Civil Rights in Mississippi (Athens, Ga., 2004), 46–67, recaps the Delta Ministry's actions from 1964 to 1967.

29. See SNCC, *The Student Voice*, October 28, 1964, 2, for a short biography of Mrs. Gray and other candidates and activities of the MFDP; Powledge, *Free At Last?* 471–73, for information on Hollis Watkins, Curtis Hayes, and Mrs. Victoria Gray in Palmers Crossing and Hattiesburg.

30. See Bob Moses memo to SNCC Executive Committee, "SNCC Mississippi Project" (n.p., September 6, 1963), for a summary of events concerning the Mississippi SNCC Project during the two years preceding the Freedom Vote.

31. See Lord, *The Past That Would Not Die*, 120–31, for a narrative of events in Hattiesburg and the battle the movement fought with Registrar Lynd; see Martin, *Count Them One by One*, 1–18, for a step-by-step picture of *United States v. Lynd (1962)* in what Martin calls "race-haunted Mississippi" as the case wended its way from the Federal District Court of W. Harold Cox up to the Supreme Court of the United States and back; SNCC, "Fact Sheet: Hattiesburg," copy in my private files.

32. Bob Moses memo to COFO.

33. See note 31, above.

34. Quoted by Silver, *Mississippi*, 303.

35. SNCC, "Fact Sheet: Hattiesburg."

36. Minnis, *Chronology*, by date.

37. Ibid.; *Mississippi Black Paper*, 42–43, affidavit by Peter Stoner.

38. Minnis, *Chronology*, by date.

39. Zinn, *SNCC*, 102–22; Branch, *Pillar of Fire*, 57–63, 214–22.

40. See Howard Zinn, "Incident in Hattiesburg," *The Nation* 198 (May 18, 1964): 501–4, for a graphic account of Oscar Chase's arrest and beating while in jail.

41. Ibid. Zinn's article provides information on Hattiesburg during Freedom Day.

42. Zinn, *SNCC*, 117–21.

43. Ibid., 118.

44. Silver, *Mississippi*, 264–65.

45. Qtd. in Len Holt, *The Summer That Didn't End* (New York, 1965), 87–94.

46. SNCC, "Hattiesburg, Miss., Freedom Day, January 22, 1964" (n.d.), copy in my files.

47. Ibid.

48. This subsection is largely based on the account of CORE's activities in Mississippi—which centered at first in Canton—provided by Meier and Rudwick, *CORE*; see Dittmer, *Local People*, 185–90, 221–24.

49. Anne Moody, *Coming of Age in Mississippi: An Autobiography* (New York, 1968).

50. See Meier and Rudwick, *CORE*.

51. Ibid.; see also Minnis, *Chronology*, by date.

52. See *The Student Voice*, October 28, 1964, 2, for biography of Mrs. Devine.

53. See subsection "The Buildup," above.

54. See Minnis, *Chronology*, by date for events and those cited below.

55. Ibid.

56. Ibid.

57. See *Mississippi Black Paper*, 30–37; Forman, *The Making of Black Revolutionaries*, 231; Jack Newfield, *A Prophetic Minority*, 57–58; Moses, taped talk; see also Burner, *Gently He Shall Lead Them*, 58–59, 63, 131–32.

58. U.S. Commission on Civil Rights, *Law Enforcement*, 54; Sobel, *Civil Rights*, 192, 247; see also Vollers, *Ghosts of Mississippi*.

59. See Meier and Rudwick, *CORE*, 273–77, for Canton Freedom Days and CORE's part in them.

60. Ibid., 277.

61. See chapter 7, below; see *Mississippi Black Paper*, 59–66; William Bradford Huie, *3 Lives for Mississippi* (New York, 1965); Louis E. Lomax et al., "Mississippi Eyewitness," *Ramparts Magazine* (special issue, 1964).

62. See chapters 3 and 5, above.

63. See Silver, *Mississippi*, and Barrett, *Integration at Ole Miss*.

64. Sobel, *Civil Rights*, 190–92.

65. See chapters 7–10, below.

66. Ibid.

67. Forman, *The Making of Black Revolutionaries*; Watters and Cleghorn, *Climbing Jacob's Ladder*, 67; Burner, *Gently He Shall Lead Them*, 130–32. This attitude was also expressed to me in private talks with movement people.

Chapter Seven

Epigraph 1: Qtd. in Sally Belfrage, *Freedom Summer* (New York, 1965), 27.
Epigraph 2: Silver, *Mississippi*, 155–56.

1. Sutherland, ed., *Letters from Mississippi*, 215.

2. Holt, *The Summer That Didn't End*, 36; Carson, *In Struggle*, 97–110; see Bruce Watson, *Freedom Summer: The Savage Season That Made Mississippi Burn and Made America a Democracy* (New York, 2010), for the latest work on Freedom Summer; McAdam, *Freedom Summer*, 3–34; Lewis, *Shadows of Youth*, 147–62; Mills, *This Little Light of Mine*, 82–85; Branch, *Pillar of Fire*, 164–65, 192–94, 271–76; see Hampton et al., eds., *Voices of Freedom*, 177–207; King, *Freedom Song*, 522.

3. See Forman, *The Making of Black Revolutionaries*, 371–86, for analysis of Freedom Summer, problems organizing it, and its meaning within SNCC's history, along with armed self-defense and its place within the Mississippi movement; Lewis, *Walking with the Wind*, 189–90; see McAdam, *Freedom Summer*, 122–23, for the move away from tactical nonviolence to self-defense; see also Dittmer, *Local People*, 242–71, for overview of "That Summer"; see also Payne, *I've Got the Light of Freedom*, 297–98, who states, "Most COFO staff, including MacArthur Cotton, Charlie Cobb, Ivanhoe Donaldson, Hollis Watkins, Willie Peacock, and Sam Block, opposed the idea [at the Greenville meeting in November 1963 of bringing in large numbers of white volunteers for the summer]"; Payne says Moses, Guyot, Dave Dennis, Mrs. Hamer, and older local leaders favored bringing in students; see Burner, *Gently He Shall Lead Them*, 131–32, for murder of Louis Allen, a deciding factor in the decision to bring in student volunteers; see also SNCC Papers, Series XV, Box 97, State Project Files, 1960–68 Folder 2: Report Concerning the Louis Allen Case by Robert Moses, n.d., Information Concerning the Killing of Louis Allen in Liberty, Miss., Amite County, on January 31, 1964.

4. Payne, in *I've Got the Light of Freedom*, 201, says, "Local adults active in COFO overwhelmingly felt that . . . the movement needed help, and white students represented help. It was clear . . . local adults were going to vote the project in"; see Jay Garnett, "SNCC Sets Drive for Civil Rights in Mississippi," *The Militant*, April 13, 1964; see also Branch, *Pillar of Fire*, 222–24, for the crucial importance of the Allen murder to push for large numbers of northern whites in the summer project.

5. Holt, *The Summer That Didn't End*, 37; Forman, *The Making of Black Revolutionaries*, 371–75; see Dittmer, *Local People*, 225–41, for information on the planning of Freedom Summer; and Richard

Woodley, "It Will Be a Hot Summer in Mississippi," *The Reporter* 30 (May 21, 1964): 21–24; *The Student Voice*, Spring 1964; see also King, *Freedom Song*, 367–436, for a personal account of Freedom Summer.

6. Forman, *The Making of Black Revolutionaries*, 375–7, SNCC national office up in Greenwood for the summer was defended at night by armed people but arms were not kept in office and SNCC workers did not carry arms; see Judson L. Jeffries, ed. *Black Power in the Belly of the Beast* (Urbana, 2006), 1–42; Wendt, *The Spirit and the Shotgun*, 100–30 ("Armed Resistance and the Mississippi Movement"); and Lance Hill, *The Deacons for Defense: Armed Resistance and the Civil Rights Movement* (Chapel Hill, 2004), 184–215; these 3 works discuss fact that local blacks armed themselves to protect their own properties but more importantly properties used by movement at Freedom Summer projects. Also some movement workers armed themselves and patrolled properties at night as well; see also Ransby, *Ella Baker*, 322–25, and Lee, *For Freedom's Sake*, 73–74, movement arming for self-defense in rural areas.

7. Forman, *The Making of Black Revolutionaries*, 376; see also, Watters and Cleghorn, *Climbing Jacob's Ladder*, 103–4, for brief sketch of Curtis C. Bryant; U.S. Commission on Civil Rights, *Hearings Held in Jackson* 2: 450, for a summary of attacks on the Bryant property in McComb.

8. Robert F. Williams, *Negroes with Guns* (New York, 1962), for Monroe story.

9. Forman, *The Making of Black Revolutionaries*, 375–77.

10. Zinn, *SNCC*, 67–68.

11. Information comes from personal experiences with mass media in fall of 1963 and as an assistant to Community Relations Director Marvin Rich at National CORE in the spring of 1964; SNCC Papers, Series VI, Box 54, Folder 2: Letter to me from Horace Julian Bond, May 5, 1964 concerning media relations for Summer Project.

12. Security Check-out Form.

13. Elizabeth Sutherland, "The Cat and Mouse Game," *The Nation* 199 (September 14, 1964): 105–8.

14. Ibid.

15. Holt, *The Summer That Didn't End*, 12; Watters and Cleghorn, *Climbing Jacob's Ladder*, 139; see also, SNCC, *Mississippi Summer Project*.

16. W. Haywood Burns, "The Federal Government and Civil Rights," in *Southern Justice*, ed. Leon Friedman (New York, 1965), 246.

17. Sobel, *Civil Rights*, 244–46, 358–59.

18. SNCC Papers, Series XIII, Box 91, Folders 4–6: Sojourner Motor Fleet documents; Sutherland, "Cat and Mouse Game"; telephone interview with Peter Orris, who helped install the CB radios throughout Mississippi in the spring and summer of 1964; see King, *Freedom Song*, 212–48, for review of methods used to maintain movement communication system, 561–65. (In 1965 I was in Selma and was saved on the night before the march reached Montgomery by one of these radio cars after I called in for help while being chased by Alabama National Guardsmen. The next night Mrs. Viola Liuzzo was killed by the Ku Klux Klan between Selma and Montgomery.)

19. Belfrage, *Freedom Summer*; Forman, *The Making of Black Revolutionaries*.

20. See Sutherland, ed., *Letters from Mississippi*, 128–33, for picture of the Harmony community.

21. McCord, *Mississippi*, 122–25; see also U.S. Commission on Civil Rights, *Hearings Held in Jackson* 2: 449–60.

22. Holt, *The Summer That Didn't End*, 47.

23. See chapters 3–4, above; see also Newfield, *A Prophetic Minority*, 48–82; Zinn, *SNCC*; Moses, taped talk; Marion Barry and Bill Higgs interviews; Forman, *The Making of Black Revolutionaries*; Robert Penn Warren, *Who Speaks for the Negro?* (New York, 1965), 48–49, 89–100.

24. See chapter 3, above.

25. See Mississippi—Subversion of the Right to Vote pamphlet (item 904, digilib.usm.edu) for a picture of the Mississippi power structure.

26. See chapter 6, above.

27. Holt, *The Summer That Didn't End*, 48.

28. Belfrage, *Freedom Summer*, 3–27; Sutherland, ed., *Letters from Mississippi*, 3–29; Holt, *The Summer That Didn't End*, 43–54; McCord, *Mississippi*, 50–77; Stephen Bingham, "Mississippi Letter" (unpublished, 1965); *The Student Voice*; Carson, *In Struggle*, 111–23; Hogan, *Many Minds, One Heart*, 155–56, 160–66; see also Branch, *Pillar of Fire*, 351–54, 360–74.

29. For an outlined plan of political activity during Freedom Summer, see COFO, "Mississippi."

30. Holt, *The Summer That Didn't End*, 49.

31. Ibid., 50; McAdam, *Freedom Summer*, 66–77.

32. Bingham, "Mississippi Letter," 1–2.

33. Holt, *The Summer That Didn't End*, 76–94.

34. Ibid., 339–40.

35. Ibid.; Forman, *The Making of Black Revolutionaries*.

36. Holt, *The Summer That Didn't End*, 87; Hilton, *Delta Ministry*; Howell, *Freedom City*; Robert W. Spike, *The Freedom Revolution and the Churches* (New York, 1965).

37. Holt, *The Summer That Didn't End*, 48–49. See McAdam, *Freedom Summer*, 3–34, for whites' and blacks' idealism for changing Mississippi's oppressive and violent nature; 35–65, for background of various summer volunteers; and 101–15, for pressures and tensions they experienced. Sutherland, ed., *Letters from Mississippi*. Forman, *The Making of Black Revolutionaries*, 379–80. See Tracy Sugarman, *Stranger at the Gates: A Summer in Mississippi* (New York, 1966), for picture of a volunteer in Ruleville in the Delta. See Tracy Sugarman, *We Had Sneakers, They Had Guns: The Kids Who Fought for Civil Rights in Mississippi* (Syracuse, N.Y., 2009), for volunteers' life in the Delta in summer 1964. *The Student Voice*, Spring 1964, special issue; July 15, 1964, 3. Mary Aickin Rothschild, "White Women Volunteers in the Freedom Summers," *Feminist Studies* 5 (Fall 1979): 475.

38. Forman, *The Making of Black Revolutionaries*, 372–74.

39. Sutherland, ed., *Letters from Mississippi*, 3–39.

40. Ibid., 5.

41. Ibid., 6.

42. Meier and Rudwick, *CORE*, 276.

43. See chapter 6, above; see also "SNCC Blasts Miss. Jailings; Demands Sheriff Be Arrested," *The Militant* 28 (April 13, 1965): 5.

44. "Mississippi: Allen's Army," *Newsweek*, February 24, 1964; see also Roberts and Klibanoff, *The Race Beat*, 351–74, for inside look at how press and reporters covered Freedom Summer, particularly the *New York Times*.

45. "Mississippi: Allen's Army," *Newsweek*, February 24, 1964.

46. See Moye, *Let the People Decide*, 119–22.

47. See appendix , below; see Holt, *The Summer That Didn't End*, 281–85.

48. See chapter 1, note 23, above.

49. U.S. Commission on Civil Rights, *Law Enforcement*, 15n3.

50. Ibid., 36–37.

51. See chapter 6, above; see also U.S. Commission on Civil Rights, *Hearings Held in Jackson* 2: 449–60; U.S. Commission on Civil Rights, *Law Enforcement*.

52. See Tucker, *Mississippi from Within*.

53. Ibid., 11.

54. Ibid.

55. Ibid.

56. Quoted by Huie, *3 Lives*, 225–6.

57. Ibid., 224.

58. McCord, *Mississippi*, 100.

59. Holt, *The Summer That Didn't End*, 72–73.

60. Silver, *Mississippi*, 304.

61. SNCC, *Mississippi Summer Project: Running Summary of Incidents, June 16–August 26, 1964* (Atlanta, n.d.).

62. The three most important published accounts of the triple lynching are Huie, *3 Lives*; Seth Cagin and Philip Dray, *We Are Not Afraid: The Story of Goodman, Schwerner, and Chaney and the Civil Rights Campaign for Mississippi* (New York, 1988); and Lomax et al., "Mississippi Eyewitness"; see Farmer, *Lay Bare the Heart*, 271–78, with his recounting of being notified of the three CORE workers' disappearance; see also Florence Mars, *Witness in Philadelphia* (Baton Rouge, 1977); see Debra L. Schultz, *Going South: Jewish Women in the Civil Rights Movement* (New York, 2001), 65–70, for an illuminating account of Bob Zellner's and Rita Schwerner's meeting with Governors Paul Johnson and George Wallace on the steps of the Mississippi capitol in Jackson, with Neshoba County Sheriff Lawrence Rainey in Philadelphia, Mississippi, and with Deputy Attorney General Nicholas Katzenbach and President Johnson in Washington.

63. Meier and Rudwick, *CORE*, 275–77.

64. Lomax et al., "Mississippi Eyewitness," 6–23.

65. Ibid., 10.

66. Quoted in *The Massachusetts Review* 6, no.1 (Autumn 1964–Winter 1965): 12, with the permission of Goodman's parents, Mr. and Mrs. Robert Goodman.

67. David M. Spain, M.D., "Mississippi Autopsy," in Lomax et al., "Mississippi Eyewitness," 43–49.

68. Ibid., 49; Sobel, *Civil Rights*, 244.

69. Lomax et al., "Mississippi Eyewitness," 46.

70. Ibid., 48.

71. Ibid., 47.

72. Ibid., 47.

73. Silver, *Mississippi*, 263–64.

74. Lomax et al., "Mississippi Eyewitness," 49.

75. "Interview with Dick Gregory," in Lomax et al., "Mississippi Eyewitness," 36–39.

76. Sobel, *Civil Rights*, 244–46, 358–59.

77. Ibid., 246.

78. Ibid., 246.

79. Ibid., 244–45.

80. Louis E. Lomax, "Road to Mississippi," in Lomax et al., "Mississippi Eyewitness," 21.

81. Ibid., 13–19.

82. David Welsh, "Valley of Fear," in Lomax et al., "Mississippi Eyewitness," 50–59.

83. David M. Spain, in Lomax et al., "Mississippi Eyewitness," 48.

84. Huie, *3 Lives*, 228–29; see also Meier and Rudwick, *CORE*, 277–78.

85. Reinhold Niebuhr, foreword to *Mississippi Black Paper*.

86. *Mississippi: Running Summary of Incidents*; see McAdam, *Freedom Summer*, 77–83, 96–101; see notes for chapter 3, above, for citations concerning movement memoirs and studies done on the Delta and other counties.

87. *The Student Voice*, October 28, 1964, l, 4; see Moye, *Let the People Decide*, 118–47, for a description of the Summer Project in Sunflower County, including Freedom School and voter registration efforts.

88. Sutherland, ed., *Letters from Mississippi*, 97–99; see Watters and Cleghorn, *Climbing Jacob's Ladder*.

89. *The Student Voice*, July 15, 1964, l, 3; see also Warren, *Who Speaks for the Negro?* 115.

90. Warren, *Who Speaks for the Negro?* 115–16; see also U.S. Commission on Civil Rights, *Hearings Held in Jackson* 1: 157.

91. Holt, *The Summer That Didn't End*, 195–96; "COFO and the Summer Project, Mississippi Project" (n.p., n.d.), in my possession; see Blackwell, *Barefootin'*, 63–173, where Mrs. Blackwell relates her participation in the movement.

92. COFO, "Mississippi," discusses techniques for fieldwork.

93. Ibid.

94. Ibid.

95. Ibid.

96. Meier and Rudwick, *CORE*, 274.

97. Mississippi: *Running Summary of Incidents.*

98. See table 2, above, for numbers of registered voters in the Delta and counties where the movement was active. The information cited on Freedom Days during the summer of 1964 is from *Mississippi: Running Summary of Incidents*; see also U.S. Commission on Civil Rights, *Hearings Held in Jackson* 1: 263–64.

99. See Lord, *The Past That Would Not Die*, 120–32.

100. See Gerald M. Stern, "Judge William Harold Cox and the Right to Vote in Clarke County, Mississippi," in Friedman, ed., *Southern Justice*, 165–86.

101. *Mississippi: Running Summary of Incidents*, by date.

102. See note 98, above.

103. See chapter 1, above.

104. See *Mississippi: Running Summary of Incidents*, by date.

105. Sutherland, "Cat and Mouse Game."

106. *Mississippi Black Paper*, 76–78; Tucker, *Mississippi from Within*, 108.

107. *Mississippi: Running Summary of Incidents*, by date.

108. See table of federal litigation in COFO, "Mississippi"; see also *Mississippi: Running Summary of Incidents.*

109. *Mississippi: Running Summary of Incidents*, by date.

110. See my Statistical Study cited in the bibliography.

111. Silver, *Mississippi*, 295.

112. Ibid., 295.

113. See chapters 9 and 10, below, for a brief description of how the Delta's African Americans organized themselves in the mid-1960s to confront this threat to their survival. See Hilton, *Delta Ministry*, and Howell, *Freedom City*, for accounts of how the Delta Ministry worked with African Americans on matters of economic organization after 1964; see Lemann, *Promised Land*, 307–39, for how the Delta and its African Americans were affected by the mechanization of cotton production.

114. Lemann, *Promised Land*.

115. Sutherland, ed., *Letters from Mississippi*, 137; *Mississippi: Running Summary of Incidents*.

116. *Mississippi: Running Summary of Incidents*, by date.

117. *The Student Voice*, July 15, 1964, 1, 4; McCord, *Mississippi*, 81–89, 122–25; U.S. Commission on Civil Rights, *Law Enforcement*; U.S. Commission on Civil Rights, *Hearings Held in Jackson* 2: 449–60; Sobel, *Civil Rights*, 247–48; Tucker, *Mississippi from Within*, 118–29; *Mississippi: Running Summary of Incidents*.

118. *Mississippi Black Paper*, 76; "Project Goes On Despite Bombing," *The Student Voice*, July 15, 1964, l, 4; McCord, *Mississippi*, 84.

119. U.S. Commission on Civil Rights, *Hearings Held in Jackson* 2: 454; *Mississippi Black Paper*, 90.

120. See *Mississippi: Running Summary of Incidents* for numbers enrolled in Freedom Schools and performances of the Free Southern Theater.

121. *Mississippi: Running Summary of Incidents*, by date.

122. Ibid.; McCord, *Mississippi*, 124–25.

Chapter Eight

1. Frederick Douglass, *Narrative of the Life of Frederick Douglass, An American Slave, Written by Himself* (1845; Garden City, N.Y., 1963), 36.

2. SNCC Papers, Series XV, Box 98, Folders 8–9: Freedom Schools, miscellaneous, July 24, 1964–67; for published sources on Freedom Schools and community centers, see Holt, *The Summer That Didn't End*, 97–128, 317–38; Sutherland, ed., *Letters from Mississippi*, 103–33; Belfrage, *Freedom Summer*, 89–92; Zinn, *SNCC*, 247–51; Jerry DeMuth, "Summer in Mississippi," *The Nation* 199 (September 14, 1964); "Progress Report I: Summer Project," *The Student Voice* 5 (July 15, 1964): 3; see also Ransby, *Ella Baker*, 326–29, 357–66, for comparison of Baker's pedagogical style to that of the Brazilian educator Paulo Freire.

3. Zinn, *SNCC*, 75–76; Lynd, *Nonviolence*, 436–40.

4. Lynd, *Nonviolence*, 437.

5. Statistical research I have compiled from U.S. Census studies.

6. Ibid.

7. Ibid.

8. DeMuth, "Summer in Mississippi."

9. See McAdam, *Freedom Summer*, 83–96, for Freedom School activity and life in the surrounding African American communities; see Sugarman, *We Had Sneakers*, 72–80, 202–9, 300–306, for a picture of Ruleville Freedom School and teachers; see also Moye, *Let the People Decide*, 122–34.

10. See Meier and Rudwick, *CORE*, 273; Zinn, *SNCC*, 247.

11. Sutherland, ed., *Letters from Mississippi*, 118–22; *Mississippi: Running Summary of Incidents*, by date.

12. Sutherland, ed., *Letters from Mississippi*, 128–32.

13. Sobel, *Civil Rights*, 265–66.

14. "Mileston Opens Community Center," *The Student Voice* 5 (October 28, 1964): 3; Silver, *Mississippi*, 267.

15. Belfrage, *Freedom Summer*, 94–97.

16. See chapters 3 and 5, above.

17. Holt, *The Summer That Didn't End*, 17–20.

18. SNCC Papers, Series II, Box 6, Folders 4–6, Executive Committee Minutes, April 19,1964, Lawyers for Mississippi Summer Project; Forman, *The Making of Black Revolutionaries*, 367–71, 380–84; Zinn, *SNCC*, 270–73.

19. Meier and Rudwick, *CORE*, 271.

20. Ibid., 296–304.

21. See Silver, *Mississippi*; Lord, *The Past That Would Not Die*; Barrett, *Integration at Ole Miss*.

22. Holt, *The Summer That Didn't End*, 87, 91.

23. See chapters 3–6, above.

24. See Holt, *The Summer That Didn't End*, 88–91.

25. Ibid.; on legal aid to the movement from private, unrecorded talks with Carl Rachlin, the attorney for National CORE, and Howard Slater of the Law Students Civil Rights Research Council.

26. For the guild's work, see Holt, *The Summer That Didn't End*, 87–94, 278–80.

27. For information on the LCDC and the NAACP Legal Defense and Educational Fund, see Holt, *The Summer That Didn't End*, 87–94; Silver, *Mississippi*, 264–67; Sutherland, "Cat and Mouse Game."

28. Silver, *Mississippi*, 264–67; Forman, *The Making of Black Revolutionaries*, 361–71, 380, 382.

29. Sutherland, "Cat and Mouse Game"; Silver, *Mississippi*, 264–65.

30. From private talks with Howard Slater, who gave me an understanding of the legal work of the Summer Project.

31. Holt, *The Summer That Didn't End*, 88.

32. Ibid., 88; see also Sutherland, "Cat and Mouse Game."

33. See essays in Friedman, ed., *Southern Justice*.

34. SNCC, *Summer Incidents*, by date.

35. See Holt, *The Summer That Didn't End*, 77–82; Belfrage, *Freedom Summer*, 97–99; Silver, *Mississippi*, 262–64; see John Dittmer, *The Good Doctors: The Medical Committee for Human Rights and the Struggle for Social Justice in Health Care* (New York, 2009), 1–130.

36. Dr. David Spain, "Mississippi Autopsy," in Lomax et al., ed., "Mississippi Eyewitness," 43–49.

37. Silver, *Mississippi*, 262.

38. Holt, *The Summer That Didn't End*, 79–80.

39. Ibid., 81–82.

40. Silver, *Mississippi*, 264.

41. Ibid., 262, 290; Holt, *The Summer That Didn't End*, 85–87; Sutherland, "Cat and Mouse Game"; see Dittmer, *The Good Doctors*, 81–156, for connections with the Delta Ministry after the summer of 1964.

42. *Mississippi Black Paper*, 79; Sutherland, ed., *Letters from Mississippi*, 139–44; Tucker, *Mississippi from Within*, 110.

43. *Mississippi: Running Summary of Incidents*, by date.

44. See chapter 10, below. See Silver, *Mississippi*, 290; Hilton, *Delta Ministry*; Howell, *Freedom City*; Forman, *The Making of Black Revolutionaries*, 399–406; see Joseph S. Vandiver, "The Changing Realm of King Cotton," *Trans-action*, November 1966; see also Gene Dattel, *Cotton and Race in the Making of America: The Human Costs of Economic Power* (Chicago, 2009).

45. Silver, *Mississippi*, 283, 286, 289.

46. See *Mississippi: Running Summary of Incidents*; Tucker, *Mississippi from Within*.

47. Holt, *The Summer That Didn't End*, 83–85, 320–21.

48. Ibid., 84–85.

49. Ibid., 82–83.

50. Holt, *The Summer That Didn't End*, 129–48; see Gregg L. Michel, *Struggle for a Better South: The Southern Student Organizing Committee, 1964–1969* (New York, 2004), 64–74, for "white folks project"; see Constance Curry et al., *Deep in Our Hearts*, 227–42, for founding of SSOC in the spring of 1964; see Sutherland, ed., *Letters from Mississippi*, 173–89.

51. Past failures during the Populist Era seemed to indicate the difficulties.

52. See Zinn, *SNCC*; see Zellner, *The Wrong Side of Murder Creek*, 300–314.

53. See Belfrage, *Freedom Summer*.

54. Holt, *The Summer That Didn't End*, 134.

55. See Stephen Bingham, "Mississippi Letter," 9.

56. Holt, *The Summer That Didn't End*, 141–43; Michel, *Struggle for a Better South*, 64–74.

57. Holt, *The Summer That Didn't End*, 143.

58. Accounts on the McGhee family can be found in Belfrage, *Freedom Summer*; Dittmer, *Local People*, 276–79; and Payne, *I've Got the Light of Freedom*.

59. See text of Civil Rights Act of 1964.

Chapter Nine

Epigraph 1: Holt, *The Summer That Didn't End*, 149.

Epigraph 2: Ibid., 168.

Epigraph 3: Forman interview.

1. See U.S. Commission on Civil Rights, *Political Participation*; see Mills, *This Little Light of Mine*, 105–71 for Mrs. Hamer's part in MFDP.

2. Stokely Carmichael and Charles V. Hamilton, *Black Power: The Politics of Liberation in America* (New York, 1967), 97–107; Holt, *The Summer That Didn't End*, 149–83, 339–51; Forman, *The Making of Black Revolutionaries*, 386–96; Hogan, *Many Minds, One Heart*, 156–60, 167–82; Carmichael, *Ready for Revolution*, 382–413; Watters and Cleghorn, *Climbing Jacob's Ladder*; Zinn, *SNCC*, 250–57; Belfrage, *Freedom Summer*, 237–46; Grant, *Black Protest*, 369–72; Sutherland, ed., *Letters from Mississippi*, 239–57; Meier and Rudwick, *CORE*, 278–81; Jennifer McDowell and Milton Loventhal, *Black Politics: A Study and Annotated Bibliography of the Mississippi Freedom Democratic Party* (San Jose, Calif., 1971), 5–19; McCord, *Mississippi*; Waskow, *Race Riot*, 265–75; Stoper, *Student Nonviolent Coordinating Committee*, 47–54; see also Dittmer, *Local People*, 279–85; see also Ransby, *Ella Baker*, 330–44.

3. See chapter 6, above.

4. Holt, *The Summer That Didn't End*, 154; Lewis, *Shadows of Youth*, 162–75.

5. See chapter 6, above. Holt, *The Summer That Didn't End*, 154.

6. Holt, *The Summer That Didn't End*, 154.

7. See note 2, above.

8. Holt, *The Summer That Didn't End*, 155–56; Meier and Rudwick, *CORE*, 320–26.

9. Meier and Rudwick, *CORE*, 320–26; Holt, *The Summer That Didn't End*, 157; Forman, *The Making of Black Revolutionaries*, 377–78.

10. See chapter 1, above.

11. Holt, *The Summer That Didn't End.* 155–57; Grant, *Freedom Bound,* 165. Ms. Baker says, "It is important you go to the convention whether you are seated or not. It is even more important that you develop a political machinery in this state. The Mississippi Freedom Democratic Party will not end at the convention. . . . You are waging a war against the closed society of Mississippi."

12. Holt, *The Summer That Didn't End,* 155–56, 161.

13. Ibid., 155.

14. Ibid., 155–56.

15. Ibid., 156.

16. Ibid.; Waskow, *Race Riot,* 268.

17. Unrecorded talks with Mrs. Eleanor Holmes Norton and Burns in 1965–66.

18. See chapters 3 and 4, above; Holt, *The Summer That Didn't End,* 156.

19. Holt, *The Summer That Didn't End,* 156–57.

20. Ibid., 157.

21. Ibid.; see Grant, *Freedom Bound,* 170, for Ms. Baker's importance in the Washington office of MFDP coordinating efforts of convention challenge.

22. Holt, *The Summer That Didn't End,* 157.

23. Meier and Rudwick, *CORE,* 320–26; facts I gathered as staff at National CORE in 1964.

24. Meier and Rudwick, *CORE,* 279.

25. Holt, *The Summer That Didn't End,* 158.

26. Ibid., 159–60.

27. Ibid., 161.

28. Ibid.

29. Ibid.

30. Ibid.; see Carson, *In Struggle,* 123–29.

31. Holt, *The Summer That Didn't End,* 161–62.

32. Ibid., 162–63; see Moye, *Let the People Decide,* 134–47.

33. Howard Shrobe, "The Mississippi Freedom Democratic Party: The Atlantic City Challenge," 1966, unpublished seminar paper, Yale University; see *Mississippi: Running Summary of Incidents,* by date; see Blackwell, *Barefootin',* 103–22.

34. *Mississippi: Running Summary of Incidents,* by date.

35. COFO, "Mississippi."

36. See Sutherland, ed., *Letters from Mississippi;* Belfrage, *Freedom Summer;* McCord, *Mississippi.*

37. See *Mississippi: Running Summary of Incidents.*

38. Sometimes the precinct meetings were held on the same day as the county convention. *Mississippi: Running Summary of Incidents,* by date; see note 33 above.

39. See *Mississippi: Running Summary of Incidents,* by date.

40. Shrobe, "The Mississippi Freedom Democratic Party."

41. Ibid.; see *Mississippi: Running Summary of Incidents;* Zinn, *SNCC,* 252; Meier and Rudwick, *CORE,* 280.

42. Sutherland, ed., *Letters from Mississippi,* 239–55; Zinn, *SNCC,* 251; McCord, *Mississippi,* 114, cites the higher figure of 80,000.

43. Holt, *The Summer That Didn't End,* 163.

44. Ibid., 163.

45. Shrobe, "The Mississippi Freedom Democratic Party"; under 1963 Mississippi statute, presidential electors were to be chosen in September of the presidential election year.

46. Shrobe, "The Mississippi Freedom Democratic Party."

47. Ibid.; Holt, *The Summer That Didn't End*, 163–64.

48. Holt, *The Summer That Didn't End*, 164; Forman, *The Making of Black Revolutionaries*, 384.

49. Holt, *The Summer That Didn't End*, 164.

50. Ibid., 164–65.

51. Forman, *The Making of Black Revolutionaries*, 384.

52. Ibid., 384.

53. *New York Times*, July 24, 1964, 9.

54. McCord, *Mississippi*, 115; Holt, *The Summer That Didn't End*, 167.

55. Quoted by McCord, *Mississippi*, 115.

56. McCord, *Mississippi*, 115.

57. Ibid., 116; Guyot interview.

58. Holt, *The Summer That Didn't End*, 167.

59. See chapter 8, above; *Mississippi: Running Summary of Incidents*.

60. Shrobe, "The Mississippi Freedom Democratic Party"; Holt, *The Summer That Didn't End*, 167.

61. Holt, *The Summer That Didn't End*, 166.

62. See Holt, *The Summer That Didn't End*, 168–78; Forman, *The Making of Black Revolutionaries*, 386–96; Zinn, *SNCC*, 252–57; Lewis, *Walking with the Wind*, 282–93; Lee, *For Freedom's Sake*, 85–102; Sutherland, ed., *Letters from Mississippi*, 255–57; Carmichael, *Black Power*, 99–103; Grant, *Black Protest*, 371–72; McDowell, *Black Politics*, 14–15; McCord, *Mississippi*, 116–18; Belfrage, *Freedom Summer*, 236–46; Watters and Cleghorn, *Climbing Jacob's Ladder*, 289–92; Waskow, *Race Riot*, 265–75; Meier and Rudwick, *CORE*, 278–80, 320–21; see also Andrew Young, *An Easy Burden; The Civil Rights Movement and the Transformation of America* (New York, 1996), 303–10; Cummings, *The Pied Piper*, 262–75; see also Dittmer, *Local People*, 285–302; Hogan, *Many Minds, One Heart*, 185–96; see also Powledge, *Free At Last?* 594–604.

63. See Holt, *The Summer That Didn't End*, 168–74.

64. Waskow, *Race Riot*, 268; Holt, *The Summer That Didn't End*, 168–69; Belfrage, *Freedom Summer*, 238; Shrobe, "The Mississippi Freedom Democratic Party."

65. Holt, *The Summer That Didn't End*, 169; Shrobe, "The Mississippi Freedom Democratic Party."

66. Holt, *The Summer That Didn't End*, 169.

67. Ibid., 169.

68. Ibid., 170; Waskow, *Race Riot*, 269.

69. Holt, *The Summer That Didn't End*, 170.

70. Ibid.; Waskow, *Race Riot*, 270; Shrobe, "The Mississippi Freedom Democratic Party."

71. Holt, *The Summer That Didn't End*, 171.

72. Shrobe, "The Mississippi Freedom Democratic Party."

73. Forman, *The Making of Black Revolutionaries*, 388.

74. Ibid., 388–89; Holt, *The Summer That Didn't End*, 171.

75. Forman, *The Making of Black Revolutionaries*, 389; Holt, *The Summer That Didn't End*, 171.

76. Forman, *The Making of Black Revolutionaries*, 389.

77. Waskow, *Race Riot*, 270–71.

78. Ibid., 269; Holt, *The Summer That Didn't End*, 172.

79. Waskow, *Race Riot*, 270–71; Forman, *The Making of Black Revolutionaries*, 388.

80. Forman, *The Making of Black Revolutionaries*, 388.

81. Waskow, *Race Riot*, 269.

82. Ibid., 271.

83. Holt, *The Summer That Didn't End*, 173; Hilton, *Delta Ministry*, 236–37; Waskow, *Race Riot*, 270–71.

84. Waskow, *Race Riot*, 271.

85. Ibid.

86. Ibid., 271–73; Holt, *The Summer That Didn't End*, 172–75; Forman, *The Making of Black Revolutionaries*, 389.

87. Qtd. in Forman, *Black Revolutionaries*, 388.

88. Silver, *Mississippi*, 344; see also, Waskow, *Race Riot*, 274.

89. Waskow, *Race Riot*, 273; Holt, *The Summer That Didn't End*, 174–78; Forman, *The Making of Black Revolutionaries*, 389–96.

90. Holt, *The Summer That Didn't End*, 171.

91. Forman, *The Making of Black Revolutionaries*, 390.

92. Waskow, *Race Riot*, 274–75; Holt, *The Summer That Didn't End*, 176; Belfrage, *Freedom Summer*, 245; Zinn, *SNCC*, 254–55.

93. The best material on the meeting is in Forman, *The Making of Black Revolutionaries*, 390–95; see also Holt, *The Summer That Didn't End*, 174–76; Zinn, *SNCC*, 255; also Shrobe, "The Mississippi Freedom Democratic Party."

94. Forman, *The Making of Black Revolutionaries*, 391.

95. Ibid., 392.

96. See chapter 7, above. Forman, *The Making of Black Revolutionaries*, 392.

97. Forman, *The Making of Black Revolutionaries*, 392; see also David J. Garrow, *Bearing the Cross: Martin Luther King, Jr., and the Southern Christian Leadership Conference* (New York, 1988).

98. Forman, *The Making of Black Revolutionaries*, 393.

99. Ibid., 393; see also Holt, *The Summer That Didn't End*, 175.

100. Forman, *The Making of Black Revolutionaries*, 393; Holt, *The Summer That Didn't End*, 175.

101. Forman, *The Making of Black Revolutionaries*, 393.

102. Ibid.

103. Ibid., 393–95.

104. Zinn, *SNCC*, 255; see also Dittmer, *Local People*, 301–2.

105. Zinn, *SNCC*, 255.

106. Holt, *The Summer That Didn't End*, 176.

107. Ibid.

108. Ibid.

109. Ibid.

110. Zinn, *SNCC*, 256.

111. Forman, *The Making of Black Revolutionaries*, 396.

112. Ibid., 396–406.

113. Holt, *The Summer That Didn't End*, 174.

114. Forman, *The Making of Black Revolutionaries*, 396–97.

115. Holt, *The Summer That Didn't End*, 171.

116. See chapters 1 and 4, above; see also Burns, *Voices of Negro Protest*.

117. Forman, *The Making of Black Revolutionaries*, 399.

118. Ibid., 399–400.

119. Warren, *Who Speaks for the Negro?* 115; Sutherland, ed., *Letters from Mississippi*, 100–101.

120. Forman, *The Making of Black Revolutionaries*, 400–402.

121. Ibid., 403–4.

122. Ibid., 404–5; see also Dittmer, *Local People*, 315–17.

123. Forman, *The Making of Black Revolutionaries*, 405.

124. Ibid., 405–6.

125. See chapters 1 and 7, above. Information on this period of violence in McComb may be found in Joseph Crespino, *In Search of Another Country: Mississippi and the Conservative Counterrevolution* (Princeton, 2007), 108–43, and McCord, *Mississippi*, 123–25; see Dittmer, *Local People*, 303–15; further material in Sobel, *Civil Rights*, 247–48; Silver, *Mississippi*, 334–37; and Tucker, *Mississippi from Within*, 118–29; see documentary materials in U.S. Commission on Civil Rights, *Hearings Held in Jackson* 2: 449–60; and *Mississippi: Running Summary of Incidents*, by date; see also Newman, *Divine Agitators*, 68–83, for Delta Ministry work, 1964–66.

126. See U.S. Commission on Civil Rights, *Hearings Held in Jackson* 2: 449–60.

127. See chapter 1, above.

128. McCord, *Mississippi*, 88.

129. Ibid., 123.

130. U.S. Commission on Civil Rights, *Hearings Held in Jackson* 2: 455–56; see also Tucker, *Mississippi from Within*, 124.

131. U.S. Commission on Civil Rights, *Hearings Held in Jackson* 2: 456–57.

132. Ibid., 457.

133. Ibid., 458; Sobel, *Civil Rights*, 247; Tucker, *Mississippi from Within*, 118.

134. U.S. Commission on Civil Rights, *Hearings Held in Jackson* 2: 457; Sobel, *Civil Rights*. 247; Tucker, *Mississippi from Within*, 118, 124; McCord, *Mississippi*, 123–25.

135. McCord, *Mississippi*, 124–25; Sobel, *Civil Rights*, 247–48.

136. U.S. Commission on Civil Rights, *Hearings Held in Jackson* 2: 458.

137. Ibid., 458; Sobel, *Civil Rights*, 248; Tucker, *Mississippi from Within*, 125.

138. Sobel, *Civil Rights*, 248; Tucker, *Mississippi from Within*, 124.

139. U.S. Commission on Civil Rights, *Hearings Held in Jackson* 2: 459–60; and Tucker, *Mississippi from Within*, 126–27.

140. Sobel, *Civil Rights*, 248.

141. Tucker, *Mississippi from Within*, 127.

142. Ibid.

143. Ibid.

144. Ibid.

145. Ibid., 128–29, including full text of McComb statement for law and order.

Chapter Ten

1. See Carmichael, *Ready for Revolution*, 414–17; see also *The Student Voice*, October 28, 1964; Moye, *Let the People Decide*, 149–51, says the MFDP was disappointed with the Democratic National Convention, but Mrs. Hamer and other activists in Sunflower continued to support the national ticket.

2. Quoted by Silver, *Mississippi*, 272.

3. Information on campaign in *The Student Voice*, October 28, 1964; William Kunstler, *Deep in My Heart* (New York, 1966), 325–27; Holt, *The Summer That Didn't End*, 178–81.

4. *The Student Voice*, October 28, 1964, 4; Kunstler, *Deep in My Heart*, 325.

5. See Moye, *Let the People Decide*, 148–51.

6. *The Student Voice*, October 28, 1964, 4.

7. "Freedom Vote Is Open to All: Balloting on Oct. 30–Nov. 2," *The Student Voice* 5 (October 28, 1964): 1.

8. Ibid., 4.

9. "MFDP to Challenge Congressional Seats," *The Student Voice* 5 (October 28, 1964): 1, 4; see also, Kunstler, *Deep in My Heart*, 324–53.

10. Holt, *The Summer That Didn't End*, 179–81.

11. Quoted by Shrobe, "The Mississippi Freedom Democratic Party," from Rauh legal brief to Credentials Committee at the convention.

12. Silver, *Mississippi*, 272.

13. Ibid.

14. Meier and Rudwick, *CORE*, 339–40.

15. Ibid., 340.

16. Ibid.

17. Ibid.

18. Forman, *The Making of Black Revolutionaries*, 439.

19. See Forman, *The Making of Black Revolutionaries*, 411–43, for changes in philosophy in SNCC; Dittmer, *Local People*, 320–31, for the period after Atlantic City up to the Waveland meeting.

20. See chapter 9, above; see Forman, *The Making of Black Revolutionaries*, 407–11, on the trip to Africa.

21. See Forman, *The Making of Black Revolutionaries*, 411–32, on the October 1964 staff meeting.

22. See note 19, above; SNCC Papers, Series II, Box 6, September 1964 Executive Committee Meeting Minutes, handwritten transcription of discussed Black Belt Project for 1965.

23. SNCC Papers, Series V, Box 26, Folder 21, SNCC Conference, Waveland Retreat Meeting Minutes, November 6–12, 1964, particularly the ongoing issue of the structure and the future projects of SNCC; Forman, *The Making of Black Revolutionaries*, 433–37, on Waveland; Lewis, *Shadows of Youth*, 182–88; Hogan, *Many Minds, One Heart*, 197–218, on Waveland; Hogan, *Many Minds, One Heart*, 273–83 (appendices E–G); McAdam, *Freedom Summer*, 123–26, on racial tensions in SNCC after Freedom Summer and debates of "structure" versus "freedom high" at Waveland; Carson, *In Struggle*, 133–52, on racial tensions within SNCC and developments about structure in SNCC at Waveland; see King, *Freedom Song*, 437–74, for role of women in the movement; Dittmer, *Local People*, 331–32.

24. Forman, *The Making of Black Revolutionaries*, 418.

25. Ibid., 419.

26. Ibid., 422–23, for "freedom high" philosophy.

27. Ibid., 422–23.

28. Ibid., 426.

29. Ibid., 435–36.

30. Ibid.

31. Meier and Rudwick, *CORE*, 340.

32. Ibid., 340.

33. Ibid., 341.

34. The Civil Rights Act of 1968 protected those involved in the voting process; the act, however, left matters of economic intimidation and protection of campaign workers uncovered. The Loyal Democrats of Mississippi represented the combined forces of the state branch of the NAACP, the Young Democrats, the Prince Hall Masons, the Mississippi Teachers Association, the state AFL-CIO, and the MFDP, which was still led by Mrs. Fannie Lou Hamer and Lawrence Guyot and made up 50 percent of the Loyal Democrats' delegation. McDowell, *Black Politics*; Carmichael, *Ready for Revolution*, 417–38; Guyot interview on April 23, 2010; see Payne, *I've Got the Light of Freedom*, 338–62, on the takeover of the movement by previously inactive middle-class African Americans.

35. Holt, *The Summer That Didn't End*, 181–82; Kunstler, *Deep in My Heart*, 328; see Dittmer, *Local People*, 338–46, for the Congressional Challenge, deposing 600 white Mississippi officials, and the dissolution of COFO.

36. Holt, *The Summer That Didn't End*, 182; Kunstler, *Deep in My Heart*, 330–31; Zinn, *SNCC*, 257–58; see Schultz, *Going South*, 74–80, for MFDP in Mississippi and Washington, D.C., gathering depositions for 1965 Challenge of Mississippi delegation; key roles played by Roberta Galler, Jan Goodman, and Lawrence Guyot.

37. Quoted by Holt, *The Summer That Didn't End*, 182.

38. Zinn, *SNCC*, 260; for steps by MFDP between December 4, 1964, and January 4, 1965, see Kunstler, *Deep in My Heart*, 331–32; Steven M. Gentine, "The Mississippi Freedom Democratic Party's Congressional Challenge of 1964–65: A Case Study in Radical Persuasion," M.S. thesis, Florida State University, 2009.

39. Holt, *The Summer That Didn't End*, 341–51.

40. Ibid., 200.

41. Zinn, *SNCC*, 260.

42. Ibid., 258; Kunstler, *Deep in My Heart*, 332–23.

43. Holt, *The Summer That Didn't End*, 341–51.

44. Ibid., 201.

45. Zinn, *SNCC*, 258–60; Kunstler, *Deep in My Heart*, 333–36.

46. Zinn, *SNCC*, 260–61; Kunstler, *Deep in My Heart*, 336–43; Curry, *Deep in Our Hearts*, 188–90; Gentine, "The Mississippi Freedom Democratic Party's Congressional Challenge."

47. Sobel, *Civil Rights*, 321; Kunstler, *Deep in My Heart*, 343, 345–50; Schultz, *Going South*.

48. Sobel, *Civil Rights*, 321; Forman, *The Making of Black Revolutionaries*, 442.

49. See SNCC Papers, Series II, Box 6, Folders 4–6, Executive Committee Minutes, February 23, 1965, for SNCC Programs for 1965, including the bringing of two thousand students to Washington, D.C., to lobby for the unseating of Mississippi congressmen.

50. McDowell, *Black Politics*, 15; Meier and Rudwick, *CORE*, 340–41; Kunstler, *Deep in My Heart*, 350–51; House Rep. James Roosevelt's remarks in appendix of Gentine, "The Mississippi Freedom Democratic Party's Congressional Challenge," taken from the *Congressional Record* 111, 18:24265f.

51. U.S. Commission on Civil Rights, *Hearings Held in Jackson* 1: 23.

52. See U.S. Commission on Civil Rights, *Hearings Held in Jackson* 1 (Voting) and 2 (Administration of Justice); U.S. Commission on Civil Rights, *Law Enforcement*, report based on those hearings.

53. See U.S. Commission on Civil Rights, *Hearings Held in Jackson*, for list of people who testified.

54. Sobel, *Civil Rights*, 286–87.

55. Ibid., 287.

56. Ibid.

57. Ibid., 288–89, for legislative history of bill.

58. Quoted by Sobel, *Civil Rights*, 289.

59. Sobel, *Civil Rights*, 289.

60. See full text of the Voting Rights Act of 1965.

61. U.S. Commission on Civil Rights, *The Voting Rights Act . . . the First Months* (Washington, D.C., 1965), 49–50; Sobel, *Civil Rights*, 290.

62. U.S. Commission on Civil Rights, *Political Participation*, 244–47.

63. Ibid., 246–47.

64. Meier and Rudwick, *CORE*, 341.

65. Ibid., 341–43.

66. Forman, *The Making of Black Revolutionaries*, 437–40; Hill, *Deacons for Defense*, 182–215, 315–22 (notes); according to Hill, Charles Evers used the protection and the threat of the deacons in Natchez to successfully negotiate with the city for desegregation by the end of 1965.

67. See Hilton, *Delta Ministry*; Howell, *Freedom City*; Spike, *Freedom Revolution and the Churches*; Newman, *Divine Agitators*, chapter 3 on Delta Ministry's actions in Hattiesburg from 1964 to 1967 and chapter 6 on work in Greenville and the Delta from 1964 to 1966.

68. Sobel, *Civil Rights*, 358–59.

69. Ibid., 359.

70. Ibid.

71. Ibid., 359–60.

72. Ibid., 368.

73. Ibid., 327.

74. Qtd. in Huie, *3 Lives*, 239.

75. Ibid.

76. U.S. Commission on Civil Rights, *Hearings Held in Jackson* 1: 6–7; see also Blackwell, *Barefootin'*, 123–32, for a contrasting picture of what the governor of Mississippi was doing in the state legislature and was saying to the U.S. Commission on Civil Rights and what on June 14 in Jackson the police were doing to the movement physically in brutalizing them before they were taken off to jail and while they were in jail for eleven days.

77. Sobel, *Civil Rights*, 329.

78. Ibid., 329.

79. Ibid., 330; Elizabeth Sutherland, "Mississippi: Summer of Discontent," *The Nation* 201 (October 11, 1965): 214.

80. Sobel, *Civil Rights*, 330.

81. Ibid., 330–31.

82. Ibid., 365.

83. Ibid.

84. See Meier and Rudwick, *CORE*, 343.

85. Ibid.; Sobel, *Civil Rights*, 320.

86. See note 67 above; Newman, *Divine Agitators*, 1–46; see also Curry, *Deep in Our Hearts*, 269–77.

87. Spike, *Freedom Revolution and the Churches*; Newman, *Divine Agitators*, 46–67.

88. Silver, *Mississippi*, 262, 290; Holt, *The Summer That Didn't End*, 85–87; Sutherland, "Cat and Mouse Game."

89. See chapter 9, above; see Forman, *The Making of Black Revolutionaries*, 391–93, 399–406.

90. Hilton, *Delta Ministry*; see Crespino, *In Search of Another Country*, 153–67, for the Delta Ministry's interaction with Mississippi church organizations.

91. Spike, *Freedom Revolution and the Churches*, 109; Howell, *Freedom City*, 113–17.

92. Hilton, *Delta Ministry*, 139–60.

93. Ibid., 14.

94. Ibid., 147.

95. Ibid., 66, 79–81; see "Showdown in the Delta." *Newsweek* 66 (June 6, 1966): 67.

96. Hilton, *Delta Ministry*, 15, 81–82; Howell, *Freedom City*, 42; "Showdown in the Delta."

97. Christopher Jencks, "Accommodating Whites: A New Look at Mississippi," *The New Republic* 154 (April 16, 1966): 20–22; see Dittmer, *Local People*, 368–82, for a recap of CDGM; see Payne, *I've Got the Light of Freedom*, 317–62, for the period after Freedom Summer in Greenwood; Blackwell, *Barefootin'*, 146–56, and Polly Greenberg, *The Devil Has Slippery Shoes: A Biased Biography of the Child Development Group of Mississippi* (New York, 1969).

98. Jencks, "Accommodating Whites"; Watters and Cleghorn, *Climbing Jacob's Ladder*, 314–15; see Crespino, *In Search of Another Country*, 135–36, on Senator Stennis and the War on Poverty.

99. Grant, *Black Protest*, 498–500; Watters and Cleghorn, *Jacob's Ladder*, 131–32; "Cotton Workers Strike in Delta," *The Student Voice* 6 (April 30, 1965): 1; Sutherland, "Summer of Discontent," 212–15; see Dittmer, *Local People*, 364–68, 383–88, for MFLU; see Lee, *For Freedom's Sake*, 121–62, for Mrs. Hamer's work with the MFLU, the Poor People's Corporation, and Freedom Farm; see Moye, *Let the People Decide*, 151–58, on MFLU and the strike of cotton workers in the Delta.

100. *New York Times*, June 4, June 7, 1965; Hilton, *Delta Ministry*, 68–76; see Moye, *Let the People Decide*, 151–54, for MFLU failure to get AFL-CIO's Claude Ramsay to support the Delta strike.

101. *New York Times*, June 4, 1965.

102. *The Student Voice*, April 30, 1965.

103. Hilton, *Delta Ministry*, 112–21, 218; Sutherland, "Summer of Discontent," 213–15; Howell, *Freedom City*; see also Blackwell, *Barefootin'*, 157–65.

104. Hilton, *Delta Ministry*, 60–61; Sutherland, "Summer of Discontent," 213; Howell, *Freedom City*; see Vandiver, "The Changing Realm of King Cotton," on the MFLU in the Delta.

105. Sutherland, "Summer of Discontent," 214.

106. Ibid.

107. Ibid.; Meier and Rudwick, *CORE*, 343.

108. See note 99, above.

109. Howell, *Freedom City*, 42.

110. Ibid.; Hilton, *Delta Ministry*.

111. Hilton, *Delta Ministry*, 145–46.

112. Ibid., 146.

113. "Violence Breaks Out with Mass Negro Registration," *The Student Voice* 6 (April 30, 1965): 1, 4.

114. Ibid., 1.

115. "Fact Sheet—Sunflower County Project, Mississippi," Jackson, Miss., n.d., in my possession.

116. Ibid.; see also U.S. Commission on Civil Rights, *Political Participation*.

117. "Miss. Negroes Run In Local Elections," *The Student Voice* 6 (April 30, 1965): 2.

118. "Big Push In ASCS Elections," *MFDP News Letter*, November 5, 1965, 1. U.S. Commission on Civil Rights, *Hearings Held in Jackson* 1: 268; 2: 478–79. Meier and Rudwick, *CORE*, 342.

119. U.S. Commission on Civil Rights, *Hearings Held in Jackson* 1: 268; 2: 478–79.

120. "Big Push in ASCS Elections," 1, 3; "Whites Use Same Tricks: Take ASCS Elections; FDP To File Suit To Void Elections," MFDP *News Letter*, December 20, 1965, 1, 4; Hilton, *Delta Ministry*, 195.

121. Forman, *The Making of Black Revolutionaries*, 442; Sobel, *Civil Rights*, 320–21; Hilton, *Delta Ministry*, 193–95; Kunstler, *Deep in My Heart*, 346.

122. Hilton, *Delta Ministry*, 194.

123. Sobel, *Civil Rights*, 291.

124. Ibid., 320–21; Forman, *The Making of Black Revolutionaries*, 442; Meier and Rudwick, *CORE*, 341.

125. Forman, *The Making of Black Revolutionaries*, 442; Sutherland, "Summer of Discontent," 215.

126. Sobel, *Civil Rights*, 320–21.

127. Ibid., 321; Dittmer, *The Good Doctors*, 103–9.

128. Sobel, *Civil Rights*, 321.

129. Ibid., 322.

130. Ibid., 289.

131. Kunstler, *Deep in My Heart*, 346; Sobel, *Civil Rights*, 291.

132. See above, concerning the implementation of the Voting Rights Act of 1965. William Leon Higgs, "LBJ and the Negro Vote: Case of the Missing Registrars," *The Nation* 201 (December 13, 1965): 460–62; U.S. Commission on Civil Rights, *Political Participation*.

133. Sobel, *Civil Rights*, 319; see Dittmer, *Local People*, 353–62, on events of Charles Evers's campaign in Natchez in fall 1965.

134. Sobel, *Civil Rights*, 319.

135. Ibid., 319–20.

136. Ibid., 320.

137. See Warren, *Who Speaks for the Negro?* 100–109, on Charles Evers; Forman, *The Making of Black Revolutionaries*, 401.

138. See U.S. Commission on Civil Rights, *Political Participation*, 21–23, 25–26, 30–35.

139. Ibid.; see also Jencks, "Mississippi II: From Conversion to Coercion," *The New Republic* 151 (August 22, 1964).

Conclusions

Epigraph 1: McCord, *Mississippi*, 122.

Epigraph 2: Lyndon Baines Johnson, remarks to a Joint Session of the U.S. Congress, March 15, 1965, in Lawson and Payne, *Debating the Civil Rights Movement*, 90–99.

1. For material on the Black Power controversy, see Forman, *The Making of Black Revolutionaries*, 447–60, 497–553; Carmichael, *Black Power*; Chuck Stone, *Black Political Power in America* (New York, 1968); McDowell, *Black Politics*; Arthur C. Littleton and Mary W. Burger, eds., *Black Viewpoints* (New York, 1971); Joseph C. Hough Jr., *Black Power and White Protestants: A Christian Response to the New Negro Pluralism* (New York, 1968); Sterling Tucker, *For Blacks Only: Black Strategies for Change in America* (Grand Rapids, Mich., 1971), 7–36; Mary L. Fisher and Elizabeth W. Miller, compilers, *The Negro in America: A Bibliography* (Cambridge, Mass., 1970); Hill, *The Deacons for Defense*, 258–73;

Jeffries, ed., *Black Power in the Belly of the Beast*, 1–42, 297–308; also Lawson and Payne, *Debating the Civil Rights Movement*, 33–39.

2. Joyce Ladner, "What Black Power Means to Negroes in Mississippi," in *The Transformation of Activism*, ed. August Meier (Chicago, 1970), 131–54; Michael Aiken and Nicholas J. Demerath III, "The Politics of Tokenism in Mississippi's Delta," *Trans-action*, April 1967.

3. Andrews, *Freedom Is a Constant Struggle*, 120–23, and fig. 1.1; see Payne, *Light of* Freedom, 317–37, for a look at the continuation of the Greenwood movement after SNCC left in fall 1964 and African American Greenwood fought for black empowerment on its own; see Frank R. Parker, *Black Votes Count: Political Empowerment in Mississippi after 1965* (Chapel Hill, N.C., 1990), for changes within Mississippi office-holding after 1965; see Jere Nash and Andy Taggart, *Mississippi Politics, The Struggle for Power, 1976–2006* (Jackson, Miss., 2006), for political changes in Mississippi after the end of the civil rights movement's organized actions from 1960 to 1965 and legal struggles fought in federal courts to defeat White Mississippi's efforts to dilute the vote attained after passage of 1965 Voting Rights Act.

4. Rogers, *Life and Death in the Delta*, and Constance Curry, *Silver Rights: A True Story from the Front Lines of the Civil Rights Struggle* (Chapel Hill, N.C., 1995), examine families who experienced the oppression of living in the Mississippi Delta. It is apparent that only the most driven and talented of these Mississippians were able to deal with such harsh living experiences and overcome them; many left the state. The result is that the Delta was and still is one of the most poverty-stricken areas in the United States.

5. See Woodward, *The Strange Career of Jim Crow*; Vernon L. Wharton, *The Negro in Mississippi, 1865–1890* (Chapel Hill, N.C., 1947); Silver, *Mississippi*; Neil R. McMillen, *Dark Journey: Black Mississippians in the Age of Jim Crow* (Urbana, Ill., 1989).

6. The organic development of the movement to a statewide phenomenon may be seen as the spreading out of political action in two Congressional primaries in 1962 to the Freedom Vote in 1963 to the establishment of the Mississippi Freedom Democratic Party as a statewide party that challenged the regular Mississippi Democratic Party at the Democratic National Convention in August 1964 and the seating of the Mississippi congressmen-elect in January 1965. Similar examples of step-by-step development can be seen in the emergence of the concept of the Freedom Schools and in the development of the Mississippi Freedom Labor Union and the Poor People's Corporation, as well as the later Poor Peoples Conference.

7. It should be remembered that Sen. James O. Eastland's influence and power as chairman of the Senate Judiciary Committee probably led to President Kennedy's appointment of W. Harold Cox to the Federal District Court in Mississippi and President Johnson's appointment of former Mississippi governor, James P. Coleman, to the Fifth Circuit Court of Appeals.

8. See chapter 10, above; see also, U.S. Commission on Civil Rights, *Hearings Held in Jackson* 1: 5–8, 9–15.

9. For a more detailed discussion of the period after 1965, see the bibliography of source materials in McDowell, *Black Politics*.

10. See Frank R. Parker and Barbara Y. Phillips. *Voting in Mississippi: A Right Still Denied* (Washington, D.C., 1981), where they state: "The report reveals that, as a result of the [1965 Voting Rights] Act, black voter registration in Mississippi has increased from 6.7 percent of the black voting-age population in 1964 to more than 60 percent at the present time [1981]. The number of black elected officials has increased from 29 in 1968 to 387 currently. Yet, a significant disparity continues to exist between the percentages of eligible whites (70.1 percent) and blacks (62.5 percent) registered

to vote. This disparity is due to the present effects of Mississippi's history of racial discrimination in voting. Moreover, blacks hold only 7 percent of the elective offices in Mississippi, and no black holds a statewide office or a Congressional seat. Indeed, in the 22 Mississippi counties in which blacks comprise a majority of the population, eight have no black representation on the county boards of supervisors, and blacks make up a majority of such boards in only two counties."

Appendix

Epigraph: Qtd in Zinn, *SNCC,* 190.

1. W. Haywood Burns, "The Federal Government and Civil Rights," in Friedman, ed., *Southern Justice,* 228–29.

2. 325 U.S. 91 (1945) in Norman Dorsen, *Discrimination and Civil Rights: Cases, Text, and Materials* (Boston, 1969), 31–41; see also McAdam, *Political Process,* 69–116, for an examination "The Historical Context of Black Insurgency, 1876–1954" and denial of African American civil rights after the Compromise of 1876 through the reinterpretation and restoration of those rights in the federal court system up to *Brown v. Board of Education* (1954).

3. Burns, in *Southern Justice,* 246.

4. 100 U.S. 371 (1879).

5. 158 U.S. 564 (1895).

6. Zinn, *SNCC,* 196–97.

7. Burns, in *Southern Justice,* 233.

8. Qtd. in John Poppy, "The South's War Against Negro Votes," *Look Magazine* 27 (May 21, 1963).

Notes on Sources

1. Barry interview; Payne, *I've Got the Light of Freedom,* 391–405, discusses the press's "tendency to frame the story in terms of Big Events, in terms of what white people did, in terms of traditional leaders and organizations, in terms of what happened after 1955, in terms of southern backwardness, in terms of violence-nonviolence, replicated biases of race, gender and class, and relegated to secondary importance the themes that would have been important from a community-organizing perspective" (403–4).

2. Huie, *3 Lives;* for local press reaction, see Tucker, *Mississippi from Within.*

3. See Lord, *The Past That Would Not Die,* 113–38.

4. See Moye, *Let the People Decide,* 1–64; Crosby, *A Little Taste of Freedom,* 1–78; Chris Myers Asch, *The Senator and the Sharecropper: The Freedom Struggles of James O. Eastland and Fannie Lou Hamer* (New York, 2008), 1–167, for a picture of how White Mississippi maintained its system of white supremacy, paternalism, and Jim Crowism through legal and extra-legal intimidation and violence.

5. Crespino, *In Search of Another Country,* 205–36, discusses how Mississippi African Americans, among them Aaron Henry, Charles Evers, and the MFDP, aligned themselves with more moderate elements of Democratic Party after the breakup of COFO and the exit of SNCC and CORE people from the state in 1965.

6. See Crosby, *A Little Taste of Freedom*, 91–254, and Moye, *Let the People Decide*, 149–204, for these local movements.

7. U.S. Commission on Civil Rights, *Law Enforcement*; *Hearings Held in Jackson*; *The Voting Rights Act . . . the first months* (Washington, D.C., 1965); *Political Participation*.

8. From SNCC and CORE's private files made available to me in Atlanta and New York in 1965–66; recorded and unrecorded interviews with key movement figures; Burns, Jenkins, Barry interviews; interview with William L. Higgs, December 19, 1965.

9. Moses, taped talk; Moses interviews in 1990; Jenkins interview.

10. Jenkins and Higgs interviews; Burns, unrecorded interview.

11. See Payne, *I've Got the Light of Freedom*, and Dittmer, *Local People*.

BIBLIOGRAPHY

Primary Sources

ORAL DOCUMENTATION

Recorded Interviews Conducted by the Author with Tape Transcriptions

Barry, Marion, Jr. Washington, D.C., December 18, 1965. Former chairman of SNCC.

Forman, James, now deceased. New York City, November 12, 1965. Former executive secretary of SNCC.

Harris, Jesse. Jackson, Miss., December 31, 1965. Former fieldworker for SNCC.

Henry, Aaron, now deceased. Clarksdale, Miss., December 28, 1965. Former president of COFO and NAACP state president.

Higgs, William Leon, now deceased. Washington, D.C., December 19, 1965. White Mississippian driven out of the state for being a movement lawyer.

Jenkins, Tim. Washington, D.C., December 18, 1965. Movement lawyer.

Lowenstein, Allard K., now deceased. New York City, July 11, 1965. White liberal who helped organize the Freedom Vote.

Mahoney, William. Washington, D.C., December 17, 1965. Former Freedom Rider and member of the SNCC staff, as well as writer.

Moses, Robert Parris. Jackson, Miss., June 20, 1963. Taped talk given to voter education meeting on SNCC and COFO's work in Mississippi from 1960 to 1963.

Smith, Rev. R. L. T. Jackson, Miss., December 30, 1965. NAACP leader who ran in the 1962 Democratic Congressional primary.

Zinn, Howard, now deceased. Boston, November 11, 1965. Professor emeritus of government at Boston University, Spelman History Department chairman, and SNCC adviser.

Interviews and Unrecorded Interviews and Talks by Author Recorded but Not Transcribed

Belfrage, Sally, now deceased. New York City, June 1966. Writer.

Bond, Julian. Atlanta, December 1965. Former SNCC communications director and

Georgia state representative and senator; professor emeritus at University of Virginia; former chairman of the NAACP.

Burns, W. Haywood, now deceased. New Haven, Conn., and New York City, 1965–1967, various working discussions involving legal aspects of the movement; taped interview September 3, 1986. Movement lawyer and writer.

Cobb, Charles, Jr. New York City, 1966. Former SNCC fieldworker.

Coffin, William Sloan, Jr., now deceased. New Haven, Conn., 1963, 1965–66. Yale chaplain and Freedom Rider.

Coleman, Val. August 28, 1986. Assistant community relations director of National CORE.

Diamond, Sigmund. Taped interview March 19, 1987. Professor of sociology, Columbia University.

Donaldson, Ivanhoe. New York City, 1965–66. Former SNCC fieldworker.

Edelman, Marian Wright. New Haven, Conn., 1965–66. Movement lawyer and founder of the Children's Defense Fund.

Farmer, James, now deceased. New York City, while on staff at National CORE in spring 1964 and also when doing research in 1965–1966. Former national director of CORE.

Forman, James, now deceased. Montgomery, Ala., 1965, and New York City, 1965–67. Former executive secretary of SNCC.

Glenn, Randy. New York City, 1964 and 1966. SNCC and CORE fieldworker.

Gordon, Bruce. Atlanta, 1964, and New York City, 1965–66. Former SNCC fieldworker.

Gore, Robert Brookings. New York City, spring 1964. National CORE staff.

Guyot, Lawrence, now deceased. Providence, R.I., April 23, 2010. Former head of MFDP.

Harrington, Donald, now deceased. New York City, 1964. Minister of Community Church.

Hill, Norman. New York City, spring 1964; taped interview August 26, 1986. Former National CORE program director.

King, Rev. Edwin. Tougaloo, Miss., December 31, 1965. Dean of students and chaplain at Tougaloo; Mississippi white who joined the movement and "ran" in the Freedom Vote in 1963. Informal talk with King, March 2011.

Lynd, Staughton. New Haven, Conn., 1965–66. Former professor of history at Yale University and Spelman College in Atlanta; the author's faculty adviser at Yale in 1965–66; director of Freedom Schools in summer 1964.

Mays, James N. Jackson, Miss., December 1965. Fieldworker for National Sharecroppers Fund.

Minnis, Jack, now deceased. Atlanta, December 1965. Former SNCC and VEP research director.

Moses, Robert Parris, New Haven, Conn., winter 1963–64 and 1990. Former SNCC Mississippi project director and COFO field director.

Murphy, Wallace. New York City, 1964–67. Former CORE fieldworker.

Norton, Eleanor Holmes. New Haven, Conn., 1965–66. Movement lawyer.

Orris, Peter. Unrecorded telephone interview, summer 2009.

Rachlin, Carl, now deceased. New York City, spring 1964. National CORE legal counsel.

Rich, Marvin. New York City, 1964–66; taped interview August 26, 1986. Former National CORE community relations director.

Ricks, Willie. Montgomery, Ala., 1965; Former SNCC fieldworker.

Rustin, Bayard, now deceased. Taped interview August 26, 1986. Former head of A. Philip Randolph Institute; deputy director of the March on Washington.

Slater, Howard. New York City, 1964. Law Students Civil Rights Research Council staff organizer.

Sutherland, Elizabeth Martinez. New York City, 1966. Movement writer and SNCC staff worker.

Travis, James, now deceased. Jackson, Miss., December 1965. Former SNCC fieldworker.

Williams, Arthur. New York City, 1964. Former CORE fieldworker.

Zellner, John Robert. New Haven, Conn., 1965–66 and 2009. Former SNCC, SCEF, and SSOC fieldworker.

Zellner, Dorothy. Former SNCC staff worker. Recorded telephone interview, summer 2009.

UNPUBLISHED DOCUMENTS

Many of the following documents, or facsimile copies, were made available to me by the respective research directors, or other appropriate officials, under the direction of James Farmer, former national director of CORE, and James Forman, former executive secretary of SNCC. The graciousness of these two organizations in letting me freely go through their files is inestimable. Unpublished materials were given to me by Professor Howard Zinn in 1989 when he was cleaning out his office at Boston University. The documents that were finally selected for use in the book and inclusion in the bibliography represent only a small fraction of the papers that I examined. Of particular importance is that little material of an exact nature had ever been published in a monographic study on the early period of the Mississippi movement when my original study was done at Yale University in 1965–66. The inexactitude of the following citations in most cases has to do with the fact that the early movement, if not the later one, paid little attention to the needs of historians and had largely left the organization of the files of SNCC and CORE to the professional archivists. In many cases, though, it was possible to guess at the origin of certain documents and position papers. The following types of documents belong to this above-mentioned category: field reports, press releases, petitions, general reports, position papers, and various other documents. They are in my private possession.

Field Reports from Mississippi

Bowman, Joan. Field report of October 23, 1963, to SNCC national office in Atlanta.

Dennis, David. Field report for March 1–31, 1963, to the National CORE office in New York City.

————. Field report for October 21–November 7, 1963, to National CORE office in New York City.

————. Field report of October 19, 1963, to National CORE office in New York City.

————. Letter—"An Abortion for a Pregnant State"—to the National Action Council of CORE, New York City, n.d.

————. Letter of November 18, 1963, to National CORE office in New York City.

Donaldson, Ivanhoe. Field report for October 30–November 5, 1963, to SNCC national office in Atlanta.

Gaither, Thomas. Field report on Clarksdale for July 20–27, 1963, to National CORE office in New York City.

Gore, Robert Brookings. Field report for October 31–November 5, 1963, to National CORE office in New York City.

Moses, Robert Parris. Memo to COFO, "Central issue in the Mississippi civil rights struggle," n.p., n.d. (From internal evidence it appears to have been written during the summer of 1963.)

————. Memo to SNCC Executive Committee, "SNCC Mississippi Project," n.p., September 6, 1963.

————. "Re-cap of the [SNCC]project's rationale," n.p., n.d.

Press Releases, Letters, Petitions, Reports, and Various Other Documents

COFO. "Freedom Vote Platform." Jackson, Miss., n.d. (Appears to have been written in October 1963.)

————. "A Petition Requesting Congress to Investigate State-Supported Denial of Constitutional Rights in Mississippi, presented to: United States Congress, Washington, D.C., November 25, 1963, by the Committee to Elect Aaron Henry Governor." Jackson, Miss., 1963.

————. Vote for Freedom directives, No. l (August 14), No. 2 (August 16), and No. 3 (August 21). Jackson, Miss., office of NAACP, 1963.

CORE. "Mississippi: The Civil Rights Commission versus The Civil Rights Movement." Washington, D.C., 1963.

————. Press release. Brandon, Miss., June 3, 1965.

————. Press release. Canton, Miss., April 1, 1965.

————. Press release. Jackson, Miss., May 29, 1963.

Mays, James N. Letter to the writer. Jackson, Miss., May 17, 1966.

————. Proposal, "Prospective For Land Development in Mississippi." Jackson, Miss., May 17, 1966.

Minnis, Jack. "Diary Notes." Atlanta, May–July 1963 (These are only some of the notes from the diary that were made available to the author.)

NAACP. Press release on Freedom Vote. Jackson, Miss., August 6, 1963.

Shrobe, Howard. "The Mississippi Freedom Democratic Party: The Atlantic City Challenge." Yale University, 1966, seminar paper.

SNCC. "Analysis of Voting Laws Passed: 1962 Regular Session of Mississippi Legislature." N.p., n.d.

———. "Fact Sheet: Hattiesburg, Mississippi." Atlanta, n.d. (Appears to have been written in early 1964.)

———. "Notes on Mississippi voter registration and sample sections of the Mississippi Constitution." N.p., n.d.

———. Press release. Atlanta, August 8, 1963.

———. Press release. Atlanta, July 30, 1963.

———. "Summary of SNCC Staff" and "Summary Personnel Report." Atlanta, n.d. (Appears to have been written in early 1964.)

Documents: Offsets and Mimeographs in Author's Possession

Bingham, Stephen. "Mississippi Letter." Berkeley, Calif., February 15, 1965.

———. "The Challenge." N.p., n.d.

COFO. "Mississippi: Handbook for Political Programs." Jackson, Miss., 1964.

———. "Do You Make under $3000.00 a Year? Then You are One of Many Poor Peoples." Jackson, Miss., n.d.

Higgs, William Leon. "Proposed Amendments to the Administration's Civil Rights Bill (HR 6400)." Washington, D.C., 1965.

McLaurin, Charles. "Notes on Organizing." N.p., n.d.

Medgar Evers Neighborhood Guild. "Poverty Program Primer; Part I: Community Action Groups." Jackson, Miss., n.d.

MFDP. "Fact Sheet—Sunflower County Project, Mississippi." Jackson, Miss., n.d.

———. "Fact Sheet—The Mississippi Freedom Labor Union." Jackson, Miss., n.d.

———. "Fact Sheet—The Poor People's Corporation." Jackson, Miss., n.d.

———. "Letter to 'All Participating Groups in the American Civil Rights Movement,'" from James Farmer, CORE, James Forman, SNCC, Dr. Martin Luther King, Jr., SCLC, Lawrence Guyot, MFDP, Re: Voting Legislation." Washington, D.C., February 27, 1965.

———. "Schedule of Mississippi Elections and Relevant Dates, February 1, 1965–November 5, 1968." Jackson, Miss., n.d.

———. "Special Note: Urgent Priority." Concerning election amendment and voting legislation. Washington, D.C., n.d.

———. "Suggested Action for Including New Elections in Voting Legislation." Washington, D.C., n.d. (Appears to have been aimed at the bill that became the Voting Rights Act of 1965.)

———. "What You Should Know about Poll Taxes." Jackson, Miss., n.d.

Robert Moses et al. v. Robert P. Kennedy and J. Edgar Hoover. U.S. District Court for the District of Columbia, filed January 2, 1963.

SNCC. "Hattiesburg, Miss., Freedom Day, January 22, 1964." Atlanta, n.d.

———. "Letter to the Student Movement." N.p., March 29, 1965.

———. "The Mississippi Power Structure, Part I: Where Their Money Comes From, Part II: Industry and Politics." Atlanta, 1964. (The probable author is Jack Minnis.)

———. "On the Long Road to Freedom." Atlanta, n.d.

———. "Operation Mississippi: One Man, One Vote Campaign." Atlanta, September 1963, written by the SNCC Mississippi staff.

———. "Proposal for a Documentary Program in Photography." Atlanta, n.d.

———. "Statistical Study of Selected Mississippi Counties." Atlanta, 1965.

———. "Testimony of the Student Nonviolent Coordinating Committee before the House Judiciary Committee, Tuesday, May 28, 1963." Atlanta, 1963.

———. "The SNCC Explosion." Atlanta, n.d.

———. "Some Notes on Education." n.p., n.d.

SRC. "The First Annual Report of the Voter Education Project of the Southern Regional Council, Inc., 1962–63." Atlanta, 1963.

———. "The Second Annual Report of the Voter Education Project of the Southern Regional Council, Inc., 1963–64." Atlanta, 1964.

Ware, Bill. "Letter to MFDP Members." Natchez, Miss., December 30, 1965.

Affidavits

Affidavits on the "Freedom Vote" campaign, October–November 1963, were made available to the writer by the following Yale University students who spent approximately two weeks in Mississippi working with the movement: Robert Ferris, Robert Haverfield, Bruce Lloyd Payne, Gary Saxonhouse, Nelson Soltman, John Anthony Speh, Jon M. Van Dyke, and Richard Van Wagenen.

Archival Materials

The King Center, SNCC Papers
Series II, Box 6, Folders 4–6, Executive Committee Minutes, Aug. 1961–Aug. 1965:
  December 27–29, 1963, Executive Committee Meeting Minutes, recorded by Jim Monsonis and Cathy Cade (5 pages).
  March 29, 1964, Executive Committee Meeting Minutes (5 pages).
  April 10, 1964, Executive Committee Meeting Minutes, recorded by Judy Richardson (6 pages).
  April 19, 1964, Lawyers for Mississippi Summer Project, discussed, full minutes, recorded by Mary King, also includes discussions on the Stall-in in New York, *The Student Voice,* and the project in Southwest Georgia (23 pages).
  September 6, 1964, Executive Committee Meeting Minutes, handwritten transcription of discussed Black Belt Project for 1965 (pages 8–23).
  February 23, 1965, Executive Committee Meeting Minutes, SNCC Programs for 1965, including the bringing of 2,000 students to Washington, D.C., to lobby for the unseating of Mississippi Congressmen, for home rule for Washington, and

simplified voting laws, restructuring of SNCC with control in field staff's hands, and holding a Southwest People's Conference (5 pages).

Series III, Box 7, Folders 1–14, August 1, 1960–October 30, 1968, Staff Meetings.

Series V, Box 26, Folder 21, SNCC Conference:

Complete Waveland Retreat Meeting Minutes, November 6–12, 1964 (45 pages).

Series VI, Box 54, Folder 2, Bookkeeping Department:

Letter to James Marshall [the author when on staff at National CORE] from Horace Julian Bond, May 5, 1964 (1 page).

Series VIII, Box 56, Folder 14:

"Life with Lyndon in the Great Society," vol. 1, nos. 1–46.

Series XIII, Box 91, Folders 4–6:

Sojourner Motor Fleet documents (8 pages).

Series XV, Box 97, State Project Files, 1960–68, Folder 2:

Report Concerning the Louis Allen Case by Robert Moses, n.d. Information Concerning the Killing of Louis Allen in Liberty, Miss., Amite County, on January 31, 1964 (7 pages).

Series XV, Box 98, Folders 11–12:

COFO, Overview of the Political Program, Jackson, October 1963, and Statement of Purpose of the Freedom Ballot for Governor, including budget, and events in Mississippi on November 1 and 2, 1963 (7 pages).

Series XV, Box 98, Folders 8–9:

Freedom Schools, miscellaneous, July 24, 1964–67.

Series XV, Box 102, Folder 4:

Operation Mississippi (25 pages).

Charles Cobb, Economic Needs and Aids in Rural Areas (2 pages).

University of Southern Mississippi (digilib.usm.edu), 1,529 digital online items by catalogue number:

(48) Agenda for SNCC staff meeting, May 1964, "Establishing Parallel Governments."

(69) Appendices C–F: The FDP and the convention challenge [July 1964] (13 pages).

(70) Appendix A: historical background summer 1964 (4 pages).

(90) Basis for the development of the MFDP (2 pages).

(108) Bob Moses West Coast Civil Rights Conference; April 23, 1964: recap of early movement up to 1964 (24 pages).

(142) Case study: statement of discipline of nonviolent movements, June 1964.

(146) Challenge of the MFDP (4 pages).

(176) COFO: What it is: what it does (6 pages).

(181) COFO Program, winter, spring 1964–65 (2 pages).

(190) Congressional Challenge: challenge by MFDP, 1965 (5 pages).

(191) Congressional Record: COFO civil rights action program in the state of Mississippi, June 16, 1964 (18 pages).

(192) Congressional Record: vol. 111, no. 1 (January 4, 1965), in House of Representatives (4 pages).

(193) Congressional Record: proceeding and debates of 89th Congress, 1st Session; September 17, 1965 (4 pages).

(197) Contacts for the White Folks Projects; supplied by Ed Hamlett (1 page).

(199) Convention Challenge; reasons for declining at-large seats and promises for 1968 and support of Johnson-Humphrey ticket (4 pages).

(206) Core-Lator, no.5, April 1964, Freedom Day in Canton (6 pages).

(212) Cotton vote in Mississippi; December 31, 1964, ASCS Election (6 pages).

(215) Cover letter of Fannie Lou Hamer and challenge of the MFDP [1964] (5 pages).

(217) Curriculum for summer project (2 pages).

(232) Development of the Mississippi Project (6 pages).

(302) FDP vote results; fall 1964 (2 pages).

(335) Sandra Adickes, Freedom School teacher, 1964 journal (15 pages).

(338) Freedom Vote Ballot.

(391) Information Sheet, Project Mississippi for summer project in 1964 (5 pages).

(399) Interview with the Honorable Charles Evers, mayor of Fayette (23 pages).

(406) It was a cool day in August 1964 waiting for the Democratic National Convention to begin (6 pages).

(437) Know Your Rights (when you are arrested) pamphlet.

(442) MFDP Congressional Challenge, January 11, 1965.

(447) Legislative history of contested election (see item 775 below; 5 pages).

(477) Moses acceptance letter to volunteers for summer project, 1964.

(485) Letter to Freedom School teachers; "Notes on Teaching in Mississippi."

(578–799) Lawrence Guyot letters on Congressional Challenge.

(727) 3 articles on 1963: "The South's War against Negroes."

(732) M is for Mississippi and Murders 1955 murders pamphlet (8 pages).

(775) Memo on contested elections for the House (5 pages).

(807) NAACP against taking part in Challenge by John Morsell.

(808) John Else of SNCC supports Challenge; Fall Freedom Vote.

(813) On Mississippi Freedom Labor Union (2 pages).

(875) Mississippi file index (32 pages).

(876) Mississippi Freedom Vote Ballot in 1963.

(881–83) MFDP brochure/sheet (15 pages).

(890) Mississippi Freedom Labor Union (3 pages).

(897) Mississippi political handbook by William L. Higgs, 1962 (49 pages).

(903) Mississippi Student Union Convention, 1964 (4 pages).

(904) Mississippi—Subversion of the Right to Vote—pamphlet (20 pages).

(978) Interview with C. C. Bryant (10 pages).

(979) Interview with Dr. Aaron Henry (58 pages).

(991) Interview with Fannie Lou Hamer (30 pages).

(998) Interview with the Honorable Unita Blackwell (51 pages).

(1012) Interview with Lawrence Guyot (30 pages).

(1021) Interview with Amzie Moore (61 pages).

(1029) Interview with Charlie Cobb (29 pages).

(1042) Interview with Hollis Watkins (44 pages).

(1049) Interview with Larry Rubin (35 pages).

(1058) Interview with R. Jess Brown (27 pages).

(1086) Interview with Winson Hudson (14 pages).

(1121) Overview of Freedom Schools (2 pages).

(1122) Overview of Political Programs (2 pages).

(1193) 5-year Anniversary of SNCC; Bob Moses questions who actually lynched the 3 movement people and would a jury ever convict them (3 pages).

(1221) Report on Challenge; July 7, 1965; difficulties in getting depositions printed and history of previous challenges of seating representatives (7 pages).

(1222) Report on Delta farm strike, August 16, 1965, by Claude Ramsay of the Mississippi AFL-CIO (6 pages).

(1275) Security Handbook, 1964; procedures to follow (3 pages).

(1292) SNCC brochure of staff and projects; 1963 (4 pages).

(1305) SNCC Staff reports, November 1, 1965, by locations (8 pages; mostly on places other than Mississippi).

(1506) What is COFO? Mississippi: structure of the movement and present operations; 1964 (8 pages).

Veterans of the Civil Rights Movement Website (crmvet.org).

This website offers biographies of civil rights martyrs and veterans, movement publications (*The Student Voice, Core-Lator,* and *Southern Courier*), SNCC/COFO WATS (Wide Area Telephone Service) Reports, COFO/MFDP documents, links to related topics, and is continually updated.

Statistical Study on the Condition of the Mississippi Negro. Based on: SNCC, *The General Condition of the Mississippi Negro,* 1963; selected reports for the U.S. Bureau of the Census, 1970–72 (see below); United States Commission on Civil Rights, *Political Participation: A study of the participation by Negroes in the electoral and political processes in 10 Southern States since passage of the Voting Rights Act of 1965;* and computations I carried out in 1975 using 1970 U.S. Census materials. I created these tables and maps, and they are in my possession; only a few of them appear in the book, but if someone wants to use them they are available for use on request.

Table I: Voter Registration in Counties of the Delta and Other Counties Where the Civil Rights Movement Was Active.

Table II: Mississippi County Breakdown of Population and Migration by Race

Table III: Vital Statistics, Median Schooling, and Median Family Income—The Delta and Adjacent Counties, Mississippi, 1970.

Table IV: Voting-Age Population for Congressional Districts, by Race—1960.

Table V: Urban-Rural Distribution, by Race, Mississippi, 1950–70.

Table VI: Voter Registration in Mississippi, by Race, 1960 to 1970.

Table VII: Elected Black Officials in Mississippi, by Office, 1967–73.

Table VIII: Comparison of Population by Selected Areas and Race—Mississippi.

Table IX: 1960 Voting-Age Population, Mississippi, Pre– and Post–1965 Voting Rights Act Registration.

Table X: Population of Mississippi, by Race, 1900–1970.

Table XI: Urban Places of More than 10,000, by Race, Mississippi, 1960 and 1970.

Table XII: Nonwhite Schooling and Housing, 1970—The Delta and Adjacent Counties, Mississippi.

Table XIII: Rural Farm and Nonfarm Population in the Delta and Adjacent Counties, Mississippi, 1970.

Table XIV: Agriculture in the Delta and Adjacent Counties, Mississippi, 1964–69.

Table XV: Agriculture in the Delta and Adjacent Counties, Mississippi, 1969.

Table XVI: Agriculture in the Delta and Adjacent Counties, Mississippi, 1969: Value of Farm Products Sold by Farms with Sales of $2,500 and Over.

Table XVII: Population of Mississippi, by Race and Age, 1950–70.

Table XVIII: Population of Mississippi, by Race and Age as a Percentage of the Population by Race, 1950–70.

Table XIX: Voter Registration in Eleven Southern States, 1960–70.

Table XX: Elected Black Officials in Eleven Southern States, by Office, 1967–72.

Table XXI: Years of School Completed by Persons Twenty-five Years and over in the South by Type of Residence, Age, Race.

Table XXII: Urban-Rural Distribution of Population for Economic Areas of Mississippi, 1970.

Table XXIII: Distribution of Population for State Economic Areas, by Race, Mississippi, 1960–70.

Table XXIV: Black Enrollment in Public Elementary and Secondary Schools for Eleven Southern States, by Increasing Levels of Isolation, 1970.

Table XXV: Population Characteristics for Eleven Southern States, 1970.

Table XXVI: Personal Income for Eleven Southern States, 1969.

Table XXVII: Housing in Eleven Southern States, 1970.

Table XXVIII: Rural Farm and Nonfarm Population in Eleven Southern States, 1970

Table XXIX: Educational Achievement of the General and Black Population in the Counties of the Delta and Other Counties Where the Civil Rights Movement Was Active, 1970.

Map: Mississippi, the Delta, 1970.

Map I: Mississippi, Nonwhite Population, by County (Percentage Distribution), 1960.

Map II: Mississippi, Net Migration, by County, 1960–70.

Map III: Mississippi, Nonwhite Population, by County (Percentage Distribution), 1970
Map IV: Mississippi, Congressional Districts prior to Redistricting, 1966.
Map V: Mississippi, Congressional Districts after Redistricting 1966.
Map VI: Mississippi, Persons over Twenty-five Years with Less Than Five Years Schooling, by County, 1970.
Map VII: Mississippi, State Economic Areas.

PUBLISHED DOCUMENTS AND PRIMARY SOURCE MATERIALS

Armstrong, Thomas M., and Natalie R. Bell. *Autobiography of a Freedom Rider: My Life as a Foot Soldier for Civil Rights*. Deerfield Beach, Fla.: Health Communications, Inc., 2011.

Bailey, D'Army, with Roger Easson. *The Education of a Black Radical: A Southern Civil Rights Activist's Journey, 1959–1964*. Baton Rouge: Louisiana State University Press, 2009.

Baldwin, James. *The Fire Next Time*. New York: Dial Press, 1963.

Barbour, Floyd B., ed. *The Black Power Revolt: A Collection of Essays*. Boston: Extending Horizons Books, 1968.

Bardolph, Richard A., ed. *The Civil Rights Record: Americans and the Law, 1849–1970*. New York: Thomas Y. Crowell, 1970.

Bell, Inge Powell. *CORE and the Strategy of Nonviolence*. New York: Random House, 1968.

Blackmon, Jeffrey, and Youth of the Rural Organizing and Cultural Center, Holmes County, Mississippi. *Minds Stayed on Freedom: The Civil Rights Struggle in the Rural South, An Oral History*. Boulder, Colo.: Westview Press, 1991.

Blackwell, Unita, with JoAnne Prichard Morris. *Barefootin': Life Lessons from the Road to Freedom*. New York: Crown Publishers, 2006.

Blaustein, Albert P., and Robert L. Zangrando, eds. *Civil Rights and the Black American*. New York: Washington Square Press, 1968.

Breitman, George, ed. *Malcolm X Speaks*. New York: Grove Press, 1965.

Broderick, Francis L., August Meier, and Elliot Rudwick, eds. *Black Protest Thought in the Twentieth Century*. 2nd ed. Indianapolis, Ind.: Bobbs-Merrill Co., Inc., 1971.

Carmichael, Stokely. *Stokely Speaks: Black Power Back to Pan-Africanism*. New York: Random House, 1971.

———, and Charles V. Hamilton. *Black Power. The Politics of Liberation in America*. New York: Random House, 1967.

———, with Ekwueme Michael Thelwell. *Ready For Revolution: The Life and Struggles of Stokely Carmichael (Kwame Ture)*. New York: Scribner, 2003.

Carson, Clayborne, David J. Garrow, Vincent Harding, and Darlene Clark Hine, eds. *Eyes on the Prize: America's Civil Rights Years, A Reader and Guide*. New York: Penguin Books, 1987.

Cohn, David. *Where I Was Born and Raised*. Notre Dame, Ind.: University of Notre Dame Press, 1967.

Curry, Constance, Joan C. Browning, Dorothy Dawson Burlage, Penny Patch, Theresa Del Pozzo, Sue Thrasher, Elaine Delott Baker, Emmie Schrader Adams, and Casey Hayden. *Deep in Our Hearts: Nine White Women in the Freedom Movement.* Athens: University of Georgia Press, 2000.

Curry, Constance. *Silver Rights: A True Story from the Front Lines of the Civil Rights Struggle.* Chapel Hill, N.C.: Algonquin Books, 1995.

Daedalus. The Negro American. 2 vols. Richmond, Va: American Academy of Arts and Sciences, Fall, 1965.

Depositions Placed before the Committee on House Administration in Order to Challenge the Seats of the Mississippi Congressional Delegation on June 2, 1965. 3 vols. Washington, D.C.: U.S. Government Printing House, 1965.

Erenrich, Susie, ed. *Freedom Is a Constant Struggle: An Anthology of the Mississippi Civil Rights Movement.* Montgomery, Ala.: Black Belt Press, 1999.

Fager, Charles E. *White Reflections on Black Power.* Grand Rapids, Mich.: William B. Eerdmans Publishing Co., 1967.

Farmer, James. *Lay Bare the Heart: An Autobiography of the Civil Rights Movement.* New York: Arbor House, 1985.

Foner, Philip S., ed. *The Black Panthers Speak. The Manifesto of the Party: The First Complete Documentary Record of the Panthers' Program.* Philadelphia: J. B. Lippincott Co., 1970.

Forman, James. *The Making of Black Revolutionaries: A Personal Account.* New York: Macmillan, 1972.

Frazier, Thomas R., ed. *Afro-American History: Primary Sources.* New York: Harcourt, Brace & World, Inc., 1970.

Friedman, Leon, ed. *The Civil Rights Reader: Basic Documents of the Civil Rights Movement.* New York: Walker, 1967.

Grant, Joanne, ed. *Black Protest: History, Documents, and Analyses, 1619 to the Present.* Greenwich, Conn.: Fawcett, 1968.

Hampton, Henry, and Steve Fayer with Sarah Flynn, eds. *Voices of Freedom: An Oral History of the Civil Rights Movement from the 1950s through the 1980s.* New York: Bantam Books, 1991.

Harkey, Ira B., Jr. *The Smell of Burning Crosses: An Autobiography of a Mississippi Newspaperman.* Jacksonville, Ill.: Harris-Wolfe, 1967.

Henry, Aaron, with Constance Curry. *Aaron Henry: The Fire Ever Burning.* Jackson: University Press of Mississippi, 2000.

Holsaert, Faith S., Martha Prescod Norman Noonan, Judy Richardson, Betty Garman Robinson, Jean Smith Young, and Dorothy Zellner, eds. *Hands on the Freedom Plow: Personal Accounts by Women in SNCC.* Urbana: University of Illinois Press, 2010.

Holt, Len. *The Summer That Didn't End.* New York: Morrow, 1965. The following documents, among others, appear in Holt's book:

COFO. "COFO and the Summer Project: Mississippi Project, 1964–65." N.p., n.d.

————. "Freedom School Data." N.p., n.d.

————. "The Mississippi Legislature, 1964." Jackson, Miss., June 2, 1964.

————. "Security Check-Out Form." N.p., n.d.

Fusco, Liz. "Freedom Schools in Mississippi, 1964." Jackson, Miss., 1964.

MFDP. "Freedom Primer No. l: The Convention Challenge and the Freedom Vote." N.p., n.d.

————. "Mississippi Freedom Democratic Party: Delegation to the Democratic National Convention." N.p., n.d.

————. "Statement of Objectives of the Mississippi Student Union–Freedom School Convention, August 1964, Meridian, Mississippi." Meridian, 1964.

Stembridge, Jane, Charlie Cobb, Mendy Samstein, and Noel Day. "Notes on Teaching in Mississippi." Jackson, Miss., 1964.

Hudson, Winson, and Constance Curry. *Mississippi Harmony: Memoirs of a Freedom Fighter*. New York: Palgrave Macmillan, 2002.

Ianniello, Lynne, ed. *Milestones along the March: Twelve Historic Civil Rights Documents— From World War II to Selma*. New York: Frederick A. Praeger, 1966.

Kennan, George F., et al. *Democracy and the Student Left*. New York: Bantam Books, 1968.

King, Mary. *Freedom Song: A Personal Story of the 1960s Civil Rights Movement*. New York: William Morrow and Co., 1987.

Lewis, John. *Across That Bridge: Life Lessons and a Vision for Change*. New York: Hyperion Books, 2012.

————, with Michael D'Orso. *Walking with the Wind: A Memoir of the Movement*. San Diego: Harcourt Brace & Co., 1998.

Lynd, Staughton. *Nonviolence in America: A Documentary History*. New York: Bobbs-Merrill, 1966.

————, and Alice Lynd. *Stepping Stones: Memoir of a Life Together*. Lanham, Md.: Lexington Books, 2009.

Minnis, Jack. *A Chronology of Violence and Intimidation in Mississippi Since 1961*. Atlanta: Student Nonviolent Coordinating Committee, 1964.

————. "Life with Lyndon." Numbers 1–46, SNCC Research, Atlanta, 1965. SNCC Papers, The King Center, Series VIII, Box 56, Folder 14.

Mississippi Black Paper: Statements and Notarized Affidavits. New York: Random House, 1965.

Moody, Anne. *Coming of Age in Mississippi: An Autobiography*. New York: Delta, 1968.

Morris, Willie. *North Toward Home*. Boston: Houghton Mifflin Co., 1967.

————. *Yazoo*. New York: Ballantine Books, 1971.

Moses, Robert P. "An Earned Insurgency: Quality Education as a Constitutional Right." *Harvard Educational Review* 79, no. 2 (Summer 2009): 370–81.

————, and Charles E. Cobb Jr. *Radical Equations: Math Literacy and Civil Rights*. Boston: Beacon Press, 2001.

Peck, James. *Freedom Ride*. New York: Simon & Schuster, 1962.

Raines, Howell. *My Soul Is Rested: The Story of the Civil Rights Movement in the Deep South.* New York: Penguin Books, 1983. Interviews with movement figures including: John Lewis, Julian Bond, Franklin McCain, James Farmer, Timothy Jenkins, Amzie Moore, Lawrence Guyot, Charles Cobb, Fannie Lou Hamer, Ivanhoe Donaldson, Hartman Turnbow, Dave Dennis, Marion Barry, and Myles Horton.

Salter, John R., Jr. *Jackson, Mississippi: An American Chronicle of Struggle and Schism.* Hicksville, N.Y.: Exposition Press, 1979.

Schultz, Debra L. *Going South: Jewish Women in the Civil Rights Movement.* New York: New York University Press, 2001.

Seale, Bobby. *Seize the Time: The Story of the Black Panther Party.* London: Arrow Books Ltd., 1970.

Sellers, Cleveland, with Robert Terrell. *The River of No Return: The Autobiography of a Black Militant and the Life and Death of SNCC.* New York: William Morrow & Co., Inc., 1973.

SNCC. *The General Condition of the Mississippi Negro.* Atlanta: Student Nonviolent Coordinating Committee, 1963.

———. *Mississippi: Subversion of the Right to Vote.* Atlanta: Student Nonviolent Coordinating Committee, n.d.

———. *Mississippi Summer Project: Running Summary of Incidents, June 16–August 26, 1964.* Atlanta: Student Nonviolent Coordinating Committee, n.d.

SRC. *The Student Protest Movement: A Recapitulation.* Atlanta: Southern Regional Council, 1961.

Stoper, Emily. *The Student Nonviolent Coordinating Committee: The Growth of Radicalism in a Civil Rights Organization.* Brooklyn, N.Y.: Carlson Publishing, Inc, 1989. Includes selected transcriptions of interviews with movement-related people: Donald Harris, Charles Jones, John Lewis, Jane Stembridge, Ella Baker, James Bevel, Julian Bond, Barney Frank, Betty Garmen, and Fannie Lou Hamer. Additional movement-related individuals include Howard Zinn, William Higgs, Timothy Jenkins, Allard Lowenstein, Elizabeth Sutherland, Bob Zellner, James Marshall, and many SNCC fieldworkers and officers including Charles Sherrod, Marion Barry, Frank Smith, Jesse Morris, Charles McDew, and Curtis Hayes.

Students for a Democratic Society. *The Port Huron Statement.* New York: Students for a Democratic Society, 1964.

Sutherland (Martinez), Elizabeth, ed. *Letters from Mississippi.* 1965. Rev. ed. Brookline, Mass.: Zephyr Press, 2007.

Tucker, Shirley. *Mississippi from Within.* New York: Arco, 1965.

U.S. Bureau of the Census. *County and City Data Book, 1972.* Washington, D.C.: U.S. Government Printing Office, 1973.

———. *General Social and Economic Characteristics: Mississippi[Report PC(1)-C].* Washington, D.C.: U.S. Government Printing Office, 1970.

———. *1970 Census of Population, Number of Inhabitants, United States Summary.* Washington, D.C.: U.S. Government Printing Office, 1971.

———. *Population Characteristics, Educational Attainment, March 1972.* Washington, D.C.: U.S. Government Printing Office, 1972.

———. *The Social and Economic Status of Negroes, 1970.* Washington, D.C.: U.S. Government Printing Office, 1971.

———. *The Social and Economic Status of Negroes, 1971.* Washington, D.C.: U.S. Government Printing Office, 1972.

———. *The Social and Economic Status of Negroes, 1972.* Washington, D.C.: U.S. Government Printing Office, 1973.

———. *Statistical Abstract of the United States, 1971.* Washington, D.C.: U.S. Government Printing Office, 1971.

———. *U.S. Census of Population: 1960, General Population Characteristics: Mississippi.* Washington, D.C. U.S. Government Printing Office, 1961.

———. *U.S. Census of Population: 1970, General Population Characteristics: United States Summary.* Washington, D.C.: U.S. Government Printing Office, 1972.

U.S. Commission on Civil Rights. *Equal Employment Opportunity under Federal Law.* Washington, D.C.: U.S. Government Printing Office, 1966.

———. *Federal Rights under School Desegregation Law.* Washington, D.C.: U.S. Government Printing Office, 1966.

———. *Hearings Held in Jackson, Mississippi, February 16–20, 1965.* 2 vols. Washington, D.C.: U.S. Government Printing Office, 1965.

———. *Law Enforcement: A Report on Equal Protection in the South.* Washington, D.C.: U.S. Government Printing Office, 1965.

———. *1964 Staff Report: Public Education.* Washington, D.C.: U.S. Government Printing Office, 1964.

———. *Political Participation: A study of the participation by Negroes in the electoral and political processes in 10 Southern States since passage of the Voting Rights Act of 1965.* Washington, D.C.: U.S. Government Printing Office, 1968.

———. *Survey of School Desegregation in the Southern and Border States, 1965–66.* Washington, D.C.: U.S. Government Printing Office, 1966.

———. *Voting in Mississippi.* Washington, D.C.: U.S. Government Printing Office, 1965.

———. *The Voting Rights Act . . . the First Months.* Washington, D.C.: U.S. Government Printing Office, 1965.

———. *The Voting Rights Act—Ten Years After.* Washington, D.C.: U.S. Government Printing Office, 1975.

U.S. Laws. Statutes. *Civil Rights Acts of 1957, 1960, 1964, 1968, and Voting Rights Act of 1965.* Washington, D.C.: U.S. Congress, House of Representatives, 1969. (91st Congress, 1st Session.)

U.S. Office for Civil Rights. *The Directory of Public Elementary and Secondary Schools in Selected Districts-Enrollment and Staff by Racial/Ethnic Group, Fall 1970.* Washington, D.C.: U.S. Government Printing Office, 1970.

Voter Education Project, Inc. *Voter Registration in the South.* Atlanta: Southern Regional Council, Inc., 1971.

Warren, Robert Penn. *Who Speaks for the Negro?* New York: Random House, 1965.

Zellner, Bob, with Constance Curry. *The Wrong Side of Murder Creek: A White Southerner in the Freedom Movement*. Montgomery, Ala.: New South Books, 2008.

BIBLIOGRAPHICAL STUDIES

Fisher, Mary L., and Elizabeth W. Miller, compilers. *The Negro in America: A Bibliography*. 2nd ed. Cambridge, Mass.: Harvard University Press, 1970.

McDowell, Jennifer, and Milton Loventhal. *Black Politics: A Study and Annotated Bibliography of the Mississippi Freedom Democratic Party*. San Jose, Calif.: Bibliographic Information Center for the Study of Political Science, 1971.

McPherson, James M., Laurence B. Holland, James M. Banner Jr., Nancy J. Weiss, and Michael D. Bell. *Blacks in America. Bibliographical Essays*. Garden City, N.Y.: Anchor Books, 1971.

Secondary Sources

MONOGRAPHS AND OTHER WORKS DEALING WITH MISSISSIPPI

Andrews, Kenneth T. *Freedom Is a Constant Struggle: The Mississippi Civil Rights Movement and Its Legacy*. Chicago: University of Chicago Press, 2004.

Arsenault, Raymond. *Freedom Riders: 1961 and the Struggle for Racial Justice*. New York: Oxford University Press, 2006.

Barrett, Russell H. *Integration at Ole Miss*. Chicago: Quadrangle, 1965.

Asch, Chris Myers. *The Senator and the Sharecropper: The Freedom Struggles of James O. Eastland and Fannie Lou Hamer*. New York: New Press, 2008.

Belfrage, Sally. *Freedom Summer*. New York: Viking, 1965.

Berry, Jason. *Amazing Grace: With Charles Evers in Mississippi*. New York: Saturday Review Press, 2nd ed., 1978.

Bowers, Rick. *Spies of Mississippi: The True Story of the Spy Network That Tried to Destroy the Civil Rights Movement*. Washington, D.C.: National Geographic, 2010.

Bruner, Eric. *And Gently He Shall Lead Them: Robert Parris Moses and Civil Rights in Mississippi*. New York: New York University Press, 1994.

Cagin, Seth, and Philip Dray. *We Are Not Afraid: The Story of Goodman, Schwerner, and Chaney and the Civil Rights Campaign for Mississippi*. New York: Macmillan Publishing Co., 1988.

Canzoneri, Robert. *"I Do So Politely": A Voice from the South*. Boston: Houghton Mifflin, 1965.

Carmichael, Stokely, and Charles V. Hamilton. *Black Power: The Politics of Liberation in America*. New York: Random House, 1967.

Carson, Clayborne. *In Struggle: SNCC and the Black Awakening of the 1960s.* Cambridge, Mass.: Harvard University Press, 1981.

Carter, Hodding, II. *So the Heffners Left McComb.* Garden City, N.Y.: Doubleday, 1965.

Carter, Hodding, III. *The South Strikes Back.* Garden City, N.Y.: Doubleday & Co., Inc., 1959.

Cobb, James C. *The Most Southern Place on Earth: The Mississippi Delta and the Roots of Regional Identity.* New York: Oxford University Press, 1992.

Crespino, Joseph. *In Search of Another Country: Mississippi and the Conservative Counterrevolution.* Princeton, N.J.: Princeton University Press, 2007.

Crosby, Emilye. *A Little Taste of Freedom: The Black Freedom Struggle in Claiborne County, Mississippi.* Chapel Hill: University of North Carolina Press, 2005.

Davies, David R., ed. *The Press and Race: Mississippi Journalists Confront the Movement.* Jackson: University Press of Mississippi, 2001.

Dittmer, John. *The Good Doctors: The Medical Committee for Human Rights and the Struggle for Social Justice in Health Care.* New York: Bloomsbury Press, 2009.

———. *Local People: The Struggle for Civil Rights in Mississippi.* Urbana: University of Illinois Press, 1994.

———. "The Politics of the Mississippi Movement, 1954–1964." In *The Civil Rights Movement in America,* ed. Charles W. Eagles. Jackson: University Press of Mississippi, 1986. 65–93.

Dorman, Michael. *We Shall Overcome: A Reporter's Eyewitness Account of the Year of Racial Strife and Triumph,* New York: Delacorte, 1964.

Evers, Charles. *Evers.* New York: World Publishing Co., 1971.

Evers, Myrlie, with William Peters. *For Us, the Living.* Garden City, N.Y.: Doubleday, 1967.

Federal Writers' Project of the Works Progress Administration. *Mississippi: A Guide to the Magnolia State.* New York: Viking, 1938.

Friedman, Leon, ed. *Southern Justice.* New York: Pantheon, 1965.

Gentine, Steven M. "The Mississippi Freedom Democratic Party's Congressional Challenge of 1964–65: A Case Study in Radical Persuasion," M.S. thesis, Florida State University, 2009.

Greenberg, Polly. *The Devil Has Slippery Shoes: A Biased Biography of the Child Development Group of Mississippi.* New York: Macmillan, 1969.

Hayden, Tom. *Reunion: A Memoir.* New York: Random House, 1988.

———. *Revolution in Mississippi.* New York: Students for a Democratic Society, 1962.

Hendrickson, Paul. *Sons of Mississippi: A Story of Race and Its Legacy.* New York: Vintage Books, 2003.

Hilton, Bruce. *The Delta Ministry.* New York: Macmillan, 1969.

Hoffman, Nicholas Von. *Mississippi Notebook.* New York: David White, 1965.

Hogan, Wesley C. *Many Minds, One Heart: SNCC's Dream for a New America.* Chapel Hill: University of North Carolina Press, 2007.

Holland, Endesha Ida Mae. *From the Mississippi Delta: A Memoir.* New York: Simon & Shuster, 1997.

Holt, Len. *The Summer That Didn't End*. New York: Morrow, 1965.

Howell, Leon. *Freedom City: The Substance of Things Hoped For*. Richmond, Va.: John Knox, 1969.

Huie, William Bradford. *3 Lives for Mississippi*. New York: WCC Books, 1965.

Kunstler, William. *Deep in My Heart*. New York: Morrow, 1966.

Katagiri, Yasuhiro. *The Mississippi State Sovereignty Commission: Civil Rights and States' Rights*. Jackson: University of Mississippi Press, 2001.

Lawyers' Committee for Civil Rights Under Law. *Voting in Mississippi: A Right Still Denied, A Report on Continued Voting Rights Denials in Mississippi*. Washington, D.C., 1981.

Lee, Chana Kai. *For Freedom's Sake: The Life of Fannie Lou Hamer*. Urbana: University of Illinois Press, 1999.

Lemann, Nicholas. *The Promised Land: The Great Black Migration and How It Changed America*. New York: Alfred A. Knopf, 1991.

Lewis, Anthony, and the New York Times. *Portrait of A Decade: The Second American Revolution; A First-hand account of the Struggle for Civil Rights from 1954–1964*. New York: Random House, 1964.

Lord, Walter. *The Past That Would Not Die*. New York: Harper & Row, 1965.

Mars, Florence. *Witness in Philadelphia*. Baton Rouge: Louisiana State University Press, 1977.

Martin, Gordon A., Jr. *Count Them One by One: Black Mississippians Fighting for the Right to Vote*. Jackson: University Press of Mississippi, 2010.

McAdam, Doug. *Freedom Summer*. New York: Oxford University Press, 1988.

McCord, William. *Mississippi: The Long, Hot Summer*. New York: Norton, 1965.

McMillen, Neil R. *The Citizens' Council: Organized Resistance to the Second Reconstruction, 1954–1964*. Urbana: University of Illinois Press, 1971.

———. *Dark Journey: Black Mississippians in the Age of Jim Crow*. Urbana: University of Illinois Press, 1989.

Meier, August, and Elliott Rudwick. *CORE: A Study in the Civil Rights Movement, 1942–1968*. New York: Oxford University Press, 1973.

Meredith, James Howard. *Three Years in Mississippi*. Bloomington: Indiana University Press, 1966.

Michel, Gregg L. *Struggle for a Better South: The Southern Student Organizing Committee, 1964–1969*. New York: Palgrave Macmillan, 2004.

Mills, Kay. *This Little Light of Mine: The Life of Fannie Lou Hamer*. New York: Dutton, 1993.

Mills, Nicolaus. *Like A Holy Crusade: Mississippi 1964—The Turning of the Civil Rights Movement*. Chicago: Ivan R. Dee, 1992.

Moye, J. Todd. *Let the People Decide: Black Freedom and White Resistance Movements in Sunflower County, Mississippi, 1945–1986*. Chapel Hill: University of North Carolina Press, 2004.

Murphree, Vanessa. *The Selling of Civil Rights: The Student Nonviolent Coordinating Committee and the Use of Public Relations*. New York: Routledge, 2006.

Nash, Jere, and Andy Taggart. *Mississippi Politics: The Struggle for Power, 1976–2006*. Jackson: University Press of Mississippi, 2006.

Newfield, Jack. *A Prophetic Minority*. New York: Signet, 1967.

Newman, Mark. *Divine Agitators: The Delta Ministry and Civil Rights in Mississippi*. Athens: University of Georgia Press, 2003.

Nossiter, Adam. *Of Long Memory: Mississippi and the Murder of Medgar Evers*. Reading, Mass.: Addison-Wesley Publishing Co., 1994.

Parker, Frank R. *Black Votes Count: Political Empowerment in Mississippi after 1965*. Chapel Hill: University of North Carolina Press, 1990.

———, and Barbara Y. Phillips. *Voting in Mississippi: A Right Still Denied*. Washington, D.C.: Lawyers' Committee for Civil Rights Under Law, 1981.

Payne, Charles M. *I've Got the Light of Freedom: The Organizing Tradition and the Mississippi Freedom Struggle*. Berkeley: University of California Press, 1995.

Polletta, Francesca. *Freedom is an Endless Meeting: Democracy in American Social Movements*. Chicago: University of Chicago Press, 2002.

Randall, Herbert, and Bobs M. Tusa, *Faces of Freedom Summer*. Tuscaloosa: University of Alabama Press, 2001.

Rogers, Kim Lacy. *Life and Death in the Delta: African American Narratives of Violence, Resilience, and Social Change*. New York: Palgrave Macmillan, 2006.

Rothschild, Mary Aickin. *A Case of Black and White: Northern Volunteers and the Southern Freedom Summers, 1964–1965*. Westport, Conn.: Greenwood Press, 1982.

Salter, John R., Jr. *Jackson, Mississippi: An American Chronicle of Struggle and Schism*. Hicksville, N.Y.: Exposition Press, 1979.

———, and Donald B. Kates, Jr. "The Necessity of Access to Firearms by Dissenters and Minorities Whom Government Is Unwilling or Unable to Protect." In: *Restricting Handguns: The Liberal Skeptics Speak Out*, ed. Donald B. Kates Jr. Croton-on-the-Hudson, N.Y.: North River Press, 1979. 185–93.

Silver, James W. *Mississippi: The Closed Society*. 1966. New Enlarged Edition (includes author's essay "Revolution Begins in the Closed Society"). Jackson: University Press of Mississippi, 2012.

Smith, Frank. *Congressman from Mississippi*. New York: Pantheon, 1964.

Sobel, Lester A., ed. *Civil Rights, 1960–66*. New York: Facts on File, 1967.

Stoper, Emily. *The Student Nonviolent Coordinating Committee: The Growth of Radicalism in a Civil Rights Organization*. Brooklyn, N.Y.: Carlson Publishing Inc, 1989.

The Student Voice. Compiled by the staff of the Martin Luther King, Jr., Project. Clayborne Carson, senior editor and director. Westport, Conn.: Meckler Corp., 1990.

Sugarman, Tracy. *Stranger at the Gates: A Summer in Mississippi*. New York: Hill and Wang, 1966.

———. *We Had Sneakers, They Had Guns: The Kids Who Fought for Civil Rights in Mississippi*. Syracuse, N.Y.: Syracuse University Press, 2009.

Vollers, Maryanne. *Ghosts of Mississippi: The Murder of Medgar Evers, the Trials of Byron*

De La Beckwith, and the Haunting of the New South. Boston: Little, Brown and Co., 1995.

Watson, Bruce. *Freedom Summer: The Savage Season That Made Mississippi Burn and Made America a Democracy.* New York: Viking, 2010.

Watters, Pat, and Reese Cleghorn. *Climbing Jacob's Ladder: The Arrival of Negroes in Southern Politics.* New York: Harbinger, 1967.

Whitfield, Stephen J. *A Death in the Delta: The Story of Emmett Till.* New York: Free Press, 1988.

Zinn, Howard. *SNCC: The New Abolitionists.* 2nd ed. Boston: Beacon, 1968.

GENERAL WORKS ON THE MOVEMENT, BLACK HISTORY, AND RELATED SUBJECTS

Adelman, Bob (photographs), and Charles Johnson (essays). *Mine Eyes Have Seen: Bearing Witness to the Struggle for Civil Rights.* London: Thames & Hudson Ltd., 2007.

Anderson, Terry H. *The Movement and the Sixties: Protest in America from Greensboro to Wounded Knee.* New York: Oxford University Press, 1995.

Bacciocco, Edward J., Jr. *The New Left in America. Reform to Revolution, 1956 to 1970.* Stanford, Calif.: Hoover Institution Press, 1974.

Ball, Howard. *A Defiant Life: Thurgood Marshall and The Persistence of Racism in America.* New York: Crown Publishers, 1998.

Berman, William C. *The Politics of Civil Rights in the Truman Administration.* Columbus: Ohio State University Press, 1970.

Blumberg, Rhoda L. *Civil Rights: The Nineteen Sixties Freedom Struggle.* Boston: G. K. Hall, 1984.

Branch, Taylor. *Parting of the Waters: America in the King Years 1954–63.* New York: Simon & Schuster, 1988.

———. *Pillar of Fire: America in the King Years 1963–1965.* New York: Simon & Schuster, 1988.

Brauer, Carl M. *John F. Kennedy and the Second Reconstruction.* New York: Columbia University Press, 1977.

Brink, William, and Louis Harris. *Black and White: A Study of U.S. Racial Attitudes Today.* 2nd ed. New York: Simon and Schuster, 1969.

———. *The Negro Revolution in America.* New York: Simon & Schuster, 1964.

Brisbane, Robert H. *Black Activism: Radical Revolution in the United States, 1954–1970.* Valley Forge, Pa.: Judson Press, 1974.

Broderick, Francis L., and August Meier, eds. *Negro Protest Thought in the Twentieth Century.* New York: Bobbs-Merrill, 1965.

Brooks, Thomas R. *Walls Come Tumbling Down: A History of the Civil Rights Movement—1940–1970.* Englewood Cliffs, N.J.: Prentice-Hall, Inc., 1974.

Burke, Joan Martin. *Civil Rights. A Current Guide to the People, Organizations, and Events.* New York: R. R. Bowker Co., 1974.

Burns, W. Haywood. *The Voices of Negro Protest in America*. London: Oxford University Press, 1963.

Cash, W. J. *The Mind of the South*. New York: Random House, 1941.

Chafe, William H. *Never Stop Running: Allard Lowenstein and the Struggle to Save America*. New York: Basic Books, 1993.

Cobb, Charles E., Jr. *On The Road to Freedom: A Guided Tour of the Civil Rights Trail*. Chapel Hill, N.C.: Algonquin Books, 2008.

Cohen, Mitchell, and Dennis Hale, eds. *The New Student Left: An Anthology*. 2nd ed. Boston: Beacon, 1967.

Coles, Robert, M.D. *Children of Crisis: A Study of Courage and Fear*. Boston: Little, Brown, 1964.

Cox, Archibald, Mark DeWolfe Howe, and J. R. Wiggins. *Civil Rights, the Constitution, and the Courts*. Cambridge, Mass.: Harvard University Press, 1967.

Crawford, Vicki L., Jacqueline Anne Rouse, and Barbara Woods, eds. *Women in the Civil Rights Movement: Trailblazers and Torchbearers, 1941–1965*. Brooklyn, N.Y.: Carlson Publishing Inc., 1990.

Cummings, Richard. *The Pied Piper: Allard K. Lowenstein and the Liberal Dream*. New York: Grove Press, Inc., 1985.

Dattel, Gene. *Cotton and Race in the Making of America: The Human Costs of Economic Power*. Chicago: Ivan R. Dee, 2009.

De Leon, David, ed. *Leaders from the 1960s: A Biographical Sourcebook of American Activism*. Wesport, Conn.: Greenwood Press, 1994.

Dellinger, Dave. *Revolutionary Nonviolence: Essays by Dave Dellinger*. Garden City, N.Y.: Double & Co., Inc., 1971.

Dollard, John. *Caste and Class in a Southern Town*. New Haven, Conn.: Yale University Press, 1937.

Dorsen, Norman. *Discrimination and Civil Rights: Cases, Text, and Materials*. Boston: Little, Brown and Co., 1969.

Du Bois, W. E. B. *The Souls of Black Folk*. New York: Barnes & Noble, 2003.

Dye, Thomas R. *The Politics of Equality*. New York: Bobbs-Merrill, 1971.

Edelman, Marian Wright. *The Measure of Our Success: A Letter to My Children and Yours*. Boston: Beacon Press, 1992.

Essien-Udom, E. U. *Black Nationalism: A Search for an Identity in America*. Chicago: University of Chicago Press, 1962.

Fairclough, Adam. *Better Day Coming: Black and Equality, 1890–2000*. New York: Viking, 2001.

Fanon, Frantz. *Black Skins White Masks*. Trans. Charles Lam Markmann. London: Granada Publishing Ltd., 1970.

———. *The Wretched of the Earth*. Trans. Constance Farrington. New York: Grove Press, Inc., 1963.

Farmer, James. *Freedom—When?* New York: Random House, 1966.

Findlay, James F., Jr. *Church People in the Struggle: The National Council of Churches and the Black Freedom Movement, 1950–1970*. New York: Oxford University Press, 1993.

Finn, James. *Protest: Pacifism and Politics; Some Passionate Views on War and Nonviolence.* New York: Vintage Books, 1968.

Forman, James. *Sammy Younge, Jr.: The First Black Student to Die in the Black Liberation Movement.* New York: Grove, 1968.

Franklin, John Hope, and Meier, August, eds. *Black Leaders of the Twentieth Century.* Urbana: University of Illinois Press, 1982.

Garrow, David J. *Bearing the Cross: Martin Luther King, Jr., and the Southern Christian Leadership Conference.* New York: Vintage Books, 1988.

Geschwender, James A., ed. *The Black Revolt: The Civil Rights Movement, Ghetto Uprisings, and Separatism.* Englewood Cliffs, N.J.: Prentice-Hall, Inc. 1971.

Gates, Henry Louis, Jr., and Nellie Y. McKay, eds. *The Norton Anthology of African American Literature.* New York: W. W. Norton & Co., 1997.

Goldschmid, Marcel L., ed. *Black Americans and White Racism. Theory and Research.* New York: Holt, Rinehart and Winston, Inc., 1970.

Grant, Joanne. *Ella Baker: Freedom Bound.* New York: Wiley, 1998.

Guthman, Edwin. *We Band of Brothers.* New York: Harper & Row, 1971.

Harding, Vincent. *There Is a River: The Black Struggle for Freedom in America.* New York: Vintage Books, 1981.

Harrington, Michael. *The Other America: Poverty in the United States.* Baltimore: Penguin Books, 1964.

Hickey, Neil, and Edwin Neil, eds. *Adam Clayton Powell and the Politics of Race.* New York: Fleet Publishing Co., 1965.

Hamilton, Charles V. *The Bench and the Ballot: Southern Federal Judges and Black Voters.* New York: Oxford University Press, 1973.

Harvey, James C. *Civil Rights During the Johnson Administration.* Jackson: University and College Press of Mississippi, 1973.

————. *Civil Rights During the Kennedy Administration.* Hattiesburg: University and College Press of Mississippi, 1971.

Hill, Lance. *The Deacons for Defense: Armed Resistance and the Civil Rights Movement.* Chapel Hill: University of North Carolina Press, 2004.

Holloway, Harry. *The Politics of the Southern Negro. From Exclusion to Big City Organization.* New York: Random House, 1969.

Hough, Joseph C., Jr. *Black Power and White Protestants: A Christian Response to the New Negro Pluralism.* New York: Oxford University Press, 1968.

Huggins, Nathan I., Martin Kilson, and Daniel M. Fox, eds. *Key Issues in the Afro-American Experience.* Vol. 2: *Since 1865.* New York: Harcourt Brace Jovanovich, Inc., 1971.

Humphrey, Hubert Horatio. *Beyond Civil Rights: A New Day of Equality.* New York: Random House, 1968.

Jackson, Esther Cooper, ed. *Freedomways Reader: Prophets in Their Own Country.* Boulder, Colo.: Westview Press, 2000.

Jacobs, Paul, and Saul Landau. *The New Radicals.* New York: Vintage, 1966.

Jeffries, Hasan Kwame. *Bloody Lowndes: Civil Rights and Black Power in Alabama's Black Belt.* New York: New York University Press, 2009.

Jeffries, Judson L., ed. *Black Power in the Belly of the Beast.* Urbana: University of Illinois Press, 2006.

Key, V. O. *Southern Politics in State and Nation.* New York: Alfred A. Knopf, Inc., 1949.

Killens, John Oliver. *Black Man's Burden.* New York: Pocket Books, 1969.

King, Martin Luther, Jr. *Where Do We Go From Here: Chaos or Community?* New York: Harper & Row, 1967.

Lassiter, Matthew D. and Joseph Crespino, eds. *The Myth of Southern Exceptionalism.* New York: Oxford University Press, 2010.

Lawson, Steven F. *Black Ballots: Voting Rights in the South, 1944–1969.* New York: Columbia University Press, 1976.

———, and Charles Payne. *Debating the Civil Rights Movement, 1945–1968.* 2nd ed. Lanham, Md.: Rowman & Littlefield Publishers, Inc., 2006.

Leiserson, Avery, ed. *The American South in the 1960s.* New York: Praeger, 1964.

Levitan, Sar A., et al. *Still A Dream: The Changing Status of Blacks Since 1960.* Cambridge, Mass.: Harvard University Press, 1975.

Levy, Charles J. *Voluntary Servitude: Whites in the Negro Movement.* New York: Appleton-Century-Crofts, 1968.

Lewis, Andrew B. *The Shadows of Youth: The Remarkable Journey of the Civil Rights Generation.* New York: Hill and Wang, 2009.

Little, Malcolm, with Alex Haley. *The Autobiography of Malcolm X.* New York: Grove, 1965.

Littleton, Arthur C., and Mary W. Burger, eds. *Black Viewpoints.* New York: Mentor, 1971.

Lomax, Louis E. *The Negro Revolt.* New York: Signet, 1962.

———. *When The Word is Given . . . : A Report on Elijah Muhammad, Malcolm X, and the Black Muslim World.* Cleveland: World Publishing Co., 1963.

Louis, Debbie. *And We Are Not Saved. A History of the Movement as People.* Garden City, N.Y.: Doubleday & Co., Inc., 1970.

Lyon, Danny. *Memories of the Southern Civil Rights Movement.* Chapel Hill: University of North Carolina Press, 1992.

Lynd, Staughton. *From Here to There: The Staughton Lynd Reader.* Oakland, Calif.: PM Press, 2010.

McAdam, Doug. *Political Process and the Development of Black Insurgency, 1930–1970.* Chicago: University of Chicago Press, 1982.

Marable, Manning. *Malcolm X: A Life of Reinvention.* New York: Viking Penguin, 2011.

———. *Race, Reform and Rebellion: The Second Reconstruction in Black America, 1945–1982.* London: Macmillan Press, 1984.

Matusow, Allen J. *The Unraveling of America: A History of Liberalism in the 1960s.* New York: Harper Torchbooks, 1984.

McCord, John H., ed. *With All Deliberate Speed: Civil Rights Theory and Reality.* Urbana: University of Illinois Press, 1969.

Mack, Raymond W., ed. *The Changing South*. Chicago: Aldine Publishing Co., Trans-action Books, 1970.

Marine, Gene. *The Black Panthers*. New York: Signet, 1969.

Marshall, Burke. *Federalism and Civil Rights*. New York: Columbia University Press, 1964.

Matthews, Donald R., and James W. Prothro. *Negroes and the New Southern Politics*. New York: Harcourt, Brace & World, 1966.

Meier, August, and Elliot Rudwick. *Along the Color Line: Explorations in the Black Experience*. Urbana: University of Illinois Press, 1976.

Meier, August, ed. *Black Experience: The Transformation of Activism*. Chicago: Aldine Publishing Co., Trans-action Books, 1970.

———, and Elliott Rudwick. *Black History and the Historical Profession, 1915–1980*. Urbana: University of Illinois Press, 1986.

———, and Elliott Rudwick, eds. *Black Protest in the Sixties*. Chicago: Quadrangle, 1970.

Mendelsohn, Jack. *The Martyrs: Sixteen Who Gave Their Lives For Racial Justice*. New York: Harper & Row, Publishers, 1966.

Miller, James. *"Democracy Is in the Streets": From Port Huron to the Siege of Chicago*. Cambridge, Mass.: Harvard University Press, 1994.

Miller, Ruth, ed. *Blackamerican Literature: 1760–Present*. Beverly Hills, Calif.: Glencoe Press, 1971.

Mirra, Carl. *The Admirable Radical: Staughton Lynd and Cold War Dissent, 1945–1970*. Kent, Ohio: Kent State University Press, 2010.

Moore, Charles, and Michael S. Durham, *Powerful Days: The Civil Rights Photography of Charles Moore*. New York: Stewart, Tabori & Chang, Inc., 1990.

Morris, Aldon D. *The Origins of the Civil Rights Movement: Black Communities Organizing for Change*. New York: Free Press, 1984.

Muse, Benjamin. *The American Negro Revolution: From Nonviolence to Black Power, 1963–1967*. Bloomington: Indiana University Press, 1968.

———. *Ten Years of Prelude: The Story of Integration Since the Supreme Court's 1954 Decision*. New York: Viking, 1964.

Myrdal, Gunnar. *An American Dilemma: The Negro Problem and Modern Democracy*. New York: Harper & Row, 1944, 1962.

Navasky, Victor S. *Kennedy Justice*. New York: Atheneum, 1971.

Oppenheimer, Martin, and George Lakey. *A Manual for Direct Action: Strategy and Tactics for Civil Rights and All Other Nonviolent Protest Movements*. Chicago: Quadrangle, 1964.

Orum, Anthony M. *Black Students in Protest. A Study of the Origins of the Black Student Movement*. Washington, D.C.: American Sociological Association, 1974.

Powell, Adam Clayton, Jr. *Keep the Faith, Baby!* New York: Trident Press, 1967.

Powledge, Fred. *Free at Last? The Civil Rights Movement and the People Who Made It*. Boston: Little, Brown and Co., 1991.

Ransby, Barbara. *Ella Baker & the Black Freedom Movement: A Radical Democratic Vision*. Chapel Hill: University of North Carolina Press, 2003.

Redding, J. Saunders. *On Being Negro in America*. New York: Bantam Books, 1964.

Roberts, Gene, and Hank Klibanoff. *The Race Beat: The Press, the Civil Rights Struggle, and the Awakening of a Nation.* New York: Vintage Books, 2006.

Rowan, Carl T. *Dream Makers, Dream Breakers: The World of Justice Thurgood Marshall.* Boston: Little, Brown and Co., 1993.

Rustin, Bayard. *Down the Line: The Collected Writings of Bayard Rustin.* Chicago: Quadrangle Books, 1971.

———. *Strategies for Freedom: The Changing Patterns of Black Protest.* New York: Columbia University Press, 1976.

Scheer, Robert, ed. *Eldridge Cleaver: Post-Prison Writings and Speeches.* London: Panther Books Ltd., 1971.

Schlesinger, Arthur M., Jr. *Robert Kennedy and His Times.* Boston: Houghton Mifflin Co., 1978.

Schuman, Howard, Charlotte Steeh, and Lawrence Bobo. *Racial Attitudes in America: Trends and Interpretations.* Cambridge, Mass., Harvard University Press, 1988.

Segal, Bernard E., ed. *Racial and Ethnic Relations: Selected Readings.* New York: Thomas Y. Crowell, 1970.

Silberman, Charles E. *Crisis in Black and White.* New York: Random House, 1964.

Sitkoff, Harvard. *The Struggle for Black Equality 1954–1980.* New York: Hill and Wang, 1981.

Spike, Robert W. *The Freedom Revolution and the Churches.* New York: Association Press, 1965.

Stanford, Barbara Dodds. *I, Too, Sing America: Black Voices in American Literature.* New York: Hayden Book Co., Inc., 1971.

Stern, Mark. *Calculating Visions: Kennedy, Johnson, and Civil Rights.* New Brunswick, N.J.: Rutgers University Press, 1992.

Sterne, Emma Golders. *I Have a Dream.* New York: Alfred A. Knopf, 1965.

Stone, Chuck. *Black Political Power in America.* New York: Bobbs-Merrill, 1968.

Strong, Donald S. *Negroes, Ballots, and Judges: National Voting Rights Legislation in the Federal Courts.* University: University of Alabama Press, 1968.

Sullivan, Patricia. *Lift Every Voice: The NAACP and the Making of the Civil Rights Movement.* New York: The New Press, 2009

Tatum, Beverly Daniel. *"Why Are All the Black Kids Sitting Together in the Cafeteria?" And Other Conversations About Race.* New York: Basic Books, 1999.

Thernstrom, Stephan, and Abigail. *America in Black and White: One Nation, Indivisible.* New York: A Touchstone Book, 1997.

Tucker, Sterling. *For Blacks Only: Black Strategies for Change in America.* Grand Rapids, Mich.: William B. Eerdmans, 1971.

Walton, Hanes, Jr. *Black Political Parties: An Historical and Political Analysis.* New York: Free Press, 1972.

Walker, Margaret. *This Is My Century: New and Collected Poems.* Athens: University of Georgia Press, 1989.

Waskow, Arthur I. *From Race Riot to Sit-in: 1919 and the 1960s.* Garden City, N.Y.: Anchor, 1967.

Watters, Pat. *Down to Now: Reflections on the Southern Civil Rights Movement.* New York: Pantheon Books, 1971.

———. *The South and the Nation.* New York: Vintage, 1969.

Weisbrot, Robert. *Freedom Bound: A History of America's Civil Rights Movement.* New York: W. W. Norton & Co., 1990.

Wendt, Simon. *The Spirit and the Shotgun: Armed Resistance and the Struggle for Civil Rights.* Gainesville: University Press of Florida, 2007.

Westin, Alan F., ed. *Freedom Now! The Civil-Rights Struggle in America.* New York: Basic Books, 1964.

Williams, Cecil J. *Freedom and Justice: Four Decades of the Civil Rights Struggle as Seen by a Black Photographer of the Deep South.* Macon, Ga.: Mercer University Press, 1995.

Williams, Robert F. *Negroes with Guns.* New York: Marzani & Munsell, 1962.

Withers, Ernest C. *Let Us March On!; selected photographs of Ernest C. Withers 1955–1968.* Boston: Afro Scholar Press, 1992.

Wofford, Harris. *Of Kennedys and Kings: Making Sense of the 1960s.* New York: Ferrar, Straus, and Geroux, 1980.

Woodward, C. Vann. *The Strange Career of Jim Crow.* 2nd ed. New York: Oxford University Press, 1966.

Young, Andrew. *An Easy Burden: The Civil Rights Movement and the Transformation of America.* New York: HarperCollins, 1996.

Young, Richard P., ed. *Roots of Rebellion: The Evolution of Black Politics and Protest Since World War II.* New York: Harper & Row, 1970.

ARTICLES ON THE MOVEMENT IN NEWSPAPERS
AND PERIODICALS

"Airlift for Greenwood." *Newsweek* 61 (March 11, 1963): 30–31.

"Allen's Army." *Newsweek* 63 (February 24, 1964): 30.

Bagdikian, Ben H. "Negro Youth's New March on Dixie." *Saturday Evening Post* 235 (September 8, 1962): 15–19.

"Big Push in ASCS Elections." MFDP *News Letter,* November 5, 1965, 1+.

Bond, Julian. "On Nonviolence." *Freedomways,* III 3 (Spring 1963): 159–68.

Burns, W. Haywood. "From Brown to Bakke and Back: Race, Law, and Social Change in America." N.p., n.d.

Carter, Barbara. "The Fifteenth Amendment Comes to Mississippi." *The Reporter* 28 (January 17, 1963): 20–24.

Carter, Barbara. "A Lawyer Leaves Mississippi." *The Reporter* 28 (May 9, 1963): 33–35.

Carter, Hodding, III. "Citadel of the Citizens Council." *New York Times Magazine,* November 12, 1961, 23+.

———. "Deluded and Still Defiant." *The Nation* 195 (October 13, 1962): 214–16.

————. "The Negro Exodus from the Delta Continues." *New York Times Magazine,* March 10, 1968, 26–27+.

————. "The Young Negro Is a New Negro." *New York Times Magazine* May 1, 1960, 11+.

Cleghorn, Reese. "Who Speaks for Mississippi?" *The Reporter* 31 (August 13, 1964): 31–34.

"COFO." *Newsweek* 64 (August 24, 1964): 30–32.

"Cotton Workers Strike in Delta." *The Student Voice* 6 (April 30, 1965): 1+.

"Court Order, SNCC Drive; Registration Jumps from 1 to 237." *The Student Voice* 5 (July 15, 1964): 1+.

DeMuth, Jerry. "Red Carpet for Beckwith." *The New Republic* 150 (May 23, 1964): 9.

————. "Summer in Mississippi: Freedom Moves in to Stay." *The Nation* 199 (September 14, 1964): 104–5+.

————. "Tired of Being Sick and Tired." *The Nation* 198(June 1, 1964): 548–51.

Evers, Medgar W. "Why I Live in Mississippi." *Ebony* 18 (September 1963):143–48.

"Evictions Follow Registration." MFDP *News Letter,* November, 5, 1965, l+.

"Facts on Mississippi Education." *Newsweek* 59 (January 22, 1962): 58.

Feagens, Janet. "Voting, Violence and Walkout in McComb, Mississippi." *New South* 16 (October 1961): 3–4+.

"Four Whites Held for Attacks on Workers." *The Student Voice* 5 (October 28, 1964): 3.

"Freedom Ride." *Newsweek* 58 (December 11, 1961): 30+.

"Freedom Summer Planned in Miss." *The Student Voice* 5 (Spring 1964): 1+.

"Freedom Vote Candidates." *The Student Voice* 5 (October 28, 1964): 2.

"Freedom Vote is Open to All." *The Student Voice* 5 (October 28, 1964):1+.

Freedomways 5 (Spring 1965): special issue on Mississippi Movement.

Garnett, Jay. "SNCC Sets Drive for Civil Rights in Mississippi." *The Militant* 28 (April 13, 1964): 1–2.

"Greenwood." *Newsweek* 61 (April 8, 1963): 25–26.

Goodman, Andrew, *The Massachusetts Review* 6, no.1 (Autumn 1964–Winter 1965): 12. Printed with the permission of his parents Mr. and Mrs. Robert Goodman.

Halberstam, David. "The Kids Take Over." *The Reporter* 24 (June 22, 1961): 22–23.

Halstead, Fred. "COFO's Miss. Election Policy. Are Northern Democrats Really Different." *The Militant* 28 (June 22, 1961): 3.

————. "Congress Faces Mississippi Issues." *The Militant* 29 (June 14, 1965): 4.

————. "Mississippi 'Freedom Vote' Drive, Freedom Democrats Run 5 Candidates." *The Militant* 28 (October 19, 1964): 2.

Herbers, John. "Communiqué from the Mississippi Front." *New York Times Magazine,* November 8, 1964, 34–35+.

Herron, Jeannine. "Underground Election." *The Nation* 197 (December 7, 1963): 387–89.

Higgs, William Leon. "LBJ and the Negro Vote: Case of the Missing Registrars." *The Nation* 201 (December 13, 1965): 460–62.

"Illiterates Vote, Negroes Barred." *The Student Voice* 5 (October 28, 1964): 3.

"Jackson." *Newsweek* 58 (August 28, 1961): 28–29.

Jencks, Christopher. "Accommodating Whites: A New Look at Mississippi." *The New Republic* 154 (April 16, 1966): 19–22.

———. "Mississippi I: When Law Collides with Custom." *The New Republic* 151 (July 25, 1964): 15–18.

———. "Mississippi II: From Conversion to Coercion." *The New Republic* 151 (August 22, 1964): 17–21.

Jones, Charles. "SNCC: Non-violence and Revolution." *New University Thought* 3 (September–October 1963): 8–19.

"Journey to Understanding: Four Witnesses to a Mississippi Summer." *The Nation* 199 (December 28, 1964): 507–16.

Kempton, Murry. "Conscience of a Convention." *The New Republic* 151 (September 5, 1964): 5–7.

King, Martin Luther, Jr. "'Let Justice Roll Down,'" *The Nation* 200 (March 15, 1965): 269–74.

Komisar, Lucille. "Mississippi: Story of an Election." *The Activist* 3 (Fall 1963): 6–8.

Kopkind, Andrew. "New Radicals in Dixie. Those 'Subversive' Civil Rights Workers." *The New Republic* 152 (April 10, 1965): 13–16.

Ladner, Joyce. "What Black Power Means to Negroes in Mississippi." In *The Transformation of Activism*, ed. August Meier. Chicago: Aldine Publishing Co., 1970, 131–54.

Lapidary, Charles J. "Ol' Massa Jim Eastland." *The Nation* 184 (February 9, 1957): 121.

Lomax, Louis E., et al., "Mississippi Eyewitness." *Ramparts Magazine* (special issue, 1964).

Long, Margaret. "A Southern Teen-Ager Speaks His Mind." *New York Times Magazine*, November 10, 1963, 15+.

———. "They Know They're Niggers." *New South*, October 1962.

Lynd, Staughton. "Freedom Riders to the Polls." *The Nation* 195 (July 28, 1962): 29–32.

———. "The Freedom Schools: Concept and Organization." In *Freedomways Reader: Prophets in Their Own Country*, ed. Esther Cooper Jackson. Boulder, Colo.: Westview Press, 2000, 94–96.

MacLeish, Archibald. "Must We Hate?" *Atlantic* 211 (February 1963): 79–82.

Matusow, Allen J. "From Civil Rights to Black Power: The Case of SNCC, 1960–1966." In *Conflict and Competition: Studies in the Recent Black Protest Movement*, ed. John H. Bracey, August Meier, and Elliot Rudwick. Belmont, Calif.: Wadsworth, 1971. 135–53.

"MFDP to Challenge Congressional Seats." *The Student Voice* 5 (October 28, 1964): 1+.

"Mileston Opens Community Center." *The Student Voice* 5 (October 28, 1964): 3.

Minnis, Jack. "The Mississippi Freedom Democratic Party, A New Declaration of Independence." *Freedomways* 5 (Spring 1965): 264–78.

"Mississippi Drive on Rights Mapped." *New York Times*, June 12, 1965, 16.

"The Mississippi Freedom Vote." *New South* 18 (December 1963): 10–13.

"Mississippi: Image and Reality." *The Student Voice* 6 (April 30, 1965): 3.

"Mississippi, Summer of 1964." *Newsweek* 64 (July 13, 1964): 18–20, cover story.

"Miss. Negroes Run in Local Elections." *The Student Voice* 6 (April 30, 1965): 2.

"Negroes Refused Place on Ballot." *The Student Voice* 5 (October 28, 1964): 1+.

"The Negro American." *Daedalus* 94 (Fall 1965): special issue.

"The Negro American—2." *Daedalus* 95 (Winter 1966): special issue.

"The Negro Protest." *Annals of the American Academy of Political Science* 357 (January 1965): special issue.

Newfield, Jack. "Revolt without Dogma: The Student Left." *The Nation* 200 (May 10, 1965): 491–95.

————. "The Question of SNCC." *The Nation* 201 (July 19, 1965): 38–40.

O'Dell, J. H. "Life in Mississippi, An Interview with Fannie Lou Hamer." *Freedomways* 5 (Spring 1965): 231–42.

Payne, Bruce. "The Quiet War." *The Activist* 4 (Summer 1964):75–80.

Poppy, John. "The South's War Against Negro Votes." *Look Magazine* 27 (May 21, 1963).

Poussaint, Dr. Alvin F. "The Stresses of the White Female Worker in the Civil Rights Movement in the South." *American Journal of Psychiatry* 123, no. 4 (1966): 401–7.

"Progress Report I: Summer Project." *The Student Voice* 5 (July 15, 1964): 3+.

"Project Goes On Despite Bombing." *The Student Voice* 5 (July 15, 1964): 1+.

Rachlin, Carl. "Return to Jackson." *Commonweal* 75 (November 17, 1961): 206–9.

"Read-in in Jackson." *Newsweek* 57 (April 10, 1961): 27.

"Rights Groups in Mississippi Help Negro Farm Strikers in Union Effort." *New York Times* June 7, 1965, 26.

Riley, David. "Who is Jimmie Lee Jackson?" *The New Republic* 152 (April 3, 1965): 8–9.

Roberts, Gene. "From 'Freedom High' to 'Black Power,'" *New York Times Magazine*, September 25, 1966, 29.

Rostow, Eugene. "The Freedom Riders of the Future." *The Reporter* 24 (June 22, 1961): 18–21.

Rothschild, Mary Aickin. "White Women Volunteers in the Freedom Summers." *Feminist Studies* 5 (Fall 1979): 466–95.

Rustin, Bayard. "From Protest to Politics: The Future of the Civil Rights Movement." *Commentary* 39 (February 1965): 25–31.

"Showdown in the Delta." *Newsweek* 66 (June 6, 1966): 67.

Silver, James W. "Mississippi Must Choose." *New York Times Magazine*, July 19, 1964, 8+.

Sinsheimer, Joseph. "The Freedom Vote of 1963: New Strategies of Racial Protest in Mississippi." *Journal of Southern History* 55 (1989): 217–44.

Slaff, George. "Five Seats in Congress: 'The Mississippi Challenge,'" *The Nation* 200 (May 17, 1965): 526–29.

"SNCC Blasts Miss. Jailings; Demands Sheriff Be Arrested." *The Militant* 28 (April 13, 1964): 5.

"SNCC Confab Set Easter Weekend in Atlanta, Ga." *The Student Voice* 4 (April 1963): 3.

"SNCC Staff Jailed as Greenwood Negroes Register in 'First Breakthrough' in Miss." *The Student Voice* 4 (April 1963): 1+.

Strickland, William. "The Movement and Mississippi." *Freedomways* 5 (Spring 1965): 310–13.

"Striking Negroes Are Evicted from Plantation in Mississippi." *New York Times*, June 4, 1965, 17.

"Summer Storms." *Newsweek* 63 (June 8, 1964): 45–46.

Sutherland, Elizabeth. "The Cat and Mouse Game." *The Nation* 199 (September 14, 1965): 105–8.

———. "Mississippi: Summer of Discontent." *The Nation* 201 (October 11, 1965): 212–15.

"Terror on Schedule." *Newsweek* 64 (October 5, 1964): 71–72.

"Three Bodies Found." *Newsweek* 64 (August 17, 1964): 28–29.

Vandiver, Joseph S. "The Changing Realm of King Cotton." *Trans-action*, November 1966.

"Violence Breaks Out with Mass Negro Registration; Injunction Aids Registration." *The Student Voice* 6 (April 30, 1965): 1+.

"Voting in Greenwood." *Commonweal* 78 (April 12, 1963): 61.

"Whites Use Same Tricks; Take ASCS Elections; FDP to File Suit to Void Elections." MFDP *News Letter* December 20, 1965, 1+.

Woodley, Richard. "Aaron Henry and His Friends." *The New Republic* 151 (October 10, 1964): 6–7.

———. "It Will Be a Hot Summer in Mississippi." *The Reporter* 30 (May 21, 1964): 21–24.

"Workers Arrested on Syndicalism Charge." *The Student Voice* 5 (October 28, 1964): 3.

Zinn, Howard. "The Double Job in Civil Rights." *New Politics* 3 (Winter 1964): 29–34.

———. "Incident in Hattiesburg." *The Nation* 198 (May 18, 1964): 501–4.

———. "The Mississippi Idea." *The Nation* 199 (November 23, 1964): 371–75.

———. "'Snick,' February 6, 2012: The Battle-Scarred Youngsters." *The Nation* 197 (October 5, 1963): 193–97.

———. "The South Revisited." *The Nation* 201 (September 20, 1965): 147–53.

INDEX

Agricultural Stabilization and Conservation Service (ASCS), xxv; elections, 190, 256n118, 257n120, 268 (212), 286, 290

Allen, Lewis: influence on selecting Summer Project volunteers, ix, 79, 206, 241n3, 241n4; murder of, 212

American Civil Liberties Union (ACLU), 122

American Jewish Committee, 122

American Jewish Congress, 122

Americans for Democratic Action (ADA), xxv; resolution on MFDP seating at Convention, 138, 140, 157

Arrests in Ruleville of Hayes, McLaurin, Surney, Block, and Cobb, 44, 65–66

Ashford, H. S. (Hinds County Circuit Clerk and Registrar), 64

Baker, Ella Josephine, x, 9, 10, 23, 75, 138–39, 143, 221; Baker interview, 274 (Stoper); on decision-making, 28, 29, 229n13, 229n17, 232n12, 233n3, 233n4, 233n7, 238n12, 239n28, 242n6, 246n2, 248n2, 249n11; on establishment of MFDP, 249n11; MFDP office, 249n21; on organizing techniques, 231n1

Ballis, George: naming of MFDP, 137

Barnett, Gov. Ross, 9; defiance of federal court orders, 46, 136, 190; founding of COFO, 34; issues federal subpoena, 174

Barrett, Russell H., 212, 228n6, 230n31, 235n29, 241n63, 247n21, 276

Barry, Marion, Jr., 5, 10, 17, 20 (qtd.), 23, 24, 50 (qtd.), 228n5, 228n6, 231 (epigraph);

232n2, 232n14, 236n11, 242n23, 259n1, 260n8, 261, 274 (Raines and Stoper)

Batesville, xxi, 89, 104, 108, 119, 141, 143, 188

Beckwith, Byron de la: murder of Evers and trial for, 49, 79, 210, 237n9, 280 (Vollers)

Bevel, Rev. James, 17, 23, 32, 47, 232n1, 274 (Stoper)

Biloxi, Harrison County, Mississippi, xxi, 13, 45, 89, 104, 116, 117, 128, 129, 143, 176, 183

Bingham, Steve: in Freedom Vote, xix, 71, 92 ("Mississippi Letter" qtd.), 243n28, 243n32, 243n55, 265

Bishop, W. J., 43

Black Belt Project and Counties, xv, 10, 11, 169, 170, 180, 207, 227n7, 253n22, 266, 283

Black Empowerment, 201, 258n3

Black Nationalism, 86, 204, 281

Black Power: sources for, 11, 199, 204, 207, 227n7, 242n6, 248n2, 250n62, 257–58, 257–58n1, 258n2, 271–72, 276, 282–84, 288–99

Blackwell, Unita, 6, 19; on reaction to SNCC and COFO, 29; on role of songs in mass meetings, 29, 231n53, 233n5, 245n91, 249n33, 255n76, 256n97, 268 (998), 271

Blackwell, Randolph, 46, 51

Block, Sam, xii, 5, 37, 43–44, 228n5, 235n24, 241n3

Blue, Rev. Willie: photography project, 127, 209

Bond, Horace Julian, xix, 10, 169, 242n11, 261, 267, 274 (Raines and Stoper), 286

Boynton v. Commonwealth of Virginia (1960), 14